Martha Brech, Ralph Paland (Hg. / Eds.)
Kompositionen für hörbaren Raum / Compositions for Audible Space

D1719881

Musik und Klangkultur

MARTHA BRECH, RALPH PALAND (HG. / EDS.)

Kompositionen für hörbaren Raum /
Compositions for Audible Space

Die frühe elektroakustische Musik und ihre Kontexte /
The Early Electroacoustic Music and its Contexts

[transcript]

Bibliografische Information der Deutschen Nationalbibliothek
Die Deutsche Nationalbibliothek verzeichnet diese Publikation in der Deutschen Nationalbibliografie; detaillierte bibliografische Daten sind im Internet über http://dnb.d-nb.de abrufbar.

Umschlaggestaltung: Kordula Röckenhaus, Bielefeld,
   unter Verwendung eines Bildhintergrundes von Martha Brech
Umschlagabbildung: © Martha Brech: Symposiumslogo, 2013
Englisches Lektorat: Peter Castine
Printed in Germany
Print-ISBN 978-3-8376-3076-3
PDF-ISBN 978-3-8394-3076-7

Gedruckt auf alterungsbeständigem Papier mit chlorfrei gebleichtem Zellstoff.
Besuchen Sie uns im Internet: *http://www.transcript-verlag.de*
Bitte fordern Sie unser Gesamtverzeichnis und andere Broschüren an unter:
info@transcript-verlag.de

Inhalt / Content

DISPOSITIVE – KOMPOSITION UND TECHNOLOGIE / DISPOSITIVES – COMPOSITION AND TECHNOLOGY

Foreword

Compositions for auditive space – the topic is less common than it might seem. Although musical space is often discussed today, especially with regard to philosophy or alongside the modern discourse of the ›spatial turn‹, the question of how space is integrated into compositions and how it is made audible in performed music only rarely arises. When it does, it is generally just as a part of analytical surveys of single compositions – more of an ornament among the multiplicity of compositional aspects than a major topic of analytical interest. Therefore, in this anthology we aim to give a rough overview on the composition of audible space.

One concession at the start: In many periods of European music history, space was of only minor interest for composers. Nevertheless, it seems to have been a topic in all ages and it became increasingly important throughout the 20th century, when human binaural perception had been explored and described by scientists, and when the first technical equipment had been invented to process the spatiality of sounds.

Composers of electroacoustic music, in particular, profited from these developments. The electronic devices invented for the production and presentation of electroacoustic music included spatial aspects. Within a short time, composers began to develop initial ideas for integrating space and spatial sound movements into their music and then, in quick pursuit, they demanded better devices in order to realize new ideas. Having obtained newer tools, they continued to develop refined spatial concepts for their music. Over the years, space became an important part of electroacoustic music, now equal in value to other musical parameters. This interaction of spatial electroacoustic compositions and analogue technology, as well as the analysis of spatial aspects in individual electroacoustic compositions, is the focus of this anthology. Spatial electroacoustic compositions, of course, were still produced in the digital era. Moreover, they usually were refined when based on this technology. Nevertheless, owing to the difference between these types of technology, and to the complex problems in documentation and readings of digital programs, in turn resulting in new problems in musical analysis, we decided not to include compositions based on digital technology. This decision has an additional advantage: The first compositional ideas for producing space by electronic means can now be studied in detail, concentrating on the music and the compositional concept of space, using the methods of historical research and its perspective. This allows one to understand these compositions and their technology as part of the time in which they were produced, rather than somehow as simplistic forerunners of today's music produced with improved technical solutions and production methods.

But technology is not restricted to the genres of art music, and so two brief excursions into the use of space in popular music and audio art are included here. Alongside historical and recent spatial music, they form the contexts of spatial electroacoustics. When space was first composed and produced with electronic means, at the same time it also became increasingly important in purely instrumental music. Moreover, both genres – instrumental and electroacoustic music – not only relied on research going back as far as the 19th century, but they also reflected traditional techniques in the composition of space, such as *cori spezzati* founded in Venice during the late Renaissance. Therefore, it seemed to be appropriate to include European music history and its treatment of space into the anthology, as well as recent instrumental and acoustic spatial compositions, in order to compare the spatial techniques and concepts of different times and genres. Are they all alike and does ›space‹ mean the same in every composition regardless of its origin – and if not, how do they differ from each other and how may auditive space be understood in the 20th century?

We asked questions like these to musicologists and experts in spatial and electroacoustic music. Their responses, first presented in a conference in July 2014 at the Technische Universität Berlin, are published here in revised and extended form. We are very grateful to all authors for their contributions and discussion and would like to thank the Deutsche Forschungsgemeinschaft (DFG) and Ernst von Siemens Musikstiftung for the support of this conference.. Additionally, we would like to thank Peter Castine (English language editor) and Ernst Strucken for their support in editing the articles.

Berlin and Hürth, April 2015   Martha Brech and Ralph Paland

Facetten des auditiven Raums /

Facets of Audible Space

Local/Field and Beyond

The Scale of Spaces

SIMON EMMERSON

TIME BECOMES SPACE

Denis Smalley has written with respect to a landscape described in sound:

>»I can collapse the whole experience into a present moment, and that is largely how it rests in my memory. [...] I ultimately sideline time's formative role. So space can be more significant than time, or at least we can profit by starting with the idea that time can be placed at the service of space rather than the reverse. Time becomes space.«[1]

But what he describes is a ›scene‹ with little foreground activity that might constitute a narrative. I have argued at a paper given recently at EMS 2014 in Berlin that, in such a continuity of sound, the listener may create a series of »moments« that might group themselves into a possible narrative. These moments may be constructed either through events articulated by change in the sound – our attention is preferentially drawn to change – or from our own concentration creating intensified instants[2].

---

1 Denis Smalley, »Space-form and the acousmatic image«, Organised Sound 12(1) (2007), pp. 35–58, here pp. 37–38.

2 Cf. Simon Emmerson, »Listening in time and over time: the construction of the electroacoustic musical experience«, in: *Proceedings of the Electroacoustic Music Studies Network Conference 2014 (EMS14)*, Berlin,
http://www.ems-network.org/spip.php?article362 (10.2.2015).

SPACE BECOMES TIME

Tim Ingold appears to reverse Smalley's collapse of time into space in his distinction between »mapping« and »wayfinding«: »Taking this view of place as my starting point, I now want to show how wayfinding might be understood not as following a course from one spatial location to another, but as a movement in time, more akin to playing music or storytelling than to reading a map.«[3]

Here is not the place to elaborate on the idea that a map is not a neutral representation but serves a particular worldview. Ingold insists here on a shift back to the in-time experience of ›dwelling‹ in a place. Time needs space, space needs time. Katharine Norman argues furthermore that space is more than mere extension, requiring sound imagination; while time also needs memory, from the personal to the collective[4].

SPACE FRAMES

The function of a diagram is to present information or ideas in a more communicative way. In 1994 I published a simple diagram, originally in response to a discussion on how composers who use live electronics can think of the new spaces they can articulate (figure 1).

It fast became both a compositional and an analytical tool, a model of spaces in general – from the enclosed studio to the wide-open environment. I wish in this paper to develop this ›tiny language‹ of symbols, intending both to represent and to stimulate discussion on how space is discussed in the electroacoustic music field. In line with the symposium theme, I will use examples from the first three to four decades of electroacoustic music, when these issues first emerged.

Figure 1 shows the original space frames delineation. In fact, it maps easily onto a basic template of an ancient Greek theatre (figure 2). The disposition of theatrical space remained relatively unchanged in the West, though increasingly bounded within structured buildings (theatres, concert halls, opera houses) until the invention of electroacoustic means and media. Such technology has allowed not simply the erosion of these boundaries, but also

---

3   Tim Ingold, *The Perception of the Environment: Essays in livelihood, dwelling and skill*, London 2000, p. 238.

4   Cf. Katharine Norman, *Sounding Art – Eight Literary Excursions through Electronic Music*, Aldershot 2004, Chapter 2.

the transformation of the spaces one into another (as well as the reduction of time delays). We shall return to this below.

Figure 1: Space Frames

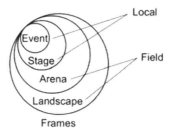

Simon Emmerson, »Aural landscape: musical space«, in: Organised Sound 3(2) (1998), pp. 135–140.

Figure 2: Ancient Greek amphitheatre plan (Epidauros)

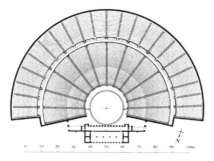

From: http://www.whitman.edu/theatre/theatretour/epidaurus/epidaurus.htm (*The Ancient Theatre Archive*), reproduced with permission of Professor Thomas Hines

DIRECTIONALITY

Humans are built with a perceptual sense of ›forward‹. Vision clearly has limited angular range with increasing detail towards a central area of focused attention; hearing (most specifically of location) is more acute in the ca. 120 degrees ›straight ahead‹. We automatically turn to face a threat, an opportunity or an invitation, and non-technological communication (including performance) is usually ›face to face‹.

Figure 3: Directionality (›Forward‹)

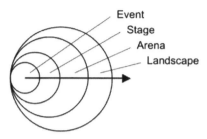

I have elsewhere written about sound's mediatized dislocation. In summary here: the ›acousmatic dislocations‹ are the consequences of the development of the new technologies of sound in the last part of the 19th century. Telephone (1876) and radio (1890s, transatlantic 1901) allow us to displace sound in space, while recording (1877) allows displacement in time. ›Dislocation‹ has a negative connotation in English – a dislocated limb needs medical attention, dislocated transport systems must be remedied. While the analogue to digital transformations in the late 20th century allowed their complete integration, the basic dislocations have not gone away – but, as we shall see, they have been reconceived as ›relocations‹. The negative connotation has steadily been eroded.

Another dislocation was to follow those defined by these new communications media. Mechanical cause of sound itself was dislocated with the invention of electronic sound synthesis[5]. This creates sound without an apparent causal real object in a real place – the answer to the question ›where is the cause?‹ is ambiguous, or at least distributed in several possible locations. The loudspeaker membrane is, strictly speaking, the cause and place. But it is a unique place that can mimic (almost) any possible sound within its defined limits of frequency and amplitude[6]. This is uncanny: it does not change shape, yet it emits almost any sound. We had not had this kind of experience before[7].

For many years the loudspeaker was seen more like an acoustic window to another world, that of an idealised performance space, maybe a real hall without audience or a specialized space adjacent to the recording studio. We

---

5   Thaddeus Cahill's *Telharmonium* see http://120years.net/wordpress/the-telharmonium -thaddeus-cahill-usa-1897 (last accessed September 2014).

6   And these steadily approach the limits defined by the ear (at its best).

7   I am not referring to *acousmatic* sound here – on the contrary I am referring to looking at the loudspeaker yet hearing it produce this vast range of sounds.

were looking at the Pythagorean veil, which covered the visual contact with the sound's apparent source. So the cause was taken to be the Berlin Philharmonic somehow performing ›behind‹ the loudspeakers. Electronic sound synthesis challenged this duality – the physical object (a musical instrument) is replaced by a circuit, the mechanical world by the electrical. The ›place‹ of the cause has become complex, effectively obscured to the listener. Maybe there is a human performer involved but maybe not. The circuit (analogue) or sequence of numbers (digital) are candidates – but where are they? The digital code of a recording may be stored near to, or far away from, the listener.

But humans learn and adapt. As the years have moved on, new generations of listeners have now extended their experience of the mechanical world of sound to embrace the loudspeaker and thus synthetic sounds, some of which have – through common use and consent – become ›recognizable‹ or at least nameable. To extend a term first developed by Smalley[8] new »indicative fields« have emerged that indicate, for example, ›sci-fi‹ sounds (from the 1950s on), ›computer game sounds‹ (from the 1980s on), mobile phone signals (from the 2000s on). We seem to have learnt to accept this sound without an original physical cause: while it has had no specific physical place in the world we now trust it to indicate a generic source – the mobile phone, for example.

Let us express this first phase diagrammatically. The electronic media of the acousmatic undermine and eventually dislocate the first simple space frame map, while direction, too, is made completely flexible.

- The ›event‹ may be isolated from its surroundings using contact or close microphone techniques.
- The ›stage‹ may become a studio construct built from the spatial relationship of such events.
- The ›arena‹ becomes a controllable variable; its shape and disposition are recreated in the mathematics of reflection and reverberation.
- The ›landscape‹ similarly may extend this to the acoustic horizon (and beyond, as we shall discuss below).

---

8   Cf. Denis Smalley, »The listening imagination: listening in the electroacoustic era«, in: Contemporary Music Review 13(2) (1996), pp. 77–107.

Figure 4: Fragmentation – dislocation

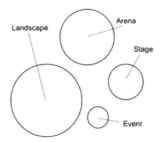

Our original diagram is now ›blown apart‹ (figure 4) allowing distance, connectivity, and reconfiguration of the components in many different combinations of local and remote. Importantly, there is now no specified direction (no ›forward‹). True, traditional music studio practice (classical or popular) has tended to preserve a constructed ›forward‹, but this is undermined in more-experimental sound art and music practices[9]. The original hall or studio was strangely empty of audience. This appears later, clearly intended to be listeners using their own technology, in their own arena and landscape (public or personal), in their own time. Recent installation and other open-work formats challenge this fundamental exclusion: an audience member may be free, after all, to ›wander into‹ the work!

CHANGE OF SCALE

Our original diagram presumed a ›real-world‹ mechanics, in which each space was progressively larger in scale. An event in personal space was smaller than the presentation stage, in turn smaller than the arena in a, possibly unbounded, *landscape*. But amplification undermines this simple size sequence. The landscape can be scaled down to an event space; an arena can become iPod sized, the amplified small sounds of John Cage or Hildegard Westerkamp can take on vast proportions, becoming the size and scale of arena and landscape. David Tudor's *Rainforest* is another paradigm case in which a swarm of tiny sounds (recorded or from oscillating circuits) fills an arena and becomes a landscape. In a work such as Cage's *Roaratorio*, the

---

9   Especially when eight-channel concert or installation works are considered.

sound landscape of Dublin is flooded into the arena from above – but then the entire arena is also the stage[10].

Figure 5: Space Frames: Change of Scale

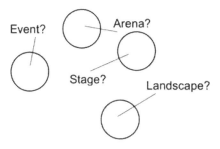

Our diagram thus reduces to a set of four potentially equal entities – and we may not be at all sure which are which, or in which direction they face. In John Cage's *Inlets*, for example, the sound of water gurgling inside beautiful large conch shells as they are rotated is highly amplified – a small ›inside sound‹ becomes a surrounding landscape.

A PROSTHESIS OF SPACE AND TIME

This use of technology has led to a feeling that live action is remote and unknowable, which might make us anxious – we cannot see it anymore. As we remarked above we need to learn to trust new systems. Given a degree of trust, dislocation can give way to relocation. Hence the notion of acousmatic dislocation can be turned on its head. New technological discoveries are an answer to distancing, not its prime cause. The new media allow us to reach out, to bridge the gap, to link together, enabling space and time ›distance‹ to be overcome. This was clearly demanded by (and enabled) the expansion of trade and empire to global outreach in the 18th and 19th centuries, driving the rapid development of telecommunications.

This is a strange equalization of the near and far – technology apparently attempts to collapse distance to a singular ›present/absent‹. But is this really true? Have we overstepped the mark to a lazy romantic notion of simultanei-

---

10 This can be seen in live performance versions of the original *Hörspiel* (1979), such as the one recorded in Peter Greenaway's movie *Four American Composers: John Cage* (1983). This film includes the 1982 London performance.

ty – the final human conquest of space and victory over the relentless passing of time? Latency is the inevitable projection of space into time. As far as we know, the speed of light cannot be exceeded: however small the distance, it takes time to traverse it. Even with pathways approaching this ideal speed of information transfer, there will remain problems of synchronization of musicians playing remotely from one another and connected via the Internet, or any of its future manifestations.

STUDIO PERFORMANCE SPACE

In the only image we have of the control room of the *Studio d'Essai* at the time of the invention of *musique concrète*, there are four turntables shown. Three are for playback and one is for recording (a cutting lathe effectively)[11]. Especially in analogue studios, where there were plenty of machines to be cued, lined up, and started or stopped, and there are faders to be manually controlled, and other knobs and dials to watch and set – the studio was often a space for a very real kind of performance. Schaeffer reports on his earliest experiments in the studio in just such language, exclaiming that he seemed sometimes to be playing the studio as he might play an instrument to create the work: »So I record a series of notes made in this way, each one on a disc. By arranging the discs on record players, I can, using the controls, play these notes as I wish [...] I have a musical instrument.«[12] And later: »The instrumentalist is no longer the winner of the Prix Conservatoire but the sound engineer.«[13] Also today's solitary user with a computer screen is an exception: most early studios provided an assistant, so there was often a duo (at least) in residence. Pierre Henry joined Schaeffer in 1949 and this collaboration produced many joint works as an outcome.

This is fully confirmed when we see that the *Groupe de Recherches Musicales* (INA/GRM) in Paris has recently released into the public domain an extract of a TV programme made in 1971[14]. In it, Schaeffer's early disc-based practice was recreated exactly as in his descriptions. It comes as some-

---

11 Carlos Palombini, »Musique concrète revisited«, in: Electronic Musicological Review 4, http://www.rem.ufpr.br/_REM/REMv4/vol4/arti-palombini.htm (1999).

12 Pierre Schaeffer, *In search of a concrete music*, translated by John Dack and Christine North, Los Angeles 2012, p. 7; original: idem, *À la Recherche d'une Musique Concrète*, Paris 1952.

13 Ibid., p. 9.

14 Available at http://fresques.ina.fr/artsonores/fiche-media/InaGrm00208/la-naissance-de-la-musique-concrete-et-electro-acoustique.html (last accessed September 2014).

thing of a surprise to see what is effectively a score and a rehearsal for a ›performance‹[15]. Schaeffer conducts the turntable performers[16] who play the »closed groove« discs – each with a number of different single rotation duration sounds[17]. They accurately cue each sound at the composer's conducting signal while Schaeffer simultaneously controls rotary potentiometers at a 1940s mixing console.

From the earliest days of *musique concrète* there appears to have been a desire to continue this process in the performance hall, to amplify the individual narrative drama and place it in a much larger shared space. This is shown in the development of the *pupitre d'espace*[18]. Schaeffer's diary first records the construction of this in an entry of 15 April 1951: »In the studio cellars Jacques Poullin is unravelling the network of tangled wires belonging to the ›potentiomètre d'espace‹ […] which should enable us to re-create the gestures of an orchestral conductor. With his left hand he will control the fine detail, and with his right he will be able to influence the trajectory of the sounds in the concert hall.«[19] While only the right hand (space control) idea seems to have been realized in the final version, performance in the studio here links seamlessly to performance in the auditorium. While the original device did not survive for long, it is brilliantly prophetic of a later generation of trackers and controllers used to control timbral and spatial trajectories[20].

There are some inspirational images of François Bayle performing in the studio at the GRM[21]. The image is blurred, thus recording and projecting the sense of moving so quickly that we are witnessing real physical performance[22]. Others have reported that while Bayle meticulously prepares all the

---

15 Schaeffer (op.cit.) has many references to these scores, and reprints quite a few extracts, yet they have received little attention.

16 Two performers, Guy Reibel and François Bayle, play two turntables each.

17 We might call these »samples«. I have discussed the remarkably similar timescales between analogue and digital samplers, as well as the rhythmic potential of these devices in: Simon Emmerson, »Pulse, meter, rhythm in electro-acoustic music«, in: *Proceedings of the Electroacoustic Music Studies Network Conference 2008 (EMS08)*, Paris, http://www.ems-network.org/ems08/paper.html (last accessed 10.2.2015).

18 Known variously as the *pupitre d'espace, pupitre de relief, potentiomètre d'espace.*

19 Pierre Schaeffer, op.cit., p. 84.

20 Images of the device in operation: Pierre Schaeffer, http://fresques.ina.fr/artsonores/parcours/0003/la-revolution-de-48-et-les-annees-50.html (last accessed September 2014); Pierre Henry (Carlos Palombini, op.cit.).

21 François Bayle, *Musique acousmatique - propositions ... positions*, Paris 1993, p. 128.

22 This sense of studio live performance is interestingly reflected in the use of the phrase »*temps réel*« in the Archives GRM CD collection, where it can refer to studio processing (used in a finally fixed work) as well as processing in live performance on stage.

possible material for a piece, his montage approach has close affinity to improvisation in the performance sense. The development of the GRM's acousmonium similarly arose from a need to complete this composition process in spatial performance terms. François Bayle, for example, continues this inventive and improvisatory performance to his asymmetric loudspeaker configurations[23].

STOCKHAUSEN'S *ROTATIONSTISCH* AND THE »COFFEE MILL« POTENTIOMETER

While much has been written on Karlheinz Stockhausen's ideas concerning space (both in composition and performance), I wish to take as an example a device with a clearly performative dimension within the studio. A *Rotationstisch* (rotation table) was first constructed in the WDR studios for work on *Kontakte* (1958–60); it was subsequently used in *Hymnen* (1966–67)[24]. A new motorized version was constructed for *Sirius* (1975–77), capable of much higher rotation speeds. This is used famously in the opening scene of the work to generate the sense of the fast-moving jets of the spaceships landing – I suggest that such higher speeds of rotation are no longer perceived as performance but as machine-like.

Here, too, a device designed for studio use was quickly extrapolated for concert sound projection. Stockhausen requested a *Rotationsmühle* (rotation mill, sometimes known colloquially as the »coffee mill«) for the massive spatialized sound system for the German Pavilion of the Osaka Word's Fair (1970)[25]. In talks shortly after he refers to rotating the sounds around the space[26].

---

23 Cf. François Bayle, op.cit.
24 While the commentary unfortunately talks about *Kontakte*, film of the table in action during the making of *Hymnen* (Stockhausen assisted by Mesias Maiguashca) was incorporated into the BBC *Omnibus* programme *Tuning In* (1981), available at http://www.youtube.com/watch?v=qGnkZnm9MPw (last accessed September 2014).
25 I am grateful to Martha Brech for clarifying the complex references to these devices. The composer's writings are not always accurate in chronology or detail.
26 Most famously when he describes the reaction of the audience in his talk to the Oxford Union 1972 »Four Criteria of Electronic Music«, available on YouTube: http://www.youtube.com/watch?v=7xyGtI7KKIY (accessed September 2014), also briefly in the BBC programme referred to above.

Figure 6: Omnidirectional Collapse

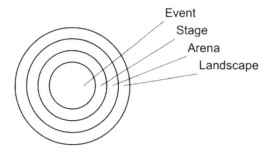

The studio and performance space have both become omnidirectional (figure 6). But this is strictly optional: recording studios retain a forward direction and the vast majority of music is still distributed in two-channel formats with a clear proscenium. The omnidirectional nature of the electronic part in *Kontakte* is reduced in the ›mixed‹ version, where the instruments (piano and percussion) are placed on stage (i.e., at the front).

BEYOND THE BOUNDARY

Studios intrinsically expand the ›sound world‹ beyond their physical boundary. A kind of Pandora's box was opened which could never again be closed. As soon as Schaeffer brought in recordings of trains and Cage the sounds of radios (and hence anything broadcast), the acoustic horizon – the effective limit of our earlier unmediated landscape – was no longer a limit. Telecommunications (as we noted above), initially a dislocation, became a relocation, a prosthesis. The studio could (and did) expand out another layer, effectively to global proportions. But this is not strictly a limit either; an increasing interest in sonification[27] allowed sound to represent atmospheric phenomena from the high stratosphere (›sferics‹), and recently a host of sonifications of ›off earth‹ phenomena, including the residual ›sound‹ of the big bang (cosmic background radiation). This is sketched in figure 7.

---

27 The mapping of parameters of non-sound phenomena to sound: a very early work for computer synthesis is Charles Dodge's *Earth's Magnetic Field* (1970) mapped to sound.

Figure 7: Studio – ›Allspace‹

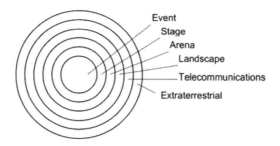

An early harnessing of this power can be found in the use of radios as sound sources in John Cage's *Imaginary Landscape IV* (1951), interestingly not as a studio resource but as live instrument. Keith Rowe of the British improvisation group *AMM* developed and extended its possibilities strongly in the 1960s. At the same time it was adopted by Stockhausen in a series of live works (notably *Kurzwellen*)[28] and in the studio work *Hymnen* (1966–67).

PROSTHESIS: EXTENDING OUR ›REACH‹ TO FAR-OFF PLACES (AND TIMES)

There is an imaginary space not indicated in this diagram. Let us call it historical and memory space. Here we might encounter the special spaces of ›plunderphonics‹ and sampling, where the sounds carry with them connotations specific to an individual or collective memory.

A classic case in which these new studio dimensions have been engaged is Stockhausen's *Hymnen*, which stretches back into the composer's memory and across the ›space of the world's musics‹. The process was started the year previously (1966) on the composer's visit to Japan and the composition of *Telemusik* in the studios of the Japan Broadcasting Corporation (NHK). The many ›world music‹ sources used in that work are often obscured in a haze of electronic »intermodulation«: we hear fleeting moments of ›other places‹ suddenly appear in the flow. In *Hymnen* the anthems (and many oth-

---

28 I suggest that the link between Cage and Stockhausen's radio use is Cornelius Cardew (through his version of Stockhausen's *Plus-Minus* for radio and piano). Cardew was a member of the free-improvisation group AMM from 1966. The relationship of radio to short-wave radio is an interesting one – the short wave bands have much greater global reach in the analogue radio world as the waves bounce more effectively off the ionosphere.

er musics and recorded environmental sounds) are heard in a recognisable form to a much greater extent: speed may be changed; fragments repeated, extended, and montaged; but this rarely obscures the origin of the sound and music heard. The anthems are not merely heard ›in the present‹. Stockhausen also mines historical recordings from his own and collective memory[29]. Heard today, what was contemporary then is now history (many of the anthems have disappeared or changed following the end of the Cold War). Thus, these layers have their own dynamic beyond the composer's control.

RELOCATION – PANDIRECTIONALITY

Schoenberg preferred the term »pantonality« to »atonality«. This might suggest ›all keys at once‹ are available – perhaps blended into one – rather than no key at all. Here, too, the ›allspace‹ of the studio has, in the first instance, no directional properties. Even today, however, it is rare to find omnidirectional studio practices in the commercial domain. While the 5.1 format developed for film and video goes some way towards pandirectionality, front is still privileged in quality – as well as normally containing the dialogue tracks.

We can think of direction in interesting ways. Figure 8 is intended to be direction sensitive, where figure 4, which showed simply a fragmentation of the space frames with their optional reassembling (in the manner of Cage), was not. I can construct a first version even without technological mediation. I might describe an imaginary listening situation. I am seated in a box at the side of, say, the Albert Hall stage in London: from behind we can hear the outside landscape through open doors and windows; in front an arena full of people; to the left a silent stage. Now, down a gangway at the left of the stage and hard left of my box, enters a perambulatory performer. This might be described diagrammatically in figure 8, where the intersection of the four circles is the listener's position[30]. Technologically mediated versions of this image are easy to imagine. Cage's dislocated versions have no unique focal point for the listener. But we might conceive of this as present in many electroacoustic works. Even mixed to stereo we hear a similar juxtaposition in works of Bernard Parmegiani and Luc Ferrari. In Ferrari's *Presque Rien*

---

29 Recordings from the British queen's coronation of 1953, and a deep and distant memory of the *Horst Wessel Lied* come quickly to mind.

30 Strictly speaking there remains no ›forward‹ in this diagram. The listener may face any of the four domains.

Nr.2 there is a juxtaposition of an outside environment with the ›inside‹ of an instrumental recording[31].

Figure 8: Relocation – Pandirectionality

CONCLUSION

The studio emerged as an increasingly sophisticated ›space controller‹ in the years following the inventions of *musique concrète* and *Elektronische Musik*, and development of technology in popular music production in the 1950s and 1960s. These controls were already inherent in telecommunications technologies themselves, yet there is some conflict between our sense of ›forward‹ and the desire to be immersed and truly pan-directional (or omnidirectional). In addition, technology can harness our desire to ›play‹ spaces with embodied movement and gesture. This article has attempted to represent some of these emerging features through simple descriptive words and diagrams.

---

31 And Ferrari's *Music Promenade* (1969) was originally for four independent tapes.

Annäherungen an Hör-Räume des Mittelalters
Klang im liturgischen Raum

INGA MAI GROOTE

Von ›Annäherungen‹ zu sprechen, ist der Vorsicht geschuldet, die Fragestellung der Tagung für Kontexte des Mittelalters überhaupt verfolgen zu
können, denn mit wachsender historischer Distanz und abnehmender Infor-
mationsdichte, was Aufführungsweisen und -bedingungen betrifft, wird es
immer schwieriger, sich räumliche Dispositive vorstellen und ihre konkrete
Rolle für musikalische Aufführungen fassen zu können. Abgesehen von den
grundsätzlichen Schwierigkeiten, historische Hörweisen zu erschließen und
zu analysieren[1], waren in vielen Fällen die betreffenden Musiken stark
funktional bestimmt und damit in ihrer *Komposition* noch einmal anderen
Bedingungen unterworfen. Um die Rolle des Raumes für mittelalterliche
Musik bestimmen zu können, ist es überdies notwendig, nach Bedingungen
und möglichen Ausdrucksweisen von Raumwahrnehmung in den behandel-

---

1 Diese Diskussion ist in letzter Zeit vor allem für Musik der Renaissance ausführlicher
geführt worden, allerdings in erster Linie bezogen auf die Faktur von Kompositionen;
vgl. besonders das von Rob C. Wegman herausgegebene Themenheft The Musical
Quarterly 82 (1998), H. 3–4, S. 427–691, *Music as heard, Listeners and listening in
late-medieval and early modern Europe (1300–1600)*. Für die Auseinandersetzung
mit konkreten Räumen Deborah Howard und Laura Moretti, *Sound and Space in Renaissance: Architecture, Music, Acoustics,* New Haven 2009. Zu Fragen des ›spirituel-
len‹ Hörens neuerdings Klaus Pietschmann, »»Polyphonie im Jenseits? Sinnendiskurs
und Musikverständnis im ausgehenden Mittelalter««, in: Die Tonkunst 6 (2012), S.
459–468; ders., »»Musik für die Sinne: Zu einem möglichen Funktionsspektrum eini-
ger Hohelied-Motetten des 15. Jahrhunderts««, in: Laurenz Lütteken, Inga Mai Groote
(Hrsg.), *Normierung und Pluralisierung, Struktur und Funktion der Motette im 15.
Jahrhundert*, Kassel u.a. 2011 (= Troja 2010), S. 87–112, sowie Melanie Wald-Fuhrmann, »»Die Motette im 15. Jahrhundert, ihre Kontexte und das geistliche Hören: For-
schungsüberblick und Perspektiven««, ebd., S. 57–86.

ten Zeiten überhaupt zu fragen, ohne indes an dieser Stelle eine umfassende Diskussion liefern zu können. Um eine weitere Perspektive zu eröffnen, soll im Folgenden versucht werden, der Frage über einen realen, aber zugleich symbolgeladenen Rahmen nachzugehen: über die räumliche Präsenz von Musik im Rahmen der Liturgie und die damit verbundenen Wahrnehmungsmodi, wofür Beispiele aus dem Hoch- und Spätmittelalter herangezogen werden können.

Trotz dieser eher skeptischen Einleitung gibt es selbstverständlich Bereiche mittelalterlicher Musik und mittelalterlichen Musikdenkens, in denen dem Raum Bedeutung zukommt und die auch im musikwissenschaftlichen Diskurs immer wieder behandelt worden sind: darunter fallen einerseits die konzeptionelle Entwicklung und Verbreitung von Raumvorstellungen, die in der theoretischen Behandlung von Musik fassbar werden, und, als besonders wichtiger Einzelfall, die Frage nach möglichen Verbindungen von gotischer Architektur und Musik. Diese Beispiele illustrieren gut die Ambivalenz von ›Raum‹ als abstrakter oder physikalischer Größe im Mittelalter: Im ersten Fall handelt es sich um gedankliche Konzeptionen, die andere Modelle ablösten und zumindest unterschwellig eine starke Wirkung bis auf den modernen Betrachter haben (die Selbstverständlichkeit, mit der wir heute von ›hohen‹ und ›tiefen‹ Tönen sprechen und es gewohnt sind, in der Notation die Verhältnisse graphisch entsprechend dargestellt zu sehen, ist eines der Resultate)[2]. Im früheren Mittelalter wäre das Begriffspaar *acutus/gravis* zu nennen, das zunächst ›schrill‹ und ›schwer‹ bedeutet und erst später die Bedeutungen ›hoch‹ und ›tief‹ annimmt; erst im 9. Jahrhundert lässt sich dann, oft in enger Beziehung zur Sprache, eine Transformation von Spannung zu Höhe als Bezugssystem festmachen, und erst mit Guidos Liniensystem kommt es zu einer wirklichen Verräumlichung der musikalischen Strukturen: daran lässt sich die allmähliche Formierung des abstrakten, gedanklichen Raumes im Bezug auf die Musik selbst nachvollziehen[3].

Physikalisch-realer Raum ist hingegen besonders in Zusammenhang mit dem sogenannten Notre-Dame-Repertoire diskutiert worden, wobei insbesondere an die Überlegungen von Christian Kaden zu erinnern ist, der von einer *Konkordanzperspektive* sprach: So wie gotische Kathedralen ihre Raumgestaltung entlang ihrer Längsachse ausrichten und damit auf den Chor

---

2   Für eine zusammenfassende Darstellung wichtiger einschlägigen Phänomene, vgl. Christian Berger, »Maß und Klang: Die Gestaltung des Tonraumes in der frühen abendländischen Mehrstimmigkeit«, in: Jan A. Aertsen u.a. (Hrsg.), *Raum und Raumvorstellungen im Mittelalter*, Berlin 1998, S. 687–701.

3   Vgl. Michael Walter, *Grundlagen der Musik des Mittelalters: Schrift – Zeit – Raum*, Stuttgart, Weimar 1994.

und die dort versinnbildlichte himmlische wie irdische Herrschermacht zielen, sei auch in der Musik eine Vektorialität erkennen. Die räumliche Konzeption zeige sich liturgisch dann beispielsweise an der Ausrichtung von Prozessionen auf die West-Ost-Achse, und in der Musik entstehe gerade im nordfranzösischen Repertoire, das geographisch in derselben Gegend entstammt wie die gotische Architektur, im modalen Rhythmus eine Verteilung der Konkordanzen, die eine nach vorn strebende Wirkung entwickele wie die Baugliederung mit dem Wechsel von Pfeilern und Freiräumen[4].

DER LITURGISCHE RAUM UND SEINE SYMBOLIK

Für Musik in Verbindung mit den gottesdienstlichen Ritualen nun findet eine Verknüpfung von musikalischen und räumlichen Ereignissen statt; dabei sind allerdings sowohl einstimmiges Choralrepertoire als auch improvisierte Mehrstimmigkeit und komponierte Polyphonie zu betrachten. Dies soll im folgenden in einigen möglichen Konstellationen skizziert werden, ohne freilich das Phänomen in allen Aspekten abdecken zu können und auch unter Heranziehung von chronologisch und geographisch voneinander entfernten Beispielen. Um den Kontext erfassen zu können, sollte sich eine Behandlung der Frage nicht ausschließlich auf Quellen mit notierter Musik stützen, sondern auch auf liturgische Bücher eingehen, die musikalische Praktiken sekundär beschreiben[5]. Gerade mit der Liturgie als Bezugsrahmen[6] bietet sich hier ein Spektrum an Quellen, anhand derer der räumliche Aspekt,

---

4   Vgl. v.a. Christian Kaden, »Gotische Musik: Polyphonie und Baukunst um 1200 als Paradigmen sozialer Orientierung«, in: ders., *Des Lebens wilder Kreis: Musik im Zivilisationsprozeß*, Basel etc. 1993, S. 104–139.

5   Ein wichtiger Quellentyp ist dabei der Liber Ordinarius; hier vgl. Franz Kohlschein, »Der mittelalterliche Liber Ordinarius in seiner Bedeutung für Liturgie und Kirchenbau«, in: Franz Kohlschein und Peter Wünsche (Hrsg.), *Heiliger Raum: Architektur, Kunst und Liturgie in mittelalterlichen Kathedralen und Stiftskirchen* (= Liturgiewissenschaftliche Quellen und Forschungen 82), Münster 1998, S. 1–25, sowie auch die Fallstudien in diesem Band. Dort auch eine spezialisierte Bibliographie, die allerdings für kirchenmusikalische Aspekte (S. 330–331) relativ schmal ist.

6   In der umfangreichen Literatur zur Beziehung von Raum und Liturgie im Mittelalter wird allerdings häufig die akustische Dimension kaum berücksichtigt; zum Thema vgl. an neueren Beiträgen etwa Frances Andrews (Hrsg.), *Ritual and Space in the Middle Ages: Proceedings of the 2009 Harlaxton Symposium*, Donington 2011 (worin der musikbezogene Beitrag von Uri Smilansky sich mit der Raumaufteilung in den Handschriften beschäftigt) sowie Anne Baud (Hrsg.), *Espace ecclésial et liturgie au Moyen Age*, Lyon 2010, und Helen Gittos, *Liturgy, Architecture, and Sacred Places in Anglo-Saxon England*, Oxford 2013.

selbst wenn er nicht explizit kommentiert wird, so doch rekonstruiert werden kann, da hier auf jeden Fall eine Interaktion mit dem Kirchenraum nötig ist. ›Kom-Position‹ wäre hier daher in weiterem Sinne als eine beabsichtigte Zusammenstellung von klanglichen Ereignissen zu verstehen.

Die dabei zu betrachtenden Räume sind allerdings teilweise imaginiert, da die zugrundeliegende Raumvorstellung in hohem Maße allegorisch-symbolisch geprägt ist. Wie sehr auch reale Kirchenräume symbolisch wahrgenommen und interpretiert wurden, zeigt sich an den existierenden mittelalterlichen Beschreibungen von Bauwerken und Zeremoniell. Typisch hierfür ist die bekannte Beschreibung des Abtes Suger von Saint-Denis (ca. 1081–1151) für den dortigen Kirchenumbau und dessen Weihe, in dem allerdings die Ausführung der Liturgie weit weniger ausführlich behandelt wird als die bauliche Anlage und Gestaltung der Kirche[7]. Dem Text zufolge gibt es jedenfalls ausgezeichnete Positionen oder Teile des Raumes, wegen der dort aufbewahrten Reliquien, der dort verehrten Heiligen oder der dort gefeierten Gottesdienste (so der Chor – der dann durch entsprechende Gerätschaften und Ausstattung zu schmücken ist). Damit ist Sugers Text ein hervorragendes Beispiel für die Mischung von bautechnischen und baumetaphorischen Begrifflichkeiten, und dafür, wie die Orientierung an funktional ausgezeichneten Bereichen die Beschreibung steuert. Für die hörbare Seite der Liturgie kommt das bei der Beschreibung der Weihe aller einundzwanzig Altäre im Jahr 1144 zum Tragen, wo es heißt, dass von den Geistlichen die Messen gleichzeitig gefeiert worden seien, sowohl in den oberen Kapellen der Chorapsis als auch in den darunterliegenden der Krypta, so dass ihr Gesang im Zusammenklang eher als himmlisch denn als irdisch gewirkt habe[8].

---

7 Abt Suger von Saint-Denis, *Ausgewählte Schriften: Ordinatio / De consecratione / De administratione*, hrsg. u. übers. von Andreas Speer u. Günther Binding, Darmstadt 2000, S. 248/249; ähnlich auch die *multimoda laus* bei der Altarweihe 1140, ebd., S. 218/219. Vgl. allgemein Hanns Peter Neuheuser, »Ne lapidum materia apparentium locus vilesceret: Die Raumvorstellung des Abtes Suger in seiner Kirchweihbeschreibung von Saint-Denis«, in: Jan A. Aertsen u.a. (Hrsg.), *Raum und Raumvorstellungen im Mittelalter*, Berlin 1998, S. 641–664.

8 Hierzu Anne Robertson Walter, *The Service-Books of the Royal Abbey of Saint-Denis: images of ritual and music in the Middle Ages*, Oxford 1991, S. 236 und 247; der Text lautet »Qui omnes tam festiui tam sollempniter tam diuersi tam concorditer, tam propinqui tam hilariter ipsam altarium consecrationem missarum sollempnem celebrationem superius inferiusque peragebant, ut ex ipsa sua consonantia et coherentia armonie grata melodia potius angelicus quam humanus concentus estimaretur [...]« / »Sie alle vollzogen die Weihe der Altäre selbst sowie die feierliche Zelebration der Messen – oben wie unten – in so festlicher Freude, so feierlich, in ihrer Verschiedenheit so einmütig, in ihrer Verbundenheit so heiter, daß aufgrund des Zusammenklangs und des

Polyphonie ist damit selbstverständlich nicht impliziert; dafür aber ein zeit-gleiches Erklingen an verschiedenen Stellen, das den Kirchenraum akustisch ausfüllt und als harmonischer Eindruck interpretiert wird.

Grundsätzlich ist diese Wahrnehmungsweise für die musikwissenschaft-liche Betrachtung insofern von Interesse, als diese Diskrepanz zwischen rea-listisch klingender und symbolisch gemeinter Beschreibung auch für die Darstellung elaborierterer musikalischer Ereignisse gelten kann. Dies deutet die Diskussionen über den Realitätsgehalt der berühmten *Oratio* von Giannozzo Manetti über die Domweihe in Florenz 1436 an, bei der Guillaume Dufays Motette *Nuper rosarum* erstmals erklang. Manettis Beschreibung sowohl des Zeremoniells als auch der musikalischen Anteile darin scheinen so stark von anderen Aussageintentionen des Autors geleitet zu sein, dass auch hier in erster Linie mit einer symbolischen Lesart zu rechnen ist. Deshalb ist die zunächst realistisch anmutende Beschreibung, dass die Musik zur Elevation den ganzen Raum der Basilika erfüllte und eher himmlische Musik zu sein schiene, mit Vorsicht zu lesen[9].

Praktisch sieht der für den Gesang in der Liturgie verfügbare Raum in mittelalterlichen Kirchen natürlich jeweils unterschiedlich aus. Es ist jedoch in der Regel davon auszugehen, dass der Chorbereich zwar der wichtigste Teil des Raumes ist, aber durch Chorgestühl und Chorschranken, die sehr massiv sein konnten, vom Schiff abgegrenzt wird, so dass außerhalb dieses begrenzten Raumes das Geschehen in dessen Innern eher schlechter zu hören ist[10]. Die Akustik im Chor selbst – so lässt sich zumindest an englischen Ka-thedralen beobachten – kann dabei für Gregorianischen Gesang durch eine Verstärkung der tieferen Lagen besonders günstig sein, während in Seiten-kapellen Polyphonie in einfacher Besetzung besser zur Geltung kommt[11].

Zusammenhalts ihrer Harmonie der wohllautende Gesang eher für eine Musik der En-gel als der Menschen hätte gehalten werden können [...]«, Suger, a.a.O., S. 248f.

9   Vgl. Sabine Zak, »Der Quellenwert von Giannozzo Manettis ›Oratio‹ über die Dom-weihe von Florenz 1436 für die Musikgeschichte«, in: Die Musikforschung 40 (1987), S. 2–32, die darstellt, wie stark Manetti die päpstliche Seite hervorhebt. Der Moment der Ausführung von Dufays Motette geht daraus nicht klar hervor, und die Beschrei-bung ist deutlich literarisch überhöht (›tantis armoniarum simphoniis, tantis insuper diversorum instrumentorum consonationibus omnia basilice loca resonabant, ut ange-lici ac prorsus divini paradisi sonitus cantusque demissi celitus [...] viderentur«).

10 Vgl. etwa die Rekonstruktionszeichnungen für den Chor von Notre-Dame in Paris, in: Craig Wright, *Music and Ceremony at Notre Dame of Paris 500–1500*, Cambridge 1989, S. 10 und 99. Vgl. für die Renaissance auch den Artikel von Dorothea Baumann in diesem Band.

11 Vgl. William Peter Mahrt, »Acoustics, Liturgy, and Architecture in Medieval English Cathedrals«, in: *Music, Dance, and Society: Medieval and Renaissance Studies in*

Zudem ist gerade zu hohen Festtagen mit einer reichen ephemere Aus-
schmückung zu rechnen, besonders durch das Aufhängen von Tapisserien
oder Stoffbahnen, die für eine eher trockene Akustik sorgten: damit kann im
hohen Mittelalter gerade eine Korrelation zwischen elaborierterer Musik
(Mehrstimmigkeit und Orgel) und Reduktion von Nachhall bestehen[12].

Normativ-symbolisch ist auch das bekannte *Rationale divinorum officiorum* von Guilelmus Durantis (Durandus, † 1296; er wirkte als Bischof von
Mende) zu verstehen[13]. Es war ein grundlegender und weithin tradierter Text
zum Liturgieverständnis, in dem der Ablauf von Messe und Stundengebet,
die einzelnen Handlungen und Gebärden des Zelebranten und der Assistie-
renden im Detail beschrieben und ausgedeutet werden, unter Erläuterung der
biblischen Bezüge und kirchenhistorischer Informationen: Daher wird bei
Durantis auch der Bereich der gesungenen Liturgie relativ ausführlich behandelt, wenngleich immer unter der Perspektive der liturgischen Funktion.
Im Zentrum steht die Beschreibung, wer wo – und fallweise auch wie – die
Gesänge der Messe auszuführen habe. Ein gutes Beispiel sind die Kapitel
über das Graduale bzw. Responsorium[14], dessen Bezeichnung bereits eine
doppelte Erklärung erhält: einerseits über den Ort, *Graduale* als auf den Stufen des Altares stattfindender Gesang, der zugleich die graduelle Annähe-
rung an Gott nachvollziehe, andererseits funktional als Antwort auf die
vorangegangene Epistel, daher *Responsorium*. Zudem kommentiert Durantis
auch die Positionierung der Beteiligten an einer Stelle im Raum für einzelne
Moment (was allerdings nicht nur die Singenden betrifft):

Memory of Ingrid G. Brainard, hrsg. von Ann Buck and Cynthia J. Cyrus, Kalamazoo
2011, S. 251–259, v.a. S. 256f. über die Vermutung, dass die damit zugleich benötigte
höhere Anzahl von Knabenstimmen einerseits den Bestand einer Kathedralschule
stützte, andererseits die Kosten für erwachsene Sänger reduzierte.

12 So pointiert Wright, a.a.O., S. 17.

13 Insbesondere das 4. Buch; für den Text s. Guilelmus Durantis, *Rationale divinorum
officiorum I–IV* (= Corpus Christianorum. Continuatio Mediaevalis 140), hrsg. von
Anselme Davril u.a., Turnhout 1995. Zum Text aus musikwissenschaflicher Sicht vgl.
Herbert Douteil, *Studien zu Durantis »Rationale divinorum officiorum« als kirchen-
musikalischer Quelle* (= Kölner Beiträge zur Musikforschung 52), Regensburg 1969.

14 Durantis, a.a.O., Cap. XIX, S. 327: »3. Dicitur autem graduale uel graduale a gradibus, scilicet humilitatis, significans ascensus nostros de uirtute in uirtutem [...]. 5.
Secundo modo dicitur graduale a gradibus altaris, eo quod in festiuis diebus in gradibus sicut et alleluya cantatur, ad notandum premissos uirtutum gradus. In profestis
uero diebus, in medio chori ante gradus altaris canatur, ad significandum quod in
corde, quod est in medio corporis, premissos gradus fundare debemus. [...] 6. Responsorium uero dicitur quia uersui uel epistole correspondere debet [...]«. Vgl. auch
Douteil, a.a.O., S. 82–94.

»Jedoch steigen Lektor und Sänger, wenn sie ihre Amtstätigkeit ausüben, eine Stufe empor, weil der Lehrer die Volksmenge durch die Vollkommenheit der Lebensführung übersteigen muss. [...] an festlichen Tagen wird das Graduale wie das Alleluja auf den Stufen gesungen, um die zuvor genannten Stufen der Tugenden zu symbolisieren. An Wochentagen singt man es mitten im Chor vor den Stufen des Altares, zum Zeichen dafür, dass wir im Herzen, welches mitten im Körper sitzt, die genannten Stufen errichten müssen.«[15]

Auch wenn die Verlagerung zwischen diesen Positionen in der Regel im Bereich weniger Meter liegt und damit akustisch noch keine großen Auswirkungen haben dürfte, fügt sich die Ausführung des Gesangs damit doch in eine Benutzung des Raumes ein, in der die konkrete Stelle bewusst gewählt und in sich aussagekräftig ist, wie etwa die Wahl von rechter oder linker Seite des Altars oder die Ausrichtung bestimmter liturgischer Handlungen nach der Himmelsrichtung. Dabei kann zwischen verschiedenen Sängern und Zelebranten unterschieden werden: wenn die Geistlichen am Ambo an höherer Stelle stehen als die Knaben auf den Stufen, die noch dem aktiven Leben angehören, wird dadurch die Unterscheidung von Graduale und Alleluja als auf das aktive bzw. kontemplative Leben bezogen und auch räumlich ausgedrückt.

Einige von Durantis' Kommentaren beziehen sich allerdings auch auf den Tonraum der Gesänge selbst:

»Jedoch wird das Responsorium, das auch als Symbol für die Verkündigung des Neuen Bundes dient, in höherer Tonlage als Lesung und Epistel gesungen, welche die Verkündigung des Alten Bundes darstellen: wenn jemand also die Ohren seines Herzens verstopft hat und sich durch die dumpf tönende Ermahnung des Alten Testaments nicht aufrütteln lässt, so möge er sich wenigstens durch den hohen Gesang des Neuen Testaments gewinnen lassen.«[16]

Wenig später heißt es »Das Graduale beginnt in mittlerer Tonlage, damit der Vers nicht allzu sehr in die Höhe steigt: damit werden jene symbolisiert, die

---

15 Ebd., S. 327: »Verumptamen et lector et cantor officium suum impleturi gradum ascendunt, quia doctor perfectione uite uulgus transcendere debet.«

16 Guilelmus Durantis, *Rationale divinorum officiorum / »Der geistliche Sinn der göttlichen Liturgie«: Prolog. Buch IV: Über die Messe*, eingel. u. übers. von Claudia Barthold, Mülheim/Mosel 2012, S. 101; der lateinische Text Durantis, S. 327: »Tamen responsorium, per quod etiam predicatio novi testamenti figuratur, altius lectione et epistola, que significant predicationem veteris testamenti, canitur; ut si quis forte, cordis auribus obturatis, depressa admonitione veteris testamenti non excitatur, saltem excelsa modulatione noui demulceatur.«

die Religion aufgrund ihrer Strenge anzunehmen scheuen. Der Vers beginnt in hoher Tonlage, womit jene bezeichnet werden die durch Fasten, Gebet und andere gute Handlungen emporsteigen [...].«[17] Höhe im Tonraum wird hier also mit spiritueller Erhöhung, mit Vervollkommnung gleichgesetzt. Ähnliches gilt für die Beschreibung, wie das *Te deum* im Stundengebet gesungen wird: nach dem Ende der Nokturn werden die Glocken geläutet und das *Te deum* mit erhobener Stimme gesungen, »[...] dass aber das Ende dieses Gesanges ab den Versen ›Per singulos dies‹ höher gesungen wird, stellt die Glückwünsche [der Nachbarinnen über den wiedergefundenen Groschen] dar.«[18] Auch hier geht es tatsächlich um die unterschiedlich hohe Rezitation verschiedener Abschnitte[19], so dass wiederum Ansätze einer bewussten räumlichen Gestaltung im ›inneren Raum‹ der Musik zu erkennen sind.

RÄUMLICHE ASPEKTE DER LITURGISCHEN GESANGSPRAXIS

Die bei Durantis erläuterten Positionierungen im Kirchenraum sind dabei keine rein abstrakten Darstellungen, sondern die beschriebenen Praktiken finden ihr Abbild in den Vorgaben für einzelne Kirchen und, in einem zweiten Schritt, in der Verwendung bestimmter Arten des Gesanges. Ein mögliches Beispiel für die Nutzung eines konkreten Raumes in dieser Art bietet der Bamberger Dom, dessen Ordinale für Heiligabend vorschreibt, dass der Chor zum letzten Responsorium der Matutin in das Schiff hinabsteige; die Knaben singen den Vers »Quem eterna« am Pult, der Chor wiederum das Melisma auf »veritate«; dann steigen sie wieder hinauf in den

---

17 Durantis, ebd., S. 102; »Graduale plane incipitur, ne nimis uersus ascendat, in quo designantur qui religionem propter eius austeritatem ingredi metuunt; uersus uero alte, in quo designantur qui, ieiunando, orando, et alia bona agendo, ascendunt [...] Et quamquam graduale timore uerses alte inchoetur [...] finito tamen uerso uox fiducialiter exaltatur, in quo significatur quod, de misericordia Dei confisi, fiducialiter omne sue actioni insistunt« (Durantis, ebd., S. 328f.).

18 Guilelmus Durantis, *Rationale divinorum officiorum* V–VI (= Corpus Christianorum. Continuatio Mediaevalis 140A), hrsg. von Anselem Davril, Turnhout 1998, S. 68: »Nocturnis finitis campanae pulsantur, et *Te deum laudamus* alta voce cantatur [...] Quod vero finis eiusdam cantici ibi *Per singulos dies* at alii versus sequentes altius canuntur, significat congratulationem vicinarum [...].«

19 Janka Szendrei, »*Altius canitur?* Durandus on the Performance of the Te deum«, in: *Studies in Medieval Chant and Liturgy in Honour of David Hiley*, hrsg. von Terence Bailay, Budapest 2007, S. 413–423.

gegenüberliegenden Georgschor und beginnen die Messe *Dominus dixit*[20]. Dadurch reagiert die Liturgie explizit auf die baulichen Umgestaltungen des mittleren 13. Jahrhunderts und nutzt die Struktur des Gebäudes mit nun zwei Chören an den Enden des Schiffes aus[21].

Aus derartigen Beschreibungen geht hervor, wie die Position im Raum mit dem ausgeführten Gesang in Relation gesetzt wird. Das klangliche Ereignis gewinnt durch seine räumliche Festlegung zusätzliche Bedeutung, vor allem, da es hierarchisch abgestufte Plätze gibt und höheres oder tieferes Stehen mit unterschiedlichen Bezugsebenen verknüpft ist. Eine entsprechende Auszeichnungslogik lässt sich dann auch bei der Verwendung von Mehrstimmigkeit anwenden, für die die Zuordnung der vierstimmigen Notre-Dame-Organa zu Weihnachten nur ein besonders plakatives Beispiel ist. Neben dieser symbolischen Bedeutung als aufwendigerer Klangraum existieren aber auch pragmatische Varianten, die Craig Wright treffend als *action chants* beschreibt[22]: wenn Teilnehmer an der Liturgie einen Weg zurücklegen müssen, kann das eine sinnvolle Stelle für die Einfügung zusätzlicher Gesänge, auch einer Motette sein, um die Zeit der währenddessen stattfindenden Handlung zu auszufüllen. Damit können auch diese Gesänge zumindest indirekt mit der räumlichen Dimension verbunden sein, denn wenn diese Handlungen Bewegungen im Raum sind, kommt der Dauer der Musik eine räumliche Sekundärbedeutung zu.

Das betrifft, nimmt man weitere Texte hinzu, nicht nur die Ausführung von Messen und Stundengebet, sondern auch andere Formen der Liturgie und ganz besonders Prozessionen, die sich durch eine Kirche oder sogar darüber hinaus in umliegende Straßen oder zu anderen Kirchen bewegen kön-

---

20 »IN SANCTA NOCTE: Ad matutinum. […] Postea incipiatur Responsorium, cum quo descendatur in monasterium et candele sex portentur cum longis candelabris. Pueri cantent versus *Quem etera* in pulpito, chorus notam super ›veritate‹ in monasterio. Deinde ascendant in chorum sancti Georgii et incipiatur missa *Dominus dixit. Kyrieleison* [c.n.]. De beata virgine. *Gloria in excelsis.* Prophetia *Populus qui ambulat.* Epist. *Apparuit gratia.* Graduale *Tecum principium. Alleluia. Dominus dixit.* Sequentia *Grates nunc omnes,* quam chorus cantet. Domini cantent notam. Ewang. *Exiit edictum. Credo in unum.*« Zit. nach Lori Kruckenberg, »Neumatizing the Sequence: Special Performances of Sequences in the Central Middle Ages«, in: Journal of American Musicological Society 59 (2006), S. 243–317, hier S. 262; dass *nota* als melodische Wendung zu verstehen ist.

21 Zudem wird dadurch auch die doppelte Bedeutung des Domes für die weltliche und wie geistliche Macht unterstrichen; dass gerade im Georgschor, der den ›weltlichen‹ Teil repräsentiert, die Beteiligung der Kanoniker explizit hervorgehoben wird, kann wohl als eine bewusste Inszenierung von Einheit gelesen werden.

22 Wright, *Music and Ceremony*, a.a.O., S. 206, in Verbindung mit der Diskussion der Pariser Königsakklamationen zu Ostern.

nen: dabei wird der Gesang von speziellen Antiphonen und Versikeln mit einer räumlichen Verlagerung kombiniert. Am Beispiel von Notre-Dame in Paris wird das besonders deutlich in den Prozessionen zu Gründonnerstag und Allerheiligen[23]. In ihnen kann es einzelne Stationen als hervorgehobene Orte geben. Zuweilen zeigt sich eine Nähe zu Elementen des geistlichen Spiels, etwa wenn im 14. Jahrundert bei der Vorprozession zum Palmsonntag das *Circumdederunt me* in St. Gertrud in Essen gesungen wird, indem sich die Prozessionsteilnehmer darum herum aufstellen und die Kanoniker damit die Antiphon gewissermaßen in ihrer räumlichen Anlage dargestellt singen[24]. Zudem ist festzuhalten, dass gerade mit der steigenden Zahl von Votivmessen und Stiftungen zunehmend mehr Zelebrationen in den Seitenkapellen stattfanden. Da Stiftungen oft Vesperpsalmen oder *Salve reginas* vorsahen, die immer häufiger polyphon ausgeführt wurden, verlagerten sich die musikalischen Aktivitäten ebenfalls in die Nebenkapellen, ganz besonders die Marienkapellen, und damit gewissermaßen an die ›Seiten‹ des Raumes. Daher ist es möglich, dass etwa in Reims der Marienaltar ›bei der Rouelle‹ mit einer Stiftung für polyphonen Gesang ausgestattet war, für die vermutlich Guillaume de Machauts Messe bestimmt war, bevor die regelmäßige Pflege von Polyphonie im Chor nachweisbar ist[25].

Dass überdies mitunter auch Interaktionen mit dem *populus*, ›dem Volk‹, also den teilnehmenden Laien als gewissermaßen irdischen ›Publikum‹, vorgesehen sind, lässt sich gut an den Quellen zur Sainte-Chapelle in Paris (vollendet 1248 und bestimmt für die durch den König Ludwig IX. erworbenen Passions-Reliquien) illustrieren. Eigentlich eine private Palastkapelle, entwickelte die Sainte-Chapelle aber gerade wegen des Ranges ihrer Reli-

---

23 Für die Prozessionsorganisation für Notre Dame vgl. bereits Jacques Handschin, »Zur Geschichte von Notre Dame«, in: Acta Musicologica 4 (1932), S. 5–17, sowie Rebecca A. Baltzer, »The Geography of the Liturgy at Notre-Dame of Paris«, in: Thomas Forrest Kelly (Hrsg.), *Plainsong in the Age of Polyphony* (= Cambridge studies in performance practice 2), Cambridge 1992, S. 45–64. Zur Zunahme von Prozessionen für Saint-Denis, vgl. Robertson, a.a.O., S. 251f.

24 Jürgen Bärsch, »Raum und Bewegung im mittelalterlichen Gottesdienst: Anmerkungen zur Prozessionsliturgie in der Essener Stiftskirche nach dem Zeugnis des Liber ordinarius vom Ende des 14. Jahrhunderts« (= Liturgiewissenschaftliche Quellen und Forschungen 82), in: Franz Kohlschein und Peter Wünsche (Hrsg.), *Heiliger Raum: Architektur, Kunst und Liturgie in mittelalterlichen Kathedralen und Stiftskirchen*, Münster 1998, S. 163–186, hier S. 170f.

25 Vgl. Anne Walters Robertson, »The Mass of Guillaume de Machaut in the Cathedral of Reims«, in: Thomas Forrest Kelly (Hrsg.), *Plainsong in the Age of Polyphony* a.a.O., S. 100–139, die betont, dass auf diese Weise Polyphonie häufig früher dort als im Chorraum selbst stattfand, besonders S. 118 und 136f., wo sie neben Reims besonders auf Beispiele aus Brüssel, Brügge und Cambrai verweist.

quien und deren Präsentationen auch eine Anziehungkraft auf größere Besu-
cherschichten und konnte damit zugleich zur Repräsentation der Königs-
macht dienen[26]. Für ihre liturgischen Abläufe wird wiederum elaboriert die
Disposition für bestimmte Gesänge beschrieben, wobei genaue Anweisungen zur Alternatim-Ausführung und die Erwähnung von bestimmten no-
tierten, in einigen Fällen wohl auch mehrstimmigen Stücken gegeben
werden[27]. Die kleinräumliche Differenzierung geschieht dabei vor allem
zwischen Vorsängern und Chor oder linker und rechter Chorhälfte[28]. Hinzu
kommen allerdings Momente, in denen die Hinwendung zu den Laien explizit erwähnt wird, etwa indem ihnen das Kreuz gezeigt oder zu ihnen hinge-
wandt gesungen wird, wobei die Ausnutzung der Anlage mit zwei Stock-
werken prozessionsartige Wege erlaubte[29].

In den bisher angeführten Beispielen stand vor allem die Verwendung
von Gesang an sich im Vordergrund. Die damit beschriebenen Praktiken be-
schränkten sich in der Regel auf Einstimmigkeit. Sie interagieren musikalisch sowohl mit dem äußeren Raum, als auch – wie das kurz erwähnte Singen bestimmter Abschnitte in höherer oder tieferer Tonlage – mit dem ›inneren‹ oder eigenen Raum der Musik. Für beides ließen sich zahlreiche zusätzliche Beispiele finden, häufig auch differenziert nach Typ des Gottes-
dienstes.

---

26 Vgl. Meredith Cohen, »An Indulgence for the Visitor: The Public at the Sainte-Cha-
    pelle of Paris«, in: Speculum 83 (2008), S. 840–883, die für eine Verstärkung des Kö-
    nigskults über die Aufwertung der Kapelle als Pilgerziel plädiert; dies wurde auch
    durch Ablässe erreicht, vgl. v.a. S. 865–868.
27 Vgl. für eine umfassende Wiedergabe der 1471 niedergelegten Bestimmungen Bar-
    bara Haggh, »An Ordinal of Ockeghem's time from the Sainte-Chapelle of Paris:
    Paris, Bibliothèque de l'Arsenal«, MS 114, in: Tijdschrift van de Koninklijke
    Vereniging voor Nederlandse Muziekgeschiedenis 47 (1997), S. 33–71.
28 Vgl. etwa zum Gründonnerstag bei der Spendung des Aschenkreuzes: »The cleric
    choirboy intones at the eagle the R. Exaudi nos, which the left choir finishes, then a
    choirboy intones the ps. Salvum mefac, which the right choir finishes, through Ani-
    mam meam. Next, that choirboy intones the an. Exaudi nos finished by the left choir,
    he intones the an. Iuxta vestibulum finished by the right choir, he intones the an. Im-
    mutemus finished by the left choir, and he intones the an. Emendemus finished by the
    right choir.« Zit. nach Haggh, a.a.O., S. 39.
29 Vgl. Cohen, a.a.O., S. 871 u. 873f. (so nach BnF lat. 1435: »ille qui facit officium […]
    ostendit crucem populo assistenti«, und nach Arsenal 114, in Ergänzung zu den von
    Barbara Haggh gegebenen Stellen: »Ile qui facit officium […] cantat antiphonam Ecce
    lignum ostendendo populo crucem praedictam«).

GESTALTUNG DES INNEREN KLANGRAUMS

Für die elaboriertere Nutzung des ›inneren‹ Raumes der Musik gibt es nun sowohl in der Faktur von Einstimmigkeit als auch durch Mehrstimmigkeit Beispiele. Die innermusikalische Auszeichnung und Differenzierung kann – neben dem alternierenden Vortrag an sic[30] – beispielsweise durch Wiederholungen oder langsameres Singen erreicht werden. Bereits im einstimmigen Gesang lässt sich entsprechendes gerade durch die Verwendung von melismatischen Passagen erreichen, die sich vom syllabischen Vortrag abheben oder durch ihre schiere Ausdehnung einen besonderen Abschnitt bilden, wie im Bamberger Beispiel mit der besonders erwähnten *nota* zu bestimmten Textabschnitten. Durantis beschreibt das als eine existierende, aber bereits veraltende Praxis, die theologisch begründet werden kann, da der Text hier ohnehin von Unsagbarem künde[31]. In Saint-Denis lässt sich aus dieser Perspektive die langdauernde Bevorzugung textloser Tropen (statt textierter oder neuer Formen von Polyphonie) interpretieren, die möglicherweise eine Analogie in der theologischen Vorstellung vom Aufstieg von der materiellen zur immateriellen Welt hat[32]. Ungeachtet, ob dort bestimmte theologische Texttraditionen wirksam werden, ist jedoch der Auszeichnungscharakter eines von Text weitgehend freien Stimmklangs erkennbar.

Dieses ausführliche Auszieren ist für unsere Diskussion von besonderem Interesse, da es stärker mit *kompositorischen* Entscheidungen verbunden ist. Das vielzitierte Beispiel Organum ist daher hierfür nur eine, schon sehr elaborierte Möglichkeit. Die dahinterstehenden Prinzipien lassen sich besonders gut an Teilen des Sequenz-Repertoires zeigen: In einigen Quellen sind Sequenzen mit eingeschobenen untextierten bzw. nur mit dem Vokal a unterlegten Passagen notiert. Dies ist als ausgedehntes Melisma zu verstehen und war als Praxis des textlosen Melismensingens nachweislich im 10. und 11. Jahrhundert in Nordfrankreich verbreitet.

---

30 Vgl. Douteil, *Studien*, a.a.O., S. 20f.

31 So zum Stichwort *neuma*, das er als wortlosen *iubilus* erklärt (Rationale, Kap. V, 32ff.), vgl. Kruckenberg, a.a.O., S. 250f.

32 Vgl. die bei Robertson, *The Service-Books*, a.a.O., S. 246f., diskutierten Aussagen, die allerdings die einschlägigen pseudo-dionysischen Interpretationen von Erwin Panofsky und Otto von Simson aufnehmen; für die Infragestellung dieser Theorien vgl. Christoph Markschies, *Gibt es eine Theologie der gotischen Kathedrale? Nochmals: Suger von Saint-Denis und Sankt Dionys vom Areopag* (= Abhandlungen der Heidelberger Akademie der Wissenschaften, Philosophisch-historische Klasse; Jg. 1995, Nr. 1), vorgelegt von Martin Hengel am 12. November 1994, Heidelberg 1995.

An einem Graduale und Sequentiar aus Rouen lässt sich dies illustrieren (Paris, Bibliothèque nationale de France, MS lat. 904)[33]. Die untextierten Abschnitte sind mit einem a mit einer zopfartigen Fortsetzung unterlegt; überdies gibt es zu zahlreichen Gesängen Rubriken, die die Aufführung genauer beschreiben. Für *Iubilans concrepa* lautet die Rubrik, dass der Text der Sequenz von fünf Knaben am Pult gesungen werden soll, dass das Melisma hingegen vom Chor (»Lit[ter]a seq[uentiae] dicatur a V pueris in pulpito pneuma t[a]m[en] dicatur a choro«)[34].

Interessant für unsere Fragestellung ist dies, weil derartige Quellen die musikalisch differenzierte Gestaltung mit der zuvor beschriebenen räumlichen Differenzierung in der Ausführung der Liturgie verbinden: Textierte und untextierte Passagen sind aufgeteilt zwischen verschiedenen Standorten, so den Knaben am Sängerpult und dem Rest des Chores oder den beiden Chorhälften. Vergleichbare Formen der räumlich getrennten Aufstellung blieben auch in späteren Zeiten üblich. Eine besonders plastische Beschreibung der räumlich getrennten Aufstellung von Sängern bieten Augenzeugenberichte der Krönung Kaiser Maximilians I. in Aachen (1486). In einem von ihnen wird ausführlich über die Feiern der Passionszeit in Aachen berichtet; hier heißt es: Am Palmsonntag sang die königliche Kapelle Figuralmusik und auch die Passion dergestalt, dass die zwei Sänger für den Evangelistenbericht und die Worte Christi vor dem gewöhnlichen Pult standen, die Worte der Jünger und anderen, also die Turbae, neben dem Altar und hinter einem Vorhang verborgen; sie sagen ebenfalls mehrstimmig. Ferner ist von Gesang vor dem Altar die Rede, überdies mit voller Stimme und mehrstimmiger Ausgestaltung ›der letzten Note‹, wobei die Sänger wieder hinter einem Vorhang verdeckt bleiben sollten[35]. Hier kommt also zur räumlichen Tren-

---

33 Vgl. hierzu Kruckenberg, a.a.O., S. 252–261, mit der dort nachgewiesenen Literatur. Unter http://gallica.bnf.fr/ark:/12148/btv1b84324657 (24.11.2014) ist das *Graduale Rotomagense* auch online einzusehen.

34 Zit. nach Kruckenberg, ebd., S. 253 (u. vgl. Abb. 4a, ebd.); vgl. als zusätzliche Beispiele »Sabb[at]o dicatur littera seq[uentie] a q[ui]nq[ue] pu[er]is pneuma t[a]m[en] dicatur a choro«; »[...] et tunc dicatur sed iubilans. ita q[uo]d dexter chorus dicat litteram et sinister pneuma« (aus der Handschrift Rouen 277); weitere Beispiele auch bei Haines, »New Light«, a.a.O., S. 60 (»in inventione sancte crucis dicatur primus versus sequentie in pulpito et reiteretur *Alleluia*, dexter chorus dicat secundum versum *Laudes crucis*«); dritter Advent: »in dextero choro dicatur littera sequentie, in sinistro pneuma«); Kruckenberg gibt auch Verweise auf Beispiele an verschiedenen Orten.

35 »In die palmarum cantores regis officium cantaverunt in figurativis et passionem hoc modo: unus ex illis verba ewangeliste, alius verba Christi, stantes ante pulpitum consuetum, discipulorum autem verba et aliorum exclamancium ceteri cantores juxta altare post cortinam absconditi diversis vocibus cum fractione notarum ad fortem.

nung der Sprechrollen eine Differenzierung in der musikalischen Faktur; Mehrstimmigkeit dient ebenfalls zur Auszeichnung – und man möchte sich die Wirkung des aufwendigeren Schlussabschnitts einerseits ähnlich wie die Unterscheidung zwischen textierten und textlosen Sequenz-Passagen vorstellen, andererseits aber auch in Verbindung mit polyphonen Praktiken.

Der Übergang in die mehrstimmige Komposition lässt sich dann an einem weiteren Beispiel aus Rouen zeigen, dem zweistimmigen *Ave virgo, virga Jesse*[36]: Das *Missale Rouen Ms. 277*, einer für die mittelalterliche Liturgie an der Kathedrale von Rouen zentralen Quelle, enthält nach dem liturgisch geordneten Hauptteil der Handschrift am Ende eine Gruppe von Sequenzen, die für bestimmte Messen zwischen Epistel und Evangelium bestimmt sind, darunter als letzte Gruppe eine Auswahl mit marianischen Texten ohne spezifische Zuordnung. Unter ihnen ist nur das allerletzte Stück, *Ave virgo, virga Jesse*, zweistimmig notiert und anderweitig wohl nur in einer einzige Quelle überliefert, also ein seltenes Stück, das möglicherweise lokalen Ursprungs ist (zumal die Kathedrale von Rouen 1214 eine neue Marienkapelle bekommen hatte)[37]. Die bereits erwähnten Aufführungsanweisungen beschreiben nicht nur die Trennung zwischen Knaben und dem Rest des Chores, sondern auch immer wieder den Wechsel von *sinister chorus* und *dexter chorus*, also das Abwechseln der Chorhälften, das letztlich natürlich auch deren räumliche Trennung ausnutzt. Im Falle unserer Motette ist das möglicherweise einkomponiert, da sie systematisch mit Stimmtausch arbeitet, der ungefähr zeitgleich auch im Traktat *Habito de ipsa plana musica* als mögliche Gestaltungsweise beschrieben wird[38]. Im Ergebnis war damit hier die sich aus liturgischen Gewohnheiten ergebende räumliche Dimension der Aufführungsweise liturgischer Musik tatsächlich einkomponiert.

Angesichts dieser Beispiele scheint sich von hier aus durchaus ein gangbarer Weg zu den Motetten im Übergang von Mittelalter zur Renaissance zu eröffnen, auch wenn nicht bei jeder Veränderung der musikalischen Textur in polyphonen Strukturen, vor allem bei der Gegenüberstellung von kleine-

---

Quarta feria sequente quatuor persone eodem modo legebant passionem, simul tamen stantes ante pulpitum, planiori voce, sed cum fractura ultime note tantummodo in consonanciam.« Zit nach Sabine Zak, »Fürstliche und städtische Repräsentation in der Kirche (Zur Verwendung von Instrumenten im Gottesdienst)«, in: Musica disciplina 38 (1984), S. 231–259, hier S. 245 (Anm. 58).

36 Hierzu ausführlich John Haines, »New Light on the Polyphonic Sequence ›Ave virgo, virga Jesse‹«, in: Early Music 34 (2006), S. 55–73.

37 Vgl. die Transkription bei Haines, ebd., S. 66f.

38 Vgl. Haines, ebd., S. 65 (»idem sonus repetitus tempore diverso a diversis vocibus«).

ren oder größeren Stimmzahlen, davon ausgegangen werden kann, dass sie vom Komponisten als räumlicher Effekt gedacht waren. Ein beträchtlicher Anteil von ihnen kann auch der Hervorhebung bestimmter Passagen, der Ausdifferenzierung der Struktur dienen, ohne den Raum explizit mitzudenken. Dennoch könnte ein Stück vom Ende des 15. Jahrhunderts wie Robert Wylkinsons *Salve regina* tatsächlich auch räumliche Wirkungen zum Ausdruck bringen – zumal hier ein Andachtsstück vorliegt (also eines, das innerhalb des Funktionsspektrums der Motette nicht so sehr politisch-huldigende Funktionen, sondern die Verstärkung individueller Andacht zum Ziel hat)[39]. Unter den Hervorhebungen fallen besonders einige statische Momente auf, etwa auf den Text »Jesum« (das Objekt, das Maria zeigen, auf das sie verweisen soll) mittels Fermaten, dann aber vor allem, indem nach einem kurzen dreistimmigen Abschnitt der Imperativ *ostende* (zeige ihn uns) neunstimmig auskomponiert wird, so dass vielleicht der Übergang in die Schau der himmlischen Sphäre erlebbar gemacht werden soll, als öffnete sich der Himmel (dadurch wird nicht nur die Symbolik der Neunzahl für die Engelshierarchien aufgegriffen, sondern auch ein klanglich deutlich unterscheidbarer Raum geschaffen). Damit scheinen sich hier realer und imaginärer, liturgischer und himmlischer Raum miteinander zu verbinden[40]. Wenn sich so der Himmel und der dort stattfindende englische Lobgesang als ein hörbar anderer Raum öffnen, kann die Musik als Medium den Beter in seiner Andacht durch eine quasi-räumliche Wahrnehmung unterstützten: wie ein Bild Heilsgegenstände vor Augen stellt, so könnten derartige Motetten sie ›vor Ohren‹ stellen.

Die Wurzeln einer solchen Denkweise lassen sich aber, das konnten uns die liturgisch ausgerichteten Beispiele zeigen, in die Praktiken des Mittelalters zurückverfolgen. Um ihre Grundlagen zu verstehen, sollten daher auch scheinbar ›einfache‹ Formen von Polyphonie oder lediglich beschriebene Praktiken in liturgischen Kontexten herangezogen werden, um die zweifellos vorhandenen liturgisch-symbolischen Raumvorstellungen in ihrer Umsetzung in musikalische Praktiken zu analysieren und damit musikalisch-kompositorisches Denken mit dem Raum unter mittelalterlichen Bedingungen rekonstruieren zu können.

---

39 Vgl. hierzu ausführlich die Interpretation bei Wald-Fuhrmann, a.a.O.

40 Der Text ist ein Gebet, keine Beschreibung, und deshalb ein – um mit Reinhard Strohm zu sprechen – aus der Perspektive des Menschen formulierter ›Sprechakt‹, der von den Musikern in der Ausführung des Gebets als gesungener Vortrag vertreten wird.

ENGLISH SUMMARY

Imagined and Liturgical Spaces
Considering Audible Spaces in the Middle Ages

The analysis of spatial aspects in the production and perception of music in the Middle Ages is rendered difficult by the types of available sources, as well as by the scarcity of precise indications concerning the role of space in performance and composition of music. Consequently, the conditions of spatial perception concerning medieval music should be outlined before trying to answer the question of how far spatial elements could be consciously employed in compositions. The material treated in this chapter consists of liturgically framed music; the music in question thus includes monophonic chant, improvised polyphony, and occasionally also composed polyphony. So, not only compositions as single works by an author have to be considered, but also the composition of musical events in space in a larger sense.

The first part of this chapter briefly recalls important questions of space in medieval music that have attracted notable interest from musicologists, as they admirably illustrate the conceptual levels on which space in medieval music can be considered: abstract or physical (in the latter case it is mostly architectural). Notwithstanding the aforementioned reservations, interest in or awareness for spatial aspects of sound and music in the Middle Ages can be deduced from different sources. In theoretical texts, the emerging treatment of ›tonal space‹ after the 9th century offers evidence for a conceptual approach that shifts from other qualities of tone or voice to the dichotomy between high and low, which is also connected to the spatial representation of music in notation. The treatment can be deduced mainly from authors who describe music or musical preferences with reference to intervallic structures. The second important topic that has been intensively discussed in relation to spatial aspects is the development of polyphony, especially the discussion of the Notre Dame repertory in relation to architectural phenomena at its centre.

Against this background of approaches to spatial qualities of music, the main part of this chapter concentrates on the relationship between music and liturgical space in the High and Late Middle Ages, as this context allows us to discuss the perception and use of music in more concrete terms, and, in a second step, to reflect on the emergence of compositional responses to spatial needs or conditions. To come closer to a potential spatial imagination in connection with polyphony, it is helpful to combine references of a different kind. Liturgy and ritual offer a good frame for approaching this problem, because they are treated in descriptive and normative sources that, even when they do not intentionally deal with the spatial use of music, contain information on practices and intentions when they offer descriptions and prescriptions for the celebration of different kinds of services. This is often intermingled with symbolic interpretations of the actual space (e.g., in Suger of Saint-Denis or in Durandus de Mende). These sources have been considered from time to time by musicologists, but usually with reference to local customs and only rarely under the perspective of information concerning the spatial dimension of musical performance in the liturgy. On this basis, two aspects are discussed: the ›outer‹ and the ›inner‹ acoustical space of music.

The connection between music and the ›outer‹ space can be reconstructed from descriptions and liturgical dispositions that mention the placement of singers for certain musical actions in a church or during a ceremony. For this, differences between different kinds of services are noticeable. The rubrics of a manuscript for Rouen Cathedral (early 13th Century) are a good example, where explicit references are made to the spatial distribution of choirs, including the performance of organum repertory. Further observations on the interaction between performers and listeners in the space of the church can be made using the example of liturgies for the Saintes-Chapelles, which include processional events and moments of interaction with the *populus*. The evidence that results from these kinds of source highlights, among other things, the importance of off-centre positions (like side chapels) and, in some cases, the spatial differentiation on several levels (inside the choir, choir versus nave, inside versus outside the church), as well as a link between movement in space and the temporal structure of the ritual.

The ›inner‹ acoustical space of music, finally, is discussed using the example of some polyphonic compositions that show an awareness of these structural moments in music implying spatial meaning. This leads on to motets in the 15th century that are of strongly devotional character and thus may intentionally have employed the acoustically powerful ›spatial‹ devices to reinforce the impact on the listener.

Music and Space in the Renaissance

DOROTHEA BAUMANN

The purpose of this article is to bring together several aspects of knowledge in order to understand the complex relations between space and music in the Renaissance. Due to restricted space, this paper concentrates only on the most important elements that converge in the analysis of two music examples: the change in concepts of space in philosophy, architecture, and visual arts; theoretical and practical knowledge in room acoustics in the Renaissance; and modern knowledge on acoustics[1].

From the 19th century onward, we have been used to thinking in terms of separate disciplines that draw on different symbolic realms with different terminology and ways of thinking[2]. Going back to the 15th and 16th centuries, however, we can situate ourselves in a world of knowledge with fewer boundaries. Music theory, mathematics, geometry, astronomy, and also painting, architecture, and the practice of music shared a common way of thinking based on theology and philosophy. That is why it is crucial in an analysis of the relation between music and space to understand the philosophical background.

---

1   This article will not treat the concept of space in the structure of music. An important paper on this aspect of space is Edward M. Lowinsky, »The Concept of Physical Space in the Renaissance«, in: *Papers of the American Musicological Society*, 1941 (ed. 1946), pp. 82–83.

2   Dorothea Baumann, »Systematische Musikwissenschaft: Eine Disziplin zwischen Kulturgeschichte und Naturwissenschaften«, in: *Musicology Today: Problems and Perspectives, a Collection of Scientific Articles, Scientific Researches*, Issue 80, edited by Olena Zinkevych, Ukrainian National Tchaikovsky Academy of Music, Kiev 2009, pp. 40–51.

THE RENAISSANCE AND PHILOSOPHY

Jacob Burckhardt, in his Civilization of the Renaissance in Italy, published in 1860, described the Renaissance as the age of »discovery of Nature and of Man«, the time »in which Man became a spiritual [intellectual] Individual and recognized himself as such«[3]. The German philosopher Ernst Cassirer, in his 1906 book *The Development of Knowledge in Modern Thought* noted that Burckhardt had written a great chapter on cultural history, which, however, was lacking a chapter on Renaissance philosophy. Cassirer showed how self-recognition became the driving force that, from the beginning of the 15th century onward, slowly changed »the balance between the particular [cultural] forces – society, state, religion, church, art, science«[4].

Cassirer was the first to recognize Nicolaus de Cusa's new view of the significance of art and the artist in building a new appreciation of art and science. Cusanus (1401–1464), cardinal, German philosopher, and mathematician, was still deeply rooted in the scholastic thinking of the Christian Middle Ages. His interest in antiquity, based on Plato's writings in the original language, is not related to poetry and rhetoric, but rather to philosophy and mathematics. His turn toward the deepening of subjectivity does not contradict the theological principles of medieval thinking, but rather builds on these very principles. Cusanus' ideas continued to influence thinking from Filippo Brunelleschi (who studied mathematics with Cusanus' close friend Paolo Toscanelli[5]) and Leon Battista Alberti (Brunelleschi's scholar), to Leonardo da Vinci, going on until Copernicus, Galileo, and Kepler.

---

3   Jacob Burckhardt, *Die Cultur der Renaissance in Italien: Ein Versuch*, Basel 1860, 2. Abschnitt, p. 131: »[Es] erhebt sich mit voller Macht das Subjective; der Mensch wird geistiges Individuum und erkennt sich als solches.« English edition: *The Civilization of the Renaissance in Italy*, transl. by S. g. C. Middlemore, 3rd ed. London 1878. With the term ›Renaissance‹ for the Italian history after the Middle Ages Burckhardt used the French translation of the original Italian term *rinascita* and followed the French historian Jules Michelet, who in 1855 published the fifth volume of his Histoire de France under the title *La Renaissance*. See Eugenio Garin, *Renaissance und Kultur*, in: *Propyläen Weltgeschichte, eine Universalgeschichte*, edited by Golo Mann, Alfred Heuß, and August Nitschke, Berlin and Frankfurt am Main 1960–64, vol. 6, p. 431.

4   Ernst Cassirer, *Das Erkenntnisproblem in der Philosophie und Wissenschaft der neueren Zeit*, Habilitationsschrift, 2 Vol., Berlin 1906–1907, Neuausgabe in: *Ernst Cassirer Gesammelte Werke* (ECW), Hamburger Ausgabe, edited by Brigit Recki, Vol. 14, Hamburg 2002, with a foreword by the author.

5   Ernst Cassirer, *Individuum und Kosmos in der Philosophie der Renaissance*, Leipzig 1927 (= Studien der Bibliothek Warburg, Vol. 10), new edition Hamburg 2013, pp. 40–41.

In *De docta ignorantia* (1440, printed in Basel 1565), Cusanus follows Plato in separating the empirical from the intellectual world in order to reach a new definition of the infinite[6]. Cassirer concludes that »this drive towards the infinite becomes a main motive entering all spheres of the spiritual life of the Renaissance.« A second main motive stems from the fact that Cusanus takes an important turn in the interpretation of the similitude between Man and God. In his creative thinking, as evident in art and science, man can approach the image of God in a steadily improving process: »God's and man's spirit belong to different categories but are related in their way of production. This is not substantial identity but analogy of acting.«[7] This view also allowed for a new appreciation of the value of mathematical physics and science which led to »the elimination of a bifurcation of knowledge in medieval philosophy (Augustin and scholasticism), the divorce between *scientia* (knowledge of natural things) and *sapientia* (knowledge of supernatural things), with primacy of *sapientia*. [Medieval] mathematics as a science of the world [could] never claim a position equal to metaphysics and theology, the sciences of the eternal.«[8] Cassirer adds that »Cusanus did not challenge the primacy of *sapientia* but opened the door towards a complex process of shifting values which also changed the concept of space. [...], with Leonardo and Galileo, mathematics became a new cultural force.«[9]

CHANGE IN CONCEPTS OF SPACE IN PHILOSOPHY, ARCHITECTURE, AND THE VISUAL ARTS

Scholastics (11th to 14th centuries) denied *intramundane* vacuum and *extramundane* space because according to Aristotle space was determined by the

6   Cassirer, ibid., p. 16.

7   Enno Rudolph, »Cassirers Rezeption des Renaissancehumanismus«, in: *Ernst Cassirers Werk und Wirkung, Kultur und Philosophie*, edited by Dorothea Frede and Reinold Schmücker, Darmstadt: Wissenschaftliche Buchgesellschaft 1997, pp. 105–121.

8   Ernst Cassirer, »Some Remarks on the Question of the Originality of the Renaissance«, 1943, reprint in: idem, *Individuum und Kosmos in der Philosophie der Renaissance*, Hamburg 2013, pp. 225–226, referring to J. H. Randall, »The Development of the Scientific Method in the School of Padua«, in: Journal of the History of Ideas I (1940), pp. 177–206.

9   Cassirer, ibid., p. 225, refers in footnote 10 to Leonardo da Vinci, Scritti letterari cavati dagli Autografi, No. 1157, London 1883, vol. II, p. 289.

surface of a body[10]. Liberated from the fully corporeal space and imaginary space[11], Renaissance philosophy finally comes to a free and infinite space that is not only extended between bodies but also exists without bodies. The development toward modern systemic space goes from Telemach (1509–1588) to Giordano Bruno (1548–1600) and Henry More (1614–1687), who defines space as infinitely extended and divisible. Only with Isaac Newton (1643–1727) the absolute, homogeneous, infinite, void space becomes one of the main basics of physics. Newton's definition of space still was compatible with the existence of God[12].

This slow and complex change in the concept of space is reflected not only in science but also in the visual arts and architecture. The medieval concept of architectural space (as in painting) is based on the aggregation of elements of corporeal space. Churches were constructed from crossings put together (aggregated) to build the main nave, side naves, transept, and presbytery. In the Renaissance, this concept of compounded architectural space was shifting toward a dynamic concept of systemic space[13] in which crossings or other units of space are not simply added but used as modules[14],

---

10 Edward Grant, *Much ado about nothing: Theories of Space and Vacuum from the Middle Ages to the Scientific Revolutions*, Cambridge 1981, p. 259: »Aristotle's denial of the existence of a separate void space must form the point of departure of any consideration of the history of spatial concepts from the Middle Ages to the Scientific Revolution.«

11 Ibid., Summary and reflections: pp. 259–264, here: p. 260: »In scholastic thought, the nature of [...] extracosmic void space was much debated. By contrast to real space, the space associated with real bodies, infinite extracosmic void was called ›imaginary‹ space, the space imagined in the absence of body.«

12 Ibid., pp. 261–262.

13 Babu Thaliat, *Perspektivierung als Modalität der Symbolisierung: Erwin Panofskys Unternehmung zur Ausweitung und Präzisierung des Symbolisierungsprozesses in der »Philosophie der symbolischen Formen« von Ernst Cassirer*, Ph.D. dissertation, Albert-Ludwigs-Universität Freiburg im Breisgau, winter semester 2002/2003, p. 345: »Die Vorstellung von einer historisch unendlichen Kontinuität der Perspektivierung gewinnt an Bedeutung, indem wir feststellen, dass die Erfindung und Etablierung der Zentralperspektive in der Renaissance tatsächlich ein vorläufiger Abschluss in der Entwicklung vom antiken Aggregatraum zum modernen Systemraum (wie Panofsky es auffasst) war, und dass sich die Perspektivität der Raumanschauung und Raumdarstellung auch nach der Renaissance historisch weiterentwickelte.« The term ›Aggregatraum‹ is defined by Erwin Panofsky, »Die Perspektive als symbolische Form«, in: *Vorträge der Bibliothek Warburg 1924/1925*, Leipzig and Berlin 1927, pp. 268–269; Erwin Panofsky, »Perspective as a Symbolic Form«, English translation by Christopher S. Wood, New York 1991, pp. 42–43.

14 The modulus is used by Vitruvius (as in footnote 19), book III, p. 72, 8: modulus and III, p. 65, 5: commodulatio.

multiplied in order to construct large spaces with coherent proportions. The structures of space, vertical piers, horizontal friezes, and flagged floors provide lines that guide the eye to perceive space in strict »natural« central perspective[15]. They also render proportions visible. The rules for proportions in architecture were described in new theoretical treatises, such as Leon Battista Alberti's *De re aedificatoria libri decem*, written from 1442 to 1452[16].

One of the first examples of the application of totally central perspective in architecture was Filippo Brunelleschi's San Lorenzo in Florence. Of all his works, this »revolutionary and forward-looking building« was »perhaps the most dogged by vicissitudes of execution.«[17] Built in the years 1421–1425 and 1442–1446, it was completed only after Brunelleschi's death by his scholar Antonio Manetti and his successors between 1446–1465. The construction plan was based on optical studies in perspective including experiments with a mirror made to gain a perspective drawing of the baptistery in Florence[18].

THEORETICAL AND PRACTICAL KNOWLEDGE IN ROOM ACOUSTICS

The rediscovery of ancient buildings in the 15th and 16th centuries sparked a new interest in Vitruvius' *De architectura libri decem*[19]. Vitruvius not only describes the ancient theatre but also gives a detailed account of sound propagation and distinguishes between helpful reflections (*reflexiones consonantes* and *reflexiones resonantes*) and disturbing reflections (*reflexiones*

---

15 Panofsky, op.cit., pp. 250 ff., English translation, op.cit., pp. 27 ff.

16 Leon Battista Alberti, *De re aedificatoria libri decem*, manuscript 1442–1452, Vatican City, Biblioteca Apostolica Vaticana and Modena, Biblioteca Estense et al., first printed edition Florentiae: Nicolai Laurentii Alamani, 1485. On Palladio and Alberti see: Rudolf Wittkower, *Architectural Principles in the Age of Humanism*, London, 2nd ed. 1952, pp. 87–88: »Optical and Psychological Factors in Palladio's Architecture.«

17 Leonardo Benevolo, *History of Architecture in the Renaissance*, London and Henley 1978, vol. I, pp. 61–65: p. 61; Eugenio Battisti, *Filippo Brunelleschi, Das Gesamtwerk*, Stuttgart und Zürich 1959, pp. 174–196.

18 Battisti, ibid., p. 109.

19 Marcus Vitruvii Pollionis, *De architectura libri decem*, first printed by Giovanni Sulpicio da Veroli, no date, no place (Rome, 1487?), see Dorothea Baumann, *Music and Space*, Bern 2011, pp. 27–28.

dissonantes and *reflexiones circumsonantes*)[20]. These remarkable definitions must have been based on exact observation[21].

Several theoretical treatises on architecture of that time contain examples of theatre construction based on the Vitruvian model. Again the most famous treatise is Leon Battista Alberti's *De re aedificatoria libri decem* of about 1450, but many treatises on theatre building published since that time address perspective, change of scenery, lighting, and other related questions[22]. This interest around 1500 led to the construction of open-air theatres in Italy and other countries. Serlio's 1545 plan for an open-air theatre (Figure 1) is an important early document on the subject[23].

Figure 1: Serlio's plan of 1545 for an open-air theatre

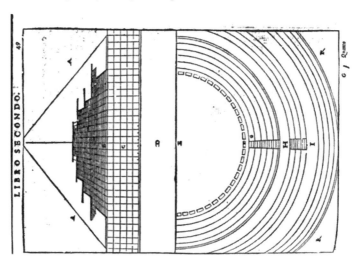

From: Sebastiano Serlio, *Tutte le opere d'architettura di Sebastiano Serlio Bolognese* (book 1–7), Venice 1584, f. 45r. (http://digi.ub.uni-heidelberg.de/diglit/serlio1584/0137)

The following music examples are taken from churches. We therefore exclude the history of the covered theatre, which starts with the *Teatro Olimpi-*

---

20 Frederick V. Hunt, *Origins in Acoustics: The Science of Sound from Antiquity to the Age of Newton*, New Haven, Connecticut 1978, pp. 34, footnote 52, and 167.

21 M. Bieber, *The History of the Greek and Roman Theatre* (2nd rev. ed. 1961), pp. 54 ff.

22 See, for instance, Iain Mackintosh, *Architecture, Actor, and Audience*, London and New York 1993, bibliography.

23 Sebastiano Serlio, *Della Architettura*, Venice 1545, vol. II, Trattato sopra le Scene, p. 48: ground plan and section.

co in Vicenza by Andrea Palladio (1580–1585, 1500 seats)[24]. However, an important idea taken from theatre construction were raked seat rows, which were also extensively used in large churches to position musicians with the goal of improving sound distribution. Leonardo da Vinci (1452–1519), who was familiar with Vitruvius' treatise, left speculative sketches for sacred rooms with steeply raked rows of seats indicated as »teatri per uldire [sic!] messa« and »loco dove si predica« (1478). In the first case the choir is placed in the center, in the second case the lecture pulpit is on a column in the centre of a circular ground plan, both based on the same idea as in the ancient theatre, namely that all listeners should see the sound source and be reached by direct sound[25].

Leonardo also left drawings of sound rays produced by hammer blows transmitted through a wall, passing through a hole in the wall and reflected off the back wall (1519)[26] (see figure 2).

A second group of important sketches on the propagation of water waves, sound waves, and light rays are directly related to observations that the angles of incident and reflected rays are equal. The drawings show the relation established between optical geometry and room acoustics. These ideas had to wait until the 17th century to be developed into a scientific theory of optics and acoustics[27], but they were used in a pragmatic way to improve acoustics.

---

24 Vincenzo Scamozzi, *Dell'Idea della Archittetura Universale*, Venice 1615, introduction to book VIII; ground plan and section.

25 Leonardo da Vinci, *Literary Works*, ed. by P. Richter (1939), Vol. 2, pp. 42–52; M. Forsyth, *Buildings for music*, Cambridge (MA) 1985, figure 1.9, facsimiles of the drawings from Paris, Institut de France, ms. B (2173), f. 55a; the same drawings and a further sketch with the title »Teatro da predicare« from ms. B, f. 52 recto also published in *Leonardo da Vinci: das Lebensbild eines Genies* (6th ed. 1972). The drawings are from 1486–88, see Leonardo da Vinci, Il Codice Arundel 263 nella British Library (1508), facsimile edition by Carlo Pedretti, transcr. and crit. comment by Carlo Vecco, Florence, 1998; see also Rudolf Wittkower, *Architectural principles in the age of Humanism*, London, 1949, p. 16, footnote 5 and plate 5.

26 Emanuel Winternitz, *Leonardo da Vinci as a Musician*, New Haven, Connecticut and London 1982, pp. 99–120. Milan, Bibl. Ambros. Codex Atlantico C.A. f. 126 ra. The drawings are from 1478 and 1519. See also Domenico Argentieri, *Die Optik bei Leonardo*, Berlin 1939, pp. 405–36.

27 The principle of Fermat, formulated by Pierre de Fermat in a letter to Cureau de la Chambre, 1 January 1662, is the mathematical basis for the proof of the law of reflection based on the shortest path. See Michael Sean Mahoney, *The Mathematical Career of Pierre de Fermat*, 1601–1665, Princeton (New Jersey), 2nd ed. 1994, p. 401.

Figure 2: Leonardo da Vinci's drawings

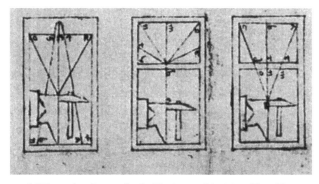

From: Emanuel Winternitz, *Leonardo da Vinci as a Musician,* New Haven and London 1982, 99–120. Milan, Bibl. Ambros. Codex Atlantico C.A. f. 126 ra

Another remarkable testimony of pragmatic acoustic knowledge is Francesco Giorgi's advice for the construction of the new church of San Francesco della Vigna in Venice in 1535:

»I recommend to have all the chapels and the choir vaulted, because the word or song of the minister echoes better from the vault than it would from rafters. But in the nave of the church, where there will be sermons, I recommend a ceiling. I should like to have it coffered with as many squares as possible, with their appropriate measurements and proportions. [...] And these coffers [...] will be very convenient for preaching: this the experts know and experience will prove it.«[28]

With the Counter-Reformation, in the second half of the 16th century, coffered ceilings were often used to improve acoustics for preaching[29]. The different effect of vaults and flat-coffered ceilings began to be discussed by organ-makers in the 17th century[30].

---

28 Francesco Giorgi, *Memorandum di S. Francesco della Vigna,* Engl. translation by Rudolf Wittkower, *Architectural Principles in the Age of Humanism* (1949), Appendix I, p. 137, from G. Moschini, *Guida per la città di Venezia, vol. I,* Venezia 1815, pp. 55–61.

29 Patrizio Barbieri, »The state of architectural acoustics in the late Renaissance«, in: *Architettura e musica nella Venezia del Rinascimento,* edited by Deborah Howard and Laura Moretti, Milano 2006, pp. 53–75, here p. 63, after Deborah Howard, Jacopo Sansovino, *Architecture and Patronage in Renaissance Venice,* New Haven, Connecticut, and London 1975, p. 70.

30 See Barbieri, op.cit., p. 67.

The positions of organs provide evidence that geometrical rules were applied to improve acoustics, first in a pragmatic way, and then, beginning in the 15th century, in a more systematic manner. From the 12th century onward, organs were placed on lofts and rood galleries, and, from the 13th century onward, in »swallows' nests« hanging on upper walls of the nave or choir, which evidently profited from the best geometrical position below a vault (figure 3).

Figure 3: Basel, Münster, organ on the west wall below a gothic vault, 15th century

From: Friedrich Jakob, *Die Orgel,* Bern 1974

Sound reinforcement from the concentration and better distribution of reflections is especially strong if the organ is raised to the bottom line of a Gothic vault, but it is also evident below Roman vaults regardless of their height above the organ (see figure 4)[31].

The position of organs and their sound distribution were planned according to the organ's specific function, which was, originally, to alternate with the priests' chant close to the altar, and then, with the development of polyphony, to play *colla parte* and, later still, the *basso seguente,* as well as to accompany singers. That is why we often see organs in or on the side wall of the choir, or a small positive organ close to the main altar or to altars in the

---

31 Dorothea Baumann, »Acoustics in gothic cathedrals: theory and practical experience in the middle ages«, in: *Actes du Colloque des orgues gothiques, Royaumont 1995,* Paris 2001, pp. 37–48, here pp. 46–47.

side naves. The large main organ in or on the west wall was certainly aimed at reaching the congregation gathered in the main nave and the side naves[32].

Figure 4: Sound reflections from Gothic and Roman vaults

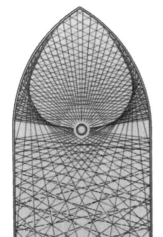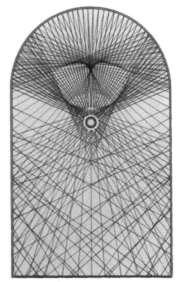

From: Thomas Baer-Loy, *Hören und Raumform,* Zürich 1986, 2nd edition

Organs from the 15th and 16th centuries produced a rich and transparent sound; however, by comparison with later organs, their sound levels were relatively limited. Due to this limitation, there was less acoustic reaction from the more distant parts of the church. Later organs gained power of sound not only by a decrease of the length-to-diameter ratio of the pipes, but also due to a change in intonation[33] and additional low notes[34]. Acoustical conditions became more fragile because of the greater acoustical activation of all parts of the church.

---

32 A study on the position of the organs in the churches of Renaissance Venice is given by Massimo Bison: »La collocazione degli organi nelle chiese veneziane del Rinascimento: implicazioni architettoniche, liturgiche, musicali e acustiche«, in: Deborah Howard and Laura Moretti 2006, op.cit., pp. 297–327.

33 Barbieri, op.cit., p. 66.

34 By 1550 the note *C* was added to a keyboard ending with *F*; by 1625 the intervening diatonic and chromatic keys were added. See Martin-Knud Kaufmann, »Le Clavier à balancier du Clavisimbalum (XVe siècle)«, in: *Actes du Colloque des orgues gothiques, Royaumont 1995,* op.cit., pp. 9–58, here: p. 43.

MODERN KNOWLEDGE ON ACOUSTICS

In geometric acoustics, the propagation of sound waves is represented by rays that reflect from the surfaces enclosing a space, according to the same laws of reflection used in optics. Each listener is located in a field of sound waves that arrive in staggered succession, radiating from a sound source at a speed of approximately 340 m/sec and reflecting off wall surfaces and sufficiently large obstacles[35]: the direct sound arrives first, followed by reflections from the nearest side walls, the ceiling, the rear wall, and further reflections from more than one surface. Not fully connected parts of a room create multiple reflections within those spaces that reach the main volume of space with delay. Such energy accumulations as occur in side naves, apses, partly closed chapels, retro choirs, etc., can strongly disturb sound perception in all parts of the church[36].

The brain produces a certain spatial perception from the time pattern of incoming sound reflections, using direct sound to locate the sound source. The initial time-delay gap between direct sound and the first reflection, as well as further early reflections, transmit information on the room's size. Aural perception combines the direct sound and the successive sound reflections to create an overall impression: we perceive the sound as more lucid and intense as the intervals between the series of reflections become closer together. Coherent reflections within a period of 50–80 msec, or under certain conditions even as much as 200 msec, enhance sound quality. Early reflections strengthen the impression of sound and improve its clarity. Reflections from the side strengthen the impression of spaciousness. They are particularly valuable as our ears are between 6 and 10 dB more sensitive to lateral sound than from other directions. Later reflections are heard as reverberation.

The reverberation time (RT), an exactly measurable value in seconds, is defined as the time required for the sound pressure level of an impulsive signal to drop to one thousandth of the initial value, corresponding to a decay of 60 dB. The reverberation time is frequency dependent and therefore has to be measured (or calculated) for every frequency and is represented in the

---

35 The geometrical law of mirrors is valid only if reflecting surfaces are clearly larger than the wavelength of incoming sound (the magnitudes here are between 1.7 cm for 20,000 Hz to 17 m for 20 Hz). Smaller obstacles cause diffraction. For detailed conditions see Jürgen Meyer, *Acoustics and the Performance of Music*, 5th ed. Berlin 2009, 1982.

36 Dorothea Baumann, »Acoustics in Sacred Buildings«, in: Rudolf Stegers, *A Design Manual: Sacred Buildings*, Basel 2008, pp. 54–59.

form of a reverberation decay curve. If the initial value is not high enough, the so-called T15-time for the decay from –5 dB to –20 dB is measured and extrapolated to –60 dB. T30- and T40-time is measured and calculated accordingly. The early decay time (ETD) corresponds to six times the decay from maximum to –10 dB[37]. The RT depends on volume and total absorption of a particular space. It is not identical with the »after-ring« of sound, which depends on sound intensity. It does not contain any information on the direction of incoming sound. There are other measurable parameters used as quality factors related to subjective attributes such as the clarity index, C80, defined as the ratio of the total energy in the signal in the first 80 milliseconds relative to the total energy from 80 msec to infinite time, measured in decibels (dB), or the lateral energy fraction (LEF), the ratio of the component of energy arriving in the direction perpendicular to the line joining source to microphone (integrated from 5 to 80 msec) to the total energy (integrated over 0 to 80 msec)[38].

Figure 5: Time pattern of sound reflections

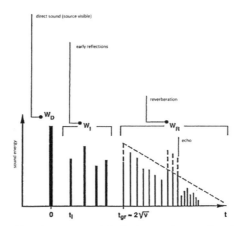

After Wolfgang Fasold and Eva Veres, *Schallschutz und Raumakustik in der Praxis,* Berlin 2003

---

37 An individual value without qualifying frequency generally denotes the mean value of the reverberation time for frequencies between 500 and 1000 Hz.

38 Davide Bonsi, Philip Garsed, Malcolm Longair, and Raf Orlofsky, »Acoustic and Audience Response Analyses of the Eleven Venetian Churches« in: Deborah Howard and Laura Moretti, *Sound and Space in Renaissance Venice*, New Haven, Connecticut, and London, 2009, pp. 214–299, here p. 219.

MUSIC EXAMPLES

The encounter between architecture and music, space, and sound often presents complex practical problems that remain to be solved. The following music examples were chosen because they stand as landmarks in the cultural history of the Renaissance and the Republic of Venice. The first analyses the history of polychoral music in the Doge's church of San Marco; the second discusses music performances in the new church San Giorgio Maggiore, built between 1565 and 1610 for the Benedictine monastery by Andrea Palladio. The discussion is based on several visits, experiments with choir singers in different positions, measurements, and sound recordings[39].

Venice, San Marco and Adrian Willaert's *Salmi spezzati*

Polychoral compositions emerged in the fifteenth century from antiphonal singing of psalms and verses of hymns alternating between Gregorian chant and polyphony, and finally polyphony for two and more choirs. The technique was not invented by Adrian Willaert, *maestro di capella* at San Marco in Venice from 1527–1562, but became well known due to his performances. This music, which at the beginning was sung by two small choirs, developed into a complex musical event by the seventeenth century, with several ensembles placed in different balconies, filling churches with impressive, splendid sound[40].

Iain Fenlon summarized documented evidence as follows:

»Any reconstruction of the *cori spezzati* style at San Marco in Venice during the sixteenth and seventeenth centuries must take account of the three musical elements: chant, improvised polyphony, and composed polyphony. Throughout the period these three co-existed. [. . .] While chant and improvised polyphony were sung by the canons of the Basilica, polyphony was performed by the professional singers of the *Cappella Marciana*. Those

---

39 My thanks go to Deborah Howard for her invitation to meetings in 2004 (Venice), 2006 (Cambridge), and 2007 (Venice). My thanks go also to the students and my colleague Stefanie Stadler Elmer for their active collaboration during two excursions to Venice in the spring of 2007 and in the spring and the fall of 2009 related to a research project and an interdisciplinary seminar at the University of Zurich (Psychology and Musicology).

40 Dorothea Baumann 2011, op.cit., pp. 8–13.

charged with performing these different strands of the musical component of the liturgical rituals inside the Basilica were located in different places at different times.«[41]

Figure 6: San Marco (1063), ground plan

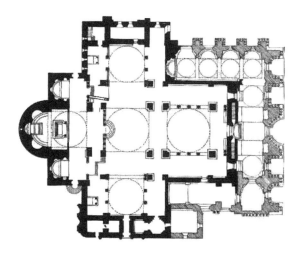

From: *Drawings of Great Buildings*, ed. Werner Blaser, Basel 1983, p. 50

The ground plan (figure 6) of the church in Byzantine style is based on a Greek cross with an arm length of 32 m (width of the transept to length of the church without the apse) and with 5 domes (maximum height 28 m, diameter 12.2 m) supported by semicircular arches (maximum height 20.85 m). The width of the main nave measures 12.5 m.

The following main positions for the musicians are documented (see also figure 7):

1) the *pulpitum magnum cantorum* or *bigonzo*, facing toward the main nave (first half of the 13th century).

2) the two pergolas, placed just behind the iconostasis within the main pier on both sides of the choir, about 2.1 m above the choir floor (constructed 1536–1537 on the north side and 1541–1544 on the south side); the distance between the two piers and the length of the iconostasis measures 10.9 m;

---

41 Iain Fenlon, »The Performance of *cori spezzati* in San Marco«, in: Deborah Howard and Laura Moretti, *Architettura e musica*, op.cit., pp. 94–95.

3) different positions on the upper level, mainly the two lofts for the organs on both sides of the choir; and

4) the usual position for liturgy held at the floor level of the choir, with singers standing or sitting on benches[42].

Figure 7: Venice, San Marco, sound distribution in the church from the upper organ loft (geometric analysis Christina Niederstätter)

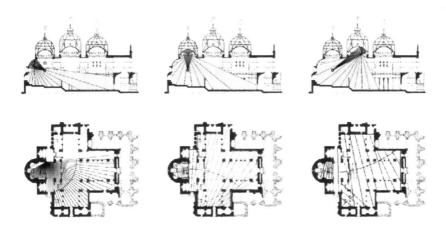

Sound example 1: Singing from the upper organ loft (Claudio Monteverdi, Salve regina)

http://www.srcf.ucam.org/~djh1000/soundandspace/index2.php?building=San%20Marco

All the positions above floor level and outside the choir benefit from a shorter distance to the reflecting surfaces: the arches, the domes, and additional supporting reflections from the apse, the vault above the apse, and the large supporting piers. As sound is surprisingly well distributed in the whole church, these positions have to cope with a relatively strong reaction from the main nave and from additional spaces in the church. That is why double-choir or polychoral coordination is more difficult between the two organ lofts than between lower positions on both sides of the choir (see figure 8).

42 Dorothea Baumann, »Geometrical Analysis of Acoustical Conditions in San Marco and San Giorgio Maggiore in Venice«, in: Deborah Howard and Laura Moretti (ed.) 2009, op.cit., pp. 117–146.

Figure 8: Venice, San Marco, sound distribution from the pergolas. (geometric analysis Christina Niederstätter)

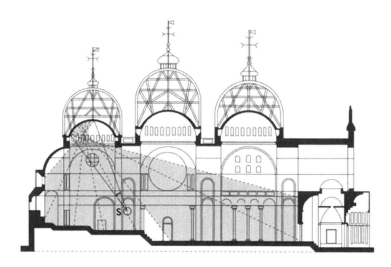

Sound example 2: Singing with two choirs from the two pergolas (Adrian Willaert, Domine probasti me).

http://www.srcf.ucam.org/~djh1000/soundandspace/index2.php?building=San%20Marco

Listening to the two small choirs (4 singers each) singing from the two per-golas makes two things evident: the main listeners (the doge close to the choir entrance and the canons in the choir) profited from excellent acoustical conditions due to the concentration of sound below the main arch and addi-tional reflections from surfaces close by, all the more so as the screen below the iconostasis was closed with marble slabs and carpets. The assembled congregation in the nave could hear music as from far away, as if it were coming down from heaven.

Venice, Palladio's San Giorgio Maggiore (Renaissance style, 1566–75, 1580–89)

San Giorgio Maggiore by Palladio is a much larger church in Renaissance style with wide open naves and clear proportions (see figure 9). The ground plan is based on a cross. The cupola is at the centre, between the west wall and the altar, and both ends of the transept. The monk's choir behind the altar was added for functional reasons[43]. Its length and height measure 18.3 m. The diameter of the central dome and the width of the main nave are about 12.2 m, with the side naves half as wide. The length of the church, without the presbytery, is the same as the total length of the transept with the oval endings (about 48.8 m).

Figure 9: Venice, San Giorgio Maggiore, ground plan

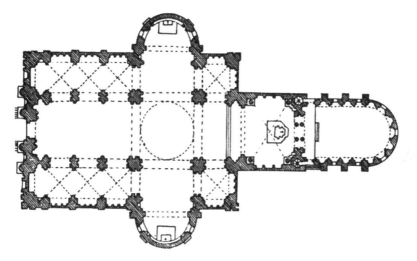

From: *Le fabbriche e i disegni di Andrea Palladio e le terme*, ed. by Editore Giovanni Rossi, Vicenza 1796

The visual transparency, due to the width of the openings between the large piers, reflects the very complex acoustic interaction between all parts of the church. This is confirmed by the listening experience: sound decay in the central nave clearly diminishes in several uneven steps because of energy accumulations arriving with time delay. The energy accumulations in these interacting parts of space are the reason for large sections with blurred acoustics and relatively few zones of clearer acoustics. As an additional factor, hard reflections from the tightly joined stone plates and piers and the central barrel vault rising to a height of more than 21 m provide high intensity to the incoherent part of the reverberation.

Sound from the retrochoir is but weakly connected with the main volume of the church because the organ loft and the organ case close about one third of the opening between the church and the monks' choir, and sound can pass

---

43 Deborah Howard and Laura Moretti (ed.) 2009, op.cit., pp. 59–76.

only below and above the organ[44]. The original organ of the late 16th century was smaller and had a lighter sound than the organ used from the mid-17th century (probably built by Pietro Nacchini), with substantial changes made by Pietro Bazzani (revision in 1887). The 16th-century organ had two façades, one toward the monks' choir and one toward the church. The range probably did not reach further down than F, while the 17th-century organ originally reached down to C (with short octave) and has but one façade toward the main nave[45].

Geometrical analysis (see figure 10) shows ›excellent‹ conditions in the monks' choir and a ›fairly good‹ situation in the chancel directly below the organ. These zones are well supplied with reflections coming from the side walls and from the ceiling. If, however, we take into account time delay and energy accumulations in the side naves, in the dome (not shown in detail in these designs), and in the transept with its two oval endings, we become aware of the danger of late sound packages coming from these spaces, which cover and blur the main and coherent part of sound in the main nave and in the chancel before the main altar. This analysis was confirmed by listening and measurements during experiments with the St. John's Choir from Cambridge in the spring of 2007[46], and during two visits in 2009 when it was possible to walk around and to enter the chancel during experiments with a students' choir and the organ[47].

Sound example 3:

http://www.srcf.ucam.org/~djh1000/soundandspace/index2.php?building=San%20Giorgio

---

44 See Deborah Howard and Laura Moretti (ed.) 2009, op.cit., pp. 247–249. On the difference of subjective impression due to the individual background of experience and the aim of perception, see Dorothea Baumann 2011, op.cit., chapter 1.4.3, pp. 66–68; on comments and results of questionnaires assessed during the organ concert by Massimo Bison on 9 September 2005, see Deborah Howard, »The Innocent Ear: Subjectivity in the Perception of Acoustics,« in: Howard and Moretti (ed.) 2009, op.cit., pp. 239–257.

45 Massimo Bison in: Deborah and Laura Moretti, *Architettura e musica*, op.cit., pp. 252–253.

46 These experiments were part of a research project conducted by Deborah Howard and Laura Moretti between September 2005 and April 2007, documented in two publications: *Architettura e musica* (2006), op.cit., and *Sound and Space* (2009), op.cit.

47 My thanks go to Pierluigi Petrobelli, Venice, and the monastery of San Giorgio Maggiore for the permission to enter the retrochoir and to play the organ, as well as to my students and their conductor, Dr. Irmgard Keldany, and to Andreas Erdös for playing the organ.

Figure 10: Venice, San Giorgio Maggiore, sound distribution from the organ in both directions (geometric analysis Christina Niederstätter)

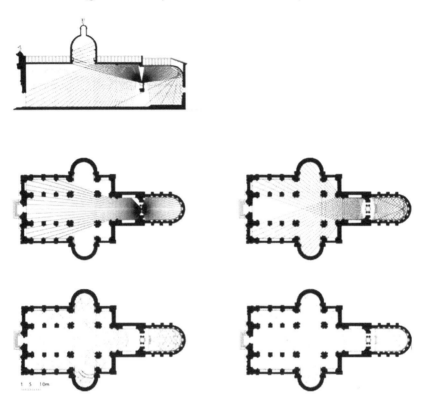

Acoustic conditions during the annual visit of the Doge for vespers on Christmas Day and the mass for St. Stephan on 26 December were certainly improved due to the presence of a large crowd, carpets, and wall hangings. This was confirmed, in the case of large public performances, by documents describing the interior alteration of San Giorgio Maggiore in 1638 held in honor of the birth of the Dauphin of France (Louis XIV), a celebration organised on behalf of the French Ambassador, Amelot de la Houssaie[48]. Two positions could be used for singing polyphony with acceptable conditions. Facing the main nave, singers and instrumentalists could be placed in the chancel in front of the main altar or on stepwise elevated podiums for two

---

48 See Andrew Hopkins, in: Howard and Moretti (ed.) 2006, op.cit., pp. 147–156 and pp. 157–159 (complete transcription of the report as in BNMVe, misc. 180.17, pp. 22–78).

choirs along both side walls[49]. Yet even here, in front or to the side of the main altar, the monks' choir would, after loud moments, send a late and disturbing echo through the open space below the organ. On the other hand, a relatively good situation can be expected for music played close to the altar for St. Stephen, at the south end of the transept, but only for listeners relatively close by. Two choirs could also have been placed on both sides of this altar. The opening to the side nave and the volume of the dome over the crossing render acoustics difficult in that part of the church. Blurring feedback from the energy accumulation at the other end of the transept, nearly 50 m distant, and from the other more distant parts of the church, could be reduced by trappings and by the audience.

This example shows that this typical Renaissance church, a basilica with central dome based on harmonic proportions, is by no means easy for musicians. Sound does not follow the same rules as visual experience. However, if conditions for music performance are set well, both aspects enhance aesthetic pleasure.

CONCLUSION

The music examples analysed leave an important question unresolved: when did the idea start that polychoral music should ›fill‹ the church with sound, and what did this idea of filling exactly mean? As outlined, the concept of space during the Renaissance changed. This also caused a change in the concept of time. The art historian Dagobert Frey speaks of »successive perception of absolute values« in the Middle Ages (analogous to Erwin Panofsky's »aggregate space«[50]) and of »simultaneous perception of relative values« specific to the Renaissance mentality (analogous to »systemic space«)[51]. If visible space became focused on a single ›viewpoint‹ it could be grasped in a single ›moment‹.

Polychoral music for several groups of musicians, and for larger groups, developed toward the end of the 16th century, constituted a new approach to music performance. The additional balconies then mounted on the side walls in the choir of San Marco prove that the idea, which started with music sung

---

49 The distance between the two side-walls of 12.2 m is about the same as the distance between the two organ lofts in San Marco and 1.3 m larger than the distance between the pergolas in San Marco.

50 See footnote 13.

51 Benevolo, op.cit., p. 264, referring to Dagobert Frey, *Die Gotik und die Renaissance als Grundlagen der modernen Weltanschauung*, Augsburg 1929.

from two small pergolas by not much more than four singers on each side, was developed further: singers and instrumentalists were placed on balconies at different levels above the floor[52]. If music was produced ›simultaneously‹ from several platforms, the church was filled with sound and the total volume of »space« became audible.

---

52 A good introduction into the later history of performance practice in San Marco is given on the CD A Venetian Coronation 1595, with the Gabrieli Consort & Players, conducted by Paul McCreesh. The reconstruction of the coronation mass for the Doge Mariano Grimani, which is in some aspects conjectural, includes settings by Andrea Gabrieli of the *Kyrie* and *Sanctus* for three choirs and the *Gloria* for four choirs, printed in 1587, as well as the motet *Omnes gentes* for four choirs by Giovanni Gabrieli, printed in 1597. Several chant items were, as usual, substituted by instrumental music, such as Giovanni Gabrieli's *Intonazioni* for one or two organs or the Canzonas for cornetti and trombones, partly played together with strings.

Klangwelten für den großen Saal

Raumkonzepte, spatiale Klangorganisation und Strategien
der Verräumlichung in der symphonischen Musik
des 19. Jahrhunderts

FABIAN KOLB

Wie im Grunde für alle Entwicklungen der Neuen Musik in der zweiten
Hälfte des 20. Jahrhunderts stellt die Kunstmusiktradition des 19. Jahrhunderts, wie sie in der Symphonik gleichsam *pars pro toto* inkarniert erscheint, gerade auch für die (frühe) elektronische Musik eine, wenn nicht die
entscheidende ästhetische Bezugsfolie dar. Als nach wie vor lebendig-
präsentes Erbe ist sie neben historistischen Rückverweisen auf die ältere
Musikgeschichte die maßgebliche (ungebrochen-gebrochene) Anknüpfungs-
und Reibungsfläche, vor der sich die Komponisten nach dem Zweiten Weltkrieg ihr eigenes ästhetisches und kompositorisches Profil generieren; und
dies gilt insbesondere auch für den schöpferisch-kreativen Umgang mit dem
musikalisch-auditiven Raum. Denn in der Tat scheinen die Potenziale einer
spezifisch spatialen Klangorganisation in nicht wort- oder bühnengebunde-
ner Orchestermusik explizit erst mit dem ausgehenden 18. Jahrhundert verstärkt in den Fokus zu rücken — dies neben genuin kompositionsgeschichtli-
chen Entwicklungen zweifellos forciert durch die Entfaltung des bürgerlichen Konzertwesens, das etwa den Bau eigener und größerer Konzertsäle
sowie die Expansion und Ausdifferenzierung des orchestralen Klangkörpers
beförderte, sowie zudem durch die auf Kategorien wie Größe, Universalität,
(Volks-)Repräsentation, Reichtum der Mittel und Wirkmacht zielenden ästhetischen Diskurse und Philosopheme, Implikationen und Postulate, wie
man sie gerade an symphonischer Musik als Inbegriff der romantisch-
idealistischen Kunstreligion festmachte. »Für große Räume, für Massenver-

einigung bestimmt, bedingt sie [die Symphonie] große Verhältnisse«[1] – »Alles [muss] großartiger gehalten seyn [...], als wirke es von der Bühne herab auf die Hörer, die nicht minder schaubegierig sind und das nicht Ferntreffende ungeschätzt, ja unbemerkt lassen«[2], heißt es etwa in den 1830er Jahren; und 1918 liest man rückblickend am Ende des ›langen‹ 19. Jahrhunderts:

> »Die sinfonische Gattung ist für den schaffenden Musiker das Mittel, sich durch die Instrumentalmusik einem größeren Hörerkreise mitzuteilen. [...] er komponiert auch gleichzeitig ein ideales Bild des Raumes und der Hörerschaft. Dieses Bild des Raumes und der Hörerschaft ist nicht etwa erst eine indirekte Folge des Kompositionsaktes, sondern es ist ein zeugendes Element dabei.«[3]

Flankiert durch die zeitgleich in den verschiedenen Disziplinen vorangetriebene Erforschung der Hörbarkeit des Raumes (Richtungs- und Raumhören) – insbesondere durch William Strutt Lord Rayleigh – macht sich im 19. Jahrhundert in der Tat eine verschärfte Tendenz bemerkbar, in instrumentalen, mithin ›rein‹-musikalischen Strukturgefügen (und das heißt *a priori* ohne Rückgriff auf szenisch-theatrale Momente, wie sie dem Musiktheater von vornherein gänzlich andere – und vielfach genutzte – Möglichkeiten bereithalten) die Ressourcen von Raumklang auszuloten bzw. Räumlichkeit zu evozieren, zu simulieren oder zu suggerieren. Nicht zuletzt eingedenk der Orientierung letztlich aller Vertreter der Neuen Musik am Bildungskanon und Konzertrepertoire ihrer Zeit, das eben maßgeblich ein Kanon der symphonischen Literatur des 19. Jahrhunderts war, mag es daher gewinnbringend sein, nach Konzepten und Strategien der Verräumlichung in ebendiesem Kanon einschlägiger Werke Ausschau zu halten.

---

1 Edmé-François-Antoine-Marie Miel, *De la symphonie, des symphonies de Beethoven et de leur exécution*, Paris 1833, zitiert nach der Übersetzung von Heinrich Panofka, »Ueber die Symphonie, ueber die Symphonie Beethoven's, und ueber ihre Ausfuehrungen in Paris«, in: Neue Zeitschrift für Musik 1 (1834), S. 101.

2 Gottfried Wilhelm Fink, Artikel »Symphonie«, in: *Encyclopädie der gesammten musikalischen Wissenschaften oder Universal-Lexicon der Tonkunst*, hrsg. von Gustav Schilling, Stuttgart 1835–1838, Bd. 6, S. 541–551, hier S. 548.

3 Paul Bekker, *Die Sinfonie von Beethoven bis Mahler*, Berlin 1918, S. 13. – Ungemein vielrezipiert, mögen von Bekkers Darstellung in der Tat entscheidende Impulse auch auf die Entwicklung nach 1950 ausgegangen sein.

JOSEPH HAYDN

Die Koppelung kompositorischer Auseinandersetzung und äußerer Aufführungsbedingungen rückt dabei exemplarisch bereits mit Joseph Haydn ins Blickfeld, und zwar in einem Maße, das über die spätestens bei Johann Joachim Quantz postulierte Forderung, der musikalische Vortrag müsse sich an die räumlichen Verhältnisse anpassen[4], deutlich hinausweist. War Haydn generell sensibel für Aspekte (imaginärer) Raumwirkungen, die auf ältere ästhetische Konzepte des 18. Jahrhunderts wie ›Klangrede‹ und Diskurscharakter von Musik rekurrieren, andererseits wie Echoeffekte, Terrassendynamik, Crescendi oder *come da lontano* eine markante Ausprägung z.B. auch bei den Mannheimer Komponisten gefunden haben, so scheinen bei ihm doch gerade die besonderen Potenziale der imposanten großstädtisch-öffentlichen Konzerträume in Paris und dann namentlich in London eine intensivierte Reflexion über den Umgang mit Raummöglichkeiten ausgelöst zu haben[5]. Während so bei den Sinfonien für Wien und Eszterháza etwa das raumgreifende Eröffnungscrescendo (prominent bereits in Hob. I:1), der ›Vorhang‹ oder der Signalbeginn im tutti *fortissimo* mit anschließendem Rückfall ins (meist solistische) *piano*, der gestaffelte dreifache Themenaufbau vom geringstimmigen Anfang bis zur Vollstimmigkeit (all dies als ›Exposition des Apparats‹) sowie die frappanten Echo-Evokationen besonders in Hob. I:72 (*Menuet*), Hob. I:38 (*Andante molto*) und Hob. I:68 (*Presto*, Coda) tendenziell durchaus noch als eher konventionelle – nichtsdestoweniger wirkmächtige – Strategien zu erklären sind, unter denen der Schluss der sogenannten *Abschiedssinfonie* Hob. I:45 mit seiner quasi-szenischen Raumvorstellung freilich einen inkommensurablen Sonderfall darstellt, lassen sich viele der berühmten ›Überraschungscoups‹ der Londoner Sinfonien in der Tat als experimentelles Spiel mit Orchesterdisposition und Raumordnung beschreiben, die dem Auditorium im Sinne Shaftesburys hier gleichsam didaktisch präsent gemacht und effektvoll vorgeführt werden.

---

4   Johann Joachim Quantz, *Versuch einer Anweisung die Flöte travasiere zu spielen*, Berlin 1752 (Nachdruck München/Kassel 1992), exemplarisch: S. 83f., 170 und 173.

5   Vgl. zur Akustik in den Aufführungsräumen Haydns Jürgen Meyer, »Raumakustik und Orchesterklang in den Konzertsälen Joseph Haydns«, in: Acustica 41 (1978), S. 145–162; ders., »Raumakustik und Orchesterklang: Zur Aufführungspraxis der Sinfonien Joseph Haydns«, in: *Musik und Raum* (= Veröffentlichungen des Instituts für Neue Musik und Musikerziehung Darmstadt 30), hrsg. von Marietta Morawska-Büngeler, Mainz u.a. 1989, S. 20–39.

Abbildung 1: Haydns in den Hanover Square Rooms etablierte Orchester-disposition

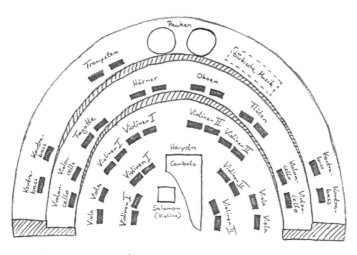

Rekonstruktion nach Neal Zaslaw[6]

Steht hierbei fraglos auch die ästhetische Zentralkategorie des Sublim-Erhabenen als Leitidee im Fokus, so bleibt als technische Grundvorausset-zung freilich die Struktur des ›klassischen‹ Satzes als mehrschichtiges Zu-sammenspiel verschiedener Ereignisebenen und heterogener Bewegungs-räume[7], wobei im Blick auf Partituranordnung und Faktur insbesondere der Bläserstimmen die Vorstellung von Nähe oder wachsender Entfernung zum Streicherklang zu dominieren scheint (entgegen der konventionellen an der Klanghöhe orientierten *colla-parte*-Praxis)[8], so dass es Haydn bei seiner fle-xiblen Orchestration offenbar wesentlich stets um immer neue Klangraum-konfigurationen mit speziellen Tiefenkonturen zu tun war. Neben einer Viel-zahl dieserart subtilerer Maßnahmen tritt nun aber für London ein spezieller dramaturgischer ›wit‹ oder ›whim‹ hinzu, der mit dem vergleichsweise groß-

---

6   in: Jack Westrup, Neal Zaslaw, Eleanor Selfridge-Field, Artikel »Orchestra«, in: *The New Grove Dictionary of Musical Instruments*, hrsg. v. Stanley Sadie, Bd. 2, London, New York 1984, S. 823–837, hier S. 829, Zeichnung: Fabian Kolb.

7   Vgl. hierzu (am Beispiel Mozarts) etwa Stefan Kunze, »Raumvorstellungen in der Musik: Zur Geschichte des Kompositionsbegriffs«, in: Archiv für Musikwissen-schaft 31 (1974), S. 1–21, hier S. 13–15.

8   Vgl. Gesine Schröder, »Über das ›klassische Orchester‹ und Haydns späte symphoni-sche Instrumentation«, in: *Joseph Haydn* (= Musik-Konzepte 41), München 1985, S. 79–97.

besetzten Klangkörper[9] bzw. der amphitheatralischen Anordnung der In-
strumente(ngruppen), auf die Haydn selbst maßgeblich gestalterischen Einfluss genommen hatte[10], plastisch raumhaft operiert.

Dem dezimierten, gleichsam konzentrisch zusammengezogenen
Streichquartett-Beginn im *Largo cantabile* von Hob. I:93[11] ist hier ebenso
eine spezifische Raumwirkung zu attestieren wie dem in das löchrig-
diffundierende Klangbild hereinplatzenden Fagott-*C* am Schluss dieses Satzes (T. 80) oder dem gewissermaßen explosionsartig-zentrifugalen *Surprise*-Schlag im *Andante* von Hob. I:94, wo das im Grunde nicht variierte
Thema dann lediglich verschiedene Orte, Regionen sowie Vordergrund-
Hintergrund-Positionen im Orchesterraum einnimmt, ehe es sich am Schluss
regelrecht im Raum verliert. Fast frappanter noch erscheint schließlich (am
Ende des ersten Londonaufenthalts) die nicht zu erwartende, sozusagen zen-
tripetale Fokussierung des musikalischen Geschehens auf den solistischen
Violino principale zu Beginn des zweiten Teils des *Presto*-Finales aus
Hob. I:98 (T. 148ff.), übertrumpft schließlich am Werkende durch die ebenso auf die Mitte des Orchesterpodiums zoomende Beteiligung des Cembalo
als dem Ort, der Haydn als ›stummer‹ Ehrenplatz zugedacht war, hier nun
aber anstelle der durch Dreiklangsbrechungen, Tremoli und Fanfaren bereits
raumfüllend ankündigten Schlussakkorde plötzlich zum Klingen gebracht
wird, und zwar primär in der Tat als ›Geräuschquelle‹, in hoher Lage mit
klirrenden Sechzehntel-Ketten.

Im Irritationspotenzial prinzipiell vergleichbar, indes nicht aufs Zentrum,
sondern auf einen gleichsam externen klanglichen Außenposten, ja ›Fremd-
körper‹ im Klanggefüge schwenkend, funktionieren die Einschaltungen der
türkischen Musik im *Allegretto* (und im Finale) von Hob. I:100, die in ihrer
Reverenz an die Bühnenmusik einer *banda* in der Tat einem ›*ex machina*‹-
Effekt gleichkommen und dabei auf ein räumliches *Separatum* verweisen.
Etwas gemäßigter scheinen dagegen die vorherrschenden Raumeffekte in
Hob. I:102 und Hob. I:103. Während die B-Dur-Sinfonie, nachdem sie im

---

9   Siehe auch Simon McVeigh, *Concert Life in London from Mozart to Haydn*, Cam-
    bridge 1993.
10 Vgl. Jack Westrup, Neal Zaslaw, Eleanor Selfridge-Field, a.a.O., sowie Simon
    McVeigh, a.a.O., S. 212. Zum Vergleich siehe auch Ottmar Schreiber, *Orchester und
    Orchesterpraxis in Deutschland zwischen 1780 und 1850*, Berlin 1938, insbesondere
    S. 99–228; Georg Schünemann, *Geschichte des Dirigierens*, Wiesbaden 1965, S. 302–
    316; sowie Daniel J. Koury, *Orchestral Performance Practices in the Nineteenth
    Century: Size, Proportions, and Seating* (= Studies in Musicology 85), Ann Arbor
    1986, S. 5–57.
11 Der Klangraum weitet sich dann periodenweise sukzessiv: Streichertutti plus Solo-
    Fagott (T. 9ff.) – volles Orchester (T. 17ff.).

Kopfsatz mehrfach den Raum mit stehenden *unisono*-Tönen in weiter Lage ausgelotet hat[12], im *Adagio* mit der satzunüblichen Beteiligung von sordinierten Hörnern und Trompeten sowie Pauken eine gleichsam nach hinten oben entrückende, durch die Dämpfung entfernt wirkende (analog zum *religioso*-Ton in die Transzendenz deutende?) Raumweitung erprobt, geht der Initialimpuls in der Es-Dur-Sinfonie mit dem solistischen Paukenwirbel am Werkbeginn in einer sozusagen umgekehrten Fluchtpunkt-Perspektive von dem hinteren oberen Extrempunkt des Klangraums aus, um sich von dort *piano sostenuto* zunächst auf die Außenpfeiler der Bassinstrumente zu erstrecken und nur zögerlich den Kern des Orchesters zu erobern[13]. (Ganz analog ist der solistische Hornbeginn im Schlusssatz zu verstehen.)

LUDWIG VAN BEETHOVEN

Ist all diesen Effekten als luzidem Spiel mit der plötzlich wechselnden Lokalisierung der Klangquellen das Spektakuläre gemein, das mit der Aufführungssituation in einem frontal konzipierten Saal[14] konvergiert, bei dem das gestaffelt in die Höhe ragende Orchester einem theaterhaften Prospekt gleichkommt (im Haymarket Theatre sicherlich noch stärker als in den Hanover Square Rooms), so rücken bei Beethoven und den Wiener Konzertstätten seiner Zeit zugleich Strategien in den Fokus, für die die beträchtliche klangliche Präsenz und physische Energie (Lautstärkevolumen/dynamisches Spektrum) ebenso zentral scheint wie vor allem auch die größere Intimität und hieraus resultierende unmittelbare Involviertheit des Publikums[15]. Denn

---

12 Schwellklänge in der *Largo*-Introduktion, *fortissimo-a* anstelle des Seitengedankens im *Vivace*-Teil, etc.

13 Pauke solo (T. 1) – Fagotte/Violoncelli/Kontrabässe (T. 2ff.) – plus Flöten und Oboen (T. 6f.) – plus Flöten, Oboen und Hörner (T. 12f.) – Violine I und II (T.14ff.) – plus Oboen, Fagotte, Hörner, Celli und Kontrabässe (T.18f.) – plus Bratsche (T. 20ff.) – Streichertutti plus alternierende Bläser (T. 24ff.). Von dieser Raumwirkung profitiert insbesondere auch der effektvolle Rückgriff auf das *Adagio* nach dem Reprisen-Abbruch (T. 201ff.).

14 Vgl. Anm. 5. Siehe vergleichend auch die Abbildungen in: Heinrich W. Schwab, *Konzert: Öffentliche Musikdarbietungen vom 17. bis 19. Jahrhundert* (= Musikgeschichte in Bildern IV/2), Leipzig 1971; sowie Michael Forsyth, *Bauwerke für Musik: Konzertsäle und Opernhäuser, Musik und Zuhörer vom 17. Jahrhundert bis zur Gegenwart*, München u.a. 1992.

15 Vgl. grundlegend Stefan Weinzierl, *Beethovens Konzerträume: Raumakustik und symphonische Aufführungspraxis an der Schwelle zum modernen Konzertwesen*, Frankfurt/M. 2002; ders., »Die Sinfonie als Ansprache an ein Massenpublikum: Konzertformate, Publikum und sinfonische Aufführungspraxis der Beethovenzeit«, in:

neben den je eigenen dramaturgischen Raumevokationen etwa der *Fünften Symphonie* (vor allem dem Durchbruchereignis zum Beginn des Schlusssatzes) und der *Sechsten Symphonie* (hier insbesondere die Bach- und Gewitterszene), wie sie in den Entwicklungs- und Prozesscharakter der Werke eingebunden sind, ist dies von Bedeutung gerade auch für Beethovens elaborierte Technik des Weiterreichens von Motiven und Melodieanteilen von einer Stimme oder Klanggruppe zur nächsten, die – durch die Nähe von Orchester und Auditorium – eine Art ›Staffellauf‹ bzw. räumliches Wandern ins Werk zu setzen vermag[16], wobei insbesondere der zeitüblichen blockhaft-antagonistischen Trennung von Streichern (links) und Holzbläsern (rechts) mit dem Bassklang in der Mitte (verstärkte Basszentrierung der Klänge!) eine dezidiert raumhafte Rolle zuwächst.

Zu besonderer Prägnanz finden die Raumeffekte bei Beethoven freilich signifikanterweise in Parallele zur Umstrukturierung des Wiener Konzertlebens im Gefolge der napoleonischen Kriege weg vom aristokratischen Mäzenatentum zu einem breiten öffentlichen Konzertwesen mit der Verlagerung von privaten Aufführungen bzw. Theaterakademien hin zu Darbietungen in solchen Fest- und Repräsentationssälen wie Redoutensaal, Universitätssaal oder Landhaus[17]. Symptomatisch scheinen hier die gemeinsamen Erstaufführungen von *Siebter Symphonie* und *Wellingtons Sieg oder Die Schlacht bei Vittoria* im Dezember 1813 / Januar 1814 in Universität und Großem Redoutensaal. Denn während Beethoven bereits in der *Siebten* systematisch die räumliche Ausdehnung des Klangkörpers zu erproben scheint – besonders deutlich etwa beim Schichtungsverfahren des zweiten Satzes –, erhebt er in *Wellingtons Sieg* sujetbedingt die konkrete Raumdramaturgie bekanntlich zur zentralen Kompositionsidee, die sich – *expressis verbis* dokumentiert durch die minutiösen Aufführungshinweise des Komponisten im Partitu-

---

Musiktheorie 26 (2011), S. 157–176 (Wiederabdruck in: *Beethovens Orchestermusik und Konzerte* (= Das Beethoven-Handbuch 1), hrsg. von Oliver Korte und Albrecht Riethmüller, Laaber 2013, S. 49–70).

16 Man betrachte im zweiten Satz der *Sechsten* beispielsweise die Sechzehntel-Linie (T. 91ff.) vom Fagott über Klarinette und Violine I bis zur Flöte.

17 Nach ersten Schüben ab 1807 (Liebhaber-Concerte) ist ein Durchbruch zu einem bürgerlichen Konzertwesen sowie damit einhergehend eine Verlagerung der Aufführungsräume im Umfeld der Befreiungskriege ab 1813/14 zu beobachten, etwa bei der Gründung der Gesellschaft der Musikfreunde 1814. Vgl. u.a. Otto Biba, »Concert Life in Beethoven's Vienna«, in: *Beethoven Performers and Critics*, hrsg. von Robert Winter und Bruce Carr, Detroit 1980, S. 77–93; Tia DeNora, »Musical Patronage and Social Change in Beethoven's Vienna«, in: The American Journal of Sociology 97 (1991), S. 310–346; sowie Weinzierl 2002, a.a.O.

rerstdruck von 1816[18] – im dichotomischen Gegenüber der beiden Harmoniemusiken sowie der Platzierung der Kanonaden manifestiert: vom Orchester deutlich separiert und für die Zuschauer explizit nicht sichtbar, so wie auch die Militärtrommeln und Trompeten, die eingangs die gegnerischen Parteiungen repräsentieren, als Ferninstrumente »von der äußersten Entfernung« allmählich näher und näher rücken sollen, während zwei weitere Trompeten »stehend im Orchester geblasen werden müssen«. Was durch zusätzlich ›einkomponierte‹ Strukturen wie das mediantische Gegeneinander von Es-Dur und C-Dur, Klangflächenkontraste und Bass-Orgelpunkte, Dialogfakturen sowie permanente Crescendi und Dynamikeffekte potenziert wird, mag als Illustratives, quasi-realistisch Geräuschhaftes zwar einen Sonderfall an Plastizität insbesondere hinsichtlich der konkreten orchesterexternen Postierung des Militär-Instrumentariums darstellen – als genuin theatrales Moment sonst einzig etwa aus der *Leonoren-Ouvertüre III* (1806) mit den hinter der Bühne platzierten Trompeten bekannt[19]. Doch geht die Verräumlichung nicht allein in einer (überdeutlichen) Programmatik auf, sondern ist durchaus konzeptuell zu werten als dezidierter Reflex auf Größe von Aufführungsort, Klangkörper und Auditorium, auf die Beethoven wiederholt hinwies[20].

Raumdisposition als Reaktion auf das Potenzial einer stark angewachsenen musikalischen Öffentlichkeit und ihrer Konzerträume: dies prägt schließlich vor allem auch die *Neunte Symphonie*, bei deren Erstaufführungen im Kärntnertor-Theater (7. Mai 1824) und Großen Redoutensaal (23. Mai 1824) der Chor – nach Vorbild etwa der 1819 inaugurierten Wiener *Concerts Spirituels* – im sonst für das Orchester reservierten Bühnenvorraum positioniert war, wohingegen für das Orchester auf der Bühne ein nach hinten aufsteigendes Podium errichtet wurde[21].

---

18 Wiedergegeben in: *Beethoven: Ouverturen und Wellingtons Sieg* (= Beethoven Werke II/1), hrsg. von Hans-Werner Küthen, München 1974, S. 124f.

19 Hinsichtlich des vieldiskutierten Einflusses von Komponisten aus den Umfeld der Französischen Revolution scheint ein Verweis auf die Verwendung von Fernensembles bei François-Joseph Gossec (*Missa pro defunctis*), Étienne-Nicolas Méhul (*Chant National du 14 juillet 1800*) und Jean-François Lesueur (*Chant du 1er Vendémiaire*) interessant.

20 Vgl. Beethovens »Bemerkungen für die Aufführung« sowie seinen Tagebuch-Eintrag zu den Aufführungen vom Januar 1814, in: Maynard Solomon, *Beethovens Tagebuch*, hrsg. von Sieghard Brandenburg, Mainz 1990, Nr. 18, S. 49.

21 Vgl. *Ludwig van Beethoven: Briefwechsel Gesamtausgabe*, hrsg. von Sieghard Brandenburg, München 1996, Bd. 5 [1823–1824], Nr. 1818, S. 308, sowie Shin Augustinus Kojima, »Die Uraufführung der Neunten Symphonie Beethovens – einige neue Tatsa-

Abbildung 2: Orchesterstellplan des Wiener Concert spirituel; Kupferstich um 1825

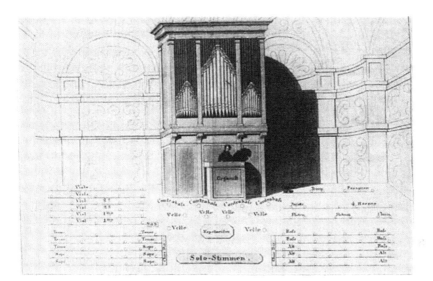

Reproduktion aus: Ferdinand Simon Gassner, *Dirigent und Ripienist für angehende Musikdirigenten, Musiker und Musikfreunde*, Karlsruhe 1844, Beilage 16.

Diese Aufstellung aber kongruiert sinnfällig mit der Werkidee: vom Eröffnungsmodus des ›Werdens aus dem Nichts‹, das ganz raumhaft sozusagen als auskomponiertes Hinführen *pianissimo* aus der Ferne des hinteren Bühnenraums zu verstehen ist, bis zum Schlusssatz, in dem sich noch einmal ein Aufbauprozess des vollen Orchestersatzes vollzieht – zunächst Bläserdominanz (hinten rechts), dann Streicherdominanz (hinten links), dazwischen Genese der späteren Gesangslinie in Celli und Kontrabässen als räumlichem Zentralklang, der später durch das Bariton-Solo gleichsam punktartig fokussiert und eine Ebene nach vorne geholt wird, schließlich die instrumentalklangliche Totale, vor der sodann der Chor – auf einer Stufe mit dem Auditorium – in gewisser Weise als direkte Näherung und finaler Nexus zwischen orchestralem Klangkörper und Publikum fungiert: dies ganz analog zu Textaussage und Ideengehalt als raumakustische Realisierung visionärer Brüderlichkeit und Humanität, als klangliche Verwirklichung des »Seid umschlungen Millionen«.

chen«, in: *Bericht über den internationalen musikwissenschaftlichen Kongress Bayreuth 1981*, hrsg. von Christoph-Hellmut Mahling, Kassel 1984, S. 390–397.

HECTOR BERLIOZ

Konkretisierte sich so um 1800 auf dem Wiener Konzertpodium Kants berühmte Formel von Musik als »Mittheilung der Gefühle in die Ferne in einem Raume umher, an alle, die sich darin befinden, und ein gesellschaftlicher Genuß, der dadurch nicht vermindert wird, dass viele an ihm teilnehmen«[22], so entwickelte sich im postrevolutionären Paris – weit mehr noch als dies im London Haydns der Fall gewesen war – eine regelrechte Monumental- und ›Massenästhetik‹ des Konzertlebens[23], die um die Jahrhundertmitte etwa zu solchen Großkonzerten wic denjenigen im Cirque Olympique, Cirque Napoléon oder dem Palais de l'Industrie führte und experimentelle Konzertsaalentwürfe wie beispielsweise den elliptischen Bau von Henry Barthélémy (1851)[24] oder den eiförmigen Saalentwurf von Adolphe Sax (1867) zeitigte. Dass Hector Berlioz – zentral involviert in all diese Entwicklungen – den akustisch-spatialen Dimensionen von Musik nicht nur in erstaunlich differenzierten theoretischen Überlegungen essentielle Bedeutung beimaß (wie sie 1843/1855 etwa in den ebenso luziden wie visionären Ausführungen zur Orchesterdisposition im Kapitel *L'orchestre* des *Grand Traité d'instrumentation et d'orchestration modernes* gipfelten[25]), sondern dass gerade auch in seinen Kompositionen ein ganzes Panorama intensiver Ausnutzung von Raumressourcen begegnet[26], findet hier seine architektur- und institutionengeschichtliche Grundierung.

22 Immanuel Kant, *Anthropologie in pragmatischer Hinsicht* [1796/1797], Königsberg ²1800, § 16 »Vom Gehör«, S. 49.

23 Vgl. zum Kontext auch Renate Groth, »Zur Idee des Monumentalen in der französischen Musik«, in: *Was hat die französische Revolution für Musik und Ästhetik bewirkt?*, hrsg. von Günter Katzenberger, Hannover 1989, S. 58–63; sowie James H. Johnson, *Listening in Paris: A cultural history*, Berkeley 1995.

24 Vgl. Françoise Boudon, »Un théâtre elliptique à Paris en 1850: Les projets d'Henry Barthélémy«, in: Bulletin de la Société de l'histoire de Paris et de l'Ile-de-France 117 (1990), S. 251–268.

25 Vgl. hierzu Fabian Kolb, »Das Orchester als Klangraum: Hector Berlioz' *le Chef d'orchestre* und seine Überlegungen zu Raumakustik und Orchesteraufstellung«, in: *Maestro! Dirigieren im 19. Jahrhundert* (= Musik – Kultur – Geschichte), hrsg. von Alessandro Di Profio und Arnold Jacobshagen, Würzburg 2015 [im Druck].

26 Vgl. etwa Wolfgang Dömling, »»En songeant au temps... à l'espace‹: Über einige Aspekte der Musik Hector Berlioz'«, in: Archiv für Musikwissenschaft 33 (1976), S. 241–260; ders., »Szenerie im Imaginären: Über dramatisch-symphonische Werke von Hector Berlioz«, in: Melos / NZ 3 (1977), S. 195–203; ders., »Les nouvelles dimensions de l'espace et du temps dans la musique d'Hector Berlioz«, in: Analyse musicale 15 (1989), S. 7–17; Jean-Pierre Bartoli, »Écriture du timbre et espace sonore dans l'œuvre de Berlioz«, in: Analyse musicale 3 (1986), S. 31–36; Mireille Hennin-

Abbildung 3: Sitzplan des Orchesters im Salle du Conservatoire, Paris

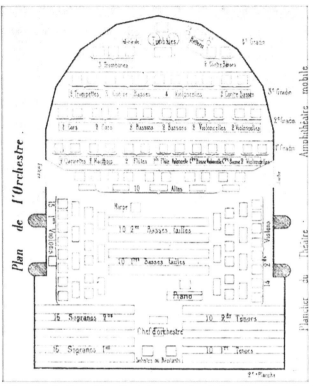

Aus: Henri Gourdon de Genouillac, *Paris à travers les siècles: Histoire nationale de Paris et des Parisiens, depuis la fondation de Lutèce jusqu'à nos jours*, Bd. 5, Paris 1881, nach S. 76.

In der Tat kann bereits in der *Symphonie fantastique* – uraufgeführt im Dezember 1830 durch das Konservatoriums-Orchester in der Salle du Conservatoire, Paradigma für Berlioz' Vorstellung eines Klangkörpers und seiner Präsentationsmatrix – eine Kumulation ganz unterschiedlicher Raumkonzepte und -effekte eruiert werden, die insgesamt dem Gedanken verpflichtet scheinen, die *idée fixe* in immer neu inszenierten Entouragen zu präsentieren, die stets auch als spezifische Raumkonstellationen gedacht werden. Von der ›Klanggenese‹ aus den *gradins* heraus (T. 1f.), den dynamischen Extremen

ger-Vial, »Une étude du temps et de l'espace dans *Les nuits d'été* de Berlioz«, in: Analyse musicale 48 (2003), S. 5–17; sowie Jean-Michel Hasler, »À la conquête de l'espace sonore«, in: *Hector Berlioz*, hrsg. von Christian Wasselin und Pierre-René Serna, Paris 2003, S. 51–63.

(insbesondere auch in den Schwellakkorden wie T. 28f. oder T. 61f.) und den skandierenden, schließlich in den Unschärfen eines Tremolo *ppp* sich verlierenden Tutti-Schlägen (T. 64ff.) in den *Rêveries*, über das wandernde, in wechselnden Präsenzgraden verschiedenen Instrumenten übereignete Auftreten der *idée fixe*, bis hin zum Ausblenden der Totale am Schluss der *Passions* (T. 492ff.: *ritardando* und *diminuendo poco a poco, tout l'orchestre aussi doux que possible, ppp*); von der markanten Verlagerung des Klanggeschehens auf den intimeren Raum von Harfen und Streichern (*plancher du théâtre*) in *Un bal*, über das Verlöschen des Walzers *pppp presque rien* (T. 117ff.) und das Hineinziehen der *idée fixe* (*1er gradin*) in den drehenden Strudel des Walzers (T. 129ff.), der nun allmählich den gesamten Orchesterraum erfüllt, bis hin zum opernhaft-dramatischen Entschwinden der *idée fixe* am Schluss (T. 298ff.: durch Kadenz suggeriertes Satzende, gewaltiges Tremolo und plötzlicher Abriss, *idée fixe un peu retenu* in der Solo-Klarinette flankiert allein durch das *a* der benachbarten Flöte und Horn): Was die ersten beiden Sätze gleichsam in extremer Pointierung an imaginärer Raumwirkung vollziehen, wendet sich mit der *Scène aux champs* schließlich ins Reale, konkret Räumlich-Szenische, wenn zu Beginn im unbegleiteten, rhythmisch-metrisch wie harmonisch frei schwebenden Alternieren von Englischhorn und Oboe der Kuhreigen zweier Hirten erklingt[27].

In räumlicher Distanz *derrière la scène* antwortet die Oboe echoartig, ehe sie zum eigentlichen Pastoralthema wieder ins Orchester zurückkehrt. Auch der Auftritt der *idée fixe* (T. 87ff.) erfolgt sodann von ferne, realisiert durch eine quasi-polymetrische Diskrepanz bzw. Störung (oder eben Raumdifferenz) zwischen dem 2/8-Duktus von Oboe/Flöte und dem 3/8-Duktus der Bässe[28], die die *idée fixe* registermäßig getrennt, räumlich indes gleichsam umschließen, bevor die Melodie bei ihrem zweiten Erklingen (T. 150ff.) ganz homogen in das 6/8-Gefüge eingepasst, dem Pastoralthema angenähert und räumlich assimiliert erscheint (Überantwortung von Holzbläsern an Violen). Wenn am Schluss der Szene (T. 175ff.) das Englischhorn schließlich wieder den Kuhreigen intoniert, antwortet nicht mehr die Oboe, sondern die Fernwirkung wird durch das Geräuschhafte des Donnergrollens (*bruit éloigné de tonnerre*) der vier Pauken umfunktionalisiert – hiermit zu den quasi-realistischen Klangeffekten und raumhaften Geräuschfaktoren von *Marche au Supplice* und *Hexensabbat* überleitend. Und auch dort stellt die Raumperspektive ein entscheidendes Moment der Bildwechsel dar: Nach der gleichsam herandrängenden Bewegungsevokation des Marsches und der

---

27 Im Programm ist der Raumbezug semantisiert: »Se trouvant un soir à la campagne, il entend au loin deux pâtres qui dialoguent un ranz de vaches«.

28 Vgl. Dömling, a.a.O., S. 267f.

Drastik der Hinrichtungsszene beginnt der Schlusssatz mit spukhaftem Flirren, erregtem Zirpen, dräuendem Paukengrollen und signalartigen, echohaft beantworteten Rufen (gestopftes Horn) aus den verschiedenen Regionen des Orchesterraumes[29], ehe sich in das düster-amorphe Tönen – angekündigt *solo lointain* durch die Klarinette (T. 21ff.) – in der Mittelebene des Podiums die verzerrte *idée fixe* lagert (T. 40ff.): eine bühnenmusikartige Blaskapellenparodie mit auskomponiertem Näherrücken (*crescendo* zum *ff*) und Sich-Entfernen (T. 86ff.: in die Tiefe absinkende *decrescendo*-Linie), in das sich mit den akustisch isolierten Glockenschlägen aus der Ferne (auch die Glocken sind *derrière la scène* zu platzieren) das nächste *tableau* einblendet (T. 102ff.).

Dieses ist abermals durch das Voreinander zweier Aktionsebenen mit divergenter metrischer Gliederung als Reflex auf die Dislokation charakterisiert, wobei vor dem Hintergrund des im Abseits unregelmäßig einsetzenden Glockengeläuts der streng gemessene Choralvortrag des *Dies irae* im hinteren Bühnenbezirk ebenso raumhaft präsentiert wird, nämlich gleichsam antiphonal in Alternatim-Praxis zwischen Fagotten plus Ophicleïde vs. Blech, das Ganze im vorderen Bühnenraum burlesk kommentiert durch Holz und Streicher. Nachdem in der *Ronde du Sabbat* sodann der Rundtanz mittels seiner Fugato-Exposition (T. 241ff.) in den einzelnen Distrikten des Orchesters konkret räumlich als drehende Klangbewegung installiert ist, wird diese Bewegungssuggestion, ist sie durch ständiges chromatisches Höherschrauben und Crescendieren einmal vollends präsent gemacht, gleichsam zu einem Bühnenprospekt, in den sich in Überlagerungstechnik erst Hornrufe (T. 328ff.) und sodann (zunächst fragmentarisch, schließlich als geschlossenes Massiv) das *Dies irae* betten (T. 331ff.) – ein Schichtungsverfahren, das im Gegenüber von Streichern und Bläsern wieder dezidiert auf den Raumebenen des Orchesters basiert und klangliche Dreidimensionalität erzeugt.

Ohne hier des Näheren auf weitere Kontexte und Strategien der Verräumlichung in Werken wie *Lélio* (unsichtbares Orchester auf der Bühne), *Harold en Italie* (Fokussierung auf den isoliert vom Orchester zu situierenden Viola-Protagonisten, Schichtenstruktur von Pilgermarsch und Serenadenszene, solistisch besetztes Streichtrio *dans la coulisse*, etc.), *Grande messe des morts* (Bläserensembles platziert in den vier Himmelsrichtungen, insbesondere zur Darstellung des Jüngsten Gerichts im *Tuba mirum*), *Roméo et*

---

29 Auch hier dominieren die Raumsituationen das Programm: »Il se voit au sabbat, au milieu d'une troupe affreuse d'ombres, de sorciers, de monstres de toute espèce, réunis pour ses funérailles. [...] cris lointains auxquels d'autres cris semblent répondre.« || »Il se voit ensuite environné d'une foule dégoutante de sorciers, de diables, réunis pour fêter la nuit du sabbat. Ils appellent au loin.«

Juliette (ausführlich-differenzierte Hinweise zur Aufstellung aller Mitwirkenden, Chöre *derrière la scène* in N° 3), der *Grande symphonie funèbre et
triomphale* (›Freiluft-Musik‹) oder dem *Te Deum* (räumliches Gegenüber
von Orchester und Orgel, Distanz zwischen Hauptchören und Kinderchor)
eingehen zu können, zeigt es sich, wie essentiell der differenzierte Umgang
mit imaginären wie auch ganz realen Raumaspekten für Berlioz' Wirkungs-
ästhetik im *genre instrumental expressif* ist.

VON FRANZ SCHUBERT ZU ANTON BRUCKNER

Auf gänzlich andere Weise offenbart sich musikalisches Raumbewusstsein
demgegenüber in der Parallelentwicklung der Symphonik Schuberts, Men-
delssohns und Schumanns, wie sie zugleich in Korrelation zur gleichsam
kontemplativen, weniger frontal-bühnenzentrierten (eher publikumsbezogen-
›parlamentarischen‹) Kommunikationssituation in bürgerlichen Konzerthäu-
sern wie dem Leipziger Gewandhaus zu verstehen ist, wo das Orchester als
weniger lokal differenzierte denn als tendenziell eher homogene, geschlos-
sen-kompakte Klangquelle fungiert, für deren klangliche Präsenz und nuancierte Klanggestalt freilich auch die vielgelobt vorbildliche Leipziger Akustik eine maßgebliche Rolle spielt — was einer weniger spektakulär als vielmehr orchesterintern ausgehandelten Raumkonzeption entgegenkommt. Sind
so bei Schubert (etwa in der *Großen C-Dur-Symphonie*) und bei Mendelssohn (etwa in der *Hebriden-Ouvertüre* sowie der *Schottischen*) vielfach
Momente einer Nobilitierung bzw. Hypostasierung von Klangphänomenen
zu beobachten, die als imaginative Raumevokationen im Sinne eines ›romantischen‹ Raumkonzepts der offen-suggestiven Weite sowie der subtil wechselnden Ferne- und Distanzgrade zu verstehen wären, so treten bei Schumann zugleich poetisch-narratologisch beschreibbare Prinzipien hervor, die
über einen spezifischen ›Ton‹ oder ein charakteristisches Idiom, die Faktur,
den Gestus, Habitus oder Duktus imaginäre Raumsituationen exponieren und
so ein quasi-episches Raumgefüge etablieren bzw. ausstaffieren (bis hin zur
plastischen Bildlichkeit etwa der *Rheinischen*).

   Während sich die Raumdimension der »tönend bewegten [sic!] Formen«[30] bei Brahms dagegen gleichsam abstrakter manifestiert und sich sozusagen subkutan ins Innere der Strukturen verlagert, um unter der Oberfläche
eine gewissermaßen multidimensional nuancierte Tiefenperspektive zu er-

---

30 So bekanntlich Eduard Hanslick, *Vom Musikalisch-Schönen: Ein Beitrag zur Revision
    der Ästhetik der Tonkunst*, Leipzig 1854 (Nachdruck Darmstadt 1965), S. 32.

öffnen, für die die trotz größeren Raumvolumens und gesteigerter Beset-
zungsstärke optimierte akustische Situation der neuen Konzertsäle im letzten
Jahrhundertdrittel freilich nicht zu unterschätzen sein dürfte (Paradigma des
Wiener Musikvereinssaals von 1871), scheint Bruckner auf die expandierende Weiträumigkeit der Konzertstätten in seiner besonderen Art der Monu-
mental- und Grandiositätsästhetik zu reagieren, greift in seinem Werk doch
symptomatisch jene signifikante Dramaturgie der sukzessiven Monumentali-
sierung, wie sie das Ausschöpfen der Ressourcen des großbesetzten Klangkörpers und das gleichsam klangliche Auskleiden des Raumvolumens im
Sinne allmählicher Imposanz und Raumerfüllung vereint.

GUSTAV MAHLER

Sozusagen in Synthese Beethovenscher, Berliozscher, Schubertscher, Men-
delssohnscher, Schumannscher und Brucknerscher Verfahren gebündelt und
potenziert scheint der Fundus symphonischer Strategien spatialer Klangorganisation um 1900 schließlich im Œuvre Gustav Mahlers, für den die Verräumlichung des Klangs im Sinne des »mit allen Mitteln der vorhandenen
Technik eine Welt aufbauen«[31] eine zweifellos herausragende Kategorie und
Grundkonstituente darstellt[32], sind seine Werke doch gespickt mit Anweisungen zur Positionierung von Instrumentalisten sowie Zusätzen zur Evokation von Raumwirkungen, und zwar als elementarer Bestandteil der jeweiligen Werkkonzepte, insofern Instrumentation »nicht dazu da [sei], Klang-
effekte zu erzielen, sondern deutlich zum Ausdruck zu bringen, was man zu
sagen hat«[33].

---

31 *Gustav Mahler in den Erinnerungen von Natalie Bauer-Lechner*, hrsg. von Herbert
   Killian, mit Anmerkungen und Erklärungen von Knud Martner, rev. und erw. Auflage,
   Hamburg 1984, S. 35.
32 Vgl. u.a. Harald Hodeige, *Komponierte Klangräume in den Symphonien Gustav Mahlers*, Berlin 2004; Laura Anne Dolp, *Mahler's landscapes: Constructions of space in
   music and the visual arts in fin-de-siecle Vienna*, Ann Arbor 2005; Erich Wolfgang
   Partsch, »Mahlers Weg ins Freie: Landschaft als ästhetischer Erlebnis- und Inspira-
   tionsraum«, in: *Mahler im Kontext / Contextualizing Mahler*, hrsg. von dems. und
   Morten Solvik, Wien/Köln/Weimar 2011, S. 165–176.
33 Natalie Bauer-Lechner, a.a.O., S. 198. Siehe zur Orchestrierung bei Mahler insgesamt
   auch Altug Ünlü, *Gustav Mahlers Klangwelt: Studien zur Instrumentation*, Frank-
   furt/M. 2006; Peter Jost, »Mahlers Orchesterklang«, in: *Mahler Handbuch*, hrsg. von
   Bernd Sponheuer und Wolfram Steinbeck, Stuttgart 2010, S. 114–126; sowie Klaus
   Aringer, »Orchesterbesetzung und Instrumentation«, in: *Gustav Mahler: Interpretationen seiner Werke*, hrsg. von Peter Revers und Oliver Korte, Laaber 2011, S. 416–
   434.

So prägt die Erzeugung von Raumklängen bereits essentiell die *Wunder-horn*-Symphonien[34], angefangen bei der imaginären Raumszenerie der Langsamen Einleitung im Eröffnungssatz der *Ersten* mit ihrem über sechs Oktaven extrem gespreizten *Naturlaut* aus flirrend-hohem Flageolett und sonorer Tiefe, in den sich neben quasi-naturalistischen Elementen wie Glockenmotiv und Kuckucksruf (»Der Ruf eines Kukuks nachzuahmen«) Signalfanfaren der Trompeten betten — Trompete I und II platziert »in sehr weiter Entfernung«, Trompete III lediglich »in der Ferne« (so die Anweisungen in der Partitur). Was hier im Sinne der werkbestimmenden Aufbruchsthematik[35] einen Prozess der Näherung und des In-Gang-Bringens initiiert (inklusive allmählicher Zunahme an Aktionsdichte, Tempo und Lautstärke), findet als Bewegungsimpuls im *Todtenmarsch in Callot's Manier* (u.a. über die Faktur eines dreistimmigen Kanons im Bassregister) zu einem – freilich grotesken – szenisch vorstellbaren Marschduktus, einer topisch-topologisch suggerierten Raumbewegung des Kondukts[36], die mit der *Zweiten* in die Position des Kopfsatzes gelangen und fortan zum beherrschenden Typus der Mahlerschen Eröffnungssätze erhoben wird[37].

Während der Aufbruch der *Ersten* dabei schließlich im Finalsatz ›erlöst‹ wird durch das verklärte Elysium eines Klanges, der klingen solle, »als wäre er vom Himmel gefallen, als käme er aus einer anderen Welt«[38], konkretisiert sich die Eschatologie in der *Zweiten* nach dem *Urlicht* und der anschließenden wild-infernalischen Raumszenerie (»Todesschrei«, Posaunensignal, Rufthema der Hörner, kondukartiges Posaunenmotiv plus irrlichternde Triller, *Dies irae*-Beginn, Marsch- und Siegestöne, schreiende Dissonanzen, höllenartige Pfiffe, etc.) sowie dem »grossen Appell« des fünften Satzes in der raumhaft-sinnlichen Evokation der Apokalypse, bei der der Einsatz eines »in weitester Entfernung aufgestellt[en]« (Z. 22) Fernensembles aus vier Trompeten, Hörnern und Schlagwerk im Sinne szenischer Tiefendimension »aus entgegengesetzter Richtung her« (Z. 29) erfolgen soll,

---

34 Ein Fernorchester begegnet zuvor schon im *Hochzeitsstück* aus *Das klagende Lied*.

35 Vgl. etwa Wolfram Steinbeck, »Erste bis Vierte Symphonie: ›Eine durchaus geschlossene Tetralogie‹«, in: Bernd Sponheuer/Wolfram Steinbeck (Hrsg.), a.a.O., S. 217–268, hier S. 220–230.

36 Vgl. Mahlers eigene Schilderung, in: Natalie Bauer-Lechner, a.a.O., S. 174.

37 Nicht unwesentlich scheint in diesem Zusammenhang, dass Mahler 1895 in einer Bearbeitung von Beethovens *Neunter* das *Alla marcia* des Finales einem allmählich näher rückenden Fernorchester anvertraut hatte; vgl. Emil Nikolaus von Reznicek, »Erinnerungen an Gustav Mahler«, in: Musikblätter des Anbruch 7–8 (1920), S. 298–300, hier S. 299. Vgl. auch Hans-Joachim Hinrichsen, »Mahler und Beethoven«, in: Nachrichten zur Mahler-Forschung 62 (2011), S. 31–40.

38 Natalie Bauer-Lechner, a.a.O., S. 27.

dies zweifellos als Allusion auf die Himmelsrichtungen, aus denen die Engel die Auserwählten sammeln, wobei sich auch hier ein nuancierter Prozess der Näherung und erneuten Entfernung vollzieht: »Der Autor denkt sich hier, ungefähr, vom Wind vereinzelnd herüber getragene Klänge einer kaum vernehmbaren Musik« (Z. 22); »aus weiter Ferne«; »etwas näher und stärker«; »viel näher und stärker«; »sehr entfernt«; »immer fern und ferner«; »sich verlierend« | »lang und verklingend« (Z. 29f.) – so lauten die entsprechenden Partiturinskriptionen.

Das dem kraftvoll-präsenten *fortissimo*-»Weckruf« von acht Hörnern *unisono* (»kräftig«, »entschieden«) folgende, vielfache und beharrliche Anrücken im Kopfsatz der *Dritten* (»kaum mehr Musik zu nennen, sondern nur ein mystischer, ungeheurer Naturlaut«[39]) dagegen stützt sich vorwiegend auf immanente, orchesterinterne Mittel wellenförmig-diskontinuierlicher Klangintensivierung. Abgesehen von der Episode mit einigen »in der Entfernung aufgestellt[en]« kleinen Trommeln (Z. 54; mit *decrescendo* zum *pppp*) und unter reicher Beteiligung solch raumakustisch determinierter Horn- und Trompetenrufe mit »Schalltrichter in die Höhe« (bzw. Holzbläserrufe »mit aufgehob. Schalltrichter«)[40] geschieht dies vor allem mittels sukzessiver Klangverstärkung vom *ppp* bis zum *fff* sowie Ambitusweitung, Ausdehnung des Klangraums und zunehmender Sonorität des zunächst nur dünn besetzten Klangkörpers (paradigmatisch in der Reprise, Z. 62ff.), wobei in quasirealistischer Plastizität über diverse martialische Marsch-, Verkündigungs- und Signaltopoi der Eindruck einer herankommenden, zwischenzeitlich sich immer wieder etwas entfernenden Militärkapelle erzeugt wird: »Wie aus weiter Ferne« (Z. 20), »Wie aus weitester Entfernung« (Z. 36) und »Wieder Alles aus weitester Ferne sich nähernd« (Z. 62), vermerkt die Partitur, damit die »Vorstellung einer räumlich bewegten Musikquelle« zum »Impuls der Form« erhebend[41].

Finden sich in dieses kaleidoskopische Aufmarschszenario bereits Kontrastmomente wie die mehrdimensionale *musica coelestis* (lichtes Choralidiom der hohen Bläser + reigenartiges Rankwerk der Violine I + Herold-Motiv der Klarinette + Wellenbewegung) einmontiert, so eröffnet das altertümliche

---

39 Ebd., S. 59. Siehe zur Raumkonstruktion in der *Dritten* auch Laura Dolp, »Voice, ground, and the construction of space in Gustav Mahler's third symphony«, in: Naturlaut 8 (2011), S. 3–11.

40 Diese Vortragsanweisung ist in der Tat ein personalstilistisches Spezifikum Mahlers; vgl. Altug Ünlü, a.a.O., S. 85.

41 Theodor W. Adorno, *Mahler: Eine musikalische Physiognomik*, Frankfurt am Main 1960, S. 110. Zur rezeptionsästhetischen Realistik dieser Raumsuggestion vgl. Peter Jost, a.a.O., S. 124.

Tempo di Menuetto des zweiten Satzes einen komplementären Raum des Rührselig-Trivialen, blendet in eine befremdlich andere Welt des illusionär Ferngerückten, das sich im dritten Satz wieder im Sinne räumlicher Distanzierung manifestiert, wenn die musikalischen Stilzitate, Zerrbilder und Topoi ungelenk-vulgärer ›Bauernmusik‹ in die Posthorn-Episode umschlagen — ein Klang von außen, aus einer ›heilen Welt‹, unerreichbar weit entrückt: zunächst suggestiv »wie aus weiter Ferne« (Z. 14) und »wie aus der Ferne (sich etwas nähernd)« (Z. 15), beim zweiten Erklingen dann sogar ganz real »in weiter Entfernung« (Z. 27). Anfänglich durch die Trompete »schnell und schmetternd wie eine Fanfare« brutal zerbrochen, findet die hier so markierte musikalische Heterotopie über die schwebenden, unwirklichen *Misterioso*-Töne des vierten Satzes[42] und die »in der Höhe postiert[en]« Glocken (plus Knabenchor) des fünften Satzes schließlich zum raumfüllend präsenten, tiefen, gesättigt-monumentalen *Adagio*-Klang des Finales: symphonische Erfüllung im *hic et nunc* reiner Musik als Antwort gleichsam auf die utopisch-illusionäre Ferne zuvor.

Was sich anhand der nachfolgenden Symphonien weiterverfolgen ließe (wobei neben der ausgesprochen ›räumlich‹-gestischen Qualität der zentralen Prägungen im Grunde aller Mahler-Symphonien insbesondere auch auf Instrumentaleffekte, Klangverfremdungen und die Ereignishaftigkeit der vielfach um Geräuschinstrumente bereicherten Orchestration einzugehen wäre), findet mit der *Achten* schließlich Eingang in eine nochmals gesteigerte Monumentalkonstruktion, die – durchaus analog zur zeitgenössischen Massenpsychologie (Gustave Le Bon) und unter abermaliger Augmentierung des Aufführungsapparats und seiner Ressourcen ins Kolossale – auf die Korrelationen von Massen- und Raumwirkung setzte[43]. »Es ist das Größte, was ich bis jetzt gemacht. [...] Denken Sie sich, dass das ganze Universum zu tönen und zu klingen beginnt. Es sind nicht mehr menschli[che] Stimmen, sondern Planeten und Sonnen, welche kreisen«[44], bekundete Mahler; und vor dieser

---

42 Tiefe Harfen vs. Flageoletts der Streicher, Modalharmonik auf *d* und *a*, Terzzüge der Oboe »wie ein Naturlaut«, ›überirdisches‹ Violin-Solo, etc.

43 Vgl. Christian Wildhagen, *Die Achte Symphonie von Gustav Mahler*, Frankfurt am Main 2000; sowie Peter Revers, »›… durchweht von den erhebenden Hochgefühlen der Sängerfeste‹: Mahlers Achte im Spannungsfeld von Oratorien- und Symphonietradition«, in: *Gustav Mahler und die Symphonik des 19. Jahrhunderts* (= Bonner Schriften zur Musikwissenschaft 5), hrsg. von Bernd Sponheuer und Wolfram Steinbeck, Frankfurt am Main u.a. 2001, S. 101–112. Vgl. auch Donald Mitchell, »Mahler's Paradoxical Eight«, in: *A ›Mass‹ for the Masses*, hrsg. von Eveline Nikkels und Robert Becqué, Rijswijk 1992, S. 185–194, hier S. 193.

44 Brief vom 18.8.1906 an Willem Mengelberg, zitiert nach: *Gustav Mahler: Briefe*, hrsg. von Herta Blaukopf, rev. Neuausgabe, Wien 1996, S. 312.

Auffassung (die auf die Konzepte von *musica mundana* und allumfassender Universalität zielt) war ihm nicht nur die optisch durchdachte Positionierung der Mitwirkenden ein Anliegen, weshalb er eigens Alfred Roller mit Disposition und Beleuchtung der Bühne betraute[45]; sondern auch die signifikanten Änderungen zwischen Autograph und Erstdruck lassen sich als Reaktion auf den voluminösen Uraufführungsraum der 1907 von Wilhelm Bertsch als Messe-Ausstellungshalle konzipierten Münchner Neuen Musik-Festhalle und die dortigen Raumwirkungen verstehen[46].

Wie Mahler dabei im Einzelnen operierte, mag exemplarisch am zweiten Teil beobachtet werden. Hatte sich der Klangraum mit Ende von Teil I aufgrund der längeren Einschaltung der Orgel (Z. 89; ab Z. 92 »volles Werk«) sowie insbesondere auch des »isoliert postierten« Fernensembles aus vier Trompeten und drei Posaunen (Z. 91) spatial geweitet, so öffnet sich der Raum mit Beginn von Teil II expositionshaft suggestiv, wenn das prägnante Zweitaktmotiv von verschiedenen Bläsern in feiner dynamischer Abstufung intoniert wird, um schließlich mittels des instrumentatorisch verstärkten, zugleich indes dynamisch reduzierten Klanggrunds wie in die Ferne entrückt zu erscheinen. Derart vorbereitet, arbeitet die Anachoreten-Szene (Z. 24ff.) mit echohaft alternierenden Repetitionen und Erwiderungen der Textworte – Sinnbild der symptomatischerweise wortgetreu mit in die Partitur übernommenen Didaskalie aus Goethes *Faust II* (»Bergschluchten, Wald, Fels, Einöde. Heilige Anachoreten, gebirgauf verteilt, gelagert zwischen Klüften. Chor und Echo.«), das hier freilich dank der sukzessiven Fragmentarisierung der sprachlich-musikalischen Syntax im Grunde rein onomatopoetisch auf die Evokation einer elementaren, naturhaft-amorphen Räumlichkeit zielt[47], ehe am Werkende – in apotheotischer Kulmination des *Chorus mysticus*, der seinerseits nach weiträumigem *morendo* im *pppp* wie im raumtranszendierenden Schwebezustand wirkt, um schließlich montage- bzw. schnitthaft in die Präsenz des *ff* einzubrechen – wieder das »isoliert postierte« Fernensemble zum Einsatz kommt: rahmend zum ersten Teilschluss als Reverenz an den *creator spiritus* (dessen Hymnus hier in final-triumphaler Verbreiterung ertönt) noch einmal realiter die Weite des kolossalen Raums durchmessend.

---

45 Vgl. Henry-Louis de La Grange, *Gustav Mahler*, Bd. IV: *A New Life Cut Short (1907–1911)*, Oxford/New York 2008, S. 951. Vgl. auch die Erinnerungen des Konzertveranstalters Emil Gutmann (»Gustav Mahler als Organisator«, in: *Gustav Mahler: Unbekannte Briefe*, hrsg. von Herta Blaukopf, Wien/Hamburg 1983, S. 87–91, u.a. S. 90): »Die äußere Gruppierung der Massen war ihm sehr wichtig«.

46 Vgl. Christian Wildhagen, a.a.O., S. 61–79.

47 Vgl. ebd., S. 308.

* * *

»Die Symphonie hat bis heute keine würdige Stätte gefunden, um vereint mit einer solchen sich uns in ihrer vollen Wirkung zu offenbaren. Während die kirchliche Tonkunst dem Schosse des Domes angehört und dort ihre harmonische Umgebung fand, während Wagner dem Drama seine Stätte im wiedergeborenen Theater der Antike anwies, fand die Symphonie nur eine unwürdige Unterkunft im Konzerthause.«[48]

Während der Münchner Architekt Ernst Haiger 1907 diese Negativbilanz stellte, um mit seinem eigenen Entwurf eines »Symphoniehauses« gegenzusteuern, das die »Wiedergeburt des Tempels aus dem Geiste der Symphonie anstrebte« und »der symphonischen Musik, die zumeist nur ein königlicher Gast in niederen Räumen ist, einen Tempel weihen« wollte[49], hatten die Komponisten das ihre getan, um mit verschiedenen musikimmanentkompositorischen Maßnahmen das spatiale Potenzial symphonischer Musik zu erproben. Wenn dabei insbesondere Mahlers Œuvre in Ballung seit Haydn entwickelter Verfahren insgesamt ein ganzes Arsenal an musikalischen Raummöglichkeiten auslotete, so findet sich hier – ergänzt um weitere Strategien etwa bei Claude Debussy[50], den Komponisten der Wiener Schule u.a. – ein Fundus, aus dem nicht nur unmittelbar die Moderne nach 1900 schöpfte, sondern der als Kulmination und Synthese der symphonischen Tradition des 19. Jahrhunderts auch die solide Basis bildete, auf dem die Komponisten nach dem Zweiten Weltkrieg mit ihren neuen technischen Möglichkeiten aufbauten.

Aus technischen Gründen musste dieser Artikel leider gekürzt werden. Die Originalfassung ist unter https:// https://www2.ak.tu-berlin.de/~akgroup/ak_pub/ 2015/KolbKlangwelten abrufbar.

---

48 Ernst Haiger, »Der Tempel: Das apollinische Kunstwerk der Zukunft«, in: Die Musik 6 (1906/1907), S. 350–356, hier S. 355.

49 Paul Ehlers, »Das deutsche Symphoniehaus«, in: *Almanach der deutschen Musikbücherei auf das Jahr 1921*, Regensburg 1920, S. 47–65, hier S. 55.

50 Vgl. etwa Peter Benary, »Das impressionistische Raumgefühl als Stilfaktor bei Debussy«, in: *Bericht über den internationalen musikwissenschaftlichen Kongreß*, hrsg. von Martin Just und Georg Reichert, Kassel 1963, S. 244–246; sowie Evelyne Andréani/Michel Borne, »Dialogue sur l'espace et le temps. Debussy / Mallarmé«, in: *Les universaux en musique*, hrsg. von Costin Miereanu und Xavier Hascher, Paris 1998, S. 233–255.

ENGLISH SUMMARY

Soundspaces for the great hall
Room concepts, spatial sound organisation and strategies of spatialisation in the symphonic music of the 19th century

Like basically for all developments in the music of the 20th and 21st century, the tradition of symphonic music of the 19th century constitutes, especially for electronic music, a decisive aesthetic role. Apart from historical cross-references to older music is it the significant link and source of friction, in front of which the composers after WWII generated their aesthetic and composing profile – and this mainly for the creativity in the way they treated auditory space.

The potentials of a specific spatial sound organisation in orchestral music explicitly turned into focus not before the 18th century was reached. This outcome had been produced on one hand by the development of a public concert scene, that promoted the building of own and greater concert halls and the expansion and differentiation of the orchestral bodies of sound and on the other by the aesthetic implications and postulates that aimed at categories like size, universality, representation, potency of effectiveness and could be identified especially in symphonic music. Recalling the orientation of all representatives of New Music on the educational canon and concert repertoire of their time, which itself is a canon of the symphonic literature from the 19th century, it can be very effective to look for concepts and strategies of spatialization in exactly this canon of relevant works.

The linkage of compositional development and outer matters of performance receives reinforced attention already with Joseph Haydn. Especially the potentials of the great concert halls in London seem to have enrolled an intense reflexion of the use of space possibilities, since they were in general quite sensible for aspects like echo effects, terrace dynamics or *como da lontano*. Hence many of the surprise coups of the London symphonies may be described as playing with orchestral dispositions and spatial order. The structure of the ›classical‹ writing/composition, the setup of the musical score, the positions of the instrument (groups) and the dramaturgy interact here.

One is also able to find interdependencies between Beethoven's ›concert hall‹ and his composed space texture (Faktur – Aufbau). Apart from the fact that Viennese concert halls overall in this time presented a higher intimacy (closeness orchestra – audience) and presence of sound (loudness, dynamic spectrum), the restructuring of the public concert lives from 1807 on revealed itself as a central aspect, in which particular space phenoma in the 5th,

6th and 7th *Symphony*, as well as in *Wellington's Victory* could be evaluated. Seemingly strong and characteristic is the concept of the *Ninth Symphony* with a frequent ›composing-out‹ of the slow approximation from afar and finally the closing, in which the choir acts as final nexus between the instrumental body and the auditorium; in this role it is very congruent to the meaning of the text and the idea of the work.

An entire panorama of plastic utilisation of space resources is encountered with Berlioz. This way an accumulation of different spatial effects may be determined already for the *Symphonie fantastique*: from various types of fading in and through diverse structures of contrasts up to screen changes and overlapping, from suggestions of movement through moments of polyrhythm up to the real spatialisation through instruments *derrière la scène*.

By contrast, in the symphonic of Schubert, Mendelssohn and Schumann the musical sense of place manifests in a completely different manner, it should rather be understood in correlation to more ›passive‹ communication situations in concert halls like the Gewandhaus Leipzig. The space dimension in Brahms's works materializes in a more abstract way and is relocated into the interior of the structures. In contrast, the symphonic by Bruckner sets its focus through its architectonic block-like shape of the movements, its wave-like enhancements, its vehement contrasts in dynamics, its agglomerations of sound, its tremendous breakthrough productions, its harsh caesuras and the abrupt inserts of quotations or choral parts into different grades of presence of the musical embossing in space, whereby a dramaturgy of successive monumentalisation and a gradual filling of the space take effect.

The fundus of symphonic strategies finally seems to be bundled and intensified around 1900 in Mahler's œuvre, in which the spatialisation of sound in the sense of »building a world with all possible means of the existing technology« represents an outstanding category, especially since his works are infused with instructions to the positioning of instrumentalists and indications in the score concerning the suggestions to spatial effects.

Starting from the »*Wunderhorn*« *symphonies* up to the 8th Mahler explores an arsenal of musical space possibilities here, which also – as synthesis of the symphonic tradition of the 19th century – provided the basis on which the composers after WWII could build upon with their fully new technical means.

Henry Brants »*Spatial Music*«

Kompositionen mit Aufführungsräumen

CHRISTA BRÜSTLE

Die Integration spezifischer Aspekte der Aufführung von Musik im Raum hat sich in den letzten Jahrzehnten zu einem selbstverständlichen Faktor der kompositorischen Arbeit entwickelt. Dabei besteht eine große Bandbreite der Möglichkeiten, die sich von einer besonderen Aufstellung der Musiker und Musikerinnen auf dem Konzertpodium bis hin zu raumfüllenden Konzertinstallationen erstreckt, ganz abgesehen von den Optionen, die mit den elektroakustischen Medien verbunden sind. Klangverteilung und Klangbewegung im Raum oder die Simulation von akustischen Verhältnissen sind nur einige wenige Gesichtspunkte, die in diesem Zusammenhang künstlerisch genutzt werden.

In der Musikgeschichte des 20. Jahrhunderts wird zumeist auf Charles Ives als Pionier der Verräumlichung von Musik hingewiesen, sei es in Bezug auf Kompositionen mit der Anlage von musikalischen Schichten, die unabhängig voneinander gespielt werden, sei es in Bezug auf Aufführungen mit einer Verteilung von (beweglichen) Klangquellen im Raum. Daneben gilt Edgard Varèse als Visionär der räumlichen Klangprojektion und als einer der ersten Komponisten, die hierfür auch die Möglichkeiten der Elektroakustik in Betracht gezogen haben[1].

Ein weiterer Komponist von Musik für den Raum, der musikhistorisch jedoch zumeist randständig behandelt wird, ist Henry Brant (geboren 1913 in

---

1 Vgl. Maria Anna Harley, *Space and Spatialization in Contemporary Music: History and Analysis, Ideas and Implementations*, PhD Dissertation, McGill University, Montreal 1994, http://www.moonrisepress.com/dissertation.html (24.08.2014), S. 123–131, sowie S. 138–144. Vgl. auch Gisela Nauck, *Musik im Raum – Raum in der Musik: Ein Beitrag zur Geschichte der seriellen Musik* (= Beihefte zum Archiv für Musikwissenschaft 38), Stuttgart 1997.

Montreal, Kanada, gestorben 2008 in Santa Barbara, Kalifornien)[2]. Er gilt in den Vereinigten Staaten von Amerika als Pionier der Spatialisierung von Musik: »A visionary of Ivesian imagination, is the leading pioneer of spatial music, music played by ensembles separated by wide distances. If he remains a rather obscure name, it is only because his music, for huge ensembles placed at wide distances, is so difficult to organize and record that few have a chance to experience it.«[3]

Im Gegensatz zu einer langen Tradition der Auffassung von Musik als reiner Zeitkunst stellte Brant seit Anfang der 1950er Jahre das Motto »*all music is space music*« ins Zentrum seiner kompositorischen Arbeit[4]. Purifizierenden Konzepten in der Musik begegnete er mit einer empirischen und experimentellen Haltung, die ihn offenbar bereits in seiner Jugend in Montreal prägte, wo er nicht nur marschierende Bands der Heilsarmee verfolgt, sondern auch ausgediente Alltagsobjekte zu Instrumenten umgebaut hat[5]. Der Vergleich mit Charles Ives wurde bereits angedeutet und stellt sich nicht zufällig ein; vielmehr hat sich Brant dezidiert auf Ives bezogen[6].

In den späten 1920er Jahren, nach Brants Musikstudium am McGill Conservatorium in Montreal, zog die Familie nach New York. Sein Vater, ein berühmter Violinist, der unter anderem bei Joseph Joachim studiert hatte, förderte den Sohn damit nachhaltig. Henry Brant wurde unter anderem ein Schüler von Aaron Copland und Wallingford Riegger, hatte jedoch auch Privatunterricht bei George Antheil. Von 1929 bis 1934 studierte er in New York am Institute of Musical Art und von 1932 bis 1934 an der Juilliard Graduate School, Vorläuferinstitutionen der Juilliard School of Music[7].

Sein Interesse an der Entwicklung von *spatial music* führte Henry Brant auf unterschiedliche Erfahrungen zurück, zunächst einmal auf seine Vorliebe

2   Vgl. das Portrait Henry Brants auf der DVD *Trajectory: A silent film for Henry Brant*, produziert von Frank Diamand, Amsterdam 1994/95. Mit einem herzlichen Dank an Frank Diamand für weitere Informationen und für die Übersendung der DVD.

3   Kyle Gann, *American Music in the Twentieth Century*, New York 1997, S. 96f.

4   Henry Brant, »Interview with Henry Brant«, in: *Soundpieces: Interviews With American Composers*, hrsg. von Cole Gagne und Tracy Caras, Metuchen (NJ) und London 1982, S. 53–68, hier S. 60.

5   Vgl. Molly Sheridan, Frank J. Oteri, »Spaced Out with Henry Brant« (Henry Brant in conversation with Frank J. Oteri, October 2002), in: *New Music Box*, Januar 2003, www.newmusicbox.org/45/interview_brant.pdf, S. 1–21, hier S. 3 (24.08.2014).

6   Vgl. dazu Maria Anna Harley, »An American in Space: Henry Brant's ›Spatial Music‹«, in: American Music 15/1, 1997, S. 70–92.

7   Vgl. Kyle Gann und Kurt Stone, Art. »Brant, Henry (Dreyfuss)«, in: *Grove Music Online*, http://www.oxfordmusiconline.com:80/subscriber/article/grove/music/03850 (25.08.2014).

für polystilistische und komplexe musikalische Strukturen. Bei der Aufführung von mehrschichtiger und komplexer Musik entstanden jedoch Probleme, die für Brant offenbar am Beispiel seiner Symphonie *Origins* (1950) für 20 Schlagzeuger, 70 Perkussionsinstrumente und Orgel überaus deutlich wurden:

»My first experience was writing a very complicated texture and they were on the stage playing it all together. Well, to tell the truth, with more than ten linear parts, I didn't know what was going on. I assumed they were playing the right notes, or approximately the right notes, but something was the matter here... [...] So I thought there's got to be some way to make complicated music intelligible.«[8]

Einen wichtigen Anstoß zur Lösung des Problems hatte Brant offenbar zum einen das Erlebnis einer Pariser Aufführung von Hector Berlioz' *Requiem* in der späten 1940er Jahren gegeben. Zudem hat er nach eigenen Angaben ungefähr zur gleichen Zeit die Musik von Giovanni Gabrieli beziehungsweise die Venezianische Mehrchörigkeit kennen gelernt, die ihn sehr beeindruckte habe[9]. Ferner sei er auf Charles Ives *The Unanswered Question* aufmerksam geworden (erste Aufführung am 11. Mai 1946 in New York[10]) und habe sich mit dessen Musik zu beschäftigen begonnen:

»Then, at Juilliard, I studied and performed *The Unanswered Question*, and other ensemble pieces of Ives. I saw that he was getting at the problem of greater polyphonic complexity in two ways: by physically separating the players, and by having them not maintain rhythmic ensemble. At that time, it seemed to me that these solutions were somewhat casual and slovenly, because my training had been like everyone else's – getting the music locked into the jail cells of bars and uniform tempi. So I attempted to find a way to apply Ives' two ideas in a more organized manner, and modified to the extent that every detail in the music must be easily and accurately playable, a restriction which Ives had never worried about.«[11]

---

8 Molly Sheridan, Frank J. Oteri, a.a.O., S. 12. Vgl. auch: Henry Brant, »Space as an Essential Aspect of Musical Composition«, in: *Contemporary Composers on Contemporary Music*, hrsg. von Elliott Schwartz u. Barney Childs, New York 1967, Reprint 1978, S. 223–242; Henry Brant 1982, a.a.O., S. 53–68.

9 Vgl. Molly Sheridan, Frank J. Oteri, ebd., S. 12, (24.8.2014).

10 Die Aufführung mit Studierenden der Juilliard Graduate School fand im Rahmen eines »all-Ives concert« an der Columbia University in New York City statt. Henry Brant unterrichtete 1945–1952 Komposition und Orchestrierung an der Columbia University.

11 Henry Brant 1982, a.a.O., S. 57.

Im Winter 1952 gab es einen weiteren Anstoß für Brants *spatial music*, als sein Schüler, der berühmte Jazzmusiker und Produzent Teo Macero, die Idee aufbrachte, ein Stück mit dem Titel *Areas* für fünf im Raum verteilte Jazzensembles aufzuführen. »Teo Macero's *Areas*, written and performed in 1952 when he was studying at Juilliard, requires five separated jazz ensembles, and includes improvisation as well as notated material. I consider it as an important landmark in the recent history of spatial music.«[12]

Einige Monate nach der Aufführung des Stücks von Teo Macero hat Henry Brant seine erste Komposition für ein großes Orchester in fünf Gruppen mit dem Titel *Antiphony One* (1953) oder *Rural Antiphonies* beendet, die er 1968 erweiterte[13]. Die fünf Gruppen, die jeweils unterschiedliche Tempi haben und in verschiedenen Tonarten stehen, sind Streicher (Violinen I, Violinen II, Bratschen, Celli, Kontrabässe), Holzbläser (drei Piccoloflöten, drei Oboen, drei Klarinetten), vier oder fünf Hörner, Blechbläserensemble (drei Trompeten, drei Posaunen, mit Dämpfer) und Schlagzeug. Im Vorwort der Partitur heisst es: »Each group situated in a different part of the hall, having its own distinct tempo, meter, and bar-line scheme.«[14]

Die Gruppen werden von fünf Dirigenten geleitet, wobei der Hauptdirigent die Streichergruppe anführt und die in der Partitur vorgegebenen Einsätze für die anderen Gruppen gibt. Die vier anderen Gruppen sollen so aufgestellt werden, dass sie jeweils nur ihren eigenen Dirigenten oder Subdirigenten sehen können:

»Only the string orchestra (or clarinet choir) should occupy the stage, but in the reverse of the usual setup. The principal conductor is downstage, facing the audience. The string (or clarinet) players face him with their backs to the audience. The four other sections should be distributed throughout the hall in effective positions, such as placing one group in a ›box‹, another in an alcove, another in a balcony, etc., depending on the size and shape of the hall. But whatever the positions, *the five groups must be widely separated.*«[15]

Das Zusammenspiel der Gruppen ist nicht zwingend exakt einzuhalten, sondern es kann approximativ sein. Die Verteilung der Orchestergruppen (sowie

---

12 Ebd, S. 57f. Vgl. Teo Maceros Erinnerungen unter dem Titel *Advice for Musicians*, http://www.artistshousemusic.org/node/5369/4937 (24.08.2014).
13 1968 hat Brant alternativ für die Streichergruppe ein Klarinettenensemble vorgeschlagen, zudem optional einen Chor mit hohen und tiefen Stimmen oder mit Frauen- und Männerstimmen eingefügt.
14 Vgl. Partitur: Henry Brant, *Antiphony One, For Symphony Orchestra*, New York, Boston, Chicago, Los Angeles 1977.
15 Vgl. ebd. »Explanatory Remarks«.

des optionalen Chores) im Raum dient erstens zur möglichst großen Unab-
hängigkeit der einzelnen musikalischen Schichten. Zweitens legte Brant großen Wert darauf, dass sich die Klangfarben nicht mischen, sondern dass
durch die Trennung der Gruppen auch eine gewisse Klarheit und Transpa-
renz der Struktur erhalten bleibt.

Die Streichergruppe spielt fast durchgehend überlappende, sich auf- und
abbauende Passagen in jeweils vier Takten, die als eine klangliche ›Grund-
stimmung‹ wie leichte Wellen erscheinen und vergehen. Die übrigen Gruppen erscheinen dazu zunächst einzeln (zunächst die Blechbläser, dann die
Hörner, danach die Holzbläser, dann das Schlagzeug), werden aber allmählich untereinander zusammen gebracht, so dass im Verlauf des Stücks eine
Verdichtung entsteht. Diese Verdichtung mit dem Spiel aller Gruppen führt
zu einem Höhepunkt und einer einmaligen Synchronisierung der Gruppen,
gefolgt von einem Ausklang (Ausblendung der Streicher und Ausdünnung
der Stimmen nach oben) und einem Triller in den höchsten Lagen[16]. In der
Coda übernehmen die Streicher den Triller und setzen ihren ›Klangteppich‹
fort, von dem dann jedoch nur ein Orgelpunkt übrig bleibt, während die anderen Gruppen nochmals kurze Einsätze haben.

Dorothy Carter Drennan interpretierte die Komposition als musikalisches
Landschaftsbild:

»*Antiphony One* (1953) is written for a symphony orchestra without bassoons or tuba. The
instruments are separated in five ensemble groups which play from different areas of the
hall. ... Each ensemble group has its own tonal relationships, timbre, and tempo, and its
own conductor, as well as a separate location in the hall. Most of the groups produce polyphonic music. None of the musical material played by any of the groups is related to the
material of any other group. No rhythmic coordination is required between the groups except at the cut-off before the Coda. Ensemble dispersion provides a directional aspect to
the sound produced by each group, which minimizes the harmonic blend between them
and helps the listener to perceive that each sound-mass is an entity. Differences in texture,
timbre, and melodic material give each sound-mass a distinctive entity. Brant uses four of
these sound-masses, alone or in contrapuntal relationships, to fashion the polyphonic texture of his composition. He uses the fifth sound-mass, the strings, mainly as an accompaniment which unifies the composition.«[17]

---

16 Vgl. ebd., S. 45f.
17 Dorothy Carter Drennan, *Henry Brant's Use of Ensemble Dispersion, as found in the
    Analysis of Selected Compositions*, Diss. University of Miami, Florida, 1975, S. 78,
    80.

Im Anschluss an *Antiphony One* hat Henry Brant zahlreiche Werke komponiert, in denen die Verteilung der Musiker und Musikerinnen im Raum eingeplant wurde. Dabei hat er immer wieder mit neuen Anordnungen experimentiert. Er hat die Gruppen nicht nur horizontal im Raum verteilt, sondern auch vertikal: hohe Register oder helle Klangfarben platzierte er auf höher gelegenen Balkonen oder Podesten, mittlere und tiefe Register oder dunkle Klangfarben unter Balkonen, im Parkett oder unter dem Parkett wie beispielsweise im Orchesterstück mit Stimme *Voyage Four* von 1963, wo er Tuba, Pauken und Glocken an drei Plätzen in offenen Schächten mit Gittern aus dem Untergrund erklingen lässt. Den Effekt beschreibt Brant wie folgt: »Far from sounding subterranean or submerged, the instruments, astoundingly, appear to be emitting their sounds from points in midair above the audience's heads.«[18]

Die Wirkung einer vertikalen Verteilung der Instrumente im Hinblick auf Tonhöhen oder Register hat Brant ebenfalls wiederholt erprobt, und er kam zu der Überzeugung:

»There is no mistaking the compelling naturalness of effect when high pitches originate in a high location (e.g. a piccolo in a top balcony), or low pitches from a low position – the latter effect being *enhanced*, not detracted from, if the sounds originate from under a projecting level (e.g. tympani placed in back of the ground floor audience section, which in many halls is under a balcony). However, the actual *pitch* need not to be high or low, as the case may be; if the *register* in which the instrument plays is *proportionately* acute or deep, this will substitute very well for absolute height or depth in pitch, and the instrument (or voice) may be situated in, respectively, high or low positions accordingly.«[19]

Mit der Idee einer vertikalen Verteilung von Musikern war für ihn auch die Vorstellung einer »Klangwand« oder die Umsetzung von »›sound travel‹ along the wall«[20] verbunden. Diesen Effekt hat Brant mehrfach getestet und seine Wirkung so beschrieben:

»If the players can be distributed vertically from floor to ceiling, playing simultaneously in an even spread over a substantial part of the area of an entire wall, the result, especially if the instruments are arranged vertically in order or pitch (lowest notes at lowest level, etc.), will be quite as hoped for – the entire wall space will seem to be sounding at once, an extremely vivid and concentrated directional effect.«[21]

---

18 Henry Brant 1978, a.a.O., S. 231.
19 Ebd., S. 232.
20 Maria Anna Harley 1994, a.a.O., S. 258.
21 Henry Brant 1978, a.a.O., S. 231.

Es erscheint daher nur konsequent, dass Brant auch mit Bewegungen von Musikern oder Musikerinnen im Raum experimentiert hat, um das Spiel mit der Bildung von »Klangwänden«, »Klangbahnen« oder »Klangwellen« im Raum zu intensivieren. Er berichtet von Versuchen mit gehenden oder laufenden Musikern, die er 1964 durchgeführt habe[22].

In einem Stück für Bläserquintett mit dem Titel *Windjammer* (1969) scheint er Bewegungen von Musikern eingeplant zu haben; die Komposition ist »a study in continuous sound-travel for live performance by a woodwind quintet«[23].

Einige Jahre zuvor bildete *Hieroglyphics* (1957) für Viola, Instrumentalensemble und Stimme eine Vorstufe, wobei jedoch nur die Bratsche ihre Positionen wechselt. Gleichzeitig hat Brant mit der Wirkung beziehungsweise mit der Wahrnehmung von Musik in abgedunkelten Räumen experimentiert. In *Hieroglyphics* ist die Anordnung bei der Aufführung: »The viola plays in three widely separated positions in a darkened hall. The other instruments each play from other widely separated positions where, in the darkness of the hall, they will be invisible to the audience.«[24] Die räumliche Wirkung der Musik scheint sich in der Dunkelheit verstärkt zu haben:

»The appearance of the soloist in different locations, moving between those locations in darkness, reinforces the concept of each musical section being a separate picture, or hieroglyphic. The framework of each picture is the particular combination of instruments chosen for the accompaniment. This framework is spatially oriented by the location of the instruments in different areas of the hall. The requirement that these obbligato instruments be invisible increases the effectiveness of the directional connections between the instruments, the sound-axes.«[25]

In der Komposition *Divinity* (1973) werden ebenfalls Bewegungen der Musiker vorgeschlagen, obwohl hier die Klangbalance im Vordergrund steht. *Divinity* besteht aus acht unterschiedlichen Dialogen zwischen einem Cembalo auf dem Konzertpodium und fünf im Raum verteilten Bläsern (zwei Trompeten weit entfernt auf Balkonen, zwei Posaunen seitlich an den Saalwänden, ein Horn im Foyer mit offenen Türen oder weit entfernt unter einem Balkon):

---

22 Vgl. ebd., S. 239–241.
23 Dorothy Carter Drennan, a.a.O., S. 59.
24 Ebd., S. 123.
25 Ebd., S. 137. »Sound-axis« wird definiert als »The aural axis formed when two instruments, each located in opposite areas of the hall, play simultaneously« (ebd., S. 15).

»*Divinity* [...], Dialogues in the Form of Secret Portraits, is for harpsichord and brass quintet. The instruments are as widely separated from each other as the hall permits. It is a multirhythmic antiphonal composition. Phrases, units, sections, and parts are combined by juxtaposition to create a dialogue texture. [...] The distribution of the instruments of the brass quintet around the hall results in a better balance between the harpsichord and the quintet. Brant always maintains balanced volumes between each of his widely separated performing elements. The placement of instruments in separate locations overcomes some of the difficulties in achieving balance between a quintet of five resonant brass instruments and the one harpsichord with limited volume of sound.«[26]

Darüber hinaus können sich die Trompeten und Posaunen optional auf ihren Plätzen bewegen. Damit sollen die vorgeschriebenen Kommunikationsrichtungen (»Klangachsen«) in den Dialogen eine größere Flexibität erhalten.

Die Versuche mit beweglichen Klangquellen ergaben für Brant auch folgende Ergebnisse:

»In his experiments which require performers to move within areas of varying sizes, Brant has found that a sound-source moving at the speed of a person walking at an average pace is not fast enough to suggest movement with any impact on the audience except in comparatively restricted space. In a small room, twenty to thirty feet square, the movement of sound from walking performers is easily perceptible. Impressions of diverging and converging separations, of increasing and decreasing distance, of decreasing and increasing volume, or of suddenly intensified resonance as a player goes from an open room into a corridor are easily perceived by the audience. Likewise, the movement of performers vertically, using stairways or ladders, is readily apparent to the listener.«[27]

Seit den späten 1970er Jahren hat Brant vor allem die Größendimension seiner kompositorischen Projekte und den Aufwand bei Aufführungen erweitert, zum Beispiel die Besetzung einer Stimme beziehungsweise einer Klangfarbe immens ausgedehnt oder die stilistischen Schichten eines Stücks erhöht. In *Orbits* (1979), »A Spatial Symphonic Ritual«, spielen 80 Posaunen und eine Orgel, zu denen eine hohe Sopranstimme (»Sopranino Voice«) hinzukommt. Der Posaunenchor wird in einem großen Kreis entlang den Wänden um das Publikum herum aufgestellt. Aus einem Bericht über die Uraufführung von *Orbits* am 11. Februar 1979 in der St. Mary's Cathedral in San Francisco lässt sich die Atmosphäre erahnen:

---

26 Ebd., S. 307f., vgl. insgesamt S. 288–309.
27 Ebd., S. 57f.

»Separated by staccato commentaries from the cathedral's pipe organ, densely dissonant sonorities clashed and blended over the listener's head. Full-throated blares, splintery muted phrases, the crooning tones of the soprano trombone, the rumble of its contrabass relative – all seemed to accelerate in a circular motion, spinning into the cathedral's 190-foot cupola like an earthly echo of the music of the spheres.«[28]

Die Komposition *Flight Over a Global Map* (1990), um ein ähnliches Stück zu erwähnen, ist für 100 Trompeten, drei Perkussionsgruppen und Klavier geschrieben[29].

In dem Stück *Meteor Farm* von 1982 wurde die stilistische Pluralität ausgedehnt. Hier sind neben einem Orchester, zwei Sopranstimmen, zwei Chören, Blechbläserensemble, zwei Schlagzeuggruppen und Jazz Band auch ein Javanisches Gamelanorchester, eine Westafrikanische Trommelgruppe sowie ein Indisches Musiktrio mit Sänger, Sitar und Tabla beteiligt, alle weiträumig getrennt voneinander aufgestellt. »It is central to the conception of the piece that these non-Western ensembles perform in their own styles and traditions, and no attempt should be made to dilute or Westernize their music.«[30]

Mit der Aufstellung oder Bewegung von Musikgruppen im Außenraum beziehungsweise im öffentlichen Raum hat Brant seine *spatial music* ebenfalls erweitert. Dabei war er zunächst gegenüber Aufführungen im Außenraum relativ skeptisch, weil er in diesem Zusammenhang feststellen musste, dass die Kalkulation von räumlichen Effekten problematisch wurde. »Brant's frequent outdoor performances can also be difficult; a 1972 New York performance of *The Immortal Combat* [2 bands] was obliterated by traffic noise, a thunderstorm and the fountain at Lincoln Center.«[31]

Die räumliche Aufstellung und Verteilung von Musikern im Außenraum beschrieb Brant daher als ein schwieriges Unterfangen:

»Live outdoor performance requires favorably placed rebounding surfaces and is sometimes diffused to the point of inaudibility by wind interference. The location of the rebounding surfaces is particularly difficult to control if the performers move. All these con-

---

28 Bericht über die Uraufführung, zit. nach CD Booklet, Henry Brant, *Orbits*, *Western Springs*, *Hieroglyphics 3*, Composers Recordings, Inc./CRI, 1999, CRI American Masters, CD 827, S. 7f.

29 Vgl. Maria Anna Harley 1997, a.a.O., S. 81.

30 Brant in seinem Aufführungskommentar zu *Meteor Farm*, zit. nach Maria Anna Harley 1994, a.a.O., S. 264.

31 Kyle Gann und Kurt Stone, a.a.O.

ditions make the calculation of effect for outdoor live music an almost hopeless task, since the probable variability in each situation is so great.«[32]

Aufgrund dieser Schwierigkeiten sprach er sich in diesem Kontext für die Verwendung von vorproduzierter Musik aus Lautsprechern aus, weil man Lautsprecher gezielt postieren und ausrichten könne[33]. Von den Möglichkeiten, bei Aufführungen elektroakustische Mittel einzusetzen, hat Brant jedoch generell abgesehen, und er hat auch in seinen Werken für den Außenraum keinen Gebrauch von Verstärkung oder Lautsprechern gemacht. Lediglich für die klangliche Integration von Mikrotönen oder Mikrointervallen hat er offenbar Aufnahmen oder elektroakustische Mittel akzeptiert[34].

Einen Höhepunkt seiner Aufführungsprojekte im Außenraum bildete *Bran(d)t aan de Amstel* (1984). Dabei wurden die Amsterdamer Grachten mit vier Booten durchfahren, in denen jeweils 25 Flötisten und Flötistinnen in zwei Gruppen (sie spielen in unterschiedlichen Tonarten) sowie unterschiedliches Schlagzeug untergebracht waren. An der Strecke der fahrenden Boote kamen an vielen Stellen weitere musikalische Schichten hinzu: Carillons von den Kirchen, Musikbands oder Chöre, eine Jugendjazzband, und zuletzt wurden vier holländische Straßenorgeln einbezogen.

»Despite the ample duration of the whole performance (4 hours) the composed ›boat music‹ lasts only for 3 minutes, requiring extensive repetitions of this material during the performance. *Bran(d)t aan de Amstel* has no score, only plans of the temporal outline of the whole spectacle. Brant's excursus through the space of Amsterdam leads away from the idea of a musical work in closed form, defined by the notation in the score. The orientation is towards a vision of music as an artistic, spatial and social event, the temporal contours of which have been designed by the composer and filled in with pre-existing musical material. The focus on space, Brant's main preoccupation, allows for a large dose of indeterminacy of details regarding the elements dispersed within this space.«[35]

Henry Brant hat in den 1990er Jahren und bis zu seinem Tod 2008 seine Ideen weiter verfolgt und noch neue Pläne entwickelt; zum Beispiel interessierten ihn bei seiner Musik zu dem Stummfilm *Trajectory* von Frank Diamand von 1994 auch die Beziehungen von bewegten Bildern und Musik – jenseits traditioneller Filmmusik, die ebenfalls zu seinem Oeuvre zählt. Darüber hinaus arbeitete er seit den 1980er Jahren an einem Plan für ein flexibel

---

32 Henry Brant 1978, a.a.O., S. 237.
33 Vgl. ebd., S. 238.
34 Vgl. Molly Sheridan, Frank J. Oteri, a.a.O.
35 Maria Anna Harley 1994, a.a.O., S. 267.

zu nutzendes Konzerthaus. In den Vereinigten Staaten von Amerika und in Holland fand Henry Brant große Anerkennung, darüber hinaus gilt er aber als Randfigur der neuen Musik. Kompositionsgeschichtlich hat er mit seiner *spatial music* allerdings einen festen Platz: in der Nähe der ersten Experimente mit der räumlichen Projektion von *musique concrète* und einige Jahre vor den Raummusik-Kompositionen von Stockhausen und Boulez[36].

---

36 Vgl. den Kommentar zu Brant und Stockhausen bei Maria Anna Harley 1997, a.a.O., S. 74.

ENGLISH SUMMARY

Henry Brant's »*spatial music*«
Compositions for Performance Spaces

In the early 1950s, the American composer Henry Brant (1913–2008), following in the footsteps of Charles Ives, began to distribute orchestras, ensembles, and soloists throughout the concert hall. From this time on he believed that »all music is space music«, as opposed to the traditional concept
of music as a purely time-related art.

I began my discussion on this topic by asking why space in traditional
music was not understood as a musical aspect, despite the fact that space –
and particularly performance space – played an important role in music.
Then I presented the work of Henry Brant and explain how the ›inner-
musical‹ space of his complex, polystilistic compositions is projected into
the performance space. Brant used the specific room acoustic of a performance space and the seating of the musicians therein to make voices, instrumental groups, registers, timbres, rhythms and tempi, and other compositional parameters more transparent to the listener. He also included the
movements of musicians and ensembles in the performance space or even a
public space.

Brant's first »space music« composition, *Antiphony One* for large orchestra (1953), is split into five groups (strings, woodwinds, horns, brass, and
percussion). Each group is »situated in a different part of the hall, having its
own distinct tempo, meter, and bar-line scheme«, as he wrote in the introduction to the score. In 1968, Brant revised and extended the piece, suggesting a clarinet ensemble instead of the string ensemble and inserting an additional choir of high and low voices. This piece will be analysed later, to
show Brant's compositional starting point and his principles of spatialization.

Brant never used electroacoustic media to compose space music, nor did
he work with electroacoustic media at all. The performance space, room
acoustics, and the spatial seating of the musicians were his elementary factors. In all the compositions following *Antiphony One*, he experimented with
new combinations of ensembles, styles, and sound impressions. In *Orbits*
(1979), for instance, 80 trombones are distributed in space, with two layers
for organ and high soprano added. *Meteor Farm* (1982) unites two soprano
voices, orchestra, two choirs, brass ensemble, two percussion groups, jazz
band, a Javanese gamelan orchestra, a West African drum ensemble, and an
Indian music trio. In *Brand(t) aan de Amstel* (1984), musicians on boats
were transported through Amsterdam. »Four boatloads of performers (25

flutists and one percussionist per boat) followed one another along a pre-designated route, traversing many canals and passing by a number of land-mark churches and bridges along the way. At each of these intermediate checkpoints, other prearranged musical levels (land based) would be added to the overall texture« (Elliott Schwartz 1984).

It is highly likely that Brant's ideas about »spatial music« influenced both John Cage and Karlheinz Stockhausen, but his mostly experimental music and his occasionally hugely dimensioned projects – based on his constantly varied spatial sound production, sound projection, and perception research – remained relatively unnoticed in Europe. A commentary on the reception of his work will close the chapter.

Spatiale Basistechnologien /

Fundamental Spatial Technologies

Von dislozierten Klängen und auditiven Räumen

Lautsprecher in der Frühzeit der Elektrophone

Sonja Neumann

1932 fand auf der Berliner Funkausstellung die Sonderschau *Elektrische Musik* statt, bei der viele neu entwickelte »elektrische« Musikinstrumente vorgeführt wurden[1]. Auf einer großen Bühne standen *Trautonium, Theremin, Hellertion, Neo-Bechstein-Flügel, Elektrochord*, Elektro-Geige und Elektro-Cello als »Orchester der Zukunft« zwar einträchtig beisammen, die Instrumente präsentierten aber jeweils unterschiedliche Technologien der Tonerzeugung, Klangfarben und Spielweisen. Eine Gemeinsamkeit teilten sie jedoch, denn zur Klangabstrahlung nutzten alle einen Lautsprecher[2].

Die Moderation dieser Veranstaltung, die auch über Rundfunk übertragen wurde, übernahm Gustav Leithäuser, Professor für Hochfrequenztechnik am Heinrich-Hertz-Institut für Schwingungsforschung. Er erläuterte nicht nur die technischen Funktionsweisen der verschiedenen Instrumente, sondern

---

1 Die Begriffe »Elektrophon« und »elektrisches« Musikinstrument werden in diesem Aufsatz synonym verwendet. Dabei entspricht die Bezeichnung »elektrische Musikinstrumente« der Begrifflichkeit der 1930er Jahre. Beide Begriffe beziehen sich auf eine Musikinstrumentengruppe, die zum einen zur Erzeugung von Tönen elektrischen Strom benötigt und zum anderen Verstärker- und Lautsprecherelemente aufweist, die den Ton hörbar machen. Zur Terminologie vgl. auch Peter Donhauser, *Elektrische Klangmaschinen*, Wien u.a. 2007, S. 12–13.

2 Die Nutzung eines Lautsprechers ist daher auch ein wichtiger Bestandteil der Definition eines Elektrophons, z.B. bei Oskar Vierling: »Unter elektrischem Musikinstrument verstehen wir nicht ein mechanisches Instrument, das nur elektrisch angetrieben wird, sondern ein Instrument, bei dem das ganze Tonspektrum aus elektrischen Tonschwingungen besteht, die über den Lautsprecher hörbar gemacht werden.« (Oskar Vierling, *Das elektroakustische Klavier*, Berlin 1936, S. 1.)

ließ sie einzeln und in kleinen ›Kammermusikensembles‹ auftreten. Immer wieder kam er dabei auf die ungeahnten Beschallungsmöglichkeiten der Elektrophone zu sprechen. Bei der Präsentation des *Trautoniums* erklärte er dem Publikum die Vielzahl technischer Geräte und Aufbauten auf der Bühne:

»Man hat hier natürlich in diesem Saal jetzt eine recht große Aufmachung gewählt. Sie sehen, wir haben hier hinter dem Instrument Großlautsprecher geschaltet, die in jener Schallwand sich befinden. Wenn wir hier das Instrument zu seiner vollen Wucht entfachen und loslassen, dann können wir hier Töne erzeugen, die diesen Raum zum Erschüttern bringen. Ich glaube, die Ersten, die hier in den Reihen vor mir sitzen, würden hier Ohrenschmerzen bekommen, wenn wir hier mit dem vollen Pulver fahren würden. Wir wollen das also lieber nicht machen oder nur nachher gelegentlich zur Kennzeichnung der überhaupt möglichen Stärke. Man kann also mit einem solchen Instrument in einer solchen Aufmachung die Hallen hier ganz leicht füllen, so werden Sie mir zugeben, dass beispielsweise auf freiem Gelände wie dem Tempelhofer Feld, wenn man da Musik im Großen machen will, ein solches Instrument durchaus das geeignete ist.«[3]

Da sich Anfang der 1930er Jahre Beschallungssysteme im öffentlichen Raum erst allmählich ausbildeten, galten die elektrischen Instrumente mit der direkten Schallwiedergabe durch Lautsprecher als eine Novität, zumal sich gerade dadurch ihr räumliches Klangpotential grundsätzlich von demjenigen der traditionellen Musikinstrumente unterschied. Da Tonerzeugung und Schallabgabe nun räumlich nicht mehr voneinander abhängig waren, der Klang damit auch disloziert realisiert werden konnte, avancierte der Lautsprecher zum konstitutiven Element des auditiven Raums.

Auch seine visuelle Präsenz war durchaus beeindruckend. Die *Klangwand* des »Orchesters der Zukunft« bestand aus einem Arsenal verschiedenster Lautsprecherkonstruktionen mit großen und kleinen Schallwänden, mit großen und kleinen Gehäusen. Dabei ist nicht eindeutig ersichtlich, welches Instrument zu welchem Lautsprecher gehörte. Ebenso scheint es kein festgelegtes Beschallungskonzept zu den jeweiligen elektrischen Instrumenten gegeben zu haben. So dokumentiert beispielsweise die Fotografie des Radiokonzertes der Berliner Funk-Stunde vom 19. Oktober 1932 eine ganz ähnliche Aufführungssituation mit nahezu den gleichen Instrumenten, aber

---

3   Mein besonderer Dank gilt Prof. Thomas Neuhaus (Institut für Computermusik und elektronische Medien, Folkwang Universität der Künste), der mir die von Elisabeth Szwarz restaurierte Audioübertragung der Berliner Funkausstellung 1932 zur Verfügung stellte.

vollkommen unterschiedlichen Lautsprechern. Die rückseitige Perspektive zeigt in diesem Fall beispielsweise auch elektrodynamische Lautsprecher ohne Schallwand, wobei berücksichtigt werden muss, dass solche Schallwandler andere Klangeigenschaften (vor allem im Tiefton-Bereich) ausbilden als Lautsprecher, die in einer Schallwand eingebaut sind.

Abbildung 1: Orchester der Zukunft 1932 / Radio-Konzert der Berliner Funkstunde 1932

Aus: »Das Orchester der Zukunft??«, in: Funkschau Nr. 32, 25.12.1932, S. 409

Während heute bei Konzerten mit elektronischen Musikinstrumenten und elektronischer Musik die akustische Beschallungssituation durch Lautsprechersysteme extrem ausdifferenziert ist, wurde die räumliche Beschallung in der Frühzeit elektronischer Klangerzeugung offensichtlich vielfach improvisiert. Dass der hörbare Raum Anfang der 1930er Jahre beschallungstechnisch noch nicht erschlossen war, lag möglicherweise aber nicht nur an der Neuheit der elektrischen Musikinstrumente, sondern auch an der Vielfalt der in Entwicklung begriffenen Lautsprecherarten und -konstruktionen. In welchem Maße die Wechselbeziehung von Elektrophon und Lautsprecher einer Dynamik unterlag, zeigt auch die allgemeine Entwicklungsgeschichte dieser Musikinstrumente. Vor allem ab Ende der 1920er Jahre wurden zahlreiche neue Elektrophone, die auf jeweils unterschiedliche Weise Elektrizität zur Klangerzeugung nutzten, patentiert bzw. der Öffentlichkeit vorgestellt. Doch erst durch die entsprechende technische Entwicklung der Beschallungstechnik konnten Elektrophone publikumswirksam präsentiert werden.

Im technisch-praktischen Sinne sowie auch im ästhetischen waren die Instrumente jedoch auf vollkommen unterschiedliche Weise mit Schallwandler-Systemen verbunden. Überraschenderweise wurde das Konzept der dislozierten Klänge vor allem bei einem der ersten modernen Elektrophone, dem berühmten elektromechanischen *Telharmonium* von Thaddeus Cahill umgesetzt, denn hier fand – mangels Verstärker und Lautsprecher – die Musikübertragung über das Telefon statt[4]. Einige Erfinder wie beispielsweise Jörg Mager experimentierten ausgiebig mit der Schallwandlertechnik, während beispielsweise Maurice Martenot die Lautsprecher auch als ästhetisch integralen Bestandteil des Instruments (*Ondes Martenot*) behandelte. Andere Konstrukteure überließen wiederum die Schallwiedergabe dem Zufall bzw. den Verhältnissen vor Ort[5].

Inwieweit Lautsprecher tatsächlich den ›Originalklang‹ bzw. Klangcharakter des jeweiligen Elektrophons prägten, welchen auditiven Raum sie herstellen konnten, lässt sich deshalb nicht pauschal festlegen. Vielmehr ist es notwendig, jedes Elektrophon und seinen Bezug zur Schallwandlertechnik gesondert zu betrachten. In dieser Hinsicht können anhand zweier Fallbeispiele zumindest die wichtigsten Entwicklungsschritte dieses wechselseitigen Verhältnisses skizziert werden. Mit dem *Theremin* und *Trautonium* rücken dabei zwei der berühmtesten elektrischen Instrumente in den Fokus. Beide Instrumente ›konzertierten‹ auf der Berliner Funkausstellung 1931 und 1932, konnten aber schon zu dieser Zeit auf eine abwechslungsreiche Entwicklungsgeschichte zurückblicken.

THEREMIN

Vor allem das *Theremin* spiegelt als eines der frühesten Elektrophone die verschiedenen Etappen der Lautsprecherentwicklung während der 1920er Jahre wider. Ein Prototyp des Instruments wurde bereits um 1917 von Lev Sergeevič Termen[6] konzipiert und gebaut. Es funktionierte nach dem Prinzip eines Schwebungssummers, indem ein hörbarer Ton durch die Überlagerung

---

4 André Ruschkowski, *Elektronische Klänge und musikalische Entdeckungen*, Stuttgart 2010, S. 20.

5 Jörg Mager experimentierte teils ausgiebig mit Lautsprecher-Membranen (vgl. Material im Bundesarchiv Berlin R 55/1142). Während Maurice Martenot seine *Ondes Martenot* nach und nach mit einer ganzen Batterie unterschiedlichster Lautsprecher ausstattete.

6 Ebenso ist die Verwendung der französisierten Version des Namens, Léon Théremin, allgemein üblich.

von zwei hochfrequenten, nicht mehr hörbaren Tönen erzeugt wird. Die Tonhöhe konnte durch eine Spielantenne gesteuert werden, die zusammen mit der Hand des Spielers einen Kondensator bildet. Dessen Kapazität wird umso größer und der Ton damit höher, je mehr sich die Hand der Spielantenne nähert[7]. Neben der Generierung der Klänge bestand bei der Konstruktion des *Theremins* die technische Herausforderung aber zunächst darin, das *Theremin* überhaupt hörbar vorzuführen. Die Problematik bestand darin, dass zur Tonwiedergabe im Europa der frühen 1920er Jahren vorrangig nur mechano-akustische Grammophontrichter und elektromagnetische Kopfhörer als Schallwandler zur Verfügung standen. Termen musste deshalb für die Tonwiedergabe seiner frühen Instrumente die damals verfügbaren einfachen elektromagnetischen Telefon- bzw. Kopfhörer nutzen. Um aber deren dürftige und im Raum kaum hörbare Tonwiedergabe zu verbessern, konstruierte er die schallabgebende (wahrscheinlich aus dünnem Metall bestehende) Membran großflächiger und fügte als akustischen Verstärker einen Papiertrichter hinzu. Dadurch erhöhte sich die Lautstärke des Instruments immerhin soweit, dass Termen eine Lautstärkeregelung mittels eines Fußpedals entwickeln und das Instrument 1921 während des *Allsowjetischen elektrotechnischen Kongresses* in Moskau erstmals einem größeren Publikumskreis vorstellen konnte[8].

Solche Behelfslautsprecher wiesen allerdings nur eine dürftige Klangwiedergabe auf, die zudem durch einen sehr hohen Klirrfaktor geprägt war[9]. Größtes Problem war dabei die generell schwache Wiedergabe der tiefen Töne, welches auch den hörbaren Ambitus des *Theremins* erheblich einschränkte. Somit blieb das *Theremin* angesichts der geringen Übertragungsbandbreite der Lautsprecher einerseits hinter seinen klanglich ›hörbaren‹ Möglichkeiten weit zurück, andererseits bestimmte der verwendete Lautsprecher durch seine spezifische Klangabstrahlungscharakteristik in einem hohen Maße den ›Originalklang‹ des *Theremins*.

Lange gab es keinen großen Qualitätssprung in Sachen Lautsprecher zu verzeichnen. Noch immer wurde die schallabgebende Membran direkt angetrieben. Bei neueren elektromagnetischen Lautsprechern, die in Europa Mitte der 1920er Jahre erhältlich waren, wurde aber zumindest die Schallabgabe

---

7 André Ruschkowski, S. 27.
8 Gleb Anfilov, *Physics and Music*, Moskau 1966, S. 144–145.
9 In den USA dagegen gab es zu dieser Zeit bereits ähnlich konstruierte Lautsprecher im Handel, wie z.B. den Lautsprecher *Chauphon* (1918) von Western Electric, der als Funktionseinheit zusammen mit einem Mikrophon als eine Art Chauffeur-Telefon für Gespräche in Limousinen entwickelt worden war.

der Membran weiterentwickelt, was zumindest zu einem höheren Wirkungsgrad führte. Doch wie kritische Zeitgenossen glaubhaft vermitteln, konnten
auch diese Konstruktionen keinen Hörgenuss bieten, denn ein »Lautsprecher
ist zunächst nichts anderes als ein großer Fernhörer mit großem Schalltrichter; er entstellt die Musik in einer ganz abscheulichen Weise – für musikalisch Empfindliche ist er ein Schreckensinstrument, das an Scheußlichkeit
ein minderwertiges Grammophon weit übertrifft.«[10]

Abbildung 2: Leon Termens Assistent George Julius Goldberg an einem frühen
»Theremin«-Modell mit Lautstärke-Pedal, Artikulationssteuerungknopf und
Schwanenhalslautsprecher. Deutschland, 29. Oktober 1927

© Bettmann/CORBIS

Die Lautsprecherqualität verbesserte sich erst ab 1926 hörbar, als effektivere
elektromagnetische Konuslautsprecher vor allem als Zungenlautsprecher-
konstruktionen auf den Markt kamen. Die Membran als eigentlicher Schall-
geber wurde nun nicht mehr direkt angetrieben, sondern durch ein bewegli-
ches Verbindungteil (Zunge) in Schwingung gesetzt, das wirkungsvoller in
den starken magnetischen Flussbereich gebracht werden konnte. Diese Lautsprecher mit konusförmiger, meist aus Pappe bestehender Membran konnten

---

10 Otto Nothdurft, *Rundfunk fürs Haus: Eine Einführung* (= Illustrierte Taschenbücher
  für die Jugend 52/53), Stuttgart 1924, S. 142.

grundsätzlich eine höhere Lautstärke erreichen, wiesen einen verbesserten Wirkungsgrad bei geringeren Verzerrungen auf und hatten eine bessere Übertragungsbandbreite, gerade auch der tiefen Töne.

Mit dieser Entwicklungsstufe waren in Bezug auf das *Theremin* im Grunde erst die Voraussetzungen für die große Europa-Tournee Termens im Jahr 1927 gegeben. Schließlich benötigte Termen in den weitläufigen Konzertsälen der europäischen Hauptstädte entsprechend leistungsstarke Schallwandler. Er konzertierte zusammen mit George Julius Goldberg nicht nur auf verschiedenen Konstruktionen seines *Theremins* (mit einer Antenne und Lautstärkepedal oder mit zwei Antennen), sondern nutzte auch unterschiedliche Lautsprecher, darunter mindestens einen herkömmlichen Schwanenhalslautsprecher und bis zu drei Dreieck-Lautsprecher. Letztere waren höchstwahrscheinlich ebenfalls noch elektromagnetische Konuslautsprecher bzw. Zungenlautsprecher, denn in Europa konnte sich der in den USA entwickelte elektrodynamische Lautsprecher wegen Patentrangeleien erst später durchsetzen.

Die Lautsprecher fungierten während der Konzerte auch als Erweiterungen der klanglichen Möglichkeiten des *Theremins*, da das Instrument selbst nur fast reine Sinustöne von sich gab und klanglich dem Publikum keine allzu große Abwechslung bot. Termen bezog offenbar die jeweiligen charakteristischen Verzerrungen der Lautsprecher bewusst als klangliche Varianten des Musikinstruments mit ein[11]. Erst später ermöglichte Termen verschiedene Klangvarianten des Instruments durch die Zuschaltung von Seitenbandfrequenzen, indem er mehrere Oszillatorpaare parallel schaltete[12].

RCA-*THEREMIN*

Als Termen unmittelbar nach seiner Europa-Tournee für einen längeren Aufenthalt in die USA weiterreiste, professionalisierte er dort auch die Vermarktung seines *Theremins*. 1928 baute er für die RCA (Radio Corporation of America) ein *Theremin*, das für einen Massenmarkt konzipiert war. Zusammen mit diesem *RCA-Theremin* wurde der *Radiola*-Lautsprecher 106 ausgeliefert, ein besonders hochwertiger externer Radio-Lautsprecher der RCA. Dieser frei stehende, mit Stoff überzogene Lautsprecher war mit einer

---

11 Albert Vincent Glinsky, *The Theremin in the Emergence of Electronic Music*, Ann Arbor 1992, S. 56/57.

12 Vgl. Leon Theremin, *Method of and Apparatus for the Generation of Sounds*, U.S. Patent 1.661.058 vom 28. Februar 1928.

elektrodynamischen Feldspule ausgestattet und wies eine offene Rückseite auf. Sein Klangbild war im Gegensatz zu den bisher von Termen verwende-ten Lautsprechern sehr ausgeglichen, charakteristisch war jedoch ein leises Hintergrundsummen bei Betrieb. Auch in Deutschland gab es Bestrebungen, das *Theremin* als Hausmusikinstrument zu vermarkten. In der Tradition des Radio-Selbstbaus wurde von Joachim Winckelmann ein Ratgeber publiziert, der eine detaillierte Bauanleitung samt Schaltplan für ein *Theremin* mit Laut-stärkepedal enthielt[13]. Ein *Ätherophon* entwickelte auch die Dresdener Firma Koch & Sterzel[14]. Ob dieses Instrument als eine Art Prototyp gebaut worden war und darüber hinaus weitere Produktplanungen existierten, ist noch un-klar. Jedenfalls waren zur Tonwiedergabe dieser *Theremine* lediglich han-delsübliche externe Lautsprecher oder Kopfhörer vorgesehen.

Doch weder in den USA noch in Deutschland konnte sich das *Theremin* als Hausmusikinstrument etablieren. Die Gründe dafür waren vielfältig. Nicht nur der hohe Preis schreckte die Kundschaft, vielmehr war die Spiel-weise des *Theremin* zu anspruchsvoll, um schnelle musikalische Erfolgser-lebnisse liefern zu können. Denn erforderlich waren ein hervorragendes mu-sikalisches Gehör, Intonationssicherheit und eine besondere Feinmotorik der Finger.

Während die Vermarktung des *Theremins* als Hausmusikinstrument weitgehend fehlschlug, gestalteten sich die Konzerte Termens in den USA wesentlich erfolgreicher[15]. Ein wichtiges Element dieser öffentlichkeitswirk-samen Auftritte war der von Termen entwickelte berühmte *Diamant*-Laut-sprecher. Dieser elektrodynamische Lautsprecher mit großer, zumeist offe-ner Schallwand war in der Lage, den großen Tonraum des *Theremins* ein-schließlich des Bassbereichs in hoher Qualität und Lautstärke zu übermitteln. Die Klangcharakteristiken des Lautsprechers wurden dabei häufig als beson-ders klar und direkt wahrgenommen, wobei sich die Größe der Schallwand

---

13 Joachim Winckelmann, *Das Theremin-Musikgerät: Selbstbau und Spielanleitung* (= Deutsche Radio-Bücherei 6), Berlin 1932. Winckelmann publizierte darüber hinaus auch eine Bauanleitung für ein *Trautonium* (1930) und für eine *Jowiphon* (1935).

14 Ein *Ätherophon* von Koch und Sterzel befindet sich im Besitz des Deutschen Muse-ums München. Es wurde offenbar eigens für das Museum angefertigt. Für diesen Hinweis danke ich Silke Berdux (Kuratorin der Musikabteilung am Deutschen Muse-um München).

15 Termen trat mit einem Ensemble aus zehn *Theremin*-Spielern auf. Darunter befand sich Lucie Bigelow-Rosen, die als *Theremin*-Solistin große Erfolge feierte. Auch Cla-ra Rockmore, die ab 1934 als *Theremin*-Solistin konzertierte, trug viel zur Berühmt-heit des *Theremins* bei.

grundsätzlich nach der Tiefe der Töne richtet, die präsent übertragen werden sollen[16].

LAUTSPRECHER IN DEUTSCHLAND UM 1930

Im Gegensatz zu den USA konnte sich der von Chester W. Rice und Edward W. Kellogg 1923/24 entwickelte elektrodynamische Lautsprecher erst Anfang der 1930er Jahre in Deutschland etablieren. Schuld an der verzögerten Einführung waren offenbar Patentstreitigkeiten. Umstritten war vor allem die sogenannte Innovationshöhe des Patents, da im elektrodynamischen Lautsprecher viele Prinzipien verwirklicht wurden, die schon seit geraumer Zeit patentiert waren. Dies betraf beispielsweise das Patent von Walter von Siemens, das bereits 1877 den elektrodynamischen Schwingspulenantrieb beschrieb, aber auch Walter von Burstyns Schallwandprinzip zur Verhinderung des »akustischen Kurzschlusses« von 1915[17]. Erst durch ein Abkommen mit General Electric konnte der elektrodynamische Rice-Kellogg-Lautsprecher durch die AEG in Deutschland zum Patent angemeldet und ab 1927 vermarktet werden[18]. Es dauerte jedoch noch einige Zeit bis der elektrodynamische Lautsprecher auch tatsächlich für den privaten Nutzer eine Alternative zu den herkömmlichen und preisgünstigeren Lautsprechern darstellte. 1931 konnte die Fachzeitschrift *Der Radiohändler* immerhin vermelden: »Einbruch des dynamischen Lautsprechers ins Heim«[19].

---

16 Inzwischen gibt es innerhalb der sehr lebendigen nordamerikanischen *Theremin*-Szene Bestrebungen, nicht nur die historischen *Theremin*-Typen wiederzubeleben, sondern auch Repliken der damals verwendeten Lautsprecher herzustellen. Führend auf diesem Sektor ist Floyd Engels, der nicht nur Nachbauten des *Theremin-Cello* und des dazugehörigen *Kabinetts* (Verstärker-Lautsprechereinheit) herstellt, sondern auch einen Bausatz für den historischen *Diamant*-Lautsprecher entwickelte.

17 Georg Sassnowski, *Die historische Entwicklung von Lautsprechern und ihres Einsatzes bei Konzertveranstaltungen*, M.A.-Abschlussarbeit, TU Berlin 2008, S. 26.

18 Zu dieser Entwicklung (und zu anderen wichtigen Aspekten der Geschichte des Lautsprechers) vgl. z.B. die Webseite von Ralf Ehlert: http://www.medienstimmen.de/.

19 »Die Entwicklung der Groß-Kraftverstärker brachte es mit sich, dass die dynamischen Lautsprecher neuerdings für verschiedene Belastungen ausgeführt werden, normal bis 3 Watt und in den sogenannten Kinotypen für Belastungen bis zu 20 Watt.« (Der Radiohändler: Fachblatt für den Handel mit Radioartikeln: Rundschau über die gesamte Radiotechnik 9 (1/1931), S. 28.)

Die meist für drei bis fünf Watt ausgelegten elektrodynamischen Laut-sprecher waren jedoch teuer[20], der ambitionierte Radiofreund musste mit rund 100 bis 140 RM rechnen. Diese Investition sollte sich jedoch lohnen, denn schließlich sei »der Lautsprecher das eigentliche Musikinstrument des Radioapparates!«[21] Angesichts der hohen Preise der elektrodynamischen Lautsprecher stellte der elektromagnetische Lautsprecher weiterhin eine günstige Möglichkeit dar – zumal als Einbaulautsprecher in Radioapparaten, wie zum Beispiel als Freischwingervariante im berühmten Volksempfän-ger[22].

So waren Anfang der 1930er Jahre zahlreiche unterschiedliche Lautspre-cherkonstruktionen für den Heimgebrauch auf dem Markt. In Werbeanzei-gen, Prospekten und Katalogen wurde als wichtigstes Verkaufsargument vor allem die Lautstärke beworben. Lautsprecherfirmen boten nicht nur Modelle namens *Fortissimo* an, sondern u.a. auch einen »Ultrakonus-Luxuslautspre-cher, der allen Belastungen gewachsen ist« oder einen »Ultra-Doppelkonus für besonders lautstarke und trotzdem naturgetreue Wiedergabe von Musik und Sprache«[23]. Zunehmend rückten aber auch die Klangeigenschaften der Lautsprecher in den Vordergrund. Vielfach wurden den Lautsprechern auch Klangcharakteristika von Musikinstrumenten (*Stradivari*) zugeschrieben. Gleichzeitig investierten die Firmen zu Beginn der 1930er Jahre verstärkt in die Produktentwicklung leistungsstarker Lautsprecher für größere Räumlich-keiten und in Beschallungssysteme für Veranstaltungen im Freien[24].

---

20 Zu berücksichtigen ist, dass Röhrenverstärker meist eine vergleichsweise geringere Ausgangsleistung hatten. Der Vergleich mit heutigen Watt-Angaben ist generell prob-lematisch, da Röhren-Watt nicht mit Transistor-Watt gleichgesetzt werden können.

21 Vgl. Der Radiohändler, S. 28.

22 »Die technische Entwicklung der elektro-magnetischen Lautsprecher ist in diesem Jahre bedeutend vorwärts gekommen. Alle großen guten Lautsprecherfirmen haben den Wirkungsgrad des Lautsprechers um etwa 100 Prozent gegenüber dem Vorjahre gesteigert. [...] Und es ist sogar gelungen, in der Wirkung der tiefen Töne an den dy-namischen Lautsprecher heranzukommen; und jetzt geht es vor allem darum, die Wir-kung der hohen Töne über 4000 Hz zu verbessern.« (Der Radiohändler, ebd.)

23 *Führer durch die Radiotechnik*, 2. neu bearbeitete Auflage, Berlin 1932.

24 In der Fachliteratur wurde hingegen versucht, Hinweise auf die praktische Umsetzung von Beschallungssystemen in Räumlichkeiten und im Freien zu geben. Vgl. Heinrich Wigge, *Technisches Hilfsbuch für Gemeinschaftsempfang, Hörerberatung und Funk-schutz*, Stuttgart 1934.

RVS-TRAUTONIUM (1930)

Auf solche unterschiedlichen Lautsprechertypen griff man 1932 während der Sonderschau *Elektrische Musik* im Rahmen der Berliner Funkausstellung zurück und versuchte, die Halle V mit ihren ca. 1.400 m^2 zufriedenstellend zu beschallen. Auch das *Trautonium* war bekanntlich Teil dieser Sonderschau. Der Ingenieur Friedrich Trautwein hatte es bereits Ende der 1920er Jahre an der *Rundfunkversuchsstelle* (*RVS*) in Berlin gebaut[25]. Dieses sogenannte *RVS-Trautonium* stellt das früheste *Trautonium*-Modell dar. Es wurde im Prinzip als eine Art Rundfunkinstrument entwickelt, d.h. die Klänge konnten direkt in den Rundfunk eingespeist werden und mussten nicht durch externe Mikrofone übertragen werden. Die Klänge, die durch eine Glimmlampenschaltung erzeugt wurden, waren obertonreich und konnten zusätzlich in ihrer Klangfarbe mittels Drehschalter verändert werden. Gespielt wurde das einstimmige Instrument auf einem Metallschienenmanual, über das ein Draht gespannt war[26]. Die Lautstärke ließ sich mittels Fußpedal regeln. Der Tonumfang des *Trautoniums* betrug gut zwei Oktaven, die allerdings auf unterschiedliche Tonregister umschaltbar waren.

Wichtig für die ›Promotion‹ des Instruments waren die öffentlichen Vorführungen, bei denen die Trautoniumsklänge nicht nur im Radio, sondern auch über Lautsprecher für ein Publikum vor Ort übertragen wurden[27]. Zum ersten Mal kam das *RVS-Trautonium* am 20. Juni 1930 im Rahmen des Festivals *Neue Musik Berlin* zum Einsatz. Für diese Gelegenheit komponierte Paul Hindemith auch ein Werk für das neue Instrument, die *Stücke für drei Trautonien: Des kleinen Elektromusikers Lieblinge*. In seiner Komposition nahm Hindemith auch bewusst Bezug zum Raum, der zweite Satz ist mit *Langsam (Fernwerk)* überschrieben – in Anlehnung an einen Klangeffekt aus der Zeit des frühen romantischen Orgelbaus, wo sich das Fernwerk als dislozierte Klangquelle an einer ›versteckten‹ Stelle befindet. Oskar Sala be-

---

25 Friedrich Trautwein hatte bereits in den 1920er Jahren verschiedene Patente angemeldet, die technische Teilbereiche der Klangerzeugung bei elektrischen Instrumenten betrafen.

26 Bereits 1928 hatten Bruno Helberger und Peter Lertes für ihr *Hellertion* ein ganz ähnliches Spielmanual entwickelt und dieses patentieren lassen.

27 Das einzige derzeit bekannte *Trautonium* der Rundfunkversuchsstelle befindet sich im Deutschen Museum in München. 1932 wurde das *Trautonium* in München bei der feierlichen Eröffnung des Bibliotheksbaus des Deutschen Museums vorgeführt. Und bei dieser Gelegenheit übergab Trautwein dem Deutschen Museum ein Exemplar des frühen *RVS-Trautoniums*, leider ohne einen zugehörigen Lautsprecher.

richtete, dass bei dem Berliner Konzert 1930 das Fernwerk durch zusätzliche, oben in der Saalmitte angebrachte Lautsprecher realisiert wurde[28].

Trautwein nutzte Anfang der 1930er Jahre jeweils unterschiedliche Lautsprecher zur Vorführung der *Trautonien*. Teils waren die Lautsprecher in offenen Schallwänden, teils in umschließenden Gehäusen eingebaut. Auch die Schallwandgeometrien, die wesentlich die Klangabstrahlung vor allem im Bassbereich beeinflussen, waren unterschiedlich ausgeprägt.

Die leistungsfähigen Lautsprecher (sogenannte Kinotypen) waren wohl hauptsächlich von der Firma Körting, die qualitativ sehr hochwertige Schallwandler produzierte[29].

Offensichtlich wurde im Rahmen der *Trautonium*-Präsentationen kein verbindliches Lautsprecherkonzept realisiert, obwohl Trautwein auch theoretische Überlegungen über die klanglichen Eigenschaften von Lautsprechern im Zusammenhang mit der Hallformantentheorie niedergeschrieben hatte. In seinem Buch *Elektrische Musik*, das im Juni 1930 parallel zur ersten öffentlichen Präsentation des *Trautoniums* erschienen war, bemerkte er: »Vielleicht ist die von manchen Lautsprecherfabriken propagandistisch ausgenutzte Beobachtung, dass gewisse Lautsprecher einzelne Musikinstrumente besonders natürlich wiedergeben, darauf zurückzuführen, dass die Hallformanten des Lautsprechers mit denen dieser Instrumente zusammenfallen. Ein solcher Lautsprecher wird auch den Klang anderer Instrumente im Sinne sei-

---

28 Vgl. das Interview von Joachim Stange-Elbe mit Oskar Sala vom 1.9.1989, http://www.klangspiegel.de/trautonium/kollegen-damals (1.10.2014). Auf die Frage nach den Lautsprechern, die bei den ersten *Trautonium*-Konzerten verwendet worden waren, antwortete Sala: »Ich kann mich nicht daran erinnern, dass das so schlecht geklungen haben mag damals, jedenfalls haben wir es geschafft, den Hochschulsaal auszuleuchten mit unseren Lautsprechern. Sogar mit dem Fernwerk da oben. Natürlich, von heute ist man verwöhnt. Solche Kritiken haben verhältnismäßig wenig Sinn, in dieser Zeit gab es einfach noch nichts richtiges, das muss man ja ehrlich anerkennen, da hat es nur die Masse gemacht, und die Masse, die hatten wir. Da waren immerhin so viele Lautsprecher, dass die ganze Wand da in den Saal strahlte, und das war ganz schön eindrucksvoll.«

29 Vgl ebd. Sala: »In der Hochschule hatten wir, soviel ich weiß, Lautsprecher von Körting. Trautwein hatte eine ganze Wand davon aufgebaut mit großen Schallwänden. Der Aufwand, der bei uns getrieben wurde, der war verhältnismäßig ungewöhnlich, weil die Lautsprecher wirklich Schallwände hatten und die Bässe wirklich abgestrahlt wurden. Das war eine ganz große Wand, ich glaube jeder Spieler von uns hat zwei oder drei so Körting-Dinger gehabt, so á 10 Watt, und damit haben wir schon ganz schön Lärm gemacht, den Hochschulsaal haben wir ganz schön gefüllt. Das war etwas ungewöhnlich für die damalige Zeit. Das kam, weil Trautwein in der Industrie war und natürlich diese Beziehungen gehabt hat und da konnte er diese Sachen aufstellen. Das konnten wir natürlich auf unseren weiteren Reisen nicht immer mitnehmen.«

ner bevorzugten Formantlage färben. [...] – durch Wahl des Lautsprechers (z.B. durch Umschaltung auf verschiedene Arten) [kann man] gleichfalls charakteristische Klangwirkungen erzielen.«[30]

Abbildung 3: »Trautonium« mit Lautsprechern, Ende 1930 im ›Probenraum‹ der Musikhochschule Berlin

Aus dem Nachlass Oskar Sala, Deutsches Museum München

VOLKSTRAUTONIUM

Für die Entwicklung des sogenannten *Telefunken-* oder *Volkstrautoniums* spielten diese Überlegungen keine Rolle[31]. Denn das auf der Berliner Funk-ausstellung 1933 präsentierte Trautoniummodell war nicht als Konzertinstr-ument konzipiert worden, sondern sollte als eine Art modernes, platzsparend

---

30 Friedrich Trautwein, *Elektrische Musik* (= Veröffentlichungen der Rundfunkversuchs-stelle bei der Staatlichen akademischen Hochschule für Musik 1) Berlin 1930, S. 18 und S. 32.
31 Mehr als zehn Exemplare sind derzeit in öffentlichen Sammlungen und Privatbesitz bekannt. Sie tragen Seriennummern zwischen 206 und 352. Vgl. Peter Donhauser, *Elektrische Klangmaschinen*, Wien u.a. 2007, S. 134–138. Das Deutsche Museum München besitzt drei Exemplare mit den Seriennummern 267, 289 und 332.

zusammenklappbares Hausmusikinstrument in Serie gefertigt und vermarktet werden[32].

Zu diesem Zweck publizierten Friedrich Trautwein, Oskar Sala, Walther Germann und Paul Hindemith für den Mainzer Musikverlag Schott eine Trautonium-Schule, die in die Spieltechnik des Instruments einführte. Darüber hinaus wurde eine Schallplatte produziert, auf der eine von Oskar Sala eingespielte Trautoniumversion des dritten Satzes eines Flötenkonzerts von Friedrich dem Großen zu hören war. Außerdem leitete Sala in der Berliner Hochschule für Musik und im Telefunken-Haus Trautoniumkurse.

Abbildung 4: Volkstrautonium mit Lautsprecher; Präsentation RVS-Trautonium, Berlin ca. 1930

Aus dem Nachlass Oskar Sala, Deutsches Museum München

Das *Volkstrautonium* wies wie seine Vorgänger-Instrumente keinen integrierten Lautsprecher auf. Es wurde an einen externen Lautsprecher, bzw. an ein Rundfunkgerät mit eingebautem Lautsprecher angeschlossen. Telefunken stellte dem *Volkstrautonium* das Telefunken Radio *»Nauen« 330WL* zur Seite. Dieses Radio war unter dem Spitznamen *Pfeifende Johanna* bekannt, inspiriert von dem Schlager *Kannst du pfeifen, Johanna?* der *Comedian Harmonists*. Das Rundfunkgerät hatte die unangenehme Eigenschaft, im Radiobetrieb Pfeifgeräusche von sich zu geben, da der Langwellensender Luxem-

---

32 Die Schallplatte erschien zur Präsentation des *Volkstrautoniums* am 2. August 1933 in der Berliner Singakademie. Bei dieser Veranstaltung waren nur Pressevertreter zugelassen.

burg ins Empfangsteil durchschlug. Dass der Absatz des *Volkstrautoniums* weit hinter den Erwartungen zurückblieb, lag allerdings nicht an der *Pfeifenden Johanna*. Deren eingebauter elektrodynamischer Lautsprecher funktionierte mit dem Musikinstrument prächtig, vielmehr war das *Volkstrautonium* bei weitem zu teuer[33].

In den folgenden Jahren entwickelte vor allem Oskar Sala das *Trautonium* entscheidend weiter. Durch ein zweites Manual, ein zweites Pedal und zusätzliche Oszillatoren war es nun mehrstimmig spielbar und wies eine Vielzahl an Klangfarben auf. Als Trautwein und Sala das Instrument 1935 einer Kommission um Propagandaminister Joseph Goebbels präsentierten, stieß aber wiederum vor allem die Tatsache, dass das Instrument mit seinem direkten Verstärker- und Lautsprecheranschluss besonders für Großveranstaltungen (im Freien) zu gebrauchen war, auf ein gewisses Interesse. So fand im Herbst 1935 auf der Berliner Dietrich-Eckart-Bühne, der heutigen Waldbühne, u.a. ein Probekonzert von Harald Genzmers *Musik für Trautonium und großes Blasorchester* mit einem Bläserkorps der Wehrmacht statt. Darüber hinaus wurden u.a. weitere Werke von Genzmer und Mozart-Streichquartette auf vier *Trautonien* mit je 150 Watt Lautsprecherleistung aufgeführt. Das Konzert mit rund 250 Musikern und 1200 Sängern diente nicht zuletzt auch dem Test einer gewaltigen Lautsprecheranlage von Telefunken, die im Hinblick die Beschallungstechnik für die Olympischen Spiele 1936 entwickelt worden war[34].

AUSBLICK: ZUKÜNFTIGE FORSCHUNGSANSÄTZE

Die Forschung im Bereich der Elektrophone konzentrierte sich bislang auf die Details der elektrischen bzw. elektronischen Klangerzeugung. Es ist also durchaus an der Zeit, den Lautsprecher als eine nicht unwesentliche Klangkomponente gerade der frühen Elektrophone in den Mittelpunkt zu stellen. Die Vielfalt und Heterogenität der Elektrophone ist allerdings zu groß, ihre Entwicklung zu individuell, um ganz allgemeine Prinzipien über Materialität, Konstruktion und Einsatz der genutzten Lautsprecher zu formulieren. Schließlich spielen in dieser Hinsicht nicht nur die technischen Details der Schallwiedergabe durch Lautsprecher, sondern auch die Kombination mit

---

33 1935 bot Telefunken das *Trautonium* für 380 RM, zuzüglich 35,25 RM für einen Röhrensatz und 15,75 RM für die Batterie an. 1937 stellte Telefunken die Produktion ganz ein; vgl. Peter Donhauser.

34 Vgl. ebd., S. 155f.

den weiteren Gerätekomponenten wie Verstärkerelemente samt Röhrenaus-
stattung (Art, Marke) eine große Rolle. Zumal grundsätzlich gilt, dass technische Angaben wie beispielsweise die Ausgangsleistung (Watt) viel Inter-
pretationsspielraum zulassen und mit weiteren Attributen wie etwa dem
Wirkungsgrad präzisiert werden müssten. Aber selbst die daraus gewonne-
nen Erkenntnisse könnten den hörbaren Raum der elektrischen Instrumente
lediglich theoretisch durchmessen. Inwieweit solche Theoreme auch tatsächlich realistische Rückschlüsse auf die Praxis zulassen, lässt sich nur unter Vorbehalt einschätzen. Zwar gibt es historische Quellen (z.B. Konzert-
berichte etc.), die als Grundlage für eine Rekonstruktion einer »historischen«
Beschallungssituation dienen können, darüber hinaus müssen jedoch auch
praktische Erfahrungen miteinbezogen werden. Letztere lassen sich allerdings ungleich schwerer herstellen, beschreiben und beurteilen. Denn auf
welche Weise beispielsweise die Elektrophone mittels Lautsprecher damals
einen Raum beschallen konnten, ist nur mit großem Aufwand rekonstruier-
bar. Diese Problematik liegt in der Materialität der technischen Gerätschaften und Bauteile begründet, die generell einem hohen Verschleiß unterlie-
gen. Selbst wenn funktionstüchtige 80 bis 90 Jahre alte Lautsprecher zur
Verfügung stünden, könnte angesichts Alterung der Bauteile und Werkstoffe
kaum eine »originale« Klangvorstellung hergestellt und könnten nur bedingt
Rückschlüsse auf die ursprüngliche Schallabstrahlung und die »Klangeigenschaften« der Lautsprecher gezogen werden[35].

Lohnenswert wäre eine Rekonstruktion der elektrischen Instrumente im
Zusammenhang mit den Verstärker- und Lautsprechereinheiten und damit
der historischen Beschallungsmöglichkeiten, gerade weil sie nicht unbedingt
der idealisierten Vorstellung einer Sprach- und Musikübertragung entspricht.
So sieht der Idealfall eine Beschallung mit einem möglichst linearen Fre-
quenzgang und linearem Phasenverhalten ohne Interferenzen vor, dabei sollen möglichst alle Punkte im Raum mit demselben Signal in ausreichendem
Pegel versorgt werden. Doch bei den frühen Elektrophonen wird deutlich,
dass Lautsprecher zwar nicht immer baulich, aber klanglich ein integraler
Bestandteil des Instruments darstellen – und in diesem Zusammenhang prä-
gen auch gewollte und ungewollte Verzerrungen sowie verbogene Frequenz-
gänge den hörbaren Raum als historische Klangschicht.

---

35 Besonders das Membranmaterial, meist Pappe, und die Aufhängung der Sicken werden im Laufe der Zeit häufig mürbe. Probleme bereiten auch generell sämtliche Dräh-
te und Kabel, denn in den kleinen dünnen Zuleitungslitzen brechen einzelne Kupfer-
adern und erhöhen dadurch den Leitungswiderstand. Aber auch Verstärkerbauteile wie
z.B. die Röhren lassen bereits nach verhältnismäßig kurzer Zeit in ihrer Leistung nach.

ENGLISH SUMMARY

Dislocated Sound and Audible Spaces
Loudspeakers in the Age of Early Electrophones

In 1932, the »orchestra of the future« was presented to the public at the Berlin radio and television exhibition. The special exhibition *Electric Music (Elektrische Musik)* was situated in a separate hall, displaying a collection of newly designed ›electric‹ musical instruments. On one large stage a *Theremin*, a *Trautonium,* a *Hellertion*, a *Neo-Bechstein* grand piano, an electro violin, and an electro cello were assembled and only separated by huge loudspeakers. But they did not play together as an ›orchestra‹. Rather, they represented, each for itself, a totality of different technologies of sound generation, timbre, and performance techniques. They had, nevertheless, one thing in common: each used its own loudspeaker (and its own audio amplification) for playback of sound in the room (see figure 1).

Therefore, the potential of sound of the so-called electrophones differs significantly from that of traditional music instruments. Since sound production and reproduction were no longer divided spatially from each, the loudspeaker advanced to being a constitutive element of the audible space. The sounds thus produced were now dislocated, or may have been used that way. Today not much is known about the performance of the early electrophones and the loudspeakers in the performance space, nor is much known about their technical, their acoustical properties, and the ›original sound‹ of the early electrophones, as defined by the specific construction, materiality, functionality, and power of the loudspeakers that were used. Even though many loudspeakers from the 1920s and 1930s still exist, they no longer reproduce their original sound. Owing to the aging of parts and materials, we can only draw limited conclusions about their original sound radiation and sound properties.

Considering the general improvement of telecommunications (c.g., telephone and radio), the development of loudspeakers seems to have been delayed. Although at the beginning of the 20th century the most important principles of sound transducers were known, the first extended tube technology as an amplifying element was needed for a breakthrough in the field of loudspeakers. In the early 1920s, mostly electromagnetic earphones were available. Their construction principle was completed with a mechanical-acoustical funnel, so the electromagnetic loudspeaker could be offered as an external funnel loudspeaker.

At the same time, many new types of ›electric‹ instruments were developed, but their constructors used loudspeakers differently. Lev Termen, for instance, used a simple electromagnetic telephone during his experimental phase from 1919 to 1920, the only sound reproduction receiver available at that time. To improve the poor (not to say almost inaudible) sound playback, he built a larger sound-emitting membrane and added a paper funnel as an acoustic amplifier. The volume was raised so much by this that one could now, at least, regulate it using a foot pedal and perform in public. This loudspeaker showed, nevertheless, poor playback quality and a high distortion factor. During his famous European Tour in 1927, Thermen performed in huge European concert halls (the Berlin Philharmonic, the Paris Opera, the Royal Albert Hall in London, etc.). There he used different constructions of the *Theremin* and more than one type of loudspeaker, including at least one swan-neck speaker (see figure 2) and up to three highly ornate and decorative triangle speakers. These devices could produce complex sounds, rich in harmonics, and could broadcast through corresponding loudspeaker technology; echo and light effects enhanced the attractiveness of the performances considerably. While constructing the *RCA Theremin* in 1928, Termen developed and patented the popular diamond loudspeaker.

Unlike the *Theremin* example, loudspeakers were not included in the development of the *Trautonium* at the conservatory in Berlin-Charlottenburg in 1930 (see figure 3), although Friedrich Trautwein knew about the sound problems of the first commercial loudspeakers (which appeared on the market at about the same time) and Paul Hindemith even incorporated spatialization, via dislocated loudspeakers, into his first compositions for three *Trautoniums* (the compositions received their first public performance in the same year). The commercial version of the instrument (*Volkstrautonium*), constructed by Telefunken 1931–1933, did not include a loudspeaker. Instead, the manufacturer recommended the use of a radio loudspeaker, colloquially known as the ›whistling Johanna‹ owing to how wireless transmission distorted sound. In combination with the *Trautonium*, however, it sounded perfect (see figure 4: *Volkstrautonium* with two different loudspeakers).

Recent Discoveries in the Spatial Thought of Early *Musique concrète*

MARC BATTIER

Musique concrète was started as a project with the specific goal of realizing a *symphonie de bruits* (›symphony of noises‹). Although this was abandoned as soon as Pierre Schaeffer started his first experiments during the spring of 1948, it remains the initial germ from which grew a whole new music. Schaeffer described the project in an internal memorandum submitted in June 1948 to the director of the French national radio broadcaster, *Radiodiffusion française* (RDF):

»My first goal, in collaboration with a musician, was to realize a *symphony of noises*, that is to say, a composition in which a large orchestra would converse with a series of noises, as in a concerto. In fact, this aim was gradually abandoned and replaced by a series of investigations not as directly effective. They can be classified into a number of categories:
a) production of noises (musical or not),
b) composition of these noises to produce works (musical or not).«[1]

In that same month of June, Schaeffer presented his first five studies under the title *Concert of Noises*[2]. On this occasion he wrote a short text, which

---

1 »Mon premier propos était, en collaboration avec un musicien, de réaliser une *Symphonie de bruits*, c'est-à-dire une composition où un grand orchestre eût donné la réplique à une suite de bruits concertants. En réalité, ce propos a été progressivement abandonné et remplacé par une suite de recherches moins directement efficaces qui peuvent être classées sous plusieurs rubriques:
a) production de bruits musicaux ou non,
b) composition de ces bruits en vue d'œuvres musicales ou non.« (Pierre Schaeffer, *Mémoire pour Monsieur le Directeur général de la Radiodiffusion Française*, Copenhagen, 28 June 1948.)
2 *Concert de bruits*, Sunday 20th June 1948, 21:00, Club d'Essai.

was read by the actor Jean Toscane, in which the question is posed, »would it be possible, from the rich material of natural or artificial noises, to take some segments, which could be used as material for an organized construction?«[3]

It is then at the very beginning that Schaeffer established the very nature of the material upon which to construct a new form of music. While producing the first five *noise studies* that constitute the initial body of works of electroacoustic music, and following that momentous event, Schaeffer developed a series of manipulation techniques to produce the ›musical noises‹ he had described to the director of RDF. Some were purely conceptual and did not require much technology, like changing the playback speed or playing a sound backwards, but others relied on techniques not readily offered by the radio studio. Hence, he was progressively led to imagining and, later, creating special equipment, so that operations on noises would lead to effective transformations, bringing the studio possibilities closer to the ideal of *musique concrète*.

What has appeared during extensive research I conducted on Schaeffer's archives is the consistency of his thought in conducting these steps. He envisioned highly structured techniques, spanning all phases of production and including the diffusion of the music and its presentation to the public.

Much of the technology developed in the years 1948–1953 was conceived by Schaeffer, together with Jacques Poullin, an engineer without whom these ideas would have been difficult to realize. Schaeffer readily acknowledges the role of his collaborator. Even in those of the patents discussed here that were signed by Schaeffer, Poullin is often named in the texts of the patents.

FIRST PATENT, 1948

In October 1948, Schaeffer filed a patent application entitled »Processes and devices for the realization of noise or musical sounds«[4]. The description of a device »for the realization of noise or musical sounds« included a system with three mono sources, to be mixed and blended to produce a complex object. One of the objectives of the patent was to describe precisely the ad-

---

3 »Serait-il possible, dans la riche matière des bruits naturels ou artificiels, de prélever des portions qui serviraient de matériaux pour une construction organisée?« (*Présentation du ›Concert de bruits‹ de Pierre Schaeffer*, Sunday 20th June 1948.)

4 Pierre Schaeffer, *Procédé et appareils pour la réalisation de bruits ou sons musicaux*, French patent 1.122.202, filed 5th October 1948, issued 4th September 1956.

vantages of a device with three channels, which converge towards a mixing device. The three mono sources were 78-rpm phonograph discs, with the option of adding sound films, as tape recorders were not yet available at RDF. The sources were thus labeled:

1, 2, 3 : discs with locked grooves *(disques à sillons fermés)*
4, 5, 6 : looped sound films *(films sonores mis en boucle)*.

The patent also described the procedures to be used with these sources to create new sounds (the notion of ›sound objects‹ does not appear in this early document). What is most interesting is that the three source devices were to be gathered in such a way that it would be easy for the musician to operate them all at once. With switches, it would be possible to inject any source and thus make various combinations. Schaeffer likened this to a new instrument, comparable to a musical keyboard. The timbres would be naturally varied according to the types of sounds played back by the phonographs. The shellac discs were described as containing fragments of sounds that were the result of sampling existing recordings to extract certain moments. The patent is very clear on this: the whole system is based on the sampling of recorded sounds. The techniques described enabled the production of new sounds from the basic manipulations offered by the devices. The three input channels and the three playback devices were individually controlled by a system akin to a musical keyboard and, in addition, a general mixer *(mélangeur général)* would ensure the blending of the samples to produce new sounds.

It is clear that this patent aimed at defining a working environment adapted to the creation of *musique concrète*. The ergonomics of the studio were reinvented to suit the new goals set by this music. In other words, *musique concrète* was an idea, and technology had to be created to realize it.

SECOND PATENT, 1951

In February 1951, a second patent was filed, called »Perfecting the devices to produce noises or musical sounds«[5]. It is based on the 1948 patent, but with an emphasis on patenting the very idea of *musique concrète*. At its heart lies the notion of the realization of sonic complexes *(complexes sonores)*. According to the patent, a sonic complex is obtained by editing operations on a recorded sound (on disc or sound film). The first step is defined as a selection of sound segments *(sélection de portions)*. From the isolated seg-

---

5   Pierre Schaeffer, *Perfectionnement aux appareils pour la réalisation de bruits ou sons musicaux*, French patent 1.033.682, filed on 26th February 1951, issued on 8th April 1953.

ments, a complex sound can be realized through the technique of locked grooves *(sillon fermé)*.

It is rather clear that Schaeffer had in mind the protection of the procedures used in creating musical sounds within the *musique concrète* aesthetics. The technology described at this point was very simple and available in any radio studio.

The patent offered, however, a number of new ideas based on devices particularly well adapted to the production of *musique concrète*. Three inventions were described in this patent. They were meant to aid in the production of »noises, sounds, and musical effects«.

A three-track tape recorder (*magnétophone à trois pistes*) was one the new devices, which was based on the three-phonograph system dating from 1948. It was composed of three tape recorders that were superimposed so that the three playback and record heads were vertically aligned. This ensured that the three tapes would be played in synchronization, provided that the playback speeds of the machines were precisely controlled.

Figure 1: Schematic of the three tapes recorders

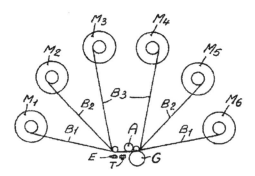

From: Pierre Schaeffer, patent FR 1033682

Although the machine was difficult to build and had many problems at first, it remained in use throughout the 1950s and was an important component of the studio for musical production and, at times, for sound diffusion.

The varispeed tape recorder (*magnétophone à vitesses multiples*) was a modified tape recorder with which the playback speed can be easily and precisely controlled, was introduced in this patent. As the 1948 device, it is based on the principle of a loop containing the sound to be processed. It was completed in April 1951[6] and was named a *phonogène*. Several models were built, with a 12-key keyboard and with a continuously variable lever. The following year, a patent was devoted entirely to this device and submitted in France, Germany[7], the United Kingdom[8], and the United States[9].

The third device was designed for ›sonic depth‹ (*relief sonore*), and was also called a ›frame‹ or ›portico‹ (*portique*[10]).

Figure 2: Schematic diagram of the ›pupitre potentiométrique de relief‹

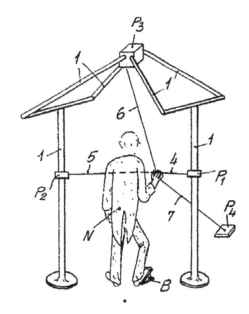

From: Pierre Schaeffer, patent FR 1.033.682

It is from this moment that the dimension of space appeared to be an essential aspect of the public performance of *musique concrète*. Schaeffer seems to have become aware of the problems of playing recorded music to a public

---

6   Pierre Schaeffer, *A la recherche d'une musique concrète*, Paris 1952, p. 97.
7   German patent 951697, 19th February 1952.
8   British patent 704,048, 5th February 1952.
9   United States patent 2,667,097, 13th February 1952.
10 French patent, 1.033.682, op.cit., p. 3. The term ›relief‹ was chosen here, as in ›potentiometric relief portico‹ (*portique potentiométrique de relief*), found in Schaeffer's 1948 patent. In this article, these terms are used interchangeably.

sitting in a theater during the performance of the *Symphonie pour un homme seul*. This took place in Paris at the *École Normale de Musique* in March 1950. During the rehearsal, Jacques Poullin played the work using phono-graphs. Meanwhile, Schaeffer wondered what kind of visual effect would be presented to the public, who would be facing the phonographs. Would it be possible to add some degree of performance, leading to an actual interpreta-tion of the music, even if this was only by adding or reducing the overall level by a few decibels? This question must have been emphasized by a sub-sequent performance of the symphony a few months later. It was held at the *Théâtre des Champs-Elysées* (famous for the premiere of Stravinsky's *Rite of Spring* in 1913) in July 1950. This was both a much larger hall than that of *École Normale de Musique* and a far more impressive venue.

At that time, the name of the system was not yet firmly established. It appears under various denominations. In the patent itself, we find a *balance potentiométrique* and a *portique*. This term, however, refers to the whole system, which in fact contains the controls for the *balance potentiométrique*. This latter term refers to the actual potentiometer configuration under the command of the operator-conductor. The name *portique d'espace* is not used in the patent. However, it is *pupitre potentiométrique de relief* which is used in a technical note[11] and portique *potentiométrique de relief* in Schaeffer's definition of *musique concrète*[12].

The device was designed by Jacques Poullin and Etienne Croix de la Valette and built by M. Raoult[13]. In the illustration included in the patent (see figure 2), a man is shown controlling three wires which are linked to po-tentiometers P1, P2 and P3. A foot pedal controls a woofer loudspeaker (be-cause »the human ear is not very sensitive to the directionality of low fre-quencies«). It can then be observed that this *portico* is in direct correspond-ence with the three sources used in the production process. It may be thought of as a device to produce sonic depth as an extension to the three-track tape recorder: »It is possible, among other things, to use this device for sonic depth. A signal is projected in depth by using two or three channels, with proper potentiometer settings.«[14]

---

11 *Notice technique*, n. d., GRMC, pp. 8–9.
12 Pierre Schaeffer, op.cit., Paris 1952, p. 108. Translation by John Dack and Christine North, *In Search of a Concrete Music*, Berkeley 2012.
13 This information appears in the *Notice technique* (see n. 11), although it also written that the device was designed by Poullin and built by M. Léon.
14 Ibid., pp. 3–4. »On peut également, entre autres usages, employer ce dispositif pour réaliser un relief sonore. Une modulation est projetée en relief par l'emploi de deux ou trois voies de départ convenablement potentiométrées«.

PUBLIC PERFORMANCE OF THE
POTENTIOMETRIC RELIEF PORTICO

The first public presentation of the *portico* took place in July 1951, at the Théâtre de l'Empire[15], for the performance of a mixed piece by Pierre Schaeffer and Pierre Henry, *Orphée ou Toute la Lyre*[16]. This piece, which belongs to the category of *musique mixte*, brought about some significant innovations. It was realized using the new special tape recorder, the *phonogène* that had been built to the specifications of Schaeffer, Poullin, and others (Galet, Chanoine), by the engineer in chief of the Tolana company, Pierre Perreau. It was, as noted earlier, made available in April of that year.

The composer and director Maurice Le Roux was in control of the *pupitre potentiométrique* for what was called a first audition in three dimensions (›première audition en relief‹). What was called the ›potentiometer balance‹ became the ›three-dimensional potentiometer portico‹ *(portique potentiométrique de relief)* for this concert.

According to the program notes, the concept of ›depth‹ or three-dimensionality has no relation to a stereophonic reproduction. That would not make sense, as *musique concrète* does not aim at presenting usual sound sources. Rather, it belongs to an unheard realm. New methods of diffusion have to be invented for it, over and above monophonic transmission, which was then the norm. *Musique concrète* must be liberated from the single loud-speaker, which constitutes a prison, as stated in the concert program.

The three-dimensional projection, which made its debut in July 1951, enabled the creation of a relationship between the musical form and the spatial form. Because *musique concrète* rejects any reference to the causal world, it should not only create its own sounds but also a new type of space, so that it would propagate around the listeners[17]. The diffusion may in fact follow two distinct paradigms: one static, with fixed points of sound projection; the other dynamic (or cinematic, to use a term employed by Schaeffer and Poullin), to create trajectories within the volume of the concert hall. Indeed, the system imagined by Schaeffer with the help of Jacques Poullin is three-dimensional: right and left projection, as well as to the rear and onto the ceiling.

---

15 The *Théâtre de l'Empire*, which later became the *Salle Wagram*, was inaugurated in 1865.

16 6th July 1951, with singers Maria Feres, Geneviève Touraine, J. Christophe Benoit, and a narrator/mime, Habib Benglia.

17 See *infra* a similar remark by Jacques Poullin.

In the performance at *Théâtre de l'Empire*, loudspeakers were hanging from the first balcony, on the edge of the stage and in the upper gallery. Schaeffer complained, however, that it had not been possible to use the potentiometers made specially for this project. The potentiometers used did not enable a precise control over the dynamic projection, so the localizations were coarse. Aside from this technical problem, the system was submitted to a general control acting on levels, to Schaeffer's satisfaction.

This is how Pierre Schaeffer described it: »Maurice Le Roux held in his right hand a ring linked to four wires. His left hand controlled the overall dynamic level. Master of the depth and of a certain range of nuances, the musician at the desk gave a long-awaited revenge on conventional ›radio mixers‹: he expanded the nuances instead of compressing them.«[18]

SPATIAL MUSIC PROJECTING DEVICE: 1952

A big step, one which has been much commented upon, was described in a patent submitted in February 1952. It introduced a device for spatial projection of music *(Dispositif de projection spatiale de musique)*. Much more elaborate than the 1951 portique, the 1952 device took all parameters of a global system into account, including the directionality of the loudspeakers. As noted above (see Footnotes 7, 8, and 9), the patent was simultaneously submitted in France, Germany, Great Britain and the United States. Its purpose was to protect several devices invented to enhance the production and performance of *musique concrète*. It is in this document that the *Pupitre d'espace* was introduced as a development of the three-track tape recorder.

The four receiver rings are 50 cm in diameter. They are preferably positioned according the actual location of the loudspeakers placed about the listening space. The operator-conductor is standing at the centre of the system. A coil is held in the right hand in front of the rings. It is 10 cm long and 2 cm in diameter, with an alternating current of 1 volt at a frequency of 5,000 Hz. By moving the coil in front of the receiver rings, four currents were induced. These were sent to the variable-gain amplifiers, thereby changing the overall loudness perceived by the public.

---

18 Pierre Schaeffer 1952, op.cit., p. 108. My translation. »Maurice Le Roux avait dans la main droite un anneau relié à quatre filins; la main gauche, elle, agissait sur l'ensemble de la dynamique. Maître du relief et d'une certaine marge de nuances, le musicien du pupitre donnait aux classiques ›mélangeurs‹ de la Radio une revanche longtemps attendue; il dilatait les nuances, au lieu de les comprimer.«

Control was done with broad gestures. The amplitude of gestures of the operator-conductor varied from 1.5 meter, corresponding to the maximum level, up to 10 cm, yielding the minimum amplification. Thus, the gestures could be quite large and theatrical.

Figure 3 shows the complete diagram, in which there are several distinctive parts: the variable amplification, following the commands provided by the gestural controls; the four rings and the coil, which is manipulated by the operator-conductor; and four loudspeakers for the spatial sound diffusion.

Figure 3: »Pupitre d'espace« and amplification, entire system

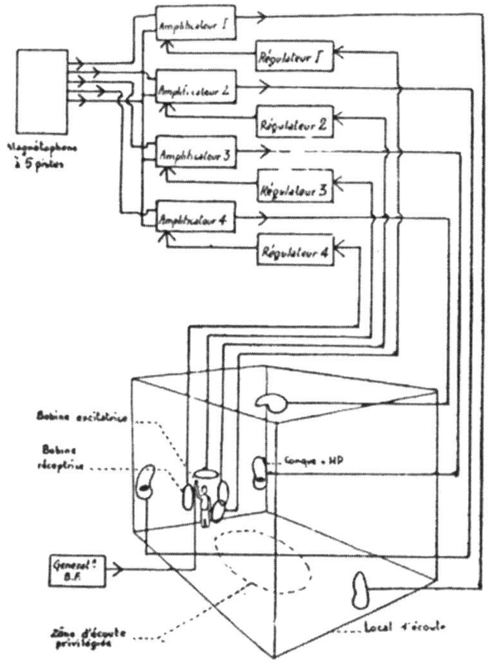

From: Jaques Pullin, *Son et Espace*, ars Sonora No. 3[19]

In this representation, the operator-conductor[20] controls the projection of several channels in a space, through the use of four loudspeakers (numbered 2, 3, 4, and 5), including one on the ceiling. It is precisely this configuration

19 http://www.ars-sonora.org/html/numeros/numero09/09f.htm.
20 *Opérateur-chef d'orchestre*, ibid., p. 206.

which was installed for the May 1952 concerts at the *Salle de l'Ancien Conservatoire* in Paris, that are discussed below.

The four rings, receiving the signal from the coil, appear in figure 4. As has already been noted, the position of the rings corresponds to the actual configuration of the loudspeakers in the diffusion space, according, at least, to the patent.

Figure 4: Pierre Schaeffer and the »Pupitre d'espace«

From: Thom Holmes, Electronic and Experimental Music, New York, London 2008, p. 41

»Spatial music. Any music which deals with the localization, in space, during the projection of works in public is called spatial music.«[21] For Schaeffer, spatial music is subdivided in two categories. He calls the first category ›static‹. It occurs when sounds are being emitted by a localized source. So the sounds are linked to the transducers, which are, in this case, the loudspeakers. Furthermore, any spatialization which may occur will have been determined beforehand, during the mixing phase, on several tracks, each one being projected from different loudspeakers. Hence, there would be various points in space, but each sound is static. The second category is

---

21 »Musique spatiale — Est dite musique spatiale toute musique qui se préoccupe de la localisation, dans l'espace, des objets sonores, lors de la projection des œuvres en public.« P. Schaeffer 1952, op.cit., pp. 205–206. See also the English translation, Dack/ North, op.cit., p. 194. My translation.

called ›cinematic‹. This is where sounds are moved in space. These are detached from their original tracks. Movements can be made to create trajectories of sounds. This is done by an operator-conductor during the performance, using a spatial device such as the one described in patent GB704,408.

Jacques Poullin, in his 1953 article[22], considers three types of sound projection. He calls the first »fixed point«, in which several tracks may be used in combination for one musical stream. The advantage is that by using several channels, the problem of masking effects which occur in dense materials may be avoided. Thus, the multichannel sound projection is a way to clarify the texture of monophonic material.

The second category is called »static stereophonic«, where a multitrack tape recorder is used. The »points of localization in space«[23] receive the signal from various tracks. They are not limited to the tracks, however, so that there are degrees of freedom in the relation between tracks, channels and loudspeakers.

This category underlines a new type of musical experience that, until then, had hardly been mentioned. It is the fact that »the listener receives acoustic impressions from all directions in the space surrounding him so that he himself is situated in the center of a volume of acoustic events. This clearly differs from the normal musical listening situation, where the orchestra generally occupies a plane in front of the public.«[24] It is this kind of situation which is now called a state of ›immersion‹, and it is quite revealing to find it described so early in the history of electroacoustic music.

The last category defined by Poullin, »kinematic stereophonics« places the emphasis on the displacement of the acoustic source in the diffusion space. This is obtained by modifying »the distribution of recording intensities on each track«[25]. Poullin then goes on to describe the system invented by Schaeffer, which he introduces as »an apparatus which would enable a playing operator to suggest acoustic paths by means of gestures performed in

---

22 Jacques Poullin, »Son et espace« (1953), in: *Vers une musique expérimentale*, (= La Revue Musicale n° 236), 1957, pp. 105–114, here p. 113. In this article, the English text is taken from the document »The Application of Recording Techniques to the Production of New Musical Materials and Forms: Applications to ›Musique concrète‹«, translated by D.A. Sinclair, *National Research Council of Canada Technical translation TT-646*, Ottawa, 1957.

23 Jacques Poullin, op.cit. (English version), p. 21.

24 Ibid., p. 22.

25 Ibid.

front of the audience«[26]. The article shows a configuration that corresponds to Schaeffer's 1952 patent, with loudspeakers located on the left and right, to the rear of the hall, and on the ceiling.

A friend of Pierre Schaeffer, writer and poet Jérôme Peignot, gave another justification to this endeavor. As he put it, »to prevent the listeners of *musique concrète* from being only seated in front of loudspeakers, the technicians of the group [Groupe de Recherche de Musique Concrète, GRMC] have devised a system of spatial projection«[27].

THE PROBLEM OF REPERTOIRE

The separation between static and cinematic spatial strategies is found in one of the earliest pieces using this system, *Timbres-Durées* by Olivier Messiaen. The question of the musical production became acute when a new opportunity was offered to Schaeffer: the organization of a retrospective of *musique concrète*, with two or three concerts to be held during the major Paris music festival *L'Œuvre du XXe siècle* organized by Nicolas Nabokov in May 1952[28].

Up to this point, from 1948 to 1951, all *musique concrète* works had been produced by Pierre Schaeffer and Pierre Henry. Several steps were taken by Schaeffer to increase production. A course for composers was organized (›Stage de *musique concrète*‹) so that young composers would learn the trade. It ran from October to December 1951, although it continued afterwards to prepare a few new pieces for the festival event. At the same time, Schaffer considered inviting well known composers to produce a piece in time for the May 1952 festival. Two composers were interested, Olivier Messiaen and André Jolivet, although the latter did not produce a piece.

Schaeffer was to be proven wrong in his exclusive approach to *musique concrète* as mere materials, when he invited Olivier Messiaen to come to the studio to realize a *musique concrète* piece. Pierre Henry became assistant to

---

26 Ibid., p. 23.
27 Peignot Jérôme, »De la ›musique concrète‹ à l'acousmatique«, in: Esprit No. 1, January 1960, pp. 111–123. »Pour éviter que les auditeurs de *musique concrète* ne se trouvent, lors des concerts, qu'en présence de haut-parleurs, les techniciens du groupe [GRMC] ont mis au point un système de ›projection spatiale‹«.
28 The festival ran from 30 April to 1st June 1952, with 29 concerts, held mostly at the *Théâtre des Champs-Elysées*, with another three concerts of *musique concrète* taking place at *the Salle de l'Ancien Conservatoire* (21st and 25th May, and a concert for a young public scheduled on 23rd May).

Messiaen. Henry had been Messiaen's student for four years (1944–1948) at the Conservatory.

Messiaen composed *Timbres-Durées*, which was realized by Henry. It was first written by Messiaen using common musical notation and, then the whole piece – with a duration of about 15 minutes – was transcribed into graphic notation, presumably by an unknown party at GRMC. The piece was performed twice during the May 1952 festival.

The concerts gave the GRMC the opportunity to present their repertoire, with a number of new pieces like the one by Messiaen, two Pierre Boulez studies, or *Jazz and Jazz* by André Hodeir. It was a way to affirm the potential offered by the *musique concrète* approach, both in terms of musical research and on the level of sound projection, defined as ›three-dimensional, static or cinematic‹.

A short document was prepared to be distributed to the press before the event. Simply titled *La musique concrète*, it emphasized two aspects which it said gave *musique concrète* some specific features and set it apart from the new German *Elektronische Musik*. One was the use of all sounds, natural or artificial, such as noises, voices, and acoustical and electronic instruments. Those sounds were to be submitted to editing, similar to the cinematographic technique. The other eminent feature was defined as the projection of sound in space, thanks to a special device. The document underlined the role of a conductor, who could move sounds about the hall by creating trajectories. It is thus interesting to note that the raison d'être of *musique concrète*, the particular use of all sounds, was placed on the same level as the spatialization processes as devised by Schaeffer and the GRMC.

The four tracks are distributed on four channels, corresponding exactly to the configuration presented in Schaeffer's patent and in the Poullin articles:

- Right
- Left
- Cinematic (*Cinématique*)
- Centre and Back

In *Timbres-Durées*, the musical signals are distributed on four tracks in a linear fashion, although the piece has a few occurrences of simultaneous tracks. It is mostly, however, a monophonic realization over four channels, as shown in figure 5.

Figure 5: Distribution of the four channels in »Timbres-Durées«

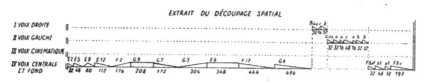

From: Jacques Poullin[29]

The three-track tape recorder was used throughout the 1950s, continuing at least until 1961. There is a mention of it as early as December 1951 (when the first *musique concrète* course was ending)[30]. Students of the ›Stage de *musique concrete*‹ were taught how to use it.

In the early 1960s, a four-track tape recorder began to be used, and the composers working at GRM immediately began to use it for several pieces, including Luc Ferrari in his *Tautologos I, II* (1961), Iannis Xenakis in *Bohor* (1962), and Van N'Guyen Tuong in *Éventail* (1963).

---

29 Jacques Poullin, »Musique Concrète«, in: Fritz Winckel (ed.), *Klangstrukturen der Musik*, Berlin 1955, pp. 111–132, here p. 129.

30 Jacques Poullin, »Séance du 4 Décembre«, internal document for the *Stage de musique concrète* (*musique concrète* course), 1951. The device is called *trois pistes* (three tracks).

Spatial Effects: Sound, Space, and Technology in Twentieth Century Popular Music

SUSAN SCHMIDT HORNING

Speaking at the February 2010 Technology, Entertainment, Design (TED) conference, musician and composer David Byrne explored the influence of architecture on musical forms, asking himself, »Do I have a venue in mind when I write music?«[1] Examining the evolution of music in different historical periods and places, he concluded that the space of a performance and the music therein produced seemed ideally matched and that certain technological developments drove musical change. His argument that musical genres evolve from the environment in which they are performed, or that they are written with a particular performance venue in mind, may seem overly simplistic and deterministic. But he does make an important point with regard to the interplay of technological and musical innovation. Whereas music evolved over time through live performance, cross-pollination of cultures, the evolution of musical instrument design, as well as the architecture of performance spaces, nothing has had a greater impact on musical evolution since the mid-twentieth century than the technology and practice of sound recording. In popular music especially, what became possible in recording dictated audience expectations of live musical performances. This had not always been true. The elusive goal in the early decades of the twentieth century of capturing an authentic and ›faithful‹ recording of a musical performance gave way by the 1960s to the imperative of reproducing the record

---

1 David Byrne, *How Architecture Helped Music Evolve*, TED Video, http:// www.ted.com/talks/david_byrne_how_architecture_helped_music_evolve, 11th February 2010, 16'00".

on stage, thus transforming the historic relationship between live performance and recorded music[2].

This chapter focuses on one very important step in that transformation,
the transition from the use of natural room reverberation to electroacousti-
cally generated reverberation and echo in popular recording during the 1950s
and 1960s. Just as twentieth-century composers increasingly integrated spatial dimensions into their compositions, so, too, recording professionals utilized the possibilities of space – both real and electronically generated – in
the recording studio. The first acoustical-mechanical recording machines
could not capture the spatial ambience of the recording room, but the introduction of electrical recording, amplification, and microphones in the 1920s
gave recording engineers the means to capture room tone and to create the illusion of space in sound recording. Although classical recording sought to
›bring the concert hall into the living room‹, some popular record producers
chose to go a step beyond recreating the live musical performance, exploiting the possibilities of studio technology to create unique sounds and exaggerated effects. These, in turn, suggested new ways of approaching musical
composition and performance. Just as the use of special effects in movies
transformed filmmaking and audience expectations, so the exploitation of
these ›spatial effects‹ in sound recording led to new sounds and styles of
music, creating a sense of space and place that bore little relation to the actual space in which the recording was made. Recording engineers and producers first began to experiment with artificially recreating the sense of
space with the use of reverberation chambers and electroacoustic devices,
techniques that had been pioneered in radio and sound film. In record production, once the illusion of presence was achieved, and engineers could
control not only volume but also levels of reverberation, that manipulation
became a creative tool.

HEARING THE ROOM

The first recording studios were laboratories in which inventors and mechanics experimented on methods of capturing sound using acoustical recording machines and various sizes and shapes of horns. As the recording

---

2 Recent books exploring the impact of recording on musical culture include Tim J.
   Anderson, *Making Easy Listening: Material Culture and Postwar American Recording*, Minneapolis, 2006; Mark Katz, *Capturing Sound: How Technology Has Changed
   Music*, Berkeley, 2004; Susan Schmidt Horning, *Chasing Sound: Technology, Culture, and the Art of Studio Recording from Edison to the LP*, Baltimore 2013.

horn gathered the sound directed into it, the sound waves moved a dia-phragm, which in turn moved the needle to engrave sound into the record. The challenge for recordists lay in positioning musicians around the horn so as to capture the sound of instruments and voices in balance, so that the re-cording was as faithful as possible to the sound of the live performance. Ear-ly recordists were aware of the importance of room size and shape and of acoustical resonance, but the science of acoustics, still in its infancy, had lit-tle impact on recording practice in the early years[3].

With the introduction of electrical recording in 1925, microphones re-placed recording horns, instruments could be amplified, and engineers gained more control over sound, bringing records that sounded vastly better. Engineers no longer had to crowd musicians around the horn, and the more sensitive microphones picked up voices and instruments, as well as reflec-tions of sound in the room. However, those reflections proved difficult to control. Consequently, radio and recording studios padded or draped the walls and carpeted the floor to eliminate resonance, but this tendency to keep reverberation time as low as possible placed a strain on musicians and sing-ers to stay in tune. In the early 1930s, broadcasters began to use ›live-end, dead-end‹ studios in which half the room was lined with sound absorbing material and the other half with hard material that reflected sound waves, thus more accurately duplicating the acoustical conditions of a hall or audi-torium. Not only did these studios provide better performing conditions for the orchestra and soloists, they gave the added effect of a much larger or-chestra with fewer musicians than was attainable in an acoustically dead stu-dio[4].

The added benefit of these acoustically ›live‹ broadcast studios was not lost on recording professionals, but few American in-house recording studios were large enough to accommodate orchestras or big bands, so record com-panies regularly used alternate venues to record large ensembles during the 1940s. Manhattan Center, the 1906 opera house for the masses built by Os-car Hammerstein and purchased in 1922 by the Freemasons, who built a grand ballroom still used today as a recording facility; Webster Hall, a dance hall once used for bohemian costume balls, society weddings, and as a speakeasy during the American Prohibition; Pythian Temple, an elaborate windowless structure built in 1926 by the Knights of Pythias; and the studios of World Broadcasting – these were some of the most popular recording

---

3   Schmidt Horning, op.cit., pp. 13–15.

4   »WCAU Uses Dead End and Live End Studios«, *Broadcast News* 5 (October 1932), p. 21; C. Gordon Jones, »Pioneer ›Live-End, Dead-End‹ Studios«, *Broadcast News* 6 (January 1933), pp. 12–13.

venues used by the major New York labels: Columbia, RCA, and Decca. All of these large rooms had natural acoustics conducive to recording symphonies and big bands, but one site in particular earned a reputation for its »distinctive big room sound« and by all accounts became the most desirable recording room throughout the 1940s[5]. Liederkranz Hall, home of the Liederkranz Club Chorus, was a spacious L-shaped room with solid wood floors and walls. In the 1930s and 1940s, Columbia Records pioneered its use for popular recording, especially big bands. One of the first recordings to exemplify this effect, *Joltin' Joe DiMaggio*, was recorded at Liederkranz Hall in 1941 by Les Brown and his Orchestra[6]. The brass section, trombone solo, the drummer's rim shots mimicking the sound of a bat striking a ball, and the male chorus shouting »Joe, Joe DiMaggio, we want you on our side« all have tremendous acoustic presence. What the live-end, dead-end broadcast studios of the 1930s did for radio orchestras, Liederkranz did for big bands. The spaciousness of the room and the reverberant quality of the wood had the effect of giving a record more presence and, seemingly, more volume. As companies sought to make their popular records stand out on radio and jukebox play, it was important to achieve volume without expanding groove dimensions; the louder the record the greater the excursion of the cutting needle and that meant wider grooves and therefore less playing time. Consequently, a studio that could lend that quality of apparent loudness without reducing playing time became extremely valued in the big band era, both aesthetically and commercially.

By 1947, room acoustics had become a primary consideration in the selection and design of recording studios, and companies sought the advice of acoustical consultants. When Liederkranz Hall was transformed into television studios in the late 1940s, Columbia engineers and recording directors canvassed Manhattan for a suitable replacement and found an ideal venue in a former Greek Orthodox Church on East 30th Street. Built on solid rock, with three layers of inch-thick maple and pine flooring providing a solid wood sounding board, Columbia's 30th Street Studio would eventually earn a reputation as »the ›Stradivarius‹ of recording studios«[7]. But that reputation came only after a good bit of acoustical tweaking by Columbia engineers, who faced the challenge of transforming a vast empty space with impressive but unruly reverberation into a functional recording studio, in which that re-

---

5 Milton T. Putnam, »A Thirty-Five Year History and Evolution of the Recording Studio«, *Audio Engineering Society Preprint 1661 of paper presented at the 66th Convention*, May 6–9 1980.

6 *Joltin' Joe DiMaggio*, OKeh Records 6377, 78 RPM.

7 Vincent J. Liebler, »A Record Is Born!« *Columbia Record* [1959], p. 4.

verberation could be controlled without altering the structure. The biggest challenge engineers faced was the room's size – 97 feet long, 55 feet wide, and 50 feet from floor to ceiling – which meant that the reverberation time was extremely long. »A string of very distinct sixteenth notes would come back as a smear«, noted one Columbia engineer, adding that it was as though »you were *immersed* in reverberation«[8].

Once the engineers figured out how to control the excessive reverberation, 30th Street became a highly desirable recording venue. In 1949, the original Broadway cast album of *South Pacific* was one of the first recordings made there, and one song in particular showcased the room's vast ambience. *Bloody Mary,* sung by the male chorus, opens with the orchestra's powerful four-beat lead-in, BUM-BUM-BUM-BUM, and the male chorus sing-shouting in unison: »Blo-ody Ma-ry is the . . . girl I love!«, followed by the orchestra's lead-in and the chorus again – a call and response repeated three times until the chorus shouts »Now ain't that too damn bad!« The voices and instruments resound with the space, enabling the listener at home to imagine the entire cast on the stage. For Goddard Lieberson, president of Columbia Masterworks, who wanted a space where he could record a Broadway show that sounded like it was live, but with the quality of studio control, 30th Street was the perfect venue. Other record producers agreed, and the ›natural sound‹ of 30th Street proved ideal for classical, jazz, and popular recording. With the new 33-1/3 RPM microgroove vinyl LP, the recently adopted Ampex magnetic tape recorders and high quality Neumann microphones, big recording rooms supplied the essential component in the creation of lush, high-fidelity sound recording in the years before stereo was introduced.

STEREO AND THE EXPLOITATION OF SPACE

By the 1950s, the use of magnetic tape for recording, the vinylite disc for playback, and better home reproduction equipment had improved the overall sound of recorded music for consumers, giving birth to the era of high fidelity records. Prior to tape, the standard method of recording on disc achieved a frequency range of 50–8,000 Hz, but tape could record flat from 30–15,000 Hz, thereby capturing not only the fundamentals but also the overtones of musical instruments and voices. While this resulted in greater clarity and depth, it was still monophonic – ›one-eared‹ listening – and thus

8   William Savory, telephone interview with author, 21st October 1999.

the ability to hear the spatial dimension of recording was limited. In 1952, two binaural systems of recording were introduced to the public, by Ampex and Magnecord, at the Audio Fair in Manhattan, an annual event sponsored by the newly formed Audio Engineering Society, where manufacturers of audio equipment displayed their latest technologies[9]. These were not the first attempts. In 1931, Alan Blumlein pioneered a binaural system that EMI used briefly at its new Abbey Road studios in London, but they shelved the technology and two decades passed before two-eared listening became a reality for audiophile listeners[10]. At the time, it was only for those who had home tape recorders, and only a few forward-thinking record companies released stereo tapes. Robin Lanier, an engineer and critic for *The New York Times*, wrote that the new system of stereophonic reproduction had the virtue of adding the ›third dimension‹ into reproduced sound, adding excitement by »increasing the illusion of space«, which included a sense that »the instruments are spread out in a sizable space«[11].

The possibilities of exploiting this illusion became irresistible to innovative musicians. Once the system for cutting stereo records was standardized, and stereo records became available to the public, dozens of stereo exploitation records were released. Conductor Enoch Light contributed to the popularization of stereo with his *Persuasive Percussion* album, conceived in 1959 as a vehicle to show the capabilities of stereophonic sound[12]. The album was a collection of instrumental versions of hit songs like *I'm in the Mood for Love* and *I Love Paris* that exploited ›ping-pong‹ stereo effects, in which the sound was panned between the left and right speakers. »This is the most unusual record you have ever put on your turntable«, boasted the liner notes, and in 1959 that was certainly true for listeners accustomed to monaural records. But it did not remain unique. A rash of other instrumental records came out around that time, exploiting both ping-pong and regular stereo, such as RCA's stereo demonstration record, *Sounds in Space* and Esquivel's *Exploring New Sounds in Stereo*[13]. Most importantly, stereo opened up new possibilities for the perception of space in recorded sound. Two-channel stereo

---

9 »2 Sound Systems on Display Here: New Binaural Methods Among High-Fidelity Equipment Shown at New Yorker«, *New York Times*, 30th October 1952. For more on the formation of the AES, see Schmidt Horning, op.cit., Chapter 3.

10 *Alan Dower Blumlein*, IEEE Global History Network, http://www.ieeeghn.org/wiki/index.php/Alan_Dower_Blumlein, (accessed 10th October 2014).

11 R. S. Lanier, »Hi-Fi: ›Stereo‹ Sound«, in: *The New York Times*, 7th July 1957.

12 Terry Snyder and the All Stars, *Persuasive Percussion*, 1959, Command Records.

13 *Sounds in Space: A Stereophonic Sound Demonstration Record*, 1958, RCA Victor Living Stereo; Esquivel, *Exploring New Sounds in Stereo*, 1959, RCA Victor Living Stereo.

was followed by three-channel stereo recording, giving even more depth to the sound and greater appreciation for the use of space.

Stereo represented a shift in the culture and technology of recording. The popularity of a ›natural sound‹ of ambient space in recording was beginning to give way to the enhanced sound of artificial reverberation, echo, and other ›spatial effects‹. Writing in *The New York Times* just four years after he heralded the illusion of space afforded by stereo, Lanier responded to a reader's criticism of a recording that sounded unnatural and hollow, asking the writer why recording engineers add reverberation instead of just recording naturally. Lanier explained that the problem was more complex than simply adding reverberation or not, that it was actually »an artistic rather than an engineering problem«, and that a sharp division existed between popular music and ›serious‹ music in their respective uses of reverberation: »The recorder of popular music has, in general, quite frankly abandoned the attempt at close naturalness to live music, in favour of ear-catching effects produced with an elaborate fake-reverberation technology«[14]. By 1961, it seems, spatial effects had already begun to dominate popular recording, but not every popular record producer embraced it. Jazz record producer John Hammond decried the use of echo chambers and other methods of achieving what he called ›phony effects‹ that he saw record companies » knocking themselves out to achieve. ... Fun for the sound engineers, maybe, but tough on the musicians. What's the good of having every instrument in a band sound as if it were being played in [New York City's] Holland Tunnel?«[15]. Although Hammond's lament may have been as exaggerated as the echo effects he criticized, these criticisms indicate the extent to which the values of record production were shifting as the technology made new things possible.

Debates about natural versus artificial sound permeated the 1950s. As stereo caught on throughout the industry, it required a new approach to recording and forced studios to modernize their existing recording equipment and to build additional facilities. These included not only stereo recorders and expanded control rooms, but, increasingly, the damping of recording studios in order to attain greater control over reverberation, which was now more frequently being achieved through the use of echo chambers‹ and other means.

---

14 R. S. Lanier, »Hi-Fi: Illusion of Reverberation«, in: *The New York Times*, 1st January 1961.
15 Quoted in »Talk of the Town«, in: *The New Yorker* (17th July 1954), p. 17.

MANUFACTURING SPACE:
THE ELECTROACOUSTIC REVOLUTION

Producers and artists who did not have access to the major labels' studios had long hoped to achieve the reverberant quality of natural acoustics on their records, so engineers devised ways to mimic the ›big hall‹ sound and vast physical space ceased to be a prerequisite. One of the first methods was by simply exploiting the most available hard-surfaced room available. The majors may have had access to the big halls, but the independent labels had bathrooms! In 1937, bandleader Raymond Scott had achieved what one listener called ›a big auditorium sound‹ on his records, simply by placing microphones in the hallway and men's room outside his record company's office, thus recreating the live-end, dead-end approach devised for radio studios[16]. The hard surface of ceramic tile provided the ideal level of reflectivity to produce the desired reverberation. In 1947, Chicago engineer Bill Putnam used the same idea when recording The Harmonicats' version of *Peg o' My Heart* at his Universal Recording studio in Chicago, but with a more exaggerated effect, making the harmonicas sound drenched in reverberation[17]. In New York, Columbia engineers at the 799 Seventh Avenue studio used the building's stairwell. William Savory described it as the brainchild of chief engineer William Bachman: »It started on the seventh floor with a microphone, and with a dual cone 15-inch loudspeaker on a landing one-half floor down the stairs. Below that, six and one-half floors of concrete and steel – *sensational!*«[18] However, the stairwell echo chamber had its drawbacks. Rather than taking the elevator, maintenance men tended to walk between floors, whistling as they went and disrupting any session in progress, necessitating stern warnings from the production and engineering staff.

Eventually, small studios began the custom building of echo chambers where space was available. Radio Recorders in Los Angeles built one on their rooftop in 1943. Capitol Records' New York studio hired a contractor to build theirs. One key element of the chamber is that no walls be parallel, so he brought in broken pieces of cinder blocks and other materials from his truck and situated them to form a ramp on the floor, which he covered with concrete, then he built a new wall at an angle at the end of the space and

---

16 Al Brackman recalled the incident in: Irwin Chusid, »Raymond Scott«, liner notes to *The Music of Raymond Scott: Reckless Nights and Turkish Twilights*, Columbia CD 53028.

17 Robert Pruter, *Doowop: The Chicago Scene*, Urbana (Ill) 1996, pp. 16–17.

18 Savory interview, 29th November 1997.

covered all room surfaces with a skin coat of very fine cement. After everything had dried he shellacked the walls to make the surfaces very smooth. The chamber performed so well that outside clients booked Capitol's New York studio specifically because they liked the sound of the echo chamber. On the West Coast, Capitol built its Tower, the first major American record label to custom-build its studios literally from the ground up. To enable greater control, design engineers minimized studio reverberation and created four sublevel-compatible reverberation chambers »to provide optimal acoustical properties«, which were intended to fulfil »the aesthetic considerations important to the artist and the practical engineering considerations of concern to the producer«[19]. Unfortunately, the musicians did not immediately appreciate the new studio. During the first sessions in February 1956, conducted by Frank Sinatra for an orchestral album entitled *Tone Poems in Color*, the musicians were appalled when they first began to play: »THUD! It was just dead as hell«, recalled clarinettist Mitchell Lurie. »I think it sounds like shit!« answered cellist Eleanor Slatkin when Sinatra asked what she thought of the playback[20]. They had been accustomed to the ambience of their previous studio on Melrose Avenue and found it difficult to get used to this new environment.

With the rise of independent studios in the 1950s and 1960s, equipment manufacturers began to market controlled reverberation in affordable, compact devices. The Audio Instrument Company of New York advertised an electronic echo chamber that occupied »2 instead of 10,000 cubic feet«, and at $1,485 promised to »pay for itself in three to five months«[21]. Another company, Fairchild Recording Equipment Corporation, drew on the reputation of Liederkranz Hall by advertising its *Reverbertron* as a means of achieving the classic Liederkranz sound: »Famous for REVERBERATION ...«, declared the advertisement's bold heading. »For years Liederkranz Hall was world renowned for its remarkable acoustic effects, and consequently it was in constant demand for recording. But even Liederkranz Hall had its limitations! Engineers could not always control the reverberation quality and time. However, if you wanted to record in Liederkranz Hall today it would be impossible because, as with most old

19 James Bayless, »Innovations in Studio Design and Construction in the Capitol Tower Recording Studios«, in: *Journal of the Audio Engineering Society* (April 1957), pp. 75–76.

20 Quoted in Charles Granata, *Sessions with Sinatra: Frank Sinatra and the Art of Recording*, Chicago 1999, p. 116.

21 *Leading Recording Organizations Use AI Electronic Echo Chambers* (Audio Instrument Company advertisement), Journal of the Audio Engineering Society (July 1958).

landmarks, it's destined for destruction. But . . . don't fret, don't worry! There's a much more practical, effective, and less expensive method to add controlled reverberation to your sound. Now reverberation comes in a compact, portable, attractive, and rack mountable package 24-1/2" high by 19" wide in . . . THE FAIRCHILD REVERBERTRON.«[22] Although neither of these devices appears to have achieved the popularity among engineers that their advertisements implied, they were representative of a growing market for technology that could achieve the big-hall sound in a more controlled, affordable, and smaller package.

Another popular means of achieving echo and reverberation utilized two tape recorders and had a slightly surreal quality. In Memphis, Tennessee, engineer and producer Sam Phillips used it to great effect recording the first Elvis Presley and Jerry Lee Lewis records, creating what came to be known as the ›Sun Sound‹. Phillips had two Ampex 350 recorders in his studio in 1954, one on the console and the other mounted on a rack behind his head. By bouncing the signal from one machine to another, with a split-second lag between the two, he created an echo effect that became the identifying sound of nearly all the records he produced for Sun, as well as for Chess and other labels. It has become an iconic sound that immediately conjures up an era, but tape slap did not create the effect considered desirable on most major-label pop and classical records of the time; it produced a distinct echo rather than the reverberant quality of a concert hall, and it worked best on small bands or singers, not orchestras or big bands. When Presley made his first RCA Victor recordings at the company's Nashville studio, the engineers there claimed they had no idea how Phillips had achieved the slapback sound[23]. They knew of echo chambers, but the distinctive sound of *Mystery Train* or *Heartbreak Hotel* did not sound like it had been achieved by an echo chamber or a big hall.

In Phoenix, Arizona, producer Lee Hazlewood also experimented with different types of tape delay to achieve echo, but he eventually created the famous sound of guitarist Duane Eddy's ›million dollar twang‹, first heard on the hit *Rumble*, by using a microphone and speaker placed at opposite ends of a cast-iron grain storage tank, a makeshift ›echo chamber‹ situated in

---

22 »*Famous for Reverberation*« (Fairchild Recording Equipment Corporation advertisement), Journal of the Audio Engineering Society 13 (Oct. 1965), p. A-234.
23 Peter Guralnick, *Last Train to Memphis: The Rise of Elvis Presley*, Boston 1994, p. 237.

the parking lot of Ramsey Recorders[24]. Both Phillips and Hazlewood, like other independent producers and engineers, had to devise affordable means to achieve the sound of the big hall on a tight budget. In the process, they came up with a sound of their own. They were open to experimentation and the recording techniques they devised became, to a great extent, the ›sound‹ of rock 'n' roll, a style that appealed to a new generation of listeners asserting their own identity and musical tastes. Born of necessity and limited technology, this new sound differed from the production quality of big band and popular singers of the post-war era. Emanating from low-fidelity car and transistor radios more often than from the home high-fidelity system, rock 'n' roll had more to do with energy and electronics than with fidelity or acoustical perfection.

One producer who sought to make records that were bigger productions of rock 'n' roll was Phil Spector, who became famous as the creator of the ›wall of sound‹ on records by the Righteous Brothers, by the Ronettes, and by Ike and Tina Turner. He did so by employing large numbers of studio-session musicians, often duplicating instruments to develop his dense sound, but also by experimental uses of studio technology. Before that, he learned some of his techniques by watching Hazlewood work in the Phoenix studio, but he surpassed his tutor in his use of studio technology to create a unique sound. During the 1960s, Spector exploited studio ambience in unique ways, working with what one collaborator called the *transparency of music* by recording with previously recorded tracks played through the studio monitors rather than headphones, allowing the sound to leak into the microphones of the performers who were singing and playing along with the prerecorded tracks. Then he would send all the sound to a chamber, creating what this collaborator called »this air effect . . . all the notes jumbled and fuzzy. This is what we recorded – not the notes. The chamber.«[25] Here, Spector used the chamber not only to provide ambience for the musical tracks, he exploited the chamber itself as an instrument.

Small studios that could not afford the space or expense of a chamber adopted a new technology, the EMT 140 Reverberation Set, developed in 1953 by Walter Kuhl of the Elektromesstechnik Company of Germany. The inspiration for the EMT came from a desire to address the needs of small studios and to improve on the technical drawbacks of existing methods,

24 Susan Schmidt Horning, »Recording: The Search for the Sound«, in: Andre Millard (ed.), *The Electric Guitar: A History of an American Icon*, Baltimore 2004, pp. 105–122.

25 Quoted in Albin J. Zak, III, *The Poetics of Rock: Cutting Tracks, Making Records*, Berkeley 2001, p. 78.

namely the expenditure and space requirements of echo chambers and the »small number of natural frequencies« in these small rooms, the disadvantages of tape slap and its discrete repetitions of sound rather than a continuous delay, and the inability to control the amount and time of reverberation in these methods[26]. The EMT used the concept of vibrating a large, tinned steel plate, which was suspended by springs from a rigid metal frame enclosed in a heavy wooden case. The system's reverberation time was controlled by a damping pad that pressed against the plate, with a reverberation time adjustable between one and five seconds. In 1961, EMT debuted the Model 140S, which added a second output pickup for a stereo effect. The EMT plate became the most popular source of reverberation and echo during the 1960s because of its portability, tunability, and size. It could fit in almost any studio and could be adjusted to the needs of the recording session. Although not easy to move, and tuning it required skill, the EMT plate offered the best option for studios with limited space. Moreover, it provided more control over reverberation than busy stairwells, men's rooms, and hallways.

* * *

Why did spatial effects come to be so desired, so exploited, so creatively adapted in popular music over the course of the twentieth century? In his rich study of the different uses of echo and reverb in popular recording up to 1960, Peter Doyle argued that no single meaning can be attached to these effects, but that their use conjures rich associations with space and place[27]. Surf music, for example, employed exaggerated reverberation, conveying the imagery of vast ocean spaces. Psychedelic rock also used excessive amounts of artificial reverberation, like that previously associated with surf music, but here the effect suggested enormous interior rather than exterior spaces and a ›depersonalization‹ of the music with excessive volume[28]. Daniel Levitin has argued that the psychological effects of reverberation in communicating emotion and creating an overall pleasing sound have been underappreciated[29]. But as this essay suggests, what can be ›pleasing‹ to one

26 Walter Kuhl, *The Acoustical and Technological Properties of the Reverberation Plate*. Lahr/Schwarzwald: Elektromesstechnik Wilhelm Franz KG, n.d.

27 Peter Doyle, *Echo & Reverb: Fabricating Space in Popular Music Recording, 1900-1960*, Middletown (Connecticut) 2005.

28 Michael Hicks, *Sixties Rock: Garage, Psychedelic, and Other Satisfactions*, Urbana 1999), p. 51 and pp. 65–66.

29 Daniel J. Levitin, *This is Your Brain on Music: The Science of a Human Obsession*, New York 2006, p. 16.

listener can be anathema to another. Spatial effects in music meant different things to different listeners at different historical moments.

During the early decades of sound recording when the equipment could neither capture nor reproduce room tone, engineers and manufacturers strove to bring the concert hall to the living room, a goal that only became achievable with improvements in the technologies of recording and reproduction. In the post-WWII years, the sound of records reached a peak as stereophonic sound made big recording rooms both desirable and available, forcing engineers to find ways to control excessive reverberation and to devise artificial means of creating it where none existed. By the time the sound of the room became perfectible, musical culture was undergoing a radical shift with the increasing popularity of unique sounds, novelty records, and rock 'n' roll, all styles that relied more on electroacoustic intervention than the ›natural sound‹ of reverberant rooms. Spatial effects, rather than natural sound, had become the new norm.

Three-Dimensional *Kunstkopf* Music and Audio Art

MARTHA BRECH

On 3 September 1973, *Demolition*, the first three-dimensional radio play, had its premiere in the German Radio Association's (ARD's) hall at the *Internationale Funkausstellung* in Berlin. Its director, Ulrich Gerhardt, had recorded it with the new *Kunstkopf*[1], a binaural microphone system that was first presented to the public on this date of 3 September. It looked like a human head, was closely modelled on human listening abilities, and allowed the recording of sounds from all sides in a seemingly natural acoustical space. Gerhardt presented the *Kunstkopf* in its full spatial abilities. When the dramatic situation of the science fiction crime story allowed it, he would place the *Kunstkopf* in the middle of the dramatic scene: the actors spoke from all around the performance space, noises came from all sides, and once, for instance, an actor threw a glass from in front of the *Kunstkopf*, with the glass flying over the *Kunstkopf* and shattering behind it against a wall.

In 1973, this kind of auditive spatiality was a sensation and soon attracted wide public attention. In the following years at least 186 radio plays were recorded with this technology at German, Austrian, and Swiss radio stations[2], and commercial music and noise recordings (LPs) were produced. All of them formed the specific genre of head-related audio art. Additionally, the company Georg Neumann GmbH began producing the *Kunstkopf* Gerhardt

---

1   The German term *Kunstkopf* is often used in literature more or less synonymously for ›*dummy head*‹. In this article, *Kunstkopf* will be used to refer to specifically German developments in the area of head-based binaural recording; the term ›*dummy head*‹ will, on the other hand, be used as a more generic term including developments outside the German-speaking world.

2   Kunstkopf-Hörspiele, Jokan-Liste: http://www.jokan.de/kunstkopf-liste.html (1.9.2014).

had used. Other *Kunstkopf* systems quickly appeared on the market, albeit with differing designs and of different technical quality[3].

It might seem as if a new technical device allowing the development of new artistic concepts and the construction of audible spaces had appeared out of nowhere. The reality was different, of course. The *Kunstkopf* introduced in 1973 was based on a long tradition of recording sounds spatially with the use of head replicas. Unlike its predecessors, the developers of the *Kunstkopf* offered the three-dimensional, ›around-the-head‹ perspective for the first time because they stood in a different research tradition. When it met with an established artistic tradition in the creation of auditive spaces a new spatial audio art appeared that centered the spatial design on the listener's head.

KUNSTKOPF AND ITS TECHNOLOGY: FUNCTIONS, HISTORY, AND SPATIAL DIMENSIONS

The basic concept of all recording systems using a head replica is the same: the imitation of the human binaural listening ability. Two microphones are placed inside a head replica and the recorded sounds are transmitted electro-acoustically to the listeners' ears by earphones, because the sounds are reproduced in best spatial quality at the position where the microphones were placed in the head replica – while the use of loudspeakers can only produce a somewhat rough and unclear two-channel stereophonic audio image.

Head replicas as spatial recording devices may be traced back to the mid-1920s. In this period, public radio broadcasts had just begun, but the quality of the monophonic sound transmission was rather poor and, therefore, subject to research worldwide. And companies that offered news and entertainment programs via telephone into private homes – among them the Theatrophone company in Paris, which was active in transmitting binaural/stereo sound from operas and theatres, a technology they had been using since 1881 – also needed new devices to compete against the rapidly growing medium of radio.

In this context, the first head replicas, called ›*dummy heads*‹, were developed. Between 1924 and 1927 at least four different systems were designed and patented in the USA and France. These relied on binaural concepts and on the desire to imitate human spatial listening abilities and were therefore

---

3   All of them were produced in German-speaking countries (Neumann, AKG, Sennheiser, Schoeps), a point that will be discussed later.

based on the distance and perceptual differences between human ears[4]. But none of these patented *dummy heads* ever seem to have been built as proposed by the authors.

The first reports of an existing *dummy head* date from 1930, when F. A. Firestone of Michigan University published results of experiments with acoustic measurements concerning audio perception. For this purpose he had built a dummy out of »a man-sized wax bust such as is used in window displays«[5], with two microphones mounted inside the head at the positions of ear canals and eardrums, and with hair felt covering for the body[6] as substitute for clothes. As an instrument for scientific research, experiments, and for measurements in subjects including acoustics, psychoacoustics, psychology, physiology, and architecture, any *dummy heads* used were built as one-of-a-kind models. This practice has continued up through to the present, and the choice of naturalistic or abstracted forms usually depends on the nature of the precise scientific research question.

---

4   Probably the first concept was proposed by the radio pioneer Franklin M. Doolittle, who in 1924 included this distance in his two-channel concept of a future broadcasting system (Franklin M. Doolittle, *Radiotelephonie*, US patent 1,513,973 (filed 21st February 1924; issued 4th November 1924)). One year later Harvey Fletcher and Leon J. Sivian of the Western Electric Company applied for a patent for a very complex sound high-quality binaural recording and transmission system (Harvey Fletcher und Leon J. Sivian, *Binaural Telephone System*, US patent 1,624,486, (filed 15th June 1925, issued 12th April 1927)), suitable for radio, telephone and phonograph recordings, that included a »dummy or artificial head« equipped with a pickup system consisting of two condenser microphones inside the head, located at the position of the ears. According to the authors, the artificial head should have the size of a natural head and its acoustic properties, although they seem to have no idea of the precise materials to be used for its construction. In 1927, W. B. Jones proposed another complex binaural recording system (W. B. Jones, *Method and means for the ventriloquial production of sound*, US patent 1,855,149 (filed 13th October 1927, issued 19th April 1932)). Jones suggested a »*dummy head* with microphones for ears« (p. 8, ll. 75–77), in which he described the microphones as substitutes for ears, located upon the head and slightly inserted to simulate the position of human ear drums (p. 6, ll. 30–45).4 His design of the *dummy head* was drawn as a ball (p. 1). Compared to these, Jean Maire's patent for a *Dispositif permettant l'audition téléphonique bi-auriculaire* (French patent 616, 677 (filed 26th June 1926, issued 5th February 1927)) seems to be more realistic and orientated at a practical use. It is reduced to the microphone bearing human looking artificial head made of gypsum, with membranes at the eardrum position. Maire proposed the use of this *dummy head* in telephonic transmission of sounds.

5   F. A. Firestone, »The Phase Difference and Amplitude Ratio at the Ears Due to A Source of pure Tone«, in: JASA 2 (October 1930), pp. 260–270, here p. 261.

6   Ibid., there are no photos of the device.

The first *dummy head* built for music recordings was made by Harvey Fletcher in 1932 from a window display wax puppet, but it looked much more civilized than Firestone's research instrument. »Oscar«, as it was named, had two microphones attached from inside the head at his jaws and was dressed like a gentleman hiding the technical equipment underneath his dinner jacket. It became famous worldwide for its concert transmissions via telephone from the Philadelphia Symphony Orchestra directed by Leopold Stokowski, where Oscar was seated among the audience in the concert hall[7].

Figure 1: »Oscar« next to a grand piano

From: Ralph E. Lapp, *Schall und Gehör*, Amsterdam 1966, p. 78

Compared to the natural-looking »Oscar«, most of the *dummy heads* built for music recordings in the laboratories of the Dutch company Philips by Kornelis de Boer and Roelof Vermeulen from the late 1930s to the early 1950s looked much less natural[8]. Although the head built by Roelof Vermeulen in

---

7   Due to the lack of synchronized two-channel recording technology in these years, the binaural aspects of the documentary gramophone recordings are lost today.

8   With only minor exceptions: A human sized female head that de Boer described as puppet head (cf. Kornelis de Boer, *Stereofonische Geluidsweedergave*, Delft 1940, pp. 17–21), and in his 1955 article Vermeulen displayed two photos of gypsum *dummy heads* that seem to be made from an artist in form of his head and his co-worker Theodor van Urk (cf. Roelof Vermeulen, »Vergleich zwischen wieder-

the early 1950s seems to resemble a human head with its ears and neck, it rather looks like an abstract object while hanging upside down in recording position above the orchestra[9].

The first and only *dummy head* used for commercial stereophonic records before 1973 was built by André Charlin in Paris. Charlin, an engineer who ran his own studio and record company, was also active in the field of (stereo) sound-film recordings. Over and above all these activities, he developed and built numerous technical devices – among them the *dummy head* that Charlin patented in the years 1963–1964[10]. But the *Tête Charlin*, as it was called, had only little in common with a human head and looked more like a flat ball.

Figure 2: a) Vermeulen »dummy head« (1955) in upright position; b) Charlin »dummy head« (1963)

 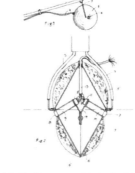

From: a) Vermeulen, op.cit., p. 192   b) Andrè Chalin, patent FR 1,375,245 (1963)

Like its predecessors for music recordings, the *Tête Charlin* – equipped with two high-quality microphones from the company Schoeps – was used for recordings in the traditional performance situation in which musicians perform in front of an audience, with the microphones having the best (or second best) place in the performance hall, next to the conductor.

---

gegebener und echter Musik«, in: *Philips technische Rundschau* 17 (1955), No. 6, pp. 191–198, here p. 192). All these human formed *dummy heads* were early prototypes.

9   Again, Leopold Stokowski conducted the recording of symphonic music that was stored on a specially designed experimental double gramophone recorder about 1955. But it is uncertain if these spatial recordings survived in the archives of the company.

10 André Marie Bernard Charlin, *Microphone stéréophonique*, French patent 1,375,245, (filed 6th September 1963, issued 7th September 1964).

Obviously, the aim was to produce a stereophonic sound recording that was concentrated on the music played by the orchestra, while the rest of the concert hall and the audience therein were ignored, just as with conventional stereophonic productions that were recorded with multiple microphones. But in recording situations like these, a natural head hanging above the orchestra's conductor was, and still is, considered unacceptable. So the design of these devices became more abstract while their acoustic properties resembled that of a natural human head. In particular, the distance between ears and absorbing qualities of skin were important – but the head's form was built with the recording function in mind.

KUNSTKOPF AS A DEVICE FOR THREE-DIMENSIONAL RECORDINGS

Figure 3: Three generations of a »Kunstkopf«. The first (second from left) was made of gypsum, covered with rubber and hair. The second generation (second from right) had a different form for the head, no hair, and with some improvements regarding the acoustical properties. The third generation was the first commercial »dummy head«, produced since 1971 (Neumann KU 80) and made of white silicon (four dummy heads in the background) and black silicon (centre) from 1973.

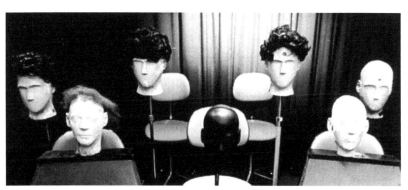

Photo: courtesy of Henning Wilkens

A look at the forms of the different generations of *dummy head* that became the Neumann-*Kunstkopf* in 1973 shows that it was not based on the existing *dummy heads* used in music recording. To precisely imitate spatial listening abilities, the first two generations were replicas of the human head. They were built in the years 1967–1968 at the Institute for Technical Acoustics at the TU Berlin[11], using moulds of human heads[12], outer ears and ear canals[13]. These moulds continued to be used for the abstract-looking sculptured heads until 1981, when a fourth generation of the system was built under the direction of the company Neumann, which had coproduced the dummy head since 1971.

The natural head form of the first two *Kunstkopf* generations refers to its use in acoustic research. Here, an independent tradition in building *dummy heads* as instruments for room acoustic measurements had begun in Germany in the mid-1950s, based on Friedrich Spandöck's proposal, dating from 1934, to use an artificial head in reduced format for the study of stereo-acoustical effects in architectural models[14]. Starting in the early 1950s, several researchers had built similar *dummy heads* in model formats, and later some researchers also built binaural *dummy heads* in natural sizes. In the 1960s the acoustic departments of five different West and East German universities (Aachen, Berlin, Dresden, Göttingen, and Munich) were experimenting with *dummy heads* for the measurement of concert-hall acoustics, and researchers in all these places were busy developing their own systems of natural-sized *dummy heads*.

In this context the first two generations of the Berlin *Kunstkopf* was originated, but it changed its function into music recording after Herbert von Karajan, who had conducted the music for the acoustic measurements, had heard the recordings and encouraged the developers to produce it as a spatial microphone system. With this change of function, the design became more abstract, too.

With the *Kunstkopf* as a three-dimensional spatial recording device, the developers – especially Georg Plenge, who was a trained conductor and experienced *Tonmeister* for music production at public radio stations – had the idea of presenting a recording system complementing the more common two-channel stereophony. This had not been fully established in the early 1970s and was still in an experimental stadium. In this technology, the virtual space between the right and the left loudspeaker allows quite a good discrimination of the instruments but has only little spatial depth. Space had to

---

11 Later, the group of developers continued its work in the Heinrich-Hertz-Institute.

12 The first mould was a second-hand use of a mould of an actor's head made in a Berlin theatre for a mask. For the next *dummy head* generation the developers took a mould of their leader's head, Georg Plenge.

13 These moulds were taken from Georg Plenge and Henning Wilkens and were made of silicon.

14 Friedrich Spandöck, »Akustische Modellversuche«, in: *Annalen der Physik*, Vol. 5, No. 4, 1934, p. 351.

be virtually constructed by electroacoustic means, and the instruments seem
to be placed like ›birds on a wire‹ between the two loudspeakers. Thus, the
creation of these virtual spaces was a challenge to every sound engineer. In
contrary to this, the three-dimensional recordings offered the listeners the
spatial impression of a concert hall, appropriate room acoustics, and the
placement of the instruments as usual as long as a good position for *Kunst-kopf* was found in the hall. In order to separate this recording technology
from the conventional one it was called »head related«.

THREE-DIMENSIONAL AUDIO ART AND MUSIC PRODUCTIONS

Radio Play Productions

To the surprise of its developers, the *Kunstkopf* was not limited to recordings
of (classical) music, but it was also used to create three-dimensional spatial
design for radio dramas such as *Demolition*, as well as other audio art.

In these art genres the design of auditive spaces turned out to be essential, because they replaced the visual scenery of the theatre and thereby became part of the creative process in the production of radio plays. Authors,
directors, and engineers in radio drama departments had constantly, since the
mid-1920s, worked together to develop techniques for producing a variety of
auditive space aspects, such as room size, distance, movement, or scene environment. In production they used artificial reverberation, echoes, noises
(original or from record or tape), tape manipulation, etc.[15]. Some of these
techniques depended on newly constructed devices or systems, others were
the result of complex experimental processes in the use of this equipment.

This was the artistic background of Ulrich Gerhardt, the director of *Dem-olition*[16] and head of the drama department at RIAS (Radio in the American
Sector) in Berlin. He asked Georg Plenge for a sample model as soon as he
had heard about the *Kunstkopf* from his colleagues in the music department[17], to experiment with it in context of other new technical devices. A

---

15 It should be remarked that Pierre Schaeffer began his *musique concrète* from his posi-
    tion as the head of the Studio d'essay – the radio play department of the French radio
    in Paris.
16 https://www.youtube.com/watch?v=2aR5PYOEeME (28.8.2014).
17 Oral report by Georg Plenge, January 2008; Gerhardt's sample is not mentioned in the
    hand-written list of deliveries kept by the Neumann company for heads made
    of gypsum, but it may have been one of the samples that were used by Henning
    Wilkens (one of the co-developers) for acoustic measurements and that were not listed

few months after the première of *Demolition* he wrote: »When I said that head-related stereophony is, for me, also the extension of artificially reproducible listening sensations, I meant the pure studio technology of multiple track recordings. Here, it is indeed possible to open up tremendous musical spaces that, up to now, could only be dreamt of and could only have been awkwardly hinted at by the use of other technologies«[18]. He continued that he had understood this as an initial result of his experiments[19].

Demolition and Its Spatial Concept

Gerhardt had chosen a rather complex topic when he and his team adopted the novel *The Demolition Man*, by the American science fiction author Alfred Bester, for the script of the first *Kunstkopf* radio drama[20]. The story recounts the planning, realization, detection, and punishment of a murder in future times[21]. The ability to read the conscious and subconscious thoughts of others, practised by a guild of specially trained persons, called ›*Esters*‹, is a prominent cultural practice. The protagonist, who is an *Ester* himself, must take this capability into account while working on his plan. In order to disguise his thoughts from other *Esters*, he buys a catchy tune from a composer. Later the melody appears in his head whenever an *Ester* is around, while his thoughts, spoken by the same actor, appear in his head when he is alone. Apart from this inside world, the story's action takes place in conventional radio play scenes and dialogues spoken in different rooms and at different occasions.

In the production process, Gerhardt was able to separate between what happens inside and outside the protagonist's head and the conventional scenes because the *Kunstkopf* allowed him to place all the inside-head parts of the script inside the head of the radio play listener, too[22]. Gerhardt and his engineers even illustrated acoustically how the protagonist ›loaded‹ the melody inside his head and they produced a short effect, a movement from out-

---

by the company. Alternately, it may have been a sample from the next generation of white *Kunstkopf* models, made of gypsum or silicon (their existence is reported in a letter form the company written in 2000).

18 Ulrich Gerhardt, »Zur Diskussion Kunstkopf Stereophonie«, in: *Funkschau*, No. 3, 1974, p. 80.

19 Ibid.

20 Jokan-Liste, op.cit. and http://www.jokan.de/kunstkopf.html#kk_demolition (8.9.14).

21 The following description is based on a listening analysis.

22 Until today, no description of the production process has been published that tells how Gerhardt managed recording and producing that inside the head impression.

side the head into the ears, at the beginning of the melody, lasting a few minutes.

Smaller excerpts of the melody appear later, when the protagonist talks to others. Then his voice appears outside his head, while the melody appears inside his head when he proceeds with his plan, or when he comments on people and dialogue partners who have just left the scene, which is marked by disappearing steps, voice, or noises. Likewise, appearing or moving of voices or objects are placed and produced carefully around the *Kunstkopf* to enable the listener the localization of these objects and their movements as well as their distance to the protagonist. Additionally, scenes are marked by sounds of different room sizes or noise atmospheres, as usual in radio drama. But this does not happen often, compared to conventional radio plays. A party, for instance, is presented with only very few party noises, such as the soft filling of drinks, murmuring, and laughs. But the clearly understandable voice of another important figure in the play can be heard in the distance at a precise point. Later still, a virtual space is constructed with musical sounds that slowly whirl around the first protagonist's head, or a naturalistic scene is described by an acoustic atmosphere of birdsong and bees humming from all around while two people are speaking only on one side.

Obviously, Gerhardt preferred to concentrate the spatial design of *Demolition* on the new possibilities offered by the *Kunstkopf*. But he did not adjust the spatial design to the protagonist's perspective, because a second protagonist appears as soon as the first has committed his crime. Now a detective takes the role of the first protagonist's opponent, and some of the scenes were recorded from his perspective. Additionally, in the final twenty minutes (out of a running time of 105 minutes) the position of voices inside or outside the head is partly unclear, probably to support the dramatic situation that culminated in the end as a conventional suspect's confession and his unconventional sci-fi punishment.

The spatial design of *Demolition* thus used the new spatial tool in much the same way as traditional techniques to describe or produce auditive spaces in radio plays, illustrating the scenes. This includes changes of auditive perspective. The order of the scenes tells the story to the listener, who is an observer, although parts of the dialogues seem to take place inside the listener's own head.

In the following years, Gerhardt directed many other *Kunstkopf* radio plays and supported authors and other directors in experimenting with the new device. But as copies of radio plays produced in public radio stations in Germany are not available on the market, analyses of the spatial design of these productions are not possible. From the list of 186 *Kunstkopf* radio plays, which offers additional abstracts for some of the productions, short hints may be extracted. In the early years until the mid-1980s, the majority of *Kunstkopf* productions were drama or literature adaptations, acoustical city and landscape portraits based on original sound recordings, and science fiction topics. The perspective of acoustical city or landscape portrait based on field recording with the *Kunstkopf* is clearly oriented towards a space outside the listener's head, and the construction of an audible space might be reduced to the composition of the recordings. In contrast, the science fiction title *Das geteilte Ich* (»The Divided Self«), an adaptation of a novel by Robert Sheckley[23], refers to an ›inside-the-head‹ spatial construction, as well as to constructions of imaginary auditive spaces around the listener's head, and to an outside world of the ›auditive-flat type‹ that has been described for *Demolition*.

Lou Reed's *Street Hassle*: A Kunstkopf-Opera and Its Spatial Design

In the middle of the 1970s public interest in *Kunstkopf* productions was at an initial peak, and *Kunstkopf* recordings entered into the field of commercial music recordings, at least for a while. The number of *Kunstkopf* recordings that were produced in these years is uncertain, and only Lou Reed's concept album *Street Hassle*[24] has remained on the market until today. In 1977–1978, the *Kunstkopf* parts of the album were recorded in the Delta Studio[25] in Wilster, a small village in Northern Germany. The high-quality *dummy head* in use here was built by Volker Mellert, a co-designer of the dummy-head system in Göttingen in the late 1960s, and his assistant, Reinhard Weber, at the nearby University of Oldenburg[26]. In contrast to the Neumann head, its design was based on the statistical average of central Europe human heads, outer ears, and ear canals, and it was equipped with microphones from the company Schoeps (figure 4).

As the Delta Studio engineers and producers were active on an international basis, they got in contact with Lou Reed while he was in search of new spatial recording technologies for his album *Street Hassle*, a kind of story-

23 Jokan-Liste, op.cit., SWR-Production, 1976, directed by Peter Michael Ladiges.
24 Lou Reed, *Street Hassle*, LP: 1C 064-60 445 (EMI) 1978, and CD: 262270-217 (Arista).
25 Reported by local newspapers and the credits printed on the album sleeve.
26 Historical Delta Studio flyers collected by Volker Mellert and handed to the author in January 2014.

telling[27] auditive opera. Its title, *Street Hassle*, refers to the late 1970s rock and punk music view on metropolitan street life: rough, aggressive, and full of violence. In the album, this is displayed from the individual perspective of the protagonist and his dark and largely nihilistic way of thinking. He is not only an observer of the scene, but also an active part of the *Street Hassle*. He perceives the atmosphere, reacts to it, and acts in it through his lyrics.

Figure 4: »Kunstkopf« by Mellert and Weber, built ca. 1976

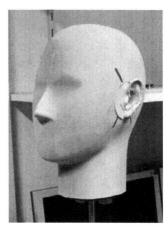

Photograph January 2014 by the authors

Hence, the album's spatial concept relies on this one perspective only and, unlike the radio plays described above, it does not change at all. From both the artistic and technological points of view, this is a consistent solution. But it might have unwanted consequences for listeners using earphones[28], because it means that they seem to take the place of the protagonist: the voice of the protagonist is placed in the middle of the listener's head. Although listeners only observe what the protagonist perceives and what he sings, they seem to be identical with him, they are part of the operatic scene. They are even attacked by the outside world through its sounds and noises, as is the protagonist. For instance, at the very beginning of the track *Dirt* an ›electric‹ sound seems to pass through the head of the listener-protagonist. But this is an extreme example of Lou Reed's artistic use of binaural or head-related recording. While listening to the record, it is possible to separate those noise attacks from Lou Reed's voice from those of the accompanying instrumental

---

27 The story is told in a song versus song technique.
28 Neither the LP nor the CD sleeve notes recommend the use of earphones.

parts of the music that appear around from different sides, either inside or next to the head. Instruments, voice, and other sounds each have their own defined places, or the move inside or outside the listener's head. This 3-D space concept continues in the next track of the album, the eponymous three-part track *Street Hassle*, which has no further sound attacks from outside, but a seemingly larger space outside the lyric self – i.e., the protagonist – and its double, the listener's self. ›Immersion‹ might be the best description for this game of identities. The listener is not only placed inside the operatic scene, but is also an integral part of it. The action happens to the listeners here, and they may feel forced, against their own will, into the album's dark virtual world with no chance to re-act themselves. So, even if the 3-D music was attractive, new, and exciting for listeners, the experience of being possessed by an unknown and strange voice inside the head – a voice that cannot be escaped – might be rather frightening, too.

The artistic design of an auditive space with *Kunstkopf* recordings does not, of course, necessarily include frightening experiences of immersion, as some radio plays produced later in the 1980s had shown (i.e., landscape portraits etc, see above). The decline of *Kunstkopf* productions since the late 1980s and early 1990s was, rather, a result of imperfect spatial images. Especially when sounds were intended to appear from the front, some listeners perceived it from the rear, while others heard it more to the right than centre. These problems were known as early as 1973, but could not be solved in the following years[29].

Listeners' Heads as Performance Space

It is only a few steps from spatial design for *Kunstkopf* recordings that include the listener's head to an art that conceives of the listener's head as a unique performance space. Although there are no direct connections to *Kunstkopf* recordings observable, in a series of art works for listener's head produced by Bernhard Leitner structural and historical similarities are obvious. Leitner is an internationally active architect and sound artist who, in the mid-1960s, began to create sounds and music as time-related sounding architecture; an activity he has continued to this very day. In 1986, after ten years of producing sound art for listeners' bodies that were transmitted by a *sound chair*, Leitner declared the human head as a projection space for his new art

---

29 The history of the *Kunstkopf* and *dummy heads* as audio recording devices will be described in full detail in a forthcoming book by the author.

series called *headscape music*[30]. As in *dummy head* recordings, listeners need earphones in order to hear the work properly.

At first Leitner produced sounds that were more or less centred in the head, with only small differences in localization occurring. Today he tries to project complex geometrical figures into listeners' heads. In 1986, as today, the sounds Leitner creates for his *headscape music* are complex, but single layered and only slowly changing, because Leitner wants to enable listeners to concentrate on the spatial aspects of his work and to perceive the creation of architecture through the moving sounds.

Today, Leitner's *headscape music* seems to be the only genuine audio art for listeners' heads that has survived. Nevertheless, for a while *Kunstkopf* art was of wide public interest. And for that reason it is one step forward in the development of spatial auditive art.

---

30 »Kopfräume«, in: Bernhard Leitner, *P.U.L.S.E.*, Ostfildern 2008, pp. 186–192, and Detlef B. Linke, »Zu den Kopfräumen«, in: op.cit., pp. 193–198.

Dispositive – Komposition und Technologie /

Dispositives – Composition and Technology

Space Impression Mediated by Sound

HELGA DE LA MOTTE-HABER

Does any music involve a space concept, though in a different manner? I start with a surprising citation from Igor Stravinsky's *Poetics of Music,* which should later be embedded in a broader context. It can be assumed that the following sentences are Stravinsky's own reflections and not those of his ghostwriter, Roland-Manuel. Stravinsky wrote:

»The *Saint Matthew Passion* of Johann Sebastian Bach is written for a chamber-music ensemble. Its first performance in Bach's lifetime was perfectly realized by a total force of thirty-four musicians, including soloists and chorus. That is known. And nevertheless in our days one does not hesitate to present the work, in complete disregard of composer's wishes, with hundreds of performers, sometimes almost a thousand. [...]The absurdity of such a practice is in point of fact glaring in every respect, and above all from the acoustic point of view. [...] Sound, exactly like light, acts differently according to the distance that separates the point of emission from the point of reception. A mass of performers situated on a platform occupies a surface that becomes proportionally larger as the mass become more sizable. By increasing the number of points of emission one increases the distances that separate these points from one another and from the hearer. So that the more one multiplies the points of emission, the more blurred will reception be.«[1]

SOUND REPRESENTED BY SPACE

It is well known that in the early modern period, solutions for the formal structure of pure instrumental music missing the support of words were emphasised by the spatial distribution of musicians. Giovanni Gabrieli's *Sonata*

---

1 Igor Stravinsky, *Poetics of Music* (1942), Cambridge (MA) 1970, pp. 129–130.

Pian e Forte and the *Symphoniae Sacrae* (both 1597) are mainly credited for
this innovation. Gabrieli arranged musicians in spatially separated groups in
the Basilica San Marco in Venice and, in this way, showed their mutual interactions, for example with softer repetitions providing the impression of an
echo, and other forms of antiphonic play. However, the real musical innovation of Gabrieli's music was the use of dynamics as a new musical form parameter. The spatial allocation of musicians was an intensification. During
the Baroque era, spatial distribution was often used for a musical performance. It disappeared with classical music. It therefore seems that the connection between spatial impressions and music no longer interested many
composers. The situation changed radically in the middle of the 1950s, when
the composers tried to overcome the punctual structure of serial music, for
which the concert hall was considered to be an empty container. A musical
structure, tone by tone, point by point, complying with the serial rule pro-
hibiting repetition, does not create a musical form. It is similar to a static
grid without a distinct beginning, middle, and end – having no formal development. Again, the search for form principles stimulated the use of spatial
effects. Karlheinz Stockhausen realized this form problem in his text »Musik
im Raum«[2] (1958): »Wenn nun alle Toneigenschaften sich beständig in glei-
chem Maß ändern, [...] so [bleibt] die Musik stehen.[...]. Und so fand man
die Lösung, verschieden lange Zeitphasen derart homogener Tonstrukturen
auf verschiedene [...] Instrumentengruppen im Raum zu verteilen. So wurde
es zunächst möglich, längere punktuelle Strukturen zu artikulieren, indem
man sie im Raum wandern ließ.« Changing the spatial position of a tone allowed the tone to be held onto for a longer time. It became possible to conceive a »*Zeitphase*« (time phase) that differs from the next state in its musical tone character. The exterior space served as an aid for creating richer
formal contrasts. Stockhausen's text referred to such important works as
Gruppen for three orchestras (1956). Many composers used spatialization in
the 1950s. Analogously to Stockhausen, Pierre Boulez noticed a standstill
produced by serial technique. He tried to overcome this through the conception of an architectural design (or representation?) that was identical to the
interior musical structure. For his *Poésie pour Pouvoir* (1958), the spiral organization of the twelve-tone series also dominated the interior structure as
the arrangement of the three orchestras and the loudspeakers. Boulez wrote,

---

2   Karlheinz Stockhausen, »Musik im Raum«, in: *Texte zur elektronischen und instru-
    mentalen Musik*, Band 1, Köln 1963, pp. 152–175, here pp. 154–155.

»the space served as an exponent of structural organization.«[3] (For a detailed analysis see the book by Gisela Nauck[4].)

For the *Diario Polacco '58*, Luigi Nono also used an arrangement of the positions of the musicians in the exterior space as a listening aid to facilitate the perception of characteristic sounding quality (»Wesensarten des Klangs«)[5].

During the 1950s, many composers were interested in the newly developed genre of electroacoustic music. Reflections on the position of loudspeakers became necessary. The idea of spatialization of loudspeakers did not differ from that of the instruments. In both cases, the space should make an inherent musical structure clear.

The first report on the *pupitre d'espace* (also called a *potentiomètre d'espace*) developed by Jacques Poullin, a coworker of Pierre Schaeffer, suggested this idea. The *pupitre d'espace* was created for the routing of monophonic *objets sonores* between five loudspeakers positioned around and above listeners (as an aside: it was used for the *Symphonie pour un homme seul*). The report on its first demonstration, made by Schaeffer himself in 1953, reads as follows: »The music thus came to one at varying intensity from various different parts of the room, and this 'spatial projection' gave sense to the rather abstract sequence of sound originally recorded.«[6] The elaboration in the architectonic space served as an enhancement for the listener's understanding of inherent musical characteristics. Nevertheless, all the pieces mentioned created veridical, additional impressions of the exterior space. Increasingly, composers tried to enrich their works through effects that required using the exterior space. *Avant la lettre*, Stockhausen created a form of Dolby Surround in *Gruppen*, forming a »*Raummelodie*« by a semi-circular arrangement of three trumpet players that fitted together, not only by pitch proximity, but primarily by overlapping *decrescendo* and *crescendo*, unifying different sounds under one amplitude envelope.

In the 1960s, Nono tried to convince the listener of the political message by such a vehemence of sound masses in the exterior space that the listener's mind and body were captivated by the music. For *A Floresta é Jovem e Chejdy de Vida* (1966), an electroacoustic piece of sampled sound (voice, in-

---

3   Pierre Boulez, *Musikdenken heute 2* (Darmstädter Beiträge zur Neuen Musik Bd. 6), Mainz 1963, p. 61.

4   Gisela Nauck, *Musik im Raum – Raum in der Musik: Ein Beitrag zur Geschichte der seriellen Musik*, Stuttgart 1977.

5   Luigi Nono, *Texte: Studien zu seine Musik*, edited by Jürg Stenzl, Zürich 1975, p. 124.

6   Peter Gradenwitz, The New York Times 9. 8. 1953, in: Elena Ungeheuer, *Wie die elektronische Musik »erfunden« wurde*, Mainz 1992, p. 152.

struments, copper plates) dedicated to the Vietnam Liberation Front, he created a combination of a virtual space with artificial reverberations and other
manipulated sounds with an intensive impact on the listeners. Loudspeakers
surrounded them; both from behind and with two 100-watt speakers at the
front. This sound bombardment from all angles was intended to have an
overwhelming effect on the listener.

The music of Iannis Xenakis should also not only be perceived as a »well
defined« object. Starting in the late 1950s (beginning with *Concrete PH* for
the Philips Pavilion at the 1958 World Fair in Brussels), but even more so in
the 1960s and 1970s, Xenakis was intrigued by the idea of dispersing sound
played by musical instruments or by loudspeakers in many different spatial
allocations. Without a doubt, *Persephassa* (1969), which had six percussionists arranged around the audience, created spatial effects. However, this
was mainly an unfolding of an interior musical space. Superimposed musical
layers are conceived as movements with different *tempi* pointing in different
directions by their increasing or decreasing dynamic level. Edgard Varèse
used similar techniques for his instrumental works. The spatial arrangement,
however, allows the listener to grasp more easily the inner structure. As Boris Hofmann[7] showed, *Persephassa* used a similar interior succession of spatial processes as *Terretektorh* – an orchestral piece where the listeners were
seated among the musicians. The audience had neither a common visual perspective, nor an acoustic one. Listeners are not confronted with sound, they
are immersed in it: they perceive a dynamic space that emerges from the
sound and envelops them. In other works, Xenakis liberates the listener from
a fixed position. In the *Polytopes* (since 1967), he became free to walk
around. Xenakis constructed the (hyperbolic) architecture by membranes in
such a way that a neutral acoustic space was created, in which the sound
could not be localized. Space served mainly to provoke the impression of an
energetic atmosphere. As with other artists, for example Edgard Varèse or
Piet Mondrian, Xenakis was influenced by the mathematical theory of space-
time. He also referred to the concept of Jean Piaget who, in opposition to
Immanuel Kant, proposed an internal coherence of time and space. Therefore, Xenakis created works with inherent spatiotemporal characteristics
based on abstract mathematical formulas valid for both categories, space and
time. The principle of rhythmical repetition, applied to the array of windows
for the monastery *La Tourette,* is the simplest one. It is also valid for chronological order, as well as for spatial sequences. A temporal musical structure

---

7   Boris Hofmann, *Mitten im Klang, Die Raumkompositionen von Iannis Xenakis aus
    den 1960er Jahren*, Hofheim 2008, pp. 116 ff.

can therefore be represented as a spatial architectonic structure, and vice versa.

The relation between the composed virtual space and the architectonic space was, and is, a special problem for electroacoustic composing. Meanwhile, good sound spatialization systems and control systems have been developed and promised to automatically transform the architectonic space into a virtual one. It is a disadvantage for the entanglement of the architectonic space with the interior musical space that electroacoustic composers work outside the performance space. Parameters of spatialization are approximated in a studio. They are adjusted during a rehearsal in the listening space, so that its architectonic space is compatible with the musical conception.

Every sound needs to appear in time and in the exterior space. Looking back to the beginning of this chapter, Stravinsky's remark shows that composers who do not intend to use sound distribution also have the spatial qualities of their work in mind. Recall the beginning of Franz Schubert's »Great« C-Major Symphony (No. 9, D. 944), with the soft and stretched repetition of the horn melody. The spatial effect of an echo is caused by the musical structure. It is not so complex that it needs to be radiated in the exterior space.

AN INTERIM SUMMARY

Compositional techniques differ to the extent that they need the exterior space.

1. There can be a constraint to reflecting the exterior space intensively if loudspeakers are employed.

2. Moreover, instrumental music with many simultaneous musical layers also becomes more easily comprehensible if these layers are projected in the architectonic space. The produced feeling of movement can, however, be provided by the rhythmic-temporal structure and, last but not least, by the dynamics. The exterior space is mostly a listening aid. Sometimes it is necessary to use the ability of the ear to locate sound at different locations in a room. For instance, the complex overlapped sound layers, text and music from various sources of Bernd Alois Zimmermann's *Requiem für einen jungen Dichter* (1967–1969) are not acoustically transparent and therefore not comprehensible itself without the assistance of spatial distribution.

3. Composers who intend immersion in the sounding field or an overwhelming effect need to fill the whole space around the audience. For them,

the exterior space is only a »better or worse« assistance to envelop the listener.

4. In all the above cases, space is comparable to an instrument – a violin, a trumpet, a drum, etc. – which has to be changed if it is inadequate. Concert halls have achieved the best quality for the performance of traditional music, yet often not for contemporary works. Therefore, many proposals are made for the best performance conditions of modern music. The new conceptions mostly have the form of a hemisphere, so that sound can be radiated from many angles. However, all the aforementioned composers present their works in different spaces. Comparable to traditional music, the independence of a specific concert hall is a guarantee for the identity of a work. The instruments or sound tools used, including the space, create only a better or worse representation. They are not directly presented. The space, as such, is not the medium in a narrower sense. I distinguish, therefore, between two different artistic intentions: on the one hand, sound represented in space, and on the other, space presented in sound. There are very few composers who present the exterior space by sound. It seems always necessary to make recourse to the music of Alvin Lucier and Maryanne Amacher.

SPACE PRESENTED BY SOUND

The American composer Alvin Lucier used the veridical acoustic information of a room for his compositions. After reading Donald R. Griffin's book *Listening in the Dark*, Lucier prepared his piece *Vespers* (1968) where an arbitrary number of performers with hand-held echolocation devices walked about in a darkened room. The echolocation devices emitted sharp fast clicks which, when sent out into the environment, returned as echoes carrying information on the shape, size, and substance of the environment and the objects in it. The performers had no orientation problems. However, *Vespers* is not only a piece that should draw our attention to spatial acoustic information processing. The listeners of the performance experience a manifold rhythmical piece. To attain additional musical relevance, Lucier used time organisation, because the repetition rate of the clicks could be changed and, thereby, the varying density of the piece gave rise to the impression of a musical form.

Amacher's compositions were space-time compositions. Loudspeakers emitted sounds blended with attributes of the space, of distances, of echoes, of structures of a staircase. Loudspeakers, sometimes directed against the wall, brought about specific frequencies. For her *Sound Joined Rooms*

(1980), Amacher explored special acoustic features by which several spaces could be connected to one another. She steered the sonic choreography of her performances through a mixing console. I assume that her play contains intuitive elements of improvisation between the sound configured by space and the listening process.

Is it the space that produces sound? John Cage's *One³* =4'33"(0'00") +♪ (1989) is very difficult to interpret. This piece is based on an instruction for a performer to arrange a sound system so that »the whole hall is on the edge of feedback, without actually feeding back«[8]. *One³* consists of the electronically amplified sound of the room, sometimes accompanied by audience noise. Nothing is performed. No measured time exists. Cage was convinced that only duration involves both sound and silence. Perhaps a moment of silence, which Cage himself could never reach, is implied in long-lasting duration. The hall itself is mirrored in sound and presented together with the idea that time is intrinsically linked with space.

In contrast to Cage, Agostino Di Scipio creates feedback loops of acoustic reflections for a new interactive, self-organized electroacoustic music. The sound of a space is mirrored again and again in the same space. The computer system ›plays‹ as if it were a new kind of music instrument«[9]. The sound is mainly an interface to show the self reference of an *Ecosystem*. The reverberating space, nevertheless, supplies the material.

REFLECTIONS ON THE LISTENER

A relationship of space and time shapes our perception of everyday life. On the one hand, the flying temporal sound event bears spatial information about a room's volume and furnishings, distances etc. On the other hand, the constitution of an object seen in our mind's eye also always implies a temporal change, a tiny change of visual viewpoint that allows the extraction of invariant components. The actual perceived space is in a continual flux. It is not an abstract geometrical construction. Moreover, reflections on space conceptions seem to be unsatisfactory without taking into account a holistic perception, because our sensory system constantly works with all of its modalities. They do not mediate just the same information, but they merge it in-

---

8   John Cage, *Complete Works*, hosted by John Cage Trust; www. johncage.org/pp/John-Cage-Works.cfm.
9   Agostino Di Scipio, »Sound I the interface: from interactive to ecosystemic signal processing«, in: Organised Sound, 8(3), 2003, pp. 269–277, here p. 269.

to each other. All our perception has a multisensory character. Beyond this entanglement of stimuli, the position and movement of a perceiver plays an important role, because any movement changes the visual, as well as the auditory, spatial impression. The *Polytopes* of Xenakis, with their luxurious light installations and, later on, sound installations, allowed the audience to experience the normal human intake action of spatial information by eye and ear.

The typically representative character of a concert fixes listeners to a seat. This artificial situation creates problems between the persistent visual and the varying auditory input of stimuli. The listening conditions are quite different, however, in the case of performing musicians or loudspeakers producing sounds. The traditional concert hall prescribes, by its almost sacrosanct atmosphere, a listening state. Moreover, elevated on the podium, musicians and their gestures attract attention[10]. Contemporary music without a podium but with a spatial distribution of musicians, whether or not it is accompanied by loudspeakers, gives similar visual input together with the sound[11].

Pure electroacoustic music is confined to one sensory modality. It represents a moving space by sound. It takes place within a hall that has additional visual spatial features. Therefore, the perceiver is confronted with the normal vision of a room and a simulated »vision« for the ear. A stopgap can be applied by suppressing the conflict between these two independent sensory inputs, e.g. extinguishing the light. In total darkness, where no action of the participants is possible (quite different from Lucier's piece), the simulated room may remind the perceiver of a nightmare. Using light installations instead of darkness turns the electroacoustic work into media art. I would like to mention briefly some effects that impede adequate information processing of pure electroacoustic music.

Vision does not dominate audition at all, except with respect to localization. Much research confirms the visual capture effect in the way that a mislocalization of the sound source takes place. That is an undesirable influence on the outcome of the artificial electro-musical design, because the virtual sounding space of electroacoustic simulation is fused with the real space. Only left-lateralized auditory cortical mechanisms ignore misalignment of

---

10 Rolf Inge Godøy and Marc Leman (ed.), *Musical Gestures, Sound Movement and Meaning*, New York 2000.

11 Before the 20th century, the listening process was not separated from visual information. The problems of iPod and similar playback devices are not the same as those of electroacoustic music. The difference, as such, is not of import here.

ear and eye in the case when we do not pay attention to the visual input[12]. This is not surprising, because the right cerebral hemisphere is responsible for the analysis of sounds and, moreover, for depth perception. The Colavita visual dominance effect[13] shows that human beings fail to respond to auditory stimuli even when visual and acoustic events are spatially co-located. Crossmodal interactions to multimodal inputs should not be disregarded at all[14]. These and other studies suggest an impact of the visible performance space on an electroacoustic performance, even though the visual information occurs outside one's focal range. In the realm of electroacoustic music, further reflections on listener's perception are necessary[15].

I conclude with a piece by Yoko Ono (1964)[16], which I pass on as a recommendation for your own private space[17]:

Tape Piece II
Room Piece
Take a sound of the room breathing
1) At dawn
2) In the morning
3) In the afternoon
4) In the evening
5) Before dawn
Bottle the smell of the room at that hour as well.

1963 Autumn

---

12 Julia A. Mossbrigde, Maria Grabowecky and Satoru Suzuki, »Seeing the Song: Left Auditory Structures May Track Auditory-Visual Dynamic«, PLOS PLoS ONE 8(10): e77201.doi:10.1371/journal.pone.0077201.
http://www.plosone.org/article/info%3Adoi%2F10.1371%2Fjournal.pone.0077201#pone-0077201-g003.

13 Francis B. Colavita, *Human Sensory Dominance*, Perception & Psychophysics 16(2), 1974, pp. 409 – 412.

14 Barry E. Stein and Alex M. Meredith, *The Merging of the Senses*, Cambridge (MA) 1986.

15 An exception is Guy Harries' doctoral dissertation, *The Electroacoustic and its Double Duality an Dramaturgy in Live Performance*, London: City University 2011; http//openaccess.city.ac.uk/1118/.

16 Yoko Ono, *Grapefruit: A Book of Instructions and Drawings*: Introduction by John Lemmon (1964); with a new introduction by the author, New York 2000 (pieces in chronological order).

17 I thank Dr. Fabian Czolbe drawing my attention to this piece.

Before and After *Kontakte*

Developments and Changes in Stockhausen's Approach
to Spatial Music in the 1960s and 1970s

ENDA BATES

INTRODUCTION

»You have overall visions, images which make demands of a kind you cannot yet realize, and they lead to the invention of new technical processes, but then the technical processes go their own way and become the starting point for other techniques which in turn pro- voke new intentions and you find yourself bombarded with images again.«[1]

Karlheinz Stockhausen is undoubtedly one of the most significant figures in the field of spatial music, and few other composers have focused so consist- ently and explicitly on this particular subject over such a long time period. Stockhausen discussed many aspects of his music in great detail throughout his long career, however, two articles published in 1958 and 1971, respec- tively, are of particular importance in terms of his approach to spatial music, namely »Music in Space«[2], and »Four Criteria of Electronic Music«[3]. The differences in these two articles illustrate how Stockhausen's approach to spatial music changed, reflecting both the significant technological changes and advances that occurred during this period, as well as the composer's changing aesthetical concerns.

Throughout Stockhausen's spatial music there is, on the one hand, a con- stant tension between the spatial effects desired by the composer and, on the

---

1 Karlheinz Stockhausen, in: *Stockhausen on Music*, Robin Maconie (ed.) London 1989.
2 Karlheinz Stockhausen, »Music in Space«, in: Die Reihe, Vol. 5 (1975), pp. 67–82, English translation by Ruth Koenig.
3 Karlheinz Stockhausen 1989, op.cit.

other, the actual capabilities of both the production tools and the particular loudspeaker array in question. While the importance of Stockhausen's *techné* has been explored elsewhere[4], this discussion has often concentrated on the composer's earliest and most well-known works. This article will therefore examine all of the electronic spatial works composed by Stockhausen during the 1960s and 70s in terms of the circular relationship between the composer's musical aesthetic and the practical means of production.

SPACE AS A MUSICAL PARAMETER

Broadly speaking, the use of space as a musical parameter can be considered in terms of three distinct categories. The first is based around the straight-forward distribution of static sources to different spatial locations. The remaining two categories are based on dynamically moving sounds, encompassing both the movement of sources at different distances from the listener, and on the horizontal (and perhaps vertical) movement of sources around the listener.

When Stockhausen began to compose works of electronic spatial music in the 1950s, he faced a dilemma as to how to actually make use of these types of dynamic spatial effects. A quite plausible (if not entirely realistic) sense of relative distance can be easily created using simple amplitude changes, spectral filtering, and artificial reverberation[5], and the technology to implement this type of effect was readily available in the 1950s. While the perceptual basis of this spatial effect was reasonably well understood, however, the very nature of this parameter made it difficult to incorporate within the overall serial framework favoured by Stockhausen at that time. As the perception of auditory distance depends on multiple variables, such as signal amplitude, spectrum, source recognition, etc., there is no single ›independent parameter‹ to be serialized. In contrast, the movement of sounds around the listener, which could seemingly be specified as a single, specific angle of orientation, or as a subset of loudspeakers, seemed very well suited to this type of compositional aesthetic. The technology to implement such dynamic spatial effects was, however, still very much in its infancy, with the only ex-

---

4 Peter Manning, »The Signficance of Techné in Understanding the Art and Practice of Electroacoustic Composition«, in: Organised Sound, 11, (2006), pp. 81–90.
5 John Chowning, »The Simulation of Moving Sound Sources«, in: Journal of the Audio Engineering Society, 19 (1971), pp. 2–6.

amples being idiosyncratic devices like the *potentiomètre d'espace*[6] or Disney's *Fantasound* system[7]. In addition, the technical and perceptual basis of stereophony was still not very well understood, and indeed its limitations would not be fully appreciated until the emergence and eventual failure of Quadraphonics, nearly two decades later[8].

Stockhausen first attempted to address these issues in the article »Music in Space«, which was published in 1958. As we shall see, certain ideas presented in this article, such as the serialization of horizontal direction, would later be abandoned as the composer gained experience with the practical limitations of the technology. In contrast, other ideas, such as the presentation of multiple layers of material from different spatial locations, would be a consistent and effective feature of his work.

BEFORE *KONTAKTE*: EARLY SPATIAL WORKS

In »Music in Space« Stockhausen suggests that the spatial distribution and movement of sounds is a necessary aspect of pointillist, serially organized music for two reasons. First, the presentation of multiple, concurrent layers of complex material from different locations allows the listener to perceive these layers as separate entities, rather than the single, dense layer that would be perceived if these layers were presented from the same location (now well known as the *cocktail party effect*). American composers such as Charles Ives or Henry Brant often made use of spatially separated sources for this reason and conceivably influenced Stockhausen's approach in this regard.

Gruppen was composed while the composer was still working on *Gesang der Jünglinge* and there are many similarities in how the composer approached the use of space in both of these works. Both works attempt to create the more fragile illusion of sounds that are dynamically moving in space, and the idea of spatial movement was highly attractive to Stockhausen as a solution to a problem which can occur when every musical parameter is serially controlled. In this type of pointillist music, »all musical elements had equal rights in the forming process and constantly renewed all their charac-

---

6   Jonty Harrison, »Sound, Space, Sculpture: Some Thoughts on the ›What‹, ›How‹ and ›Why‹ of Sound Diffusion«, in: Organised Sound, 3(2), 1999, pp. 117–127.

7   William E. Garity and Hawkins, J.N.A., »Fantasound«, in: Journal of the Society of Motion Picture Engineers, August 1941.

8   Günther Theile and Georg Plenge, *Localization of Lateral Phantom Sources*, in: Journal of the Audio Engineering Society, Vol. 25, 1976, pp. 196–200.

teristics from one sound to the next«[9]. If the pitch, duration, timbre, and dynamic of each sound are constantly changing, this can actually lead to a static texture in which ›the music stands still‹. One solution to this stasis is to let one parameter dominate for some time, however, this would undermine the very aesthetic of total serialism, which gave rise to this problem in the first place. Stockhausen's solution, therefore, is to use the dynamic spatialization of sounds to create and articulate longer structures from this serially organized material.

The movement of sounds in both these works was achieved using a basic form of amplitude panning. In *Gruppen,* and the later instrumental work *Carré* (1959–1960), this was attempted using similar instrumentation in three or four spatially distributed groups, with somewhat mixed results[10]. For the electronic work *Gesang der Jünglinge,* horizontal spatial movement was achieved using simple fader adjustments. For faster or more complex trajectories, the source material would be first played back at half speed while the required fader movements are applied and recorded, before finally playing back the recording at double speed to achieve the required tempo.

Gesang der Jünglinge was initially based on five channels of audio and five associated loudspeakers but was later mixed down to just four tracks. It is often reported that this fifth loudspeaker was to be suspended from the ceiling[11], however, recent research strongly suggests that this may not have been the case and that all five loudspeakers were actually intended to be placed around the audience[12]. It is worth noting that in the accompanying CD booklet Stockhausen places equal importance to distributed static sources, horizontal movement, and distance effects[13], and indeed, the spatial distance – especially of the boy's voice – is clearly a highly important aspect of this work. Here the composer links the spatial distance to the comprehensibility of the voice. In this way, Stockhausen was able to serialize the parameter of distance in this particular work, by relating this parameter to a scale of lexical comprehensibility. As we can see from his writing on the

9 Karlheinz Stockhausen 1975, op.cit.

10 Cornelius Cardew, »Report on Stockhausen's ›Carré‹«, in: The Musical Times, 102, No. 1424 (Oct., 1961), pp. 619–622.

11 E.g. Michael Manion 1994, *From Tape Loops to MIDI: Karlheinz Stockhausen's Forty Years of Electronic Music,* http://www.stockhausen.org/tape_loops.html (3.06. 2014).

12 Pascal Decroupet, Elena Ungeheuer, and Jerome Kohl, »Through the Sensory Looking-Glass: The Aesthetic and Serial Foundations of ›Gesang der Jünglinge‹«, in: Perspectives of New Music, 36, No. 1 (1998), pp. 97–142.

13 Karlheinz Stockhausen, *Electronic Music 1952–1960,* translated from Stockhausen 1964 by Richard Toop, Text booklet for Stockhausen Complete Edition CD 3 1992.

topic from this time, however, it was not clear to Stockhausen how this approach could be extended to instrumental or electronic sounds without an associated text.

STOCKHAUSEN'S DILEMMA

At the time of writing »Music in Space«, Stockhausen was therefore faced with a number of technical and perceptual challenges in terms of how these types of dynamic spatial effects could be incorporated effectively within a serially organized work. As we have seen, the exact way in which spatial distance was to be used within this type of serialist aesthetic was also still uncertain. Stockhausen largely avoids the latter issue in »Music in Space«, merely stating that as spatial distance depends on a number of different factors, it cannot be treated as an independent parameter and therefore cannot be serially controlled, outside of certain limited conditions[14]. Stockhausen has often been criticized for dismissing every type of spatialization except for horizontal direction[15,16]. There is indeed a certain contradiction between the limited discussion of spatial distance in this article, and the extensive use of this parameter by the composer in his music at that time. But while Stockhausen certainly does state that spatial distance is not suitable for serialization, this is not at all the same as dismissing this parameter entirely.

While Stockhausen's description of the perception of spatial distance is quite accurate, in »Music in Space« he does not describe how this parameter might be used in a work of spatial music. In contrast, horizontal spatial movements are discussed in great detail as Stockhausen attempts to create an analogy between proportions of time (pitch, duration, timbre) and space, using proportional changes in horizontal direction around a notional, continuous circle surrounding the listener[17]. This idea of ›serializing the circle‹ has been widely criticized, and with some justification. Critics argue that the absolute directions specified on paper will not be perceived by the audience[18,19], and this view is supported by a significant amount of experimental

---

14 Stockhausen 1975, op.cit.
15 Maria Anna Harley, »Spatiality of Sound and Stream Segregation in 20th-Century Instrumental Music«, in: Organised Sound, 3(2) (1998), pp. 147–166.
16 Timothy Schmele, *Exploring 3D Audio as a New Musical Language*, Master's Thesis, Music Technology Group, Department of Information and Communication Technologies, Universitat Pompeu Fabra, 2011.
17 Stockhausen 1975, op.cit.
18 Jonty Harrison, op.cit.
19 Anna Maria Harley 1998, op.cit.

data[20]. It is now known that significant variations in perceived source direction will occur with electronic spatialization systems when only four loudspeakers are used, particularly for sounds to the sides or rear, and a reliable and absolute perception of direction is difficult to achieve in practice. It is therefore extremely difficult to see how the scale of localities proposed by Stockhausen in »Music in Space« could be achieved with sufficient resolution. However, although it is clear now that this approach is problematic, it is important to remember the time period in which it was proposed. The limitations of stereophony were not at all fully understood in 1958 and, in fact, would not be for many years to come. While Stockhausen undoubtedly overestimated the capabilities of stereophony in this case, this misplaced optimism was perhaps understandable. And, as we shall see, the composer would move away from this idea quite quickly.

Stockhausen would attempt to put these ideas into effect in *Kontakte*, which is – in many respects – the last attempt by the composer to implement a totally organized music in which every parameter (timbre, pitch, intensity, duration, movement, and location) is serially controlled. The composition of this work, however, also involved a significant amount of practical experimentation in the studio and the creation of new production tools such as the famous *rotation table* (*Rotationstisch*), which would have a significant influence on Stockhausen's entire approach to spatialization.

FIRST WE SHAPE OUR TOOLS …

The change in character and increase in extent of dynamic spatial effects in *Kontakte*, compared to *Gesang der Jünglinge*, is quite noticeable even in the stereo versions of these works. These dynamic spatial effects were created using one of the most unusual and notable aspects of this piece, namely the rotating loudspeaker mechanism. This device, which was created for Stockhausen in 1959 by the technicians at WDR, was in many respects a highly unusual approach to adopt. A constant-power panpot had been developed years previously for Disney's *Fantasound* system[21] and the technicians at WDR were certainly aware of other possible approaches[22]. The decision to develop a spatialization device based on a physically rotating loudspeaker

---

20 Enda Bates, E. *The Composition and Performance of Spatial Music*, PhD thesis, Trinity College Dublin 2009.
21 Garity and Hawkins, op.cit.
22 Peter Manning 2006, op.cit.

must therefore have been a deliberate choice which raises some interesting questions in terms of the imperatives behind this decision.

The original *rotation table* device consisted of a circular plate mounted on ball bearings, which could be rotated by hand at speeds of up to approximately 5 to 6 rps[23]. The horizontal facing loudspeaker was about 8 inches in diameter and fitted with an extended cone to increase the directionality of reproduced sound. A single, monophonic channel of audio was routed to the rotating loudspeaker while four microphones positioned around the table were used to record the panned signal onto a four-track tape machine. If the four channels of the tape machine were played back on consecutive loudspeakers, this would result in a rotational trajectory, however, Stockhausen also attempted to create other trajectories by adjusting the routing of the tape machine to the array. As with *Gesang der Jünglinge,* faster trajectories were achieved by first playing the source signal into the *rotation table* at half speed, recording the desired movement and then finally playing back the four-channel recording at double speed[24]. The differences between this type of approach and simple amplitude panning should not be underestimated, as the physically rotating loudspeaker mechanism used here will alter the source material in a quite complex manner. Recording a real, moving source will result in complex Doppler effects, time varying filtering, phase shifts, off-axis coloration as the speaker changes position, and other distortions that are difficult to recreate using solely electronic means.

The initial sketches for *Kontakte* contain performance plans, which describe in detail how these different spatial movements were to be implemented with the *rotation table*[25]. As pointed out by Manning and others[26], the manual operation of the *rotation table* was an important and sometimes overlooked aspect of this device, as these physical gestures supported the expressive performance of spatial movements. The rotating electronic sounds in *Kontakte* do not move at fixed, static speeds but instead speed up and slow down in a highly expressive and musical fashion that is a direct result of this ›physical performance‹ with the *rotation table*. Indeed, Stockhausen's performance plans for the *rotation table* include comments such as *accell.* and *rit.* which are more commonly associated with tempo changes in

---

23 Karlheinz Stockhausen, »Die Zukunft der elektroakustischen Apparaturen in der Musik«, Summary of a presentation at the 9th Tonmeistertagung 1972 in Cologne, in: Musik und Bildung, Nr. 7–8 (1974).

24 ibid.

25 Paul Miller, *Stockhausen and the Serial Shaping of Space.* Ph.D. diss. Rochester, Eastman School of Music 2009.

26 Manning 2006, op.cit.

instrumental performances[27]. As we shall see, Stockhausen would always seek to retain some form of manual control over spatialization, even once digital technologies had developed to the point where the trajectories and rotation speeds could be precisely specified in advance.

In *Kontakte*, distance is often used in a structural sense to delineate different sections, however, the most important use of this type of spatial effect developed in *Kontakte* is the creation and the contrasting of different layers of material at different spatial distances. Stockhausen would return to this idea in later works, and it would play an important part in the composer's later approach to spatial music and, particularly, the idea of the »multi-layered spatial composition«[28]. Although the *rotation table*, owing to its manual operation, could only achieve speeds of up to approx. 5–6 rps, faster rotation speeds (up to about 30 rps) could be achieved by using repeated tape speed adjustments, as before[29]. Although this first version of the *rotation table* was somewhat limited in its ability to achieve such high-speed rotations, the idea was clearly attractive to Stockhausen and would play an important part in later works.

LIVE ELECTRONIC MUSIC & *TELEMUSIK*

Stockhausen's musical aesthetic changed in many ways through the 1960s, reflecting perhaps the significant cultural and political changes which occurred during this decade. In particular, the composer would move away somewhat from totally organized music to embrace new ideas such as live electronics, indeterminacy, and variable forms. The use of live electronics was a particular focus for the first half of the decade, and the spatial projection of these sounds would be a major influence on the composer's approach to spatialization in subsequent performances at the 1970 World's Fair at Osaka.

In the period from 1964 to 1965 Stockhausen composed a trio of works, namely *Mixtur* (1964), *Mikrophonie I* (1964), and *Mikrophonie II* (1965), in which electronic processes and transformations are realized in real-time during the performance. In each of these works, live performers are manually processed using different filters and modulation processes before being spatialized to a four-channel loudspeaker system. The composer himself would often serve as the sound projectionist for these works, using multiple poten-

---

27 Paul Miller 2009, op.cit.
28 Karlheinz Stockhausen 1989, op.cit.
29 Karlheinz Stockhausen 1974, op.cit.

tiometers to control the distribution and, to a certain extent, the movement of sounds around the four loudspeakers. The experience of composing, rehearsing and performing these works must have been quite informative and revealing in terms of the practical abilities and limitations of four-channel spatial audio systems, particularly in a performance context.

Telemusik (1966) was Stockhausen's first studio-based electronic composition since *Kontakte* six years before. In terms of its spatialization, however, this piece is in many respects much closer to the antiphonal interaction of spatially distributed sounds in *Gesang der Jünglinge*. Stockhausen did not, of course, have access to the *rotation table* while in Japan, and this is perhaps one of the reasons why horizontal movement plays such a small role in *Telemusik*. Throughout this work, Stockhausen uses spatial distance to differentiate multiple layers of material, but also to articulate sounds in a highly expressive manner, such as, for example, the repeated percussive sound that starts in the left channel at 8'50" before moving off into the distance as its timbre undergoes extensive modulation.

HYMNEN

Hymnen (1966–67) was constructed from numerous recordings of national anthems, combined with a wide variety of synthesized and found sounds. There are four movements, which the composer describes as ›regions‹ (which are in turn divided into different centres), with a total duration of approximately two hours. In much the same way as *Kontakte*, *Hymnen* exists as both a purely electronic work for four loudspeakers, and as an electroacoustic work for live instruments and tape.

In certain respects, *Hymnen* is an extension of the ideas and techniques developed in both *Telemusik* and *Kontakte*. Stockhausen's original intention for *Kontakte* was for the live musicians to freely respond and imitate material on the tape, however, this proved difficult in practice and so the idea was abandoned and a fixed score was used instead. National anthems were therefore deliberately chosen as the primary source material in *Hymnen* to provide highly recognizable material (for both the players and the audience), which could be more readily imitated[30]. As with *Telemusik*, a variety of rhythmic, harmonic, and dynamic modulation processes are used to forge connections between different types of material, but the material is here ar-

---

30 Robin Maconie, *Through the Looking Glass: Robin Maconie Revisits Hymnen, Karlheinz Stockhausen's Electroacoustic Classic of the 1960s*, in: The Musical Times, 139, no. 1863, 1998.

ranged in a much more elaborate ›spatial polyphony‹, in which both horizontal movement and distance are used extensively. The way in which the
movement and distribution of sounds is integrated within the dreamlike, radio drama of *Hymnen* is, however, very different to the totally organized approach of earlier works such as *Kontakte*. Instead of a top–down approach in
which different parameters (spatial or otherwise) are organized according to
an abstract, numerical scale, in *Hymnen* the spatialization – and indeed the
entire form of the work – was created from the bottom–up in a largely intuitive manner[31]. Distance effects are used extensively in *Hymnen*, both to differentiate multiple layers of material, and also to expressively articulate material and create a sense of perspective. In addition, spatial distance is used
as a large-scale structural device, as extended periods of very distant and
therefore very quiet material is generally used to transition between the different centres of each region.

The use of very fast trajectories and rotational effects, first briefly explored in *Kontakte,* is quite prominent in *Hymnen*, and Stockhausen would
subsequently return to this idea many times. This technique did, however,
reveal some limitations of the original four-channel *rotation table*, as these
fast trajectories tended to result in a significant amount of Doppler shift and
a certain choppiness in the resulting sound. The latter distortion was somewhat disguised in *Hymnen* by the various amplitude and modulation processes used in the piece, which produced a somewhat similar audible result,
albeit without a Doppler shift (one example of this distortion can be found
right at the end of Region II). This issue, along with the nonsuitability of this
device for live performances, meant that new spatialization devices would be
subsequently developed for works such as *Sirius*.

Stockhausen had expressed a desire for new types of concert halls specifically designed for the performance of electronic spatial music as far back
as 1958[32] and a few years after *Hymnen* he would get his wish. The elaborate
auditorium built specifically for Stockhausen at the 1970 World Fair in Osaka was a dramatic improvement on the basic four-channel system he had
used up to this point, and the auditorium was unsurprisingly extremely well
suited to the types of spatial effects of interest to the composer at that time.

---

31 Karlheinz Stockhausen 1989, op.cit.
32 Karlheinz Stockhausen 1975, op.cit.

OSAKA 70 AND LIVE SPATIALIZATION

»New halls for listening must be built to meet with demands of spatial music. My idea would be to have a spherical chamber, a platform, transparent to both light and sound, would be hung for the listeners. They could hear music coming from above, from below and from all directions.«[33]

The spherical auditorium in which Stockhausen performed during the 1970 World Fair in Osaka was, in many respects, a realization of the composer's ideal form of venue for spatial music. The building consisted of a geodesic dome constructed from a steel frame and multiple layers of acoustically absorbent material. Inside the auditorium, the audience was positioned on an acoustically transparent platform just below the centre of the sphere and seated on benches facing the centre of the platform. The loudspeakers were arranged in seven layers at different heights; two layers of five loudspeakers each at the top and bottom – and, hence, narrowest in diameter – of the sphere, and three layers of ten loudspeakers at the widest portion of the sphere.

The custom-built control desk in the German Pavilion at Osaka received the microphone signals from the soloists and the multichannel output of a tape machine, and these could then be spatialized to the loudspeaker array in two different ways. First, a number of push buttons could be used to quickly position a signal at a single loudspeaker by routing that mixer channel to one of seven master channels (which could be allocated to any of the loudspeakers in the array). Alternatively, a signal could be routed to one of two *rotation mills*, specially designed for Stockhausen, which could then pan the signal around a subset of loudspeakers in the array. Each *rotation mill* consisted of a rotary handle that, when manually turned at a maximum speed of approximately 6–7 rps, would consecutively route the monophonic input signal among ten outputs. These outputs could be connected to any of the loudspeakers in the array. In this way, a large number of different trajectories could be achieved by altering which loudspeakers were connected to the outputs of the *rotation mill*, in much the same way as the *rotation table*[34]. While repatching the outputs of the *rotation table* could, however, produce diagonal and other nonrotational trajectories (whose effectiveness over four loudspeakers is questionable), the spherical nature of the venue at Osaka and its multiple rings of loudspeakers could potentially support many different

---

33 Karlheinz Stockhausen 1975, op.cit.
34 Karlheinz Stockhausen *Spiral, für einen Solisten, Nr. 27* (UE14957), Wien 1973.

types of rotational trajectories. Apart from simple clockwise or counter-clockwise rotations in the horizontal plane, Stockhausen could now create vertical or diagonal rotations, or even spiral effects if used in conjunction with distance effects[35]. While this type of three-dimensional spatialization was certainly possible at Osaka, when Stockhausen later attempted to create similar effects using a much smaller number of loudspeakers, the results were far less effective, illustrating how the effectiveness of any spatial strategy depends greatly on the particular loudspeaker array in question.

THE MULTILAYERED SPATIAL COMPOSITION

Following the performances at Osaka 70, Stockhausen published a new article describing his approach to spatialization entitled »Four Criteria of Electronic Music«. Instead of the prescribed, numerical organization of space presented earlier, Stockhausen now proposed a much less systematic approach, in which horizontal direction, distance, and trajectory are all used in a far more relative fashion. In place of a fixed perspective (perhaps such as the ›scale of localities‹ proposed earlier), Stockhausen now proposed the idea of a ›multilayered spatial composition‹ and the creation of multiple, different perspectives through the positioning and movement of different layers of material. While we have already seen how Stockhausen used different static locations to distinguish and clarify different, concurrent layers of material, he now suggests that spatial distance can be used in a similar fashion. Instead of a concurrent presentation, different layers can be consecutively presented by cutting a dense foreground layer to reveal another layer at a greater distance[36].

Stockhausen's article also describes how different types of trajectories (rotations, spirals, loops, alterations, etc.) can be used to characterize and distinguish different sounds. In this way, specific trajectories can be used, like static locations and spatial distance, as another means of articulating different layers of material, rather than in an absolutist fashion which requires the recognition or relating of specific spatial paths. While this avoids the overly absolutist and systematic organization of space proposed earlier, there is no doubt that this approach was strongly influenced by the experience of performing at Osaka. It is not surprising that a venue built largely to Stockhausen's own specifications would be well suited to this type of spatializa-

---

35 Jonathan Cott, *Stockhausen: Conversations with the Composer*, New York 1973.
36 Karlheinz Stockhausen 1989, op.cit.

tion, the effectiveness of this approach with a more basic loudspeaker array is far from assured. The spherical venue at Osaka was particularly appropriate for rotational trajectories, as the multiple layers of loudspeakers supported not only horizontal rotations but also diagonal and even vertical rotations around the audience. In later works such as *Oktophonie* (1991), Stockhausen would again attempt to create similar trajectories using a much more basic eight-channel system (consisting of two vertically separated four-channel arrays). This reliance on stereophonic panning to position sounds at different heights and to create trajectories with a vertical component is, however, problematic, as amplitude panning is unreliable in the vertical domain[37]. In the horizontal domain as well, the experience of Osaka must have been quite revealing as the performance of even a single horizontal layer, which at Osaka contained ten loudspeakers, would have been a significant improvement on the rather minimal, four-channel system employed previously. Clearly some compromise between these two extremes was needed, and Stockhausen outlined the requirements of such a system in an article from 1972 entitled *The Future of Electroacoustic Apparatus in Music*[38]. In this article, Stockhausen recommended the adoption of an eight-loudspeaker system as a new standard, and this arrangement would in fact be used by him for the rest of his career, beginning with his next major electronic work, *Sirius* (1975–77).

The description of the other desired improvements in spatialization hardware discussed in this article is quite revealing in terms of Stockhausen's priorities at the time when it came to spatialization. The creation of very high-speed trajectories had long been of interest to Stockhausen, and he repeatedly mentions the need for continuous user-control of the speed of different preplanned trajectories. All of these recommendations would be realized in the new hardware designed for Stockhausen just a few years later. These new tools would be used in the composition of *Sirius*, which was also one of the first works by Stockhausen to employ commercial synthesizers, namely the EMS Synthi 100. In many respects this composition was a highpoint of the analogue era, particularly in terms of Stockhausen's electronic music, which would, from that point on, enter a period of technological flux in which analogue and digital hardware were both in use.

---

37 V. Pulkki, and M. Karjalainen, »Directional Quality of 3-D Amplitude-Panned Virtual Sources«, in: *Proceedings of the Seventh International Conference on Auditory Display* (ICAD 2001), pp. 239–244.

38 Karlheinz Stockhausen 1972, op.cit.

SIRIUS AND THE END OF THE ANALOGUE ERA

»Sirius is based entirely on a new concept of spatial movement. The sound moves so fast in rotations and slopes and all sorts of spatial movements that it seems to stand still, but it vibrates.«[39]

The Synthi 100 used in *Sirius* was one of the first analogue synthesizers with a built-in sequencer that could be used to store and execute control voltages. Although quite difficult to program, this functionality was well suited to the intermodulation processes of interest to Stockhausen at the time. The speed at which sequences were played back could be controlled by a clock or could be manually adjusted using either the five-octave keyboard, faders, or joysticks. The ability to speed up melodic and rhythmic material to the point at which it is perceived instead as timbre had also long been of interest to Stockhausen, and this process would be used extensively in *Sirius*. Although Stockhausen does not explicitly state the connection, the ability to similarly control the speed of spatial trajectories is clearly another way of creating this idea of a unified time structure discussed earlier[40].

To implement these very high-speed spatial trajectories, a new version of the four-channel *rotation table* was designed that could be rotated by a remote-controlled motor[41]. The increased number of channels, and the high speeds that could be achieved using the motor (up to approximately 35 rps) could be used to rotate sounds at such a velocity that the perception of a clear trajectory disappears (clearly audible in the opening of *Sirius)*. As with previous versions of this device, the mechanical rotation of the loudspeaker resulted in complex Doppler effects and modulation of the spatialized sound. However, *Sirius* would also be the first time that Stockhausen made use of joystick-style panners, which would not contain these types of Doppler effects, namely the *Quadrophonic Effect Generator* (*QUEG*) developed by EMS. This change in interface was perhaps intended to support the movement of sounds through the listening area, rather than just around or beyond the edges of the loudspeaker array, something which had long been a goal of Stockhausen's. However, this approach is potentially problematic as although a joystick interface could be positioned at points inside the listening area, the fact remains that simple stereophony cannot really create sounds that are closer than the loudspeakers. The *QUEG* device used here, just like

---

39 Felder, D. and K. Stockhausen, *An Interview with Karlheinz Stockhausen*, in: Perspectives of New Music, 16, No. 1, (1977), pp. 85–101.
40 Karlheinz Stockhausen 1989, op.cit.
41 Karlheinz Stockhausen 1974, op.cit.

many panners used in digital audio workstations (DAWs), attempts to create the impression of sounds inside the array by simply feeding the source signal into a greater number of loudspeakers. While this may be reasonably effective for fast movements through the listening area, it is not the case that stereophony can create reliable phantom images inside the array, and this is particularly true in a performance context.

CONCLUSION

»Some time ago I suffered a terrible shock listening to my *Elektronische Studie II* (Electronic Study II) in the electronic music studio at Stockholm University, which has a very up-to-date synthesizer. It was a performance realized, according to the instructions published in the score, but without my collaboration. Well, what happened? It was awful. A farce, to say the least, a caricature of the work. Why? Because they let the computer handle the dynamic curves of the sound (Hüllkurven) which I had regulated, on the contrary, with manual controls. Hence the static quality.«[42]

It is often said that first we shape our tools, and thereafter our tools shape us. This is particularly true in the context of spatial electronic music, however, this fact is often overlooked in today's digital age. The staggering capabilities of today's computers can sometimes disguise the way in which software lock-in and specific design choices have a profound influence on how we approach composing music. A composer's relationship with the materials, form, and spatialization of a particular work of music is ultimately mediated by both the means of production and of reproduction. The particular panning device used will influence the types of spatial trajectories created, however, the particular loudspeaker array ultimately used to perform the piece is also critically important. Much of Stockhausen's spatial music displays a tension between the types of trajectories and spatialization he could implement in the studio and what was actually effective in a performance context. This is the primary difficulty with space as a musical parameter, as what might be possible for a single listener, or with a particular array, may not work in other contexts.

The preceding discussion has outlined some of these difficulties in terms of Stockhausen's early works of spatial music. What, however, does this imply for modern DAW-based spatialization tools? Graphical interfaces often deceptively suggest that a source can be positioned at any point inside the array with the same degree of accuracy and reliability as sources placed on its

---

42 Mya Tannenbaum, *Conversations with Stockhausen*, Oxford 1987.

boundaries, and the graphical depiction of spatial trajectories can similarly be quite misleading. For example, the trajectories shown below are visually different, but if these are implemented using a simple stereophony, how audible will these differences actually be? In reality, trajectory (c) will audibly manifest as a smoother version of trajectories (a) and (b), and not as the closer trajectory suggested by the graphic. Tools such the *rotation table* and *sound mill* are far more restrictive in their focus on simple rotations, but they are perhaps also less deceptive in terms of their actual capabilities.

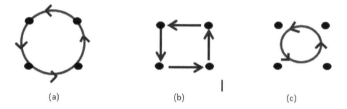

(a)   (b)   (c)

Stockhausen's insistence on a hands-on working method in the studio is perhaps one of the most significant aspects of his approach to spatialization. Although his writings often suggest a conception of musical space based on absolute numerical specifications of angle, speed, or distance, Stockhausen's actual working method involved a large degree of experimentation in which different spatial effects and trajectories were manipulated by hand in the studio. This physical performance created a sense of gesture that Stockhausen considered to be absolutely vital, as evidenced by the quote at the start of this article.

Throughout his long career, Karlheinz Stockhausen constantly tested the limits of the musical parameter of space. Although at times his demands were based on incorrect assumptions, or were greater than what the technology could actually deliver, these errors are as revealing as his successes in terms of what they uncover about the composition and performance of spatial music. Understanding how and why Stockhausen's approach changed over the years can provide valuable insights into the circular relationship between the composer's musical aesthetic, and the practical means of production; an issue as relevant today as it was fifty years ago.

Aspects of Space in Luigi Nono's *Prometeo* and the Use of the *Halaphon*

MARTHA BRECH AND HENRIK VON COLER

Luigi Nono integrated space into his music since his earliest compositions. While he worked in the Freiburg Experimental Studio at the SWR (1980 to 1990) he came to know the electroacoustic devices that were invented there for concerts with live electronic music. In particular, the *Halaphon* for controlling spatial sound movements (constructed by the head of the Experimental Studio, Hans Peter Haller, together with his friend, the engineer Peter Lawo) had a significant impact on Nono's work. The *Halaphon* enabled both automatic and interactive movement of sound by amplitude panning, organized in user-defined programs. It was designed specifically for live performances and concerts, and so was unique among all other devices for sound movement in this period. With its use, Nono made further developments in both his lifelong work on space composition and his broader concern with ›wandering‹ into a disembodied movement of sound in the concert hall.

Among Nono's compositions of the Freiburg period, *Prometeo, tragedia dell'ascolto (Prometheus, Tragedy of Listening,* composed 1984–1985) has special significance. It is regarded as one of the most elaborate spatial compositions of its time and is still performed today. For its first performances a huge wooden construction was built, containing both the audience and the performers. Orchestra, soloists, and choir were seated in different locations and levels that were ›connected‹ by electroacoustic sounds that wandered or were sometimes distant. Although room acoustics, localization of sources, and sound movements within the audible space are essential, they are rarely mentioned in the literature about *Prometeo.*

In this chapter, we will take initial steps to fill this gap in the literature and to show with a few examples how Nono composed audible space as an integral part of *Prometeo.* To this end, the presentation of both the compositional and the technological aspects of the work are essential. Because the collaboration between Nono and Haller was based in its day on a strict separation of the musical and technological components, most of the *Prometeo* material is currently located in different places. To reconstruct the sound movements and aspects of audible space in the composition, the material kept in both Nono's and Haller's archives, and in other places, has to be carefully combined. Additionally, the *Halaphon* should be described. Of course, the acoustical properties of the wooden construction built for this performance are also important.

Figure 1: »Prometeo« Performance space (»arca«, »struttura«) in San Lorenzo, Venice 1984. It was subdivided by the Baroque-style iconostasis, where Nono, Haller, and the sound director were seated on a scaffold above the audience, which was, in turn, seated below. The musicians and singers are to be seen at the first and second levels at the balconies.

From: Jürg Stenzl, *Luigi Nono*, Reinbek 1998, p. 114

THE TECHNOLOGY OF THE *HALAPHON*

The *Halaphon* was used to control spatial sound movements, rather than to otherwise process the sounds. After first experiments with electromechanical devices for sound diffusion, the general principle of the *Halaphon* had been developed using analogue circuitry at the end of the 1960s[1]. In the course of its development, the *Halaphon* increasingly made use of digital technology. Of special interest for the performances of *Prometeo* are the *Halaphon III* (constructed in 1976) and the *Halaphon IV* (constructed autumn 1984), which were used in Venice and Milan, respectively. Both devices were similar in principle but different in operation and capabilities.

Basically, the sound movements controlled by the *Halaphon* work on the principle of phantom sound sources: a sound seems to move because the balance of volume within a configuration of loudspeakers is altered. In a two-channel set-up, a movement from left to right would be produced when the loudspeaker on the left-hand side is constantly reduced in volume while the volume is increased at the loudspeaker on the right-hand side. Therefore, the function of the *Halaphon* is to control the volume of each loudspeaker included in a sound path (see below for *Prometeo*). In the *Halaphon* this is done by the use of a combination of ›envelopes‹ and ›gates‹ as shown in figure 2. ›B‹ marks the input of the ›envelope‹ to a ›gate‹, a voltage controlled amplifier (VCA) that increases or decreases the volume of the sound to be moved (›A‹) and is directly routed to a loudspeaker.

Figure 2: Sound level at ›A‹ is controlled by signal ›B‹ in ›gate‹

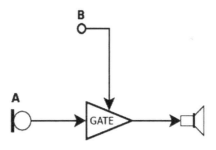

The ›envelopes‹ of infrasonic frequencies control[2] the speed of the sound movement, while their curves control their mode (see figure 3).

---

1 Hans Peter Haller, *Das Experimentalstudio der Heinrich-Strobel-Stiftung des Süd-westfunks Freiburg 1971–1989: Die Erforschung der Elektronischen Klangumformung und ihre Geschichte* (2 volumes), volume 1, Baden-Baden 1995, p. 20.

2 »Die Hüllkurvengeneratoren kontrollieren die elektronischen Regler (Gates)« (ibid., p.78).

Figure 3: Example of envelopes at ›B‹

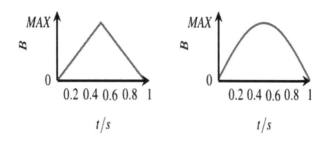

Depending on whether they are inverted or normal, the volume of the ›gate‹ will decrease or increase the volume of the sound to be moved at ›A‹ (see figure 4).

Figure 4: Signal at loudspeaker either inverted or normal of a triangular ›envelope‹

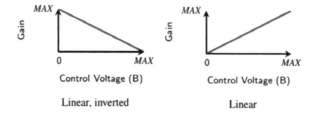

PROGRAMMING

The complete movement of a sound source within a loudspeaker set-up was programmed as a sequence of envelopes. The *Halaphon III* could store 20 of these programs, while the *Halaphon IV* could store an unlimited number of sound-path programs. A program contained the shape, starting point, and length of each envelope. The position of the envelopes in time is defined relatively: each envelope starts at a given fraction (defined in terms of 16 steps) of the length of the preceding envelope. An example for the realization of a ›circular‹ movement in a four-channel loudspeaker setup is given in figure 5. It shows the use of four ›gates‹. The corresponding triangular envelopes with an overlap of 50% are also plotted.

Figure 5: Circular movement (a) and forms of four envelopes to generate that movement (b)

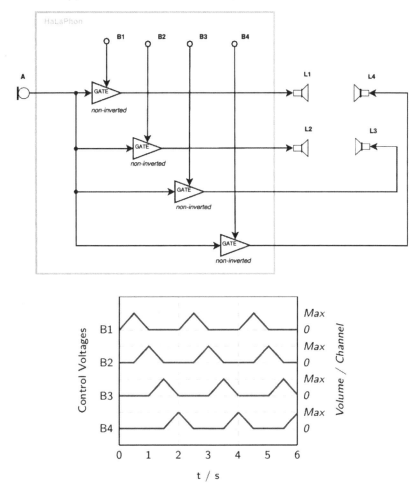

As indicated, such movements could be used in an ongoing way, repeating the rotation endlessly. Additionally, the device allowed the general tuning of a program to the acoustics of a concert situation. Consequently, all the envelopes of a movement could be changed in length without changing their position in time. The overlap is controlled, which can help to create a smooth sound movement in environments with different reverberation times. Synchronization between audio and sound spatialization is an important aspect for use in live performances. One means for synchronization was given by the trigger input. Depending on an audio signal, a program could be triggered when the input exceeded a threshold. The threshold could be tuned manually in the *Halaphon III*. This enabled a synchronized start of sound and program. While running, the program's speed could be adjusted manually by the sound engineer to prevent drifting apart. Additionally, the musicians could follow their position within the program on a digital display.

USING THE *HALAPHON* WITH PERIPHERALS

The *Halaphon* was part of a larger studio or live set-up, used in combination with other equipment, such as analogue sound processing devices built in Freiburg or a switching matrix (called a *Koppelfeld* in German) that was linked directly to the *Halaphon* via analogue multicore connectors and digital control buses.

Figure 6: Freiburg Studio devices; the Halaphon and the switching matrix, third from right

From: Hans Peter Haller 1995, op.cit., volume 2, p. 78

This device, also invented by Haller and Lawo, managed the routing of all audio signals. Source and destination could be connected in a matrix on the front panel of the device by tapping with an electric pen. Once set, the switching matrix could save all connections as programmed presets. In addition, audio effect devices such as reverberators and harmonizers were used to strengthen spatial impressions.

PROMETEO, TRAGEDIA DELL'ASCOLTO

When Luigi Nono worked on his composition *Prometeo* (1978–1985) he was well aware of the technical capabilities of the Freiburg Studio, as described above[3], and after he began to work there he became increasingly experienced with its functions. Moreover, Nono's first visit to the Freiburg Studio in 1980 must have been, at least in part, planned to support his ideas of a spatial composition for *Prometeo*, which had originally been an opera project. As the theatre dramaturge and opera director Klaus Zehelein reported, in autumn 1979 Nono changed his plans for a *Prometeo* from an opera on a closed stage to a composition for space[4]. At this stage, Nono had already received a libretto from Massimo Cacciari. The character of Prometo, based on the figure from ancient Greek cosmology, is presented here not only as the well-known immortal half-god, half-Titan personality, who – against the will of Zeus – supplied mankind with fire and, as punishment for this, was subjected to never-ending torture.

At the same time, Cacciari and Nono interpreted Prometeo on a metaphorical level as a supporter and creator of human culture, who constantly suffers from the world. He is a wanderer, a person both searching as well as constantly on the move[5]. For his libretto, Cacciari compiled antique Greek text sources and combined them with modern texts by Walter Benjamin and Friedrich Hölderlin. He formed them into different blocks and arranged them in a series or network of ›islands‹.

---

3 Hans Peter Haller, »Erinnerung an Venedig: Wege zu Nonos Prometeo«, in: *Luigi Nono: Prometeo*, Inventionen 2000, Programmbuch, Berlin 2000, pp. 42–45, here p. 42.

4 Klaus Zehelein, »Prometeo, die heimliche Szene«, in: Klaus Kropfinger (ed.), *Komponistenportrait Luigi Nono*, Berliner Festwochen, Berlin 1988, pp. 37–43, here p. 37.

5 Lydia Jeschke, *Prometeo: Geschichtskonzeptionen in Luigi Nonos Hörtragödie*, Stuttgart, 1997, pp. 19ff., suggested some additional metaphorical interpretations of the *Prometeo* material as understood by Nono and Cacciari, such as the journeys of Odysseus or the antique Jewish mythology.

Figure 7: Cacciari, sketch of Prometeo

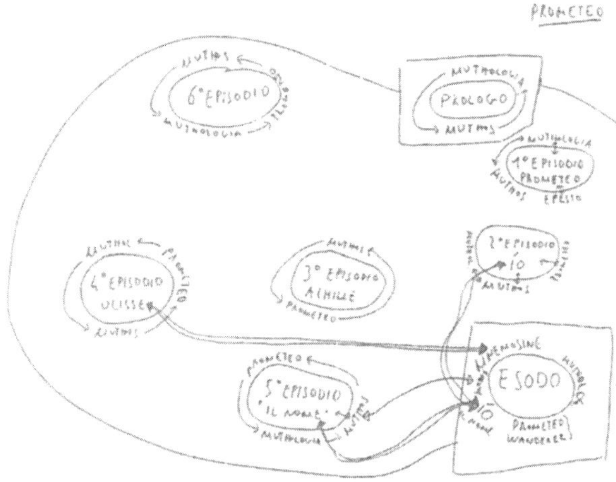

From: Lydia Jeschke, *Prometeo: Geschichtskonzeptionen in Luigi Nonos Hörtragödie*, Stuttgart 1997, p. 210

Nono kept to this basic idea over the years and projected it into the space of a concert hall by musical and compositional means without dramatic effects. There is only one exception: at one point the speaker, who symbolizes Prometeo, is to walk silently for a certain distance. All other spatial movements in the composition are purely acoustical.

In 1984 Nono finished the first complete version of *Prometeo, tragedia dell'ascolto*. Although there are differences to the second, »Milan version«, the basic spatial concept remains the same. It consists of different elements.

THE *ARCA*: THE PERFORMANCE SPACE FOR *PROMETEO*

Both versions were performed in the same wooden construction built by the Italian architect Renzo Piano. It was called either *arca* (»arch«) or *struttura* (»structure, building«) and was designed to house the audience as well as the musicians and singers who were placed on different points of the balconies next to the wall above the listeners. Photos and verbal descriptions of the Venice performance as well as Piano's plan show that the *arca* stood on stilts about 1.5–1.8 m in height[6], so that its upper edge almost touched the domed roof of San Lorenzo, a former church with a Baroque-style interior.

---

6   Zehelein, op.cit., p. 41, described its height as »*mannshoch*« (»human sized«).

For the acoustic of the *arca* it is important to note that some of its walls were built in carved concave forms, giving a natural resonance to the sounds produced by the musicians or singers[7]. All this indicates that the *arca's* function was intended to fulfill acoustical needs more than just visual ones. Acoustic reflections could be minimized and controlled much better than sounds reflected in unaltered rooms of different sizes. Therefore, the *arca* has an important part in the spatial design of *Prometeo* and the use of the *Halaphon* or other spatial technology used herein in order to create moving sounds and variable audible space impressions.

Figure 8: »Arca« in San Lorenzo built on stilts

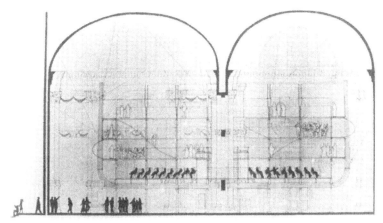

From: Jeschke, op.cit., p. 180

THE CONCEPT OF AUDIBLE SPACE IN *PROMETEO*

There are several aspects of space, as it was composed or used:

- fixed places of Instruments, singers and loudspeakers;
- the movement of sounds in different speeds and between different ›locations‹ or complete circles produced by the *Halaphon* and peripheral devices;
- variable room dimensions provided by different kinds of artificial reverberation; and
- external sounds.

---

7   Hans Peter Haller called them *Resonanzschalen* (»resonator bowls« or, perhaps more appropriately in this case, »resonance walls«) for solo singers and choir (op.cit., volume 2, p. 165).

Placement of Musicians and Loudspeakers

Solo voices, choir, speaker (Prometeo), solo musicians, and orchestra were distributed across two levels of the balconies, roughly as sketched out in figure 9, and seem to have followed a symmetrical order[8].

Figure 9: Sketch of musicians and loudspeaker placement (compilation from different manuscripts[9]). The »arca« is reduced to the ground floor and two floors of the balconies.

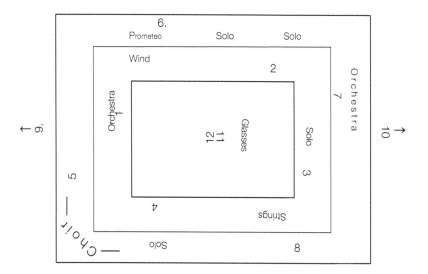

Arca: Exterior Sounds and Interior Sound Paths

The loudspeakers outside the *arca* might also have been used for the production of precise sound paths. But it is certain that they were used to project less precise musical structures, such as the *coro lontanissimo* (remote choir). This was conceived by Nono for *Prometeo*[10] and consists of female voices from the chamber choir, positioned in the *arca*, singing extremely softly (*ppppppp*). The voices were picked up and reverberated for an unnaturally long time (8 to 15 seconds). The projection on the indirectly positioned loud-

---

8 Additionally, the glasses were placed on the floor.
9 See, for instance, Haller 1995, op.cit., volume 2, pp. 199 ff., or http://www.hp-haller.homepage.t-online.de/ab_2_27.jpg (19.2.2015).
10 Hans Peter Haller 1995 op.cit., volume 2, p. 91.

speakers resulted in what Haller described as an effect of a vague, blurred audible space, seeming to enter the *arca* from nowhere.

Figure 10: Sound paths in the »arca«

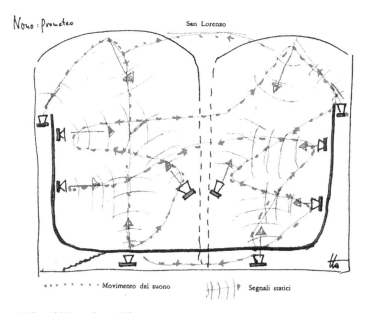

From: Haller 1995, op.cit., p. 163

In contrast to these distant and ›atmospheric‹ sound effects, the acoustic space inside the *arca* was defined much more clearly, although artificial reverberation was still in use. Obviously, Nono's aim was to design an elaborate and exact definition of sound, sound sources, and an impression of audible space.

This can be demonstrated for the first part of the composition, the *Prologo*. It begins with the *coro lontanissimo*, described above (bars 1–22)[11]. Following this, bowed strings and speaker take over, with the sound initially concentrated opposite the choir (bars 23–27). In a third spatial step, speakers, choir, and solo musicians are active differently concentrating the partly reverberated sounds on three parts (of four) of the *arca* (bars 28–33). This spatial design stays more or less the same for quite a while (including short inserts of *coro lontanissimo* and *Halaphon* motion).

---

11 Luigi Nono, *Prometeo* (Versione 1985), Partitura, Milano.

At the end of the *Prologo* (from bar 151) the music culminates in a complex sound movement from the *Halaphon* that transports the music of solo woodwinds, brass, and strings in two ›circles‹ resembling Haller's vertical sketch and there seems to be a journey of sound through the complete *arca*.

Here, the spatial design of the *Prologo* might be interpreted as support for the dramatic context: the music enters the acoustic stage from outer space, stays there and describes certain places before it starts to wander about, symbolizing Prometeo's journey. This begins in the following part, entitled *primo isola* (»first island«). A complete analysis of *Prometeo* – which is planned as a future project – will show in detail how Nono integrated space into other parts of his composition.

Space, Sound, and Acousmatic Music

The Heart of the Research

ANNETTE VANDE GORNE

The spatial projection of music for acousmatic listening – the sound in space – enables the space of the future to open up to a fifth dimension of expression in music: the space of sound.

The listening conditions of acousmatic music (with no real established sound source) approach those of a blind person, who senses space by close listening to the acoustic qualities of his or her physical environment. The ›eyes closed‹ approach abolishes the physical limits of the performance space, and it allows the imagination to deploy its spatial sensations.

SPECIES OF SPACES:
THE FOUR MAIN SPATIAL CATEGORIES

Four categories of space emerge from this particular practice of interpretation and knowledge of the acousmatic repertoire: (1) the ›ambiophonic‹ or ›surround space‹ immerses the listener in a ›bath‹ of sound; as opposed to (2) the ›sound source‹ space, in which sounds may be localized; (3) the ›geometry space‹ in a work structures planes and volumes; and (4) ›space illusion‹, works in the traditional stereo format. The first three categories relate mostly to multichannel recordings. In contrast, the fourth category, the traditional stereo form, creates both a phantom sound source (possibly moving) and an illusion of spatial depth across the distance of two loudspeakers, regardless of whether that depth is consciously perceived as such. This sonic image resembles a film that displays spatial depth in the central perspective format on a screen.

(1) Ambiophonic Space

A space is termed ambiophonic if we cannot determine where sounds come from, so that the auditor is bathed in a diffused ambiance. Listening achieves a ›mixing‹ of all events hinted at. One can draw an analogy to Byzantine churches: these include domes covered with gold tesserae, which redistribute what little ambient light there is equally across the whole church, but the source cannot be localized.

For ambiophonic diffusion, we surround the audience with identical speakers, relatively equidistant to each other, so that there is no acoustic ›hole‹. The encircling takes place in every plane; the sphere is the ideal model. If the audience is encircled on only one plane, then the circle becomes the appropriate model. Dolby and THX cinema systems can also be classified in this category: three different channels at the screen but the sides and rears share one or two channels. The sound projection should be done with identical loudspeakers surrounding the audience. There should be only little movement realized with the aid of the console.

(2a) Source Space: Pointillism

In contrast to the previous category, the ›pointillist‹ type of space pinpoints the source of the sound, which can be monophonic, two track, or multitrack (but not stereo[1]). The movements and the localization of the sound are what matter. We may also want to make the audience feel the differences in colour and power of each speaker.

Pierre Henry was probably the first to explore the musical possibilities of this philosophy of space, during both the compositional process and the concert. In this context, he often contrasts the right and left channels and tracks (›biphony‹) using the geography of the space as an organizational principle (cf. figure 1). Today, the most common use of the source space is the multiphony from a multitrack player.

Creating a source space involves placing sounds with attack transients sufficiently delineated for localization, even if these transients are very short. The composition then becomes a pointillist environment, playing with masses, the occasional phrasing, and variations in density. Multitrack dialogues and sequence overlays assigned to the same speakers are another kind of this source-space aesthetic, which highlights sonic characters or counterpoint.

---

1   In contrast to stereo, two-track recordings have different sounds on each track, while stereo works carry interrelated information on their two channels.

Sound projection can work with identical or with a diverse range of loud-speakers, selected according to the musical situation. Only little movement with the console is required for realizing this type of space.

Figure 1: Loudspeaker distribution of Pierre Henry's »Histoires naturelles«, Paris, Radio France, Olivier Messiaen Hall, 1997

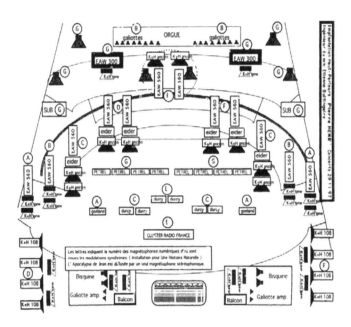

From: Annette Vande Gorne, »L'interprétation spatiale: Essai de formalisation méthodo-logique«, in: Revue Demeter, Université Lille 3, 12/2002, www.univ-lille3.fr/revues/demeter/interpretation/vandegorne.pdf (4/2015), p. 4[2]

(2b) Source Space: Movement

Anything in movement is also part of the source space, an audible trajectory in ›outer space‹, generated by the interpreter or written by the composer on the multitrack tape (›inner space‹). As Aesop's tongue, the movement itself can be the worst or the best thing. Indeed, it has always seemed useless to try to save a poor composition, one without internal energy, by applying move-ments or external ›agitations‹. The movement remains mere ornamentation,

---

2   reprinted in: *La spatialisation des musiques électroacoustiques*, edited by Pottier Lau-rent, Université de Saint-Étienne 2012, p. 57.

not integrated into the music, nor is it justified by musical structure or phrasing. But if we consider the musical expression from the point of view of energy, the trajectories may strengthen the internal energy of the sound. Western music history is strewn with works that give importance to agogics themselves as a factor in expression (think of Claudio Monteverdi and his *stile concitato,* of word painting, particularly in the work of Johann Sebastian Bach or the *Symphonie fantastique* by Hector Berlioz) and a structural factor (Igor Stravinsky's *Rite of Spring,* Arthur Honegger's *Pacific 231,* Giacinto Scelsi, etc.). If you forgive a banal example, an orbit around the audience, or any other pivot, will highlight to the ears any rotary motion of a spinning top, a swivel, or a repetition.

Finally, the application of a swinging spatial movement to a neutral, abstract sound gives it a special meaning, that of a lullaby for example. It may be recalled here how much time, space and motion are related: fast or slow rotations do not generate the same meaning, and if a rotation gradually moves to a faster tempo, it changes its shape and becomes a spiral. This movement space would especially have an ornamental or metaphorical function to sustain: expressive sounds themselves in which it provides a spatial support. In the nineteenth century, timbre and melody maintained the same relationship.

Sound projection is based on identical loudspeakers in a multichannel set. The various colours and movements of this type should be strengthened or created at the console.

(3) Geometry Space

If we consider space from a structural point of view, we can imagine it as the intersection of different lines and planes, as surface or volume interspersed with lines that are bisected biphonically, obliquely, vertically, laterally, etc. From multiple sources (multichannel), think of the sound in terms of composition of the space (monophonic, two track, quadrophonic, triple stereo, dual quadrophony, octophonic, etc., or in any combination possible) applied to a single acoustic chain or to many, simultaneously or sequentially, in close or distant planes. This gives space the equivalent parameter status of the other four parameters. The movement is part of the form when it becomes a figure, a repetition, a transition, a rupture, a trigger, etc. Here, space geometry is not a carrier; it is a real and abstract musical object that leads the perception of listening and structure, with its evolution over time.

This organized and controlled space requires a diagram of the diffusion system and the choice of the spatial patterns to appear on the tape, for example, within the sound systems of specific venues or installations. Too much complexity (number of tracks, the possible spatial variations) will affect the transparency of the architecture. My current perceptual experience is limited to four movements or four differentiated geometric spaces. The disposition *a priori*, writing space for itself from multiphonic point sources, generates a stabilizing musical thought that binds the space to the form, so once again, to time.

Sound projection of this kind has to work with identical loudspeakers and a diverse choice of situations by sequences.

(4) Illusion Space

This type of sound projection is based on the illusion of spatial depth and uses stereo technology and its capability to create so-called phantom sound sources (which may be heard in fixed positions or moving between a pair of loudspeakers), thereby building a sonic plane. The sound is no longer perceived as a real object, but as an image or as a representation. We enter the world of media coverage, a world of photos, film, video, radio, etc.

Technologically, phantom sound sources appear in the interrelation of two sound tracks. This must be considered throughout the entire chain of production, and the two channels should stay connected to each other. The creation of an imaginary space is based on multiple pairs of loudspeakers; each pair forms its own sound plane in the three-dimensional concert hall.

Therefore, perspectives need to be created and depth planes need to be multiplied, highlighted by multiple phase screens (pairs of loudspeakers), by their staged disposition in at least three positions (near, middle ground, and distant), and by at least three different types of spatial width (very large calibre, medium, and very thin). One may play different calibre registers on a single plane or in 3-D space to enhance the centre of a wide phase screen (static) or to effect a movement of expansion or contraction (dynamic).

The direction of the loudspeakers relative to the audience may or may not specify the contours of sounds as they converge towards one another and towards the centre of the cone of the audience's presence or, on the other hand, diverge as the loudspeakers project sound live. Conversely, the projectors may radiate the sound towards reflective surfaces indirectly, or fill the entire space.

The colour (i.e. the spectral response of the transducers, from low to hyper-high frequencies), also plays an important role. The transducers are divided into five families:

- the basses, called ›double basses‹ (10–400 Hz) in a very wide stereo that covers the whole field of the room, or in the centre if there is only one subwoofer;
- the ›hollow‹ midrange (250–1000 Hz) is used to fill the space;
- the ›clear‹ midrange (400–3000 Hz) is responsible for maximum audibility of the message, and especially of the human voice;
- the ›bright‹ midrange (3000–8000 Hz) reinforces the presence of microscopic life of sonic beings;
- a multiplied group of very high-frequency loudspeakers or tweeters (8000–16000 Hz), which specify the edges. We will use small tweeters to refine the contours present in the audience. The very high pitched speakers or trumpets are used to help locate a set placed far away. The bass is diffuse. Speakers of poor quality (hollow medium) will smoothly play a role of diffuse mass (radiators).

All combinations of placement, calibre width, colour, and directivity give to each pair or group a different musical role, like orchestration: soloists (a pair of references, often in close and converging focal length), mass (distribution of loudspeakers in reflection, on a large area), referential stereo (large width calibre, all frequencies), double basses (bass), and effect (vertical stereo, ceiling, presence in the public etc.).

This projection instrument designed to enhance existing space on the tape (the internal space) and reach the imagination and emotion of the listener was developed by François Bayle in 1974, who named it an *Acousmonium* (cf. figure 2). The last step of the acousmatic production, the *GRM Acousmonium*, counted more than 80 speakers by 2002.

The *Acousmonium* of *Musiques & Recherches*, Brussels, founded in 1980, had more than 70 speakers in 2014. It combines the interpretation of the imaginary space with that of the multiphonic space source.

The sound projection works with a variety loudspeakers. Spatial figures and situations of the internal space need to be reinforced from the mixing console.

Figure 2: The first version of the »Acousmonium«, by François Bayle, Espace Cardin, Paris, 1974

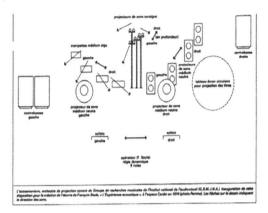

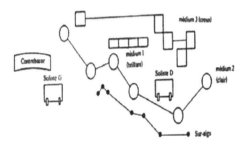

From: François Bayle, »L'acousmatique ou l'art des sons projetés«, *Encyclopaedia Universalis*, Paris 1984, p. 216[3]

SPATIAL INTERPRETATION:
STEREO-BASED SPATIAL PERFORMANCE

The console of projection (fader, multitouch surface, interactive gestures, etc.) is a musical instrument, and its ›operator‹ is a performing musician. This requires some virtuosity on the part of the interpreter, taking into account not only the chosen speaker system but also the ergonomics of the sound projection instrument, stylistic knowledge of the repertoire, a graphic statement of the simplified works and relevant to their spatialization, and maximum memorization of the works.

---

3 reprinted in: François Bayle, *Musique Acousmatique, propositions... positions*, Paris 1993, annexe XIV.

The interpretation of acousmatic music tends to bind different spatial figures that reinforce the writing of the work; the figures highlight existing figures or create new ones. The stereo works also offer more freedom of choice to the interpreter. Sixteen figures are listed, with their musical function:

Crossfading

Crossfading is a slow or imperceptible transition of sounds between pairs or larger groups of loudspeakers. The gesture must be careful to avoid digging any acoustic ›hole‹. Start to move up the faders to be faded in before bringing down the first set of faders, and find a balance point.

Musical function: strengthening the existing crossfade on the tape by changing the plane or depth calibre. Draw a path by successive crossfades if, for example, this sound evokes a moving object (ball, car, plane, etc.).

Unmasking

This is a sort of ›upside-down crossfade‹ from a given mass; we hear the desired pair or group of loudspeakers by reducing the amplitude of other speakers or by removing them from the mix entirely. The gesture can be gentle, imperceptible, or brutal, using the mute buttons for example.

Musical function: to strengthen an existing unmasking effect on the tape, to change the plane or the depth calibre, or to impose a trajectory on the sound by successive unmasking if, for example, this sound evokes a moving object (ball, car, plane, etc.) and the starting spatial situation is a *tutti* or a mass encompassing the public.

Emphasis

This is the highlighting of a specific location (the soloists, for example) or a group forming a particular space, volume, or a new calibre, by slightly increasing the amplitude of the chosen speakers without modifying the others. The amplitude of departure (the basis) is important because it determines the overall level. We balance it from the stereo reference pair (also called ›the principals‹).

Musical function: this approach can be applied to a specific passage of the work or to a general strategy of projection, in which case we slightly open all the main faders (which thus provide the basis) and then we increase some points following the structure or sections of the work, the desired effect on the listener's perception. This is the general strategy used by François Bayle. Emphasis is a soft, light, and relaxed way to play on the console.

Sparkling

This figure consists of fast, cascading operations highlighting a given mass (and back). Random play of the amplitude within the acousmonium, play on the spectrum (by filtering) in the context of the *Cybernéphone*, developed by Christian Clozier at the *Institut International de Musique Electroacoustique de Bourges* (IMEB) in 1973. To ensure continuity, also keep some channels open and fixed.

Musical function: the spatial equivalent of a *tremolo*, to create liveliness ›inside‹ a thick and smooth mass by digging, or lightly increasing spectral and dynamic fragmentation. This can also highlight a moment composed by micro-montage or pointillist (granular) techniques.

Oscillation

Rapid and regular alternation between two loudspeakers or two groups of loudspeakers; the dynamic and the spectrum are subject to alternation. The effect of ›vibration‹ given by a very rapid regularity is only possible on an automated console. A low frequency oscillator (LFO) could serve as a controller.

Musical function: the spatial equivalent of the trill, agitation preparing an explosion, a burst, or otherwise, creating a lively reflux or a fermata.

Swinging

Slow and gestural alternation between two loudspeakers or two groups of loudspeaker; subject to alternation are the dynamic and the spectrum.

Musical function: highlighting the composed musical dialogue, delimitation of spatial landmarks, lullaby.

The Wave

A ›round trip‹ that runs through crossfades or successive unmasking gestures, a series of speakers in a line. For example, from the backstage to the front of the stage, or along the sides, or to the back of the room and back again to the front.

Musical function: the effect of moving mass and of predictable unidirectionality. This gesture has the advantage of joining a known agogic archetype.

Rotation

Circular trajectory between four speakers on stage or, more often, around the audience, with a gesture slightly highlighting each of the points by successive crossfades.

Musical function: evidence of the sound's internal rotation (then we must keep the pace of this internal motion) or creating movements to give, for example, a sense of confinement.

The Spiral
A circular trajectory onto which is applied an acceleration or a deceleration, where the endpoint would be somewhere other than the start.

Musical function: a preparation, an announcement, or a goal-oriented or conclusive trajectory.

Rebound
A quick jump from one point in space to another, from one group to another, or from a soloist to a group (and *vice versa*), by effectuating a quick, alternating gesture on the console or by using a set of mute buttons. The rebound is even more effective when both poles are distant.

Musical function: launch (or relaunch) of a triggering sound; going into another spatial region without any transition.

Insertion (Rupture)
In an area that has already been established, and over a sufficiently long period, a sudden shift or overlap (by unmuting) of a characteristic space or a different width. For example, inserting a directional solo of narrow width into a large and diffuse mass.

Musical function: a rhetorical figure, highlighting written inserts on the tape; an accentuation. The rupture can be used as an abrupt and contrasted departure to another state.

Appearance (and Disappearance)
An unprepared burst or closing from a different spatial state, superimposed on or following the preceding state. The use of mute buttons is the best way to proceed.

Musical function: surprise, ›magic‹, or awakening the listening.

Explosion
The sudden passage from a narrow or directional space to a large and environmental space: not diffused.

Musical function: highlighting an eruptive mass, or a characteristic and energetic morphology.

Accumulation

The successive addition of planes or calibres on top of each other to achieve a spatial *tutti*.

Musical function: the highlighting of a corpuscular sound material (e.g., grains) or the progressive enlargement of a frame.

Invasion

A rapid accumulation, an accumulative trajectory oriented towards the audience.

Musical function: similar to the Lumière brothers' *Arrival of a Train at La Ciotat Station*, an effect of subjective aggression.

Empty and Full

A game playing with the density of the stereo ramp, planes, or volumes. A stereo ramp bounded by two distant speakers seems ›empty‹ or transparent, compared to the same thing when it is filled by other pairs of loudspeakers placed on the same front (as in the case of wave field synthesis, WFS). The same choice is also possible between depth planes or volumes that incorporate an additional dimension of height, away from one another or filled by intermediate loudspeaker pairs.

Musical function: to clarify or strengthen a sonic mass, akin to a symphonic orchestration. Note, however, that a spatial *tutti* destroys any sensation of space.

THE MULTIPHONIC SPATIAL PERFORMANCE

The interpretation of multiphonic works raises new requirements, both in terms of technology (including drivers, interfaces, and types of transducers) and in terms of aesthetics. This becomes evident in an examination of interpretations of stereo works.

Today, the means of access (for example, multitouch tablet) and multitrack recording of a sound or sequence, in real time, allow for greater accuracy of trajectory and positioning in space. Each sound can receive a precise spatial identity in the studio. Space truly becomes a musical parameter equivalent to others, if the composer so desires. In concert situations, however, the interpretation is less free and creative than in the case of a stereo work. Unless we multiply the total number of loudspeakers by eight – octophony has become a *de facto* standard in electroacoustic music – with one group of eight loudspeakers controlled by a single fader (cf. BEAST in its

second version, for which Jonty Harrison has completed a piece of 72 channels (*BEASTiary*), is the precursor system), it reduces the possibilities of
choice in the play on the projection console and it also decreases the diversity of colours offered by the *acousmonium* ›*à la française*‹; indeed, to fulfil
the spatial balance of the composition, we must give the same colour, so the
same loudspeakers in each group. The *acousmonium* used at *Musiques &
Recherches*, Brussels, solves these two requirements (diversity of colours
and groups of eight speakers) with an ›*à la belge*‹ compromise.

Stylistic Aspects

Depending on the character of each piece, one can, for a different work space,
focus on some aspect of the writing, for example, iconicity, movement, ›unmixing‹ of polyphony, phrasing changes, matters of subjectivity, or the fluidity of
the trajectories.

- image, or iconicity: The ›phonographic‹ image is viewed, understood and re-
  framed, and enlarged with appropriate dimensions to present its content. We do
  not give the same emphasis, the same calibre to an outdoor soundscape, or to a
  vocal character's portrait, or to a sonic representation of an interior.
- movement: The energy, the inherent movement in the nature of a sonic sequence or a thread, will be all the more apparent if it is translated by a correlated spatial movement of the same nature.
- ›unmixing‹ of contrapuntal writing: The mixing is ›stripped‹ from the original,
  after it has been analysed for specific spatial placement of types of sounds. If
  the writing gives more importance to an individual sonic element, this can be
  highlighted from a pair of loudspeakers inside a larger group.
- phrasing and variations: The structure of the work – its phrasing, rhythm, and
  variations – are made explicit by an interpreter who has internalized the work
  and who now ›relives‹ it, playing it as if interpreter and composer were one
  and the same person. This is ›acousmatic modality‹ applied to interpretation.
- subjectivity: Often, in works with text, for example, it comes to making the listener feel the internal situation of which a character speaks. A kind of › subjective camera ‹, it is the balance between different points of space, defined and
  fixed, which the internal space (often reinforced by the tone of voice in the
  presence of a text) clearly differs.
- matter: The roughness, grain, or flow, the density and mass of the materials
  will be enhanced by the proximity, distance, number, and density of the loudspeakers.

• mobility: Create fluid and unpredictable trajectories by a set of successive crossfades separating stereo into two mono channels that are placed independently on different numbers, locations, and qualities of loudspeakers.

A NEW PROFESSION: THE SPATIALIZATION INTERPRETER

The concert stereo projection of sonic images on phase screens that are pairs of loudspeakers – this is undoubtedly the form of spatial interpretation that is most flexible, varied, and free. This new interpretative profession requires both experience and learning.

It takes the knowledge of the work, which may be helped by its graphic transcription and a well-founded knowledge of the response of each pair of speakers in the acoustic of a given space. The act of interpretation begins with the design of the sound system and its placement, the orientation and the role given to each loudspeaker, the ergonomic allocation of these on the potentiometers of the console. The interpreter then becomes familiar with the system and memorizes the configuration of the console to acquire gestural reflexes that are both lively and reliable.

Then, the rehearsal will take into account the internal space of the work, movements, highlighting speeds will increase, clarifying planes in the depth of field. I still assign other functions to the spatialization in the context of the interpretation itself in concert, as well as part of the multichannel composition in the studio. This is to clarify to the listener the structure of the work and its sections, for example, by attributing to each a different spatial configuration. It will then perform spatial figures within each configuration. This is also to strengthen the perception of memory games, by returning to the same spatial configuration or location with the resumed signal sounds or identical sequences in the different times of the composition.

Multichannel works, for which the writing space is already defined, leave, *de facto*, less freedom or fluidity for the interpretation in concert. The task, then, is to set in place the ratios of tracks on a system, of which the number of speakers is greater than the number of tracks, and to play varying combinations of groups, ensuring that all tracks are always audible: indicate in this design, the track number on the console of projection.

These are just a few aspects of the profession of the spatialization interpreter, which responds, just like any other instrumental discipline, to the combination of competence and performance: technical knowledge of the instrument, analytical and memorized knowledge of the work, and the desire of forward following the ›feeling‹ of the moment, the emotion experienced during the concert.

LEVELS OF COMPOSED SPACE

As for any musical element, the space of sound is attributed a level of musical function determined by the composer. Nowadays, technology allows for any variation in the use of space, from a micro-event (static or dynamic spatial location for each sound) to a macro-structure (whole spatial structure, dynamic or static, monophonic or polyphonic for each section, phrases, or group of events). Among other possible levels, I have selected the following six that, to me, are particularly useful and expressive:

- The abstract level of space, conceived of planes, volumes, movements, or geometric figure.
- The structural level of space, used to emphasise sections, transitions, or recall.
- The decorative level of space, often in movement, added to an event to strengthen its meaning or temporary function.
- The figurative level, relating space to the imagination, the key feature, the metaphor.
- The archetypal level of some obvious space figures, such as the wave (rocking movement), circle (locked-in effect), etc.
- The ›madrigal‹ level of the expressive strengthening of elements external to the music itself (text, image, etc.): through figures, movements, and appropriate spatial situations.

Abstract Level

In stereo, depth planes lighten and clarify the sonic orchestration, the mix. The space becomes an active agent, as well as terracing pitch registers and tonal colorations in orchestral writing. Spatial differentiations allow a form of variation on the same material.

Without going back to the 1950s and the 1960s (Karlheinz Stockhausen's *Gesang der Jünglinge*, from 1956, and *Kontakte*, from 1960) or 1972 (John Chowning's *Turenas*), abstract multichannel writing evolved in the 1990s, with digital 8-track player-recorders. In 1989, *Lune Noire*, by Patrick Ascione, composed and mixed at the *GRM* on analogue 16-track, 2-inch tape, installs a dual-space movement swirling around the audience and on stage. The same year, *Terre*, the fifth element of Annette Vande Gorne's

TAO, combines geometric figure spaces in and around the public on 8-track, analog, 1-inch tape.

Structural Level

The choice of movement helps to clarify a form or section, highlighting a particular moment. For example, a double-mirror section, of which events and materials are similar, but inverted spatial movement accentuates an inverted form, for example in *Combattimento: sous les coups de ta croupe, et le lait de tes reins,* the second act of *Yawar Fiesta*[4].

Ornamental Level

Space or added movement strengthen the interest of a sound figure. As with a *mordent* or trill, the path directs attention to perceptual elements among others. This space allows source-type »background and figure« writing. For example, in *Condor*, the first act of *Yawar Fiesta*, a circlular movement takes place on the word »Taureau«, in order to fight the bull.

Figurative Level

The imagination, which is based on recognition, recreates space, movement and location. In *Voyage*, from Annette Vande Gorne's *Paysage/Vitesse*, the movement from left to right is artificially applied to a cicada sound; what does one hear more: the source or the movement?

Archetypal Level

Certain movements, by their mere presence, qualify the meaning of the message, the context, and the communication. Examples for such archetypal movements are:

- the wave (as a representation of a round trip, a hesitation, a rocker), for instance, in the final monologue (»les dieux«) from *Yawar Fiesta*;
- the circle (as a representation of confinement), for example, in the final monologue, »les mêmes tains ont dit«, from *Yawar Fiesta*; and
- the explosion, for instance, in the first part of *Terre*, fifth part of *TAO*, to express the primordial big bang.

---

4   *Yawar Fiesta*, acousmatic opera (2009–2012), libretto by Werner Lambersy, music by Annette Vande Gorne.

Madrigal Level

The abstract architectures of polyphonic music have evolved towards expressiveness, thanks to the passage of the text and its immediate naive relationship developed in the 16th century madrigal. I aimed for a similar relationship in my opera *Yawar Fiesta*, assigning this role to spatial movements, or spatial illusion. In the women's choir *combattimento* from the second act, the words »nous rêvons« (»we dream«) are illustrated with reverberation on all channels; the phrase »sound of your hoof« is depicted with rhythms on the fragmented words; and the sentence »We have fed our souls on it« is expressed with a movement far away in front and with medium-high frequencies on the word »soul«. Also, in the final of the third act such ›madrigalisms‹ are to be found. So, for example, in the following sentence: »Here at least where words are sung all meet up again for the games (full space), of darkness (empty space rear) and light (solo front center)«.

CONCLUSION

The spatial projection of music for acousmatic listening – sound in space – enables the space of the future to open up to a fifth dimension of expressive music: the space of sound.

»Compare to Other Spaces, Real or Imagined« (Pauline Oliveros 1969)

Acoustic Space in North American Experimental Music of the Late 1960s

JULIA H. SCHRÖDER

Considering the title of this book, *Compositions for Space: The Early Electroacoustic Music and its Contexts*, Pauline Oliveros's live-electronic composition *In Memoriam Nikola Tesla, Cosmic Engineer* (1969) is not only a composition *for* space, it is also *about* the spatial and acoustic characteristics of the individual performance space. Typically for the late sixties, it also asks the performers to move about both in the inside and the outside of the performance space, to project the outside soundscape to the inside, and to verbalize their auditory experience of the space. Most interestingly, it is a reflection about spatial experiences, when Oliveros asks the performers to »compare [the performance space's sound] to other spaces, real or imagined«[1].

In the following, Oliveros's composition will be compared with works by Alvin Lucier from the same period and with works by Maryanne Amacher[2].

---

1 Pauline Oliveros, *In Memoriam Nikola Tesla, Cosmic Engineer* (verbal score, 1969), typescript published in: Julia H. Schröder, *Cage & Cunningham Collaboration: In- und Interdependenz von Musik und Tanz*, Hofheim 2011, pp. 241f.

2 All three are American experimental composers from the same generation: Pauline Oliveros (*1932), Alvin Lucier (*1931), Maryanne Amacher (1938–2009).

RESONANCE DISASTER

Pauline Oliveros's composition *In Memoriam Nikola Tesla, Cosmic Engineer* (1969) refers to a so-called resonance disaster, i.e., the destruction of the performance hall through mechanical vibrations in the hall's resonant frequency. Tacitly, the performers re-enact an event in the physicist Nikola Tesla's life, as told by his biographer[3]: In John O'Neill's *Prodigal Genius: The Life of Nikola Tesla* (1944), an experiment with mechanical vibrations of a small oscillator in Tesla's New York laboratory in 1898 is described as follows:

»In 1896 while [Tesla's] fame was still on the ascendant he planned a nice quiet little vibration experiment in his Houston Street laboratory. [...] The quiet little vibration experiment produced an earthquake [...]. In an area of a dozen square city blocks [...], there was a sudden roaring and shaking, shattering of panes of glass, breaking of steam, gas and water pipes. Pandemonium reigned as small objects danced around rooms, plaster descended from walls and ceilings, and pieces of machinery weighing tons were moved from their bolted anchorages and shifted to awkward spots in factory lofts.«[4]

It is the biographer who dramatizes the incident in a way that might have sparked the composer's interest. (O'Neill also claims that this experiment was the first systematic research of vibrations since Pythagoras[5].) After the whole neighbourhood was shaking and the populace suspected they had witnessed an earthquake[6], the police finally rushed to Tesla's lab where they found him smashing the oscillator:

»There was a sense of impending doom – that the whole building would disintegrate – and their fears were not relieved by the sound of smashing glass and the queer roars and screams that came from the walls and floors. [...] They arrived just in time to see the tall gaunt figure of the inventor swing a heavy sledge hammer and shatter a small iron

---

3 Although this is not mentioned in the score, and only the title and the instruction to project a photo of Tesla allude to it, Tesla's experiment is explicitly referred to elsewhere (cf. Pauline Oliveros in: James Klosty (ed.), *Merce Cunningham*, New York 1975 pp. 79f.; also: Heidi von Gunden, *The Music of Pauline Oliveros*, Metuchen (NJ) 1983, pp. 63f.).

4 John J. O'Neill, *Prodigal Genius: The Life of Nikola Tesla*, New York 1944, and London 1968, p. 155.

5 Ibid., p. 158.

6 The shaking of the whole neighbourhood seems to be local oral history; it is part of New York City lore.

contraption mounted on the post in the middle of the room. Pandemonium gave way to a deep, heavy silence.«[7]

In Oliveros's 1969 homage to this event, the performers first discuss the acoustic properties of the hall, then they test the acoustics of the performance space, and comment on their findings, they search for the resonant frequency of the space[8]. In the last part low frequencies are being sent into the space, as if to bring it down[9]. Oliveros writes in 1975: »If the search for the resonant frequency has been successful, then the frequency of the generators selected by the musicians can cause the performance space to add its squeaks, groans, and other resonance phenomena to the general sound. Thus the space performs in sympathy with the musicians.«[10] Or as an earwitness describes it: »When [the performers] had found the resonant frequency, they tried to match it with their instruments. If they succeeded, the air in the hall would vibrate, producing a deep pulsing sound.«[11]

---

7   John J. O'Neill, op.cit., p. 161.
8   Cf. Pauline Oliveros: »The compositional problem was to include, extend, expand, explore, compare, store, and manipulate the auditory space within Cunningham's philosophy, which allows a natural rather than an imposed relationship to arise between the music and the dance. This philosophical relationship is embodied in the following description of a Tesla experiment and the response of the environment and its inhabitants from which the central tasks of the score are derived: Tesla's experiment with mechanical resonance in his New York City laboratory (near the present location of the Cunningham studio) nearly ended in disaster. He adjusted an oscillator to the resonance of the building and then began to give the machine more power. This caused a minor earthquake which terrorized the neighborhood and brought the police out in full force just as Tesla perceived the magnitude of his procedure and smashed his oscillator before the building began to fall apart.« (James Klosty (ed.), op.cit., pp. 79f.)
9   »I could feel my seat vibrating in the final moments of [Canfield]«. (Stephen Smoliar, »Merce Cunningham in Brooklyn«, (1970), in: Ballet Review 3/3 (1970), reprinted in: Richard Kostelanetz (ed.), *Merce Cunningham: Dancing in Space and Time: Essays 1944–1992,* Chicago 1992; pp. 77–92, here p. 91.)
10 Pauline Oliveros in: James Klosty (ed.), op.cit., pp. 79f.
11 David Vaughan, *Merce Cunningham: Fifty Years,* edited by Melissa Harris, Chronicle and Commentary by David Vaughan, New York 1997, p. 171. See also reviews: Marcia B. Siegel, »Come in, Earth. Are You There?« (1970), in: *At the Vanishing Point,* New York 1972, reprinted in: Richard Kostelanetz (ed.), op.cit., pp. 71–76; Stephen Smoliar, op.cit., pp. 77–92.

RESONANCE FREQUENCIES

Similarly, but less threateningly, in Alvin Lucier's composition *I am sitting in a room* (1970) higher resonance frequencies of a smaller space are evoked by speech.

»In *I am Sitting in a Room* (1970), several paragraphs of human speech are used to expose sets of resonant frequencies implied by the architectural dimensions of various sized rooms. By means of a pair of tape recorders, the sound materials are recycled through a room to amplify by repetition those frequencies common to both the original recording and those implied in the room. As the repetitive process continues and segments accumulate, the resonant frequencies are reinforced, the others gradually eliminated. The space acts as a filter. We discover that each room has its own set of resonant frequencies.«[12]

Lucier uses the architectural space as an instrument, as Martin Supper has put it[13], since the acoustics of each performance space shape the sonic outcome and appearance of the composition; he states, »the space does all kinds of processing due to its dimensions and materials«[14]. Lucier »was also struck by how space intrudes its personality on the sounds that [one] produce[s]«[15].

A comparative analysis by Miguel Presas of different realizations of Lucier's composition shows that different performance rooms (and speakers) indeed elicit different resonant frequencies[16]. Inherent in Lucier's concept is the comparison of different rooms[17].

---

12 Alvin Lucier, »The Propagation of Sound in Space: One Point of View« (1979), in: idem, *Reflections: Interviews, Scores, Writings 1965–1994* (English and German), edited by Gisela Gronemeyer and Reinhard Oehlschlägel, 2nd, revised edition, Cologne 2005; pp. 416–423, here p. 418.

13 Martin Supper, *Elektroakustische und Computermusik. Geschichte – Ästhetik – Methoden – Systeme*, Hofheim 1997, pp. 122–123. Supper also distinguishes between virtual and simulated acoustics, the former being imaginary rooms or halls, the latter existing in the real world.

14 Alvin Lucier in interview with Douglas Simon, »›...and listen to the ocean again‹, Chambers 1968«, in: Alvin Lucier 2005, op.cit., pp. 62–73, here p. 64 and p. 66.

15 Ibid., pp. 65f.

16 Miguel A. Presas, »Scipios Realisation von Luciers Raumkomposition: Zu Alvin Luciers *I am Sitting in a Room*«, in: kunsttexte.de/auditive_perspektiven, (2011/3), http://edoc.hu-berlin.de/kunsttexte/2011-3/presas-miguel-a.-3/PDF/presas.pdf (11/2014).

17 Lucier writes in the performance text: »I am sitting in a room different from the one you are in now«, noting the difference between recording space and performance

TESTING THE ACOUSTICS

In order to discover those resonant frequencies of the performance space, Oliveros asks the performers in the second part of *In Memoriam Nikola Tesla* to test the acoustics with standard acoustic testing devices: cap pistol, slide whistle, and short melodic fragments, *tattoos*, played on a brass instrument[18]. In this listing of performance materials, the performers' names, David (Tudor) and Gordon (Mumma), next to John Cage, are part of the verbal score. They were the musicians, specializing in live electronics and experimental music, who performed with the Merce Cunningham Dance Company, which had commissioned the composition from Oliveros. It was performed at the same time as a dance, *Canfield*, by Merce Cunningham.

Another composition, in which the performers walk through the performance space, was used to accompany the dance *Objects* (1970), also by Cunningham[19]. In that composition by Alvin Lucier, *Vespers* (1968), echolocation devices are employed[20]. In *Vespers* the blindfolded performers move through the performance space with the aid of »Sondols«. These are echolocation devices, formerly produced by Listening, Inc., of Arlingon, Massachusetts, using pulsing sounds that were also employed in acoustic testing to measure reverberation times[21].

In their prose scores, both composers ask the performers to discuss or contemplate the acoustic environment or the soundscape:

space – or playback space. The fact that he did not consider *I am Sitting in a Room* a ›mere‹ tape-piece, and published a performance score, shows that he planned for it to be realized in different rooms, thereby comparing the resonant frequencies of several rooms, and becoming more sensitive to acoustic characteristics of rooms in general.Alvin Lucier, *I am Sitting in a Room* (prose score), in: idem 2005, op.cit., pp. 312–315.

18 »In one experiment [...] Mumma was sent up on stage (off in the wings) to play a bugle while turning in a circle. As he turned, the sound bounced off walls, sank into curtains, and was even affected by the dancers. One was reminded that such a procedure provides the necessary data by which bats navigate.« (Stephen Smoliar, op.cit., p. 78.) Smoliar seems to connect the testing in Oliveros' *Canfield* with the bat's orientation in Lucier's *Vespers*.

19 Cf. David Vaughan, *Merce Cunningham: Fifty Years*, edited by Melissa Harris, Chronicle and Commentary by David Vaughan, New York 1997, p. 179.

20 Cf. Helga de la Motte-Haber's chapter in this volume, as well as her publications on space in music and the arts, which have been instrumental to the development of this text.

21 Alvin Lucier 2005, op.cit., p. 418. Cf. idem, *Music 109*, op.cit., pp. 84–88.

»I. Begin a discussion of the acoustic environment in which you are performing. (Use Lavaliers [lapel microphone] or equivalent at first so that your discussion is heard through the Public Address system.)

Hypothetize, criticize, air opinions, compare to other spaces, real or imagined. (i.e. an underwater theater, anechoic theater, a plastic theater.)«[22]

What strikes me as particularly interesting is the combination of facts and imagination Oliveros asks for in the above quoted excerpt from *In Memoriam Nikola Tesla*: What might an imaginary space sound like? What would the acoustics in an underwater theatre be like?

In the score, the following list of »possible subject matter« for the performers' mediated (and amplified) discussion deals with building features and other parameters that influence the acoustics. It is a technical discussion about the space's sound qualities, which is implied in these subjects.

»Possible subject matter:
    The shape and dimension of the space
    The way the audience is seated
    The absorption quality of the audience
    The temperature
    The weather
    The surface materials
    Sound reflection, directivity, reverberation, Interference
    Resonance
    External noise sources
    Masking
    Sound-focusing effects
    Transmission loss
    Air borne versus structure borne sound
    The effect of open or closed doors and windows
    Other.«[23]

In *(Hartford) Memory Space* (1970) Lucier asks the performers to record a soundscape – by memory, written notation, or tape recordings – and then imitate it in a performance space[24]. One presumes that would include the

---

22 Pauline Oliveros, *In Memoriam Nikola Tesla, Cosmic Engineer*, op.cit.
23 Ibid.
24 »Go to outside environment (urban, rural, hostile, benign) and record by any means (memory, written notations, tape recordings) the sound situation of those environments. Returning to an inside performance space at any later time, re-create,

acoustics of the outside environment. In re-creating the environmental sounds in another room, the performers' imaginative abilities – in this case, improvisatory abilities – are called for. Imagination becomes a creative task.

ROOMS WITHIN ROOMS: RESONATING CONTAINERS

In yet another composition, *Chambers* (1968)[25], Lucier demonstrates that each resonating object is a ›room‹, a notion that may also include, for instance, a large cave or a cistern. The acoustic characteristics of a room, which alter any sound produced inside, operate similarly in smaller containers – in fact, in any vessel. In *Chambers*, the size of the resonant object used for filtering the sounds should have a wide variety, from pots to football stadia[26]. Playing a recording of a Beethoven symphony from a teapot or Debussy's *Prélude à l'après-midi d'un faune* from a vase means that the low frequencies are not transmitted, since neither the teapot nor the vase is large enough[27]. But the altered sound raises the listener's awareness of the change of the size of a space, e.g., from a concert hall, where the recording was made, to a vase, in which it is played back.

»Collect or make large and small resonant environments.

    Sea Shells

    Rooms

    Cisterns

    Tunnels […]

    Others.

Find a way to make them sound. […]

    Talking

---

solely by means of your voices and instruments and with the aid of your memory devices (without additions, deletions, improvisations, interpretations) those outside situations.« (Alvin Lucier, *(Hartford) Memory Space* (prose score, 1970), in: idem 2005, op.cit., p. 316.)

25 Lucier had *Chambers* performed as well as installed. An example of the latter was the exhibition »Chambers« with works by Alvin Lucier and Sol LeWitt at Stadtgalerie Kiel, Germany (27 October until 26 November 1995). A photo of a performance in the Museum of Modern Art, New York 1968 – with audience sitting on the floor – by Peter Moore is published in: Alvin Lucier 2005, op.cit., p. 69.

26 Alvin Lucier/Douglas Simon, »›…and listen to the ocean again‹«, in: Alvin Lucier 2005, op.cit., p. 66.

27 Ibid.

Singing
Whistling
Walking [...] .«[28]

INSIDE AND OUTSIDE

»I notice now that many composers in their work have not a person but a place
(environment) in mind. This is true of Pauline Oliveros's work, *In Memoriam Nikola
Tesla*.«[29]

Acoustic resonance is an important part of Pauline Oliveros's work, both in
the periods before and after *In Memoriam Nikola Tesla*. From the 1970s
onward, Oliveros improvised with her *Deep Listening Band* in cisterns and
watertanks. For her early tape music of the sixties, which was recorded in
real-time, she used her bathtub and wooden apple boxes for resonance or
paper tubes for filtering effects[30]. Small or large, the scale of the resonating
container matters in terms of the result, but a cistern and a teapot both adhere
to the container model of space. Accordingly, there are the inside and the
outside of the performance space to be considered. Typically of the 1960s,
with the evolving idea of environment and land art, and with the influence of
performance art on music (or vice versa), both ›inside‹ and ›outside‹ are
performed in, when the musicians walk through the audience's space for
acoustic testing[31] and discussing their findings via walkie-talkies. Oliveros's

---

28 Alvin Lucier, *Chambers* (prose score), in: idem 2005, op.cit., pp. 289–303. There is a
certain resemblance to Pauline Oliveros's *Apple Box Double* (1965), which she
performed with David Tudor: »The composer was fond of the resonance of apple
boxes. She placed small vibrant objects on the boxes amplified by Piezo contact
microphones. Each performer selected his or her own objects and methods of
performing.« (Pauline Oliveros, in: David W. Bernstein (ed.), *The San Francisco Tape
Music Center: 1960s Counterculture and the Avant-Garde*, Berkeley 2008, p. 299.)

29 John Cage, »The Future of Music« (1974), in: idem, *Empty Words: Writings '73–'78*,
Middletown 1979, p. 85.

30 »I didn't really work in the studio at all. I created that first tape piece [*Time
Perspectives*, 1961] with my Sears and Roebuck Silvertone tape recorder and a
microphone. I used mechanical devices to simulate filters and reverberation. [...]
Cardboard tubes. And a bathtub, and using the wall or a box for amplification.«
[Pauline Oliveros interviewed by David W. Bernstein and Maggi Payne, in: David W.
Bernstein (ed.), op.cit., p. 100f.]

31 »Examine the whole space and its contents, both internal and external.« (Pauline
Oliveros, *In Memoriam Nikola Tesla, Cosmic Engineer*, op.cit.)

In Memoriam Nikola Tesla also asks for the various parts of the performance space to be amplified[32]:

»Internal and external environments as follows (Amplification by air microphones):
1. The stage or dancer's area
2. Back stage (aim for dancers' off-stage comments)
3. The lobby
4. The out-of-doors
5. Other adjoining spaces.«[33]

Continuing the aesthetics of John Cage and Merce Cunningham of a »multiplicity of centers«[34], the musical performance is decentralized. Later, recordings of an earlier part of the performance are also played back.

As we have seen, there are remarkable similarities between Oliveros's prose score and similar prose scores by Alvin Lucier from the same time, the late 1960s[35]. They employ acoustic testing devices, they ask the performers to contemplate the soundscape or acoustic environment, they aim to show the effect of the size of a room upon the sound played in it. From an ›outside‹ they transmit sound in real-time to a listening place, and – via recordings – from the past.

»During the second section of [*In Memoriam Nikola Tesla*] the performers are asked to test the environment in order to find the resonance frequency of the space, to report any interesting facts via walkie-talkie, and occasionally to broadcast particularly interesting features through the PA system. The differences in quality between the sound of moving

---

32 In earlier concerts organized by Oliveros, loudspeakers can also be found in the au-
    dience space: »the Sonics I concert [1961] was announced as a ›bring your own
    speaker‹ event. [Due to the limited number of loudspeakers available.] As speakers
    arrived, they were dispersed around the auditorium and wired to a specially
    configured keyboard. This allowed the composers to ›play‹ their works spatially
    throughout the room and the adjacent corridor.« (David W. Bernstein, »The San
    Francisco Tape Music Center«, in: idem (ed.), op.cit., pp. 5–41, here p. 12.)
33 Pauline Oliveros, *In Memoriam Nikola Tesla, Cosmic Engineer*, op.cit.
34 Cf. Julia H. Schröder, op.cit., pp. 51–58. Interestingly, Cunningham's dance stays on
    the stage, whereas the musicians explore the whole building and make it audible for
    the audience.
35 Oliveros and Lucier met through their mutual friend, the pianist David Tudor in 1966.
    Shortly afterwards, Lucier composed *Chambers* in 1967 when he was invited by
    Oliveros to stay at the University of San Diego; cf. Pauline Oliveros, »Poet of
    Electronic Music: Preface«, in: Alvin Lucier 2005, op.cit., pp. 12–15, here p. 14.

walkie-talkies and the stationary PA system are essential in the increasing collection and comparison of auditory phenomena.«[36]

MEDIATED SPACE

In Oliveros's score a differentiation between »structure-borne sounds« and »airborne sounds« is listed, which can be correlated to the imagining of underwater theatre acoustics, and which was most important in Maryanne Amacher's installed music. If sound is transmitted through the air, it travels at a different velocity than sound that is transmitted via stone walls or water. In fact, transmission is also part of Lucier's *Quasimodo* »for any person who wishes to send sounds over long distances through air, water, ice, metal, stone, or any other sound-carrying medium, using the sound to capture and carry to listeners far away the acoustic characteristics of the environments through which they travel«[37].

In Maryanne Amacher's works, the installation or performance space was always acoustically tested. It mattered where the loudspeakers were placed, whether they faced a wall, and she performed her electronic music at the mixing desk herself. In her *City-Links* series (1967–1980)[38] she transmitted soundscapes from public places like the Boston harbor to her studio or to concert spaces. If different cities were connected sonically, there was a »city-link«. In that way a sonic presence of a space was translocated to a different space. Later, Amacher introduced the term »sonic telepresence«, referring to Virtual Reality[39].

In 1995 Amacher mentioned a scientific project, current at the time, that measured acoustic resonance in the sun, and concluded that the sound changes with different transmitters.

---

36 Pauline Oliveros, in: James Klosty (ed.), *Merce Cunningham*, op.cit., pp. 79f.

37 Alvin Lucier, *Quasimodo the Great Lover* (prose score, 1970), in: Alvin Lucier, *Chambers: Scores by Alvin Lucier: Interviews with the composer by Douglas Simon*, Middletown (CT) 1980, pp. 55–57.

38 Cf. Volker Straebel, »Zur frühen Geschichte und Typologie der Klanginstallation«, in: Ulrich Tadday (ed.), *Klangkunst* (= Musik-Konzepte Sonderband), München 2008, pp. 24–46, especially pp. 35f.

39 In many of the later works, the listener should move through a series of rooms, for example in the *Sound-Joined Rooms* installation, realized in the staircase and rooms of the bell tower of the Berlin Parochialkirche in 2006; cf. Carsten Seiffarth, Markus Steffens (eds.), *Singuhr – Hoergalerie in Parochial: Sound Art in Berlin: 1996 bis 2006*, Heidelberg 2010.

»For music students, I hope that Cage's influence gets deeper and deeper, that right now we've only touched the tip of the iceberg and that one day we'll have minds for music. Imagine, there are six listening posts where people are currently studying sound on the sun in a project called ›The Gong‹[40]. In the last few decades, interferometry techniques have revealed defined patterns of acoustic oscillations corresponding to a series of harmonics produced as sound waves reflect off the thermal boundaries surrounding the sun's core. Separated from us by 93 million miles of vacuum, the sun is in effect a big silent gong. In its interior, middle C (which on our earth has a wavelength of roughly four feet in air at room temperature) has a length of about one half mile. Imagine the sound.«[41]

Although we cannot listen to music performed on the sun, we can try to fathom the difference to our regular experience, if we use our imagination. More precisely, if we use our imagination informed by the state of scientific research of our time. It should be noted that Amacher was informed on the helioseismological research one year before the magazine *Science* published a special issue on it.

IMAGINING SONIC SPACES

This active interest in contemporaneous scientific research triggered Amacher's imagination and provided ideas for her creative work. Similarly, Pauline Oliveros had been inspired by the experiments of a physicist, Tesla, and Alvin Lucier by books on auditory perception in bats[42], etc.

In the late 1960s influences on art could come – as Oliveros writes – from culture, from the natural world, from the technological world, and from personal imagination.

»My own music has passed through various stages in the 25 years that I have been composing. [...] Traditional, Improvisational, Electronic, Theatrical [...], Meditational,

---

40 »Global Oscillation Network Group (GONG)«, cf. *Science* Vol. 272 (31 May 1996).

41 Maryanne Amacher et al., »Cage's Influence: A Panel Discussion« (1995), in: David W. Bernstein, Christoph Hatch (eds.), *Writings Through John Cage's Music, Poetry and Art*, Chicago 2001; pp. 167–198, here p. 197.

42 Lucier names the following book as inspiration for *Vespers*: Donald Griffin, *Listening in the Dark: The Acoustic Orientation of Bats and Men*, New Haven 1958. For the composition, which visualizes resonance patterns after Chladni, he refers to the photos in: Hans Jenny, *Cymatics*, Basle 1967, 1974. The latter work deals with problems similar to the helioseismological research Maryanne Amacher later explored, i.e., the measurement and visualization of acoustic waves; cf. ibid. p. 12.

now moving into what I call software for people. My materials have come from four major sources:

1. All the music I have ever heard.
2. All the sounds of the natural world I have ever heard including my own inner biological sounds.
3. All the sounds of the technological world I have ever heard.
4. All the sounds from my imagination.«[43]

To compare spaces – in this case, the auditory impressions of spaces – means remembering the acoustics of a space and compare it to a current space. Thus, it is an exercise in sensibility. Once it is mastered, it can be extended into the imaginary realm. If you know how a violin tune sounds in a small room compared to how it sounds in a large room, you can imagine what it will sound like in a different space. If you can compute acoustic properties, you can also compute those of an imaginary room.

In the late 1960s, space concepts of the experimental music scene incorporated elements of performance art: the performers move through the whole space and include the audiences' space in their explorations, thus overcoming the traditional boundaries between stage and auditorium. Often the experimental compositions were performed in art galleries, rather than in concert halls.

The acoustic exploration of the individual performance space is part of the composition, as is the procedural character of testing[44]. The individual acoustics of the performance space become apparent and form the unique appearance of the composition's performance. That allows for comparison of different spaces and different performances.

If the focus is on the spatial characteristics, the compositions tend to develop into sound installations, contrary to their original proximity to performance pieces. The immersive quality of the whole building resonating in its resonant frequency is independent of the performers' acting who merely serve as engineers for the listeners' experience. It is a physical experience the composer provides for the listener.

Imagination, on the other hand, can conceive the utopian. It could be argued that it is part of the avant-garde concept of progress, and it adds an

---

43 Pauline Oliveros, *Software for people*, [no date] p. 3.
44 This process-based form of Lucier's *I am Sitting in a Room* or the test for the resonant frequency in Oliveros's *In Memoriam Nikola Tesla* differ from ritual forms. The performers are supposed to carry out the acts in a distinctly matter-of-fact manner, and not at all like play-acting or as in a trance.

artistic or metaphysical dimension. Paradoxically, there is no strong distinction between the real and the imaginary acoustic spaces, if you only read the verbal score that provided the basis of this chapter[45]. One must imagine the sound.

45 Although there have been more than sixty performances of Cunningham's *Canfield* with Oliveros's music between 1969 and 1972, to the best of my knowledge there is no published audio documentation of Pauline Oliveros's *In Memoriam Nikola Tesla, Cosmic Engineer.*

Theorie und Praxis der Raumkomposition /

Theory and Practice of Spatial Composition

Vom Finden zum Erfinden

Stockhausens Theorie von der »Musik im Raum«
durch die Brille seiner Werke *Gesang der Jünglinge,
Gruppen, Kontakte* und *Carré* betrachtet

PASCAL DECROUPET

Seit Jahrzehnten wird auf den Aufsatz »Musik im Raum« Karlheinz Stockhausens verwiesen, in der Hoffnung, aus ihm die Elemente einer Theorie des
Raums herauslösen zu können. Aus diesem Grunde ist es auch hier unum-
gänglich, diesen Aufsatz als solchen zu thematisieren, doch ist der vorlie-
gende Ansatz ein umgekehrter: anstatt den Aufsatz als eine (für *Gesang der
Jünglinge* und *Gruppen*) nachgereichte bzw. (für *Kontakte* und *Carré*) prä-
skriptive Theorie zu betrachten, vor dessen Hintergrund sich die effektiven
Kompositionen verstehen lassen, werden hier die Informationen gleichsam
aufgespalten. Einerseits wird die eigene Geschichtlichkeit des Aufsatzes ge-
klärt, andererseits wird aus den Werken herausgelesen, welches die musikalisch operierenden Raumstrategien sowie die eventuell dahinterliegenden
Raumvorstellungen sind. Da der Aufsatz »Musik im Raum« 1958 in seiner
›definitiven‹ Fassung formuliert wurde, ergibt sich im Vergleich mit den hier
zur Diskussion vorgeschlagenen Werken folgende Situation: *Gesang der
Jünglinge* und *Gruppen* sind uraufgeführt, für *Kontakte* arbeitet Stockhausen
seit dem Frühjahr 1958 an der Erforschung neuer Klangproduktionsmög-
lichkeiten und wird sich wohl auch schon einige Gedanken gemacht haben,
nach welchen Kriterien die so hergestellten Klänge zu musikalischem Zusammenhang zusammengefügt werden können, während *Carré* noch gar
nicht zur Debatte steht. Zwar entwarf Stockhausen im Herbst 1957, also parallel zur Fertigstellung bzw. Reinschrift der Partitur der *Gruppen* eine neue
räumliche Komposition, *Hörkreis* genannt, doch blieb diese in den ersten
Gedankenskizzen stecken.

1. DER AUFSATZ »MUSIK IM RAUM«
Erfahrungsbericht mit historischer Einbettung
wie auch Skizze für weitere Projekte

Am 4. September 1958 hielt Stockhausen bei den Darmstädter Ferienkursen für neue Musik seinen Vortrag »Musik im Raum«. Vorausgegangen waren am 30. Mai 1956 die Uraufführung von *Gesang der Jünglinge* sowie am 23. März 1958 die Uraufführung der *Gruppen* für drei Orchester. Im Oktober 1958 erschien in einem auf die bevorstehenden Donaueschinger Musiktage für zeitgenössische Tonkunst der Zeitschrift *Melos* zugeschnittenen thematischen Heft zur Frage des Raumes eine erste schriftliche Fassung des Aufsatzes, welche anschließend auch in den *Darmstädter Beiträgen zur neuen Musik* publiziert wurde. In Heft 5 von *Die Reihe* folgte dann 1959 jene lange Fassung, die später auch in den ersten Band von Stockhausens *Texten* aufgenommen wurde[1]. Für die CD-Ausgabe seiner nunmehr gesprochenen Schriften im Jahre 2007 fügte Stockhausen insbesondere in diesen Text einige Zusätze ein, von denen später ausführlich die Rede sein wird, sowie, gleichsam als zusätzlichen, eigenständigen Abschnitt, einen kommentierten Durchlauf der *Gruppen*, welcher aber (ebenfalls) kaum eine Grundlage zu einer Theorie des Raumes bei Stockhausen in der zweiten Hälfte der fünfziger Jahre darstellt.

In seiner langen Druckfassung umfasst der Aufsatz vier Schwerpunkte: (1) eine historische Einleitung mit Beispielen von Raummusik aus früheren Jahrhunderten, (2) einen Abschnitt zu *Gesang der Jünglinge* und *Gruppen*, (3) weitere Ausführungen zu *Gruppen* und spezifische Überlegungen zu neuen Aufführungsstätten, sowie (4) einen theoretischeren Teil, in dem Stockhausen den Raum als fünften Parameter zu etablieren beabsichtigt. Insbesondere die dort in der zweiten Hälfte prominenten graphischen Beispiele verweisen auf das frühe Skizzenstadium von *Kontakte* sowie auf die Entwürfe zu *Hörkreis*. Die Texte zu den Abschnitten (2) und (3) hatte Stockhausen zuvor als Einführungstexte zu den Ursendungen der beiden Kompositionen im Musikalischen Nachtprogramm des Westdeutschen Rundfunks verwendet.

---

1 Kleinere Streichungen bzw. eine leicht abgewandelte innere Untergliederung werden hier nicht thematisiert. Als Referenztext dient die Ausgabe in Karlheinz Stockhausen, *Texte 1*, Köln 1963, S. 152–175.

Abbildung 1: Die verschiedenen veröffentlichten Fassungen des Aufsatzes »Musik im Raum«

	I	II	III	IV	[V]
	Vorgeschichte	*Gesang/ Gruppen*	*Gruppen* Fortsetzung + Klammer zu Räumen	»Theorie«	
Rundfunk	/	Fragmente als Einleitungen zu /*Gesang*/ in: WDR 7.11.56 BR 27.11.56 BR 16.3.59 /*Gruppen*/ in: WDR 23.4.58	in: WDR 23.4.58 (Erstsendung *Gruppen*)	/	
Melos 10/1958	/	komplett außer §12–13	komplett außer Klammer §3	/	
Darmstädt. Beitr 1959	/	komplett	komplett	/	
die Reihe 5 (1959)	bezeichnet als »I« komplett	bezeichnet als »II«, komplett außer II §12–13 und III §2 [identisch mit Fassung *Melos*]		bezeichnet als »III« komplett	
Texte 1, 1963	komplett	komplett	komplett	komplett	
Texte gelesen auf CD, 2007		*3 Zusätze*	*1 Zusatz am Ende*	*3 Zusätze*	*Durchlauf der Gruppen für drei Orchester*

Einige Überlegungen aus den im letzten Abschnitt aufgestellten theoretischen Ansatzpunkten sind für den vorliegenden Aufsatz nicht zentral. Aus diesem Grund ist der folgende Punkt auf *Kontakte* konzentriert in der Absicht, den theoretischen Äußerungen jene praktischen Elemente beizustellen, die für ein konkretes Verständnis kaum umgangen werden können.

2. KONTAKTE
Veränderung der Raumplanung entsprechend der Wandlung des Projektes im Laufe des Kompositionsprozesses

Die aus dem Aufsatz bekannten Dreiecke mit Kreuz in der Mitte stammen offensichtlich aus den Skizzen zu *Kontakte*. Wie die Strukturskizzen zeigen, bestimmte Stockhausen den Tonort dort als obersten Ausarbeitungsparameter nach Festlegung der Abschnittsdauern. Wie bereits von Helmut Kirchmeyer beschrieben[2], beabsichtigte Stockhausen zunächst, die Komposition als mobile Partitur für elektronische Klänge, Klavier (Kreuz) und drei Schlagzeuger (die Spitzen des Dreiecks) anzulegen. Schwierigkeiten bei den ›Testproben‹ haben Stockhausen dazu bewogen, die Interaktion zwischen Tonband und Musikern neu zu überdenken. Daraus resultierte das bekanntgewordene Werk mit kontinuierlichem Tonband und Instrumentalpartien für nur zwei Musiker.

Nichtsdestotrotz können aus dem Planungsstadium der *Kontakte* Erkenntnisse zu Stockhausens Raumdenken gewonnen werden. Zunächst bedeutet der Tonort gleichsam als Tonraumpunkt eine diskrete Bestimmung: der Wechsel geschieht von einem Klangort zu einem oder mehreren anderen, und der zu beobachtende Unterschied ist Teil einer Skala von Veränderungsgraden, die von der kleinsten, gerade noch wahrnehmbaren Variation bis hin zu maximalem Kontrast reicht. Nach Aufgabe des Gedankens der Verräumlichung der Spieler wurde quasi die ›Raumuhr‹ wieder auf Null gestellt, und in dieser Situation fand Stockhausen neue, dem nunmehr kontinuierlichen Vierspurtonband adäquate Lösungen, u.a. in Form des bekannten *Rotationstisches*. Was im *Gesang der Jünglinge* noch durch langwierige Montagearbeit realisiert werden musste, konnte in *Kontakte* anders angegangen werden, denn die Verteilung über die Lautsprecher konnte fortan in einem einzigen zusätzlichen Arbeitsschritt nach der endgültigen Montage der Klänge realisiert werden – auch wenn dies bekanntlich von Hand geschah. Dadurch erweitert sich das Spektrum der verfügbaren Raumstrategien, denn zusätzlich zu den statischen Tonorten können nun auch dynamische Raumbewegungen (Kreise oder Schleifen) komponiert werden, wobei neben der Drehrichtung auch die Drehgeschwindigkeit als Parameter berücksichtigt werden kann. Die folgende Aufstellung zeigt, wie Stockhausen für die einzelnen Abschnitte übergeordnete Raumverhalten festlegt, wodurch die Momente nun als zusammenhängende Einheiten auch räumlich charakterisiert werden, was sowohl ihre Individualität im Verband der Großform steigert als auch großformale Zusammenhänge herstellt. Wie bei Stockhausen in den fünfziger Jahren üblich, werden zu Beginn der Komposition die wesentlichen Variationsmöglichkeiten in kompakter Weise vorgestellt, so dass alle späteren sich auf diese Besonderheiten beziehenden Abschnitte als ›Auskomponierungen‹ verstanden werden können.

---

2   Helmut Kirchmeyer, »Zur Entstehungs- und Problemgeschichte der *Kontakte* von Karlheinz Stockhausen«, Einführung zu WERGO 60009 [1963]; ohne Abbildungen wieder veröffentlicht in: Neuland 3 (1982/83), S. 152–176.

Abbildung 2: Transkription der Verräumlichungsstrategien für das Vierspurton-
band von »Kontakte« (Abschnittszählung nach Partitur und Analyse, nicht nach
Skizze)

I	in Laut- sprecher »Mitte«	in allen Ver- schiedenes	alternierend	in allen dasselbe	Rotation	Flutklang
II	einzelne wechselnd					
III	Bewegung zwischen einzelnen					
IV	in einzelnen		in allen dasselbe		alternierend	
V	Rotationen					
VI	Schleifen [1–2–4–3–1–2–4–3...] + fixiertes in allen dasselbe					
VII	in allen dasselbe					
VIII	Flutklang + in allen verschiedenes					
IX	alternierend (2. Teil rasend schnell) – räumliche Tiefe					
X	Bewegung zwischen einzelnen					
XI	Rotation (Schwärme)					
XII	Einschub					
XIII	Schleifen, Fenster, Raum voll MG / »Schüsse« aus allen verschiedenes (sehr dichte Metallschübe, Schläge) hohes Klirren					
XIV +XV	in allen dasselbe, stampfend und kurze Stücke Rotation					
XVI	Flutklang					

3. CARRÉ
Räumliches Verhalten als Gliederung der Großform

Es mag paradox anmuten, dass der Raumgestaltung in *Carré* anscheinend
eine untergeordnete Rolle zukommt, denn in der Strukturskizze zu *Carré*
taucht der Raum als Parameter gar nicht auf. Stockhausen beschränkt sich
dort auf acht in jeweils vier Varianten unterteilte Parameter: Typ, Ein-
schwing[akzent in einem bestimmten Instrument], Gestaltveränderung,
Dichte (der Tonhöhen), Lage, Dauer, Lautstärke und Farbe[3]. Entstanden sind
diese ersten Skizzen eindeutig sowohl nach dem Vortrag »Musik im Raum«
als auch nach den letzten Korrekturen an der Partitur der *Gruppen* (deren definitive Fassung erstmals am 17. Juni 1959 in Wien erklang). In der Tat, erst
für den nächsten Schritt der Ausarbeitung, jene berühmt berüchtigten ›Kärt-

---

3 Diese Skizze ist abgedruckt auf dem Cover der Partitur zu Chor und Orchester I, sowie in: Richard Toop, *Six Lectures from the Stockhausen Courses Kürten 2002*, Kürten 2005, S. 173.

chen‹ für jeden Moment, die Stockhausen Cornelius Cardew zur Ausarbeitung vorlegte[4], erscheint die räumliche Verteilung, nun aber an prominenter Stelle. Andere Arbeitsunterlagen zeigen, wie Stockhausen in *Carré* eine Ebene der Großform in vier Teile gemäß unterschiedlicher Raumverteilungsstrategien zu gliedern beabsichtigte. Wie aus den auf der Titelseite der Partitur zu Chor und Orchester II abgedruckten Skizzen unmittelbar zu ersehen ist, sieht Stockhausen vier qualitativ unterschiedliche Raumverhalten vor: fixe Positionen (Anschluss), Rechtsdrehung, Linksdrehung und einen in seinem Raumverhalten dort nicht näher ausgeführten Abschnitt. Gerade die Drehungen lassen Stockhausens Problemstellung deutlich erkennen, da er dort eine gerichtete Bewegung einerseits mit seriellen Gleichverteilungskriterien andererseits zu vereinbaren sucht.

Der serielle Verteilungsrahmen ist von fast verstörender Einfachheit. Jede Drehung sieht 48 Raumpunkte vor, also 4x12, wobei jeder der vier Raumpunkte in jeder Gruppierung (ein einzelnes Orchester, oder 2, oder 3, oder 4) 3 Mal vertreten sein muss. Diese statistische Gleichverteilung berücksichtigt Stockhausen auf allen Ebenen. Die Rechtsdrehung erscheint als erste, und das Bewegungsmuster ist dort sehr deutlich durchgeführt: außer den beiden Diagonalstellungen 2–4 und 1–3 (ca. zu Beginn des letzten Drittels des Abschnitts), führen alle Verläufe das Prinzip der Rechtsdrehung aus, wenngleich die regelmäßige Rotation manchmal in einem Tonort stockt (ein neuer Moment also in einem Tonort beginnt, der bereits im vorherigen erreicht wurde) oder sogar um eine Position zurückspringt (was aber kaum als eine Linksdrehung gedeutet werden kann), bevor eine neuerliche eindeutige Rechtsdrehung einsetzt. Bei der Linksdrehung stehen die beiden Diagonalpaare im ersten Drittel des Abschnitts unmittelbar nebeneinander. Diese Drehungen gelten sowohl für die Beziehung zwischen den Momenten als auch innerhalb der Momente. Die in den folgenden Tabellen gezeigten Zahlenfolgen weichen von jenen in Stockhausens Skizzen ab, da der Komponist dort lediglich auf die Gleichverteilung der Zahlen bedacht war und die effektive Bewegung erst später in der graphischen Skizze ausführte, während hier beide Informationen in die Zahlenfolgen integriert wurden.

---

4   Vgl. Cornelius Cardew, *Report on Stockhausen's Carré*, in: The Musical Times 102 (Nr. 1424), Oktober 1961, S. 619–622; auch in: *Cornelius Cardew (1936–1981): A Reader*, hrsg. von Edwin Prévost, Matching Tye/Essex 2006, S. 23–30.

Abbildung 3: »Carré«, Verläufe zu den Rechts- und Linksdrehungen in Zahlen; jede Spalte bezieht sich auf einen Moment (Positionen: 1 oben, 2 rechts, 3 unten, 4 links; X = Diagonalstellungen)

Rechtsdrehung

3	4			3	4	1		3				4	1	2		2			2	1	
	41					12		34		42					23		31				
342			412										341					23		231	
								1234							4123				2341		
									X								X				

Linksdrehung

1	4	3	2							2	3		1	4	3	2	1	4			
				42	13		43	14	32												21
142						143					243								321		
			1432				2143										3214				
			X	X																	

4. GRUPPEN
Raumbewegungen und räumliche Konzentration

Der Ausgangspunkt für die Komposition der *Gruppen* ist eindeutig eine Überlegung zur Zeitgestaltung – jene ›Korrektur‹ an der »chromatischen« Dauernskala, wie sie in den allerersten seriell multidimensionalen Kompositionen aus den Jahren 1951–52 angewendet worden war. Doch auch die Verräumlichung der Schallquellen hat Stockhausen bereits zu einem sehr frühen Stadium beschäftigt, und so bietet denn auch der erste Entwurf eines im Maßstab gezeichneten Zeitplans erste grundlegende Einsichten in die Beziehung zwischen Zeit- und Raumkomposition, die einerseits auf eine freie Wahl des Komponisten schließen und andererseits bestimmte durch das Material aufgezwungene Einschränkungen erkennen lassen. Ich werde hier versuchen, die wesentlichen Arbeitsschritte des Komponisten chronologisch nachzuzeichnen, so dass die entsprechenden räumlichen Situationen als Resultate bestimmter Entscheidungen während des Kompositionsprozesses erkennbar werden. (Dies bedeutet z.B., dass die später hinzugefügten Soli als Markierungen innerhalb des Formverlaufs zunächst selbstverständlich unberücksichtigt bleiben müssen. Es wird später zu sehen sein, wie sich das Einfügen der Soli ebenfalls auf die Raumstrukturierung ausgewirkt hat.)

Zunächst also der Zeitplan in seiner ersten Fassung[5]. Dieses Dokument liegt in jener Form vor, wie es am Ende des Kompositionsprozesses erhalten

---

5   In Faksimile nachzuschlagen in Karlheinz Stockhausen, *Kompositorische Grundlagen Neuer Musik: Sechs Seminare für die Darmstädter Ferienkurse 1970*, hrsg. von Imke Misch, Kürten 2009, S. 56.

geblieben ist. Die dort verschränkten unterschiedlichen chronologisch auf-einanderfolgenden Arbeitsschritte lassen sich an den Farben bzw. den ver-schiedenen Stiften oder Schriften erkennen. Entfernt man alle durch die Analyse als »später« identifizierbaren Eintragungen, so erhält man den sozu-sagen ›nackten‹ Zeitplan mit der Verteilung der Ereignisse über die drei Or-chester.

Abbildung 4: »Gruppen«, Rekonstruktion der chronologisch ersten Schicht des Zeitplans. Die durchgehenden Linien stehen für die Gruppenlängen, die gestrichelten für die Verbindungen zwischen den Gruppen. Die Nummern kennzeichnen die einzelnen Gruppen nach Stockhausens erster Zählung. Die drei Orchester sind wie folgt innerhalb eines Systems überlagert: oben, O. I (links); in der Mitte, O. II (vorne); unten, O. III (rechts). Eine Rechtdrehung verläuft graphisch von oben nach untern, eine Linksdrehung, von unten nach oben.

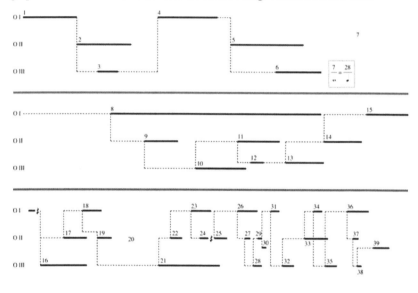

Zu Beginn ist die Situation relativ überschaubar: unabhängig von der effek-tiven Dauer der Klanggruppen und der sie trennenden Pausen ist es möglich, die Klangereignisse in eine einzige Richtung drehen zu lassen, nämlich im Uhrzeigersinn. Aufeinanderfolgende Gruppen überlagern sich oder werden durch Pausen getrennt. Aufgrund der Proportionen im Zeitplan entsteht nach Gruppe 6 aber eine unvergleichlich längere strukturelle Pause als bisher, was einen eindeutigen Einschnitt markiert (Stockhausen vergibt dort folglich unmittelbar eine Gruppenzahl, die 7). Außerdem wirkt sich diese lange Pau-se beim Wiedereintritt des Klanges dahingehend aus, dass die nächste Klanggruppe (8 in der ersten Fassung des Zeitplans, 9 in der veröffentlichen

Partitur) entsprechend ausgedehnt ist, so dass eine erhebliche Zahl von darauffolgenden Gruppen räumlich nichts als ein ständiges Pendeln zwischen den beiden verbleibenden Orchestern darstellen können. Dieser durch die Zeitstruktur diktierte qualitative Wandel hat ferner zur Folge, dass sich Stockhausen beim Wiedereintreten einer schnelleren Aufeinanderfolge der Gruppen (ab Gruppe 13, welche nur unwesentlich später endet als Gruppe 8) für eine Rotation in gegenläufiger Richtung entscheidet (die dann aber bei Gruppe 25, wiederum durch eine lange Gruppe, diesmal in Orchester III, zum Stocken kommt). Insgesamt ergibt sich also für den Beginn der Komposition eine ganz einfache Dreiteiligkeit: Rechtsdrehung, Pendeln vor stabilem Hintergrund in Orchester I, Linksdrehung. Die Tatsache, dass die gedehnte Klanggruppe in Orchester I steht ist bezeichnend, denn betrachtet man das jeweils dominierende Orchester über den gesamten Verlauf des Stückes, so ist ebenfalls eine allmähliche Rechtsdrehung auszumachen: zu Beginn dominiert Orchester I, in der Mitte Orchester II und am Ende Orchester III. Diese globale Verschiebung kann eindeutig als serielles Anliegen bezeichnet werden, nämlich eines Wandels der inneren Hierarchie entsprechend des Verlaufs der Großform.

Bei den nächsten Arbeitsschritten verteilt Stockhausen über diesen Zeitplan charakterisierende Merkmale auf zwei Ebenen: zunächst 4 unterschiedliche Texturmerkmale, die seriell permutiert über die gesamte Komposition verteilt werden; später und komplementär dazu dann noch die Chromatik unterschiedlich färbende Intervalle, die die Intervallproportionen der Grundreihe des Zeitplans in größter Spreizung einmal über die Gesamtdauer der Werkes als Tonhöhenintervalle hörbar machen. Wie von Imke Misch gezeigt wurde, entsprechen die Schnittpunkte den Tritoni im Zeitplan[6]. Der erste Schnitt fällt somit zwischen die Gruppen 15 und 16: hier soll der statistische chromatische Charakter der Harmonik zu Beginn des Werkes verlassen werden und ein erstes färbendes Intervall, die fallende große Terz, als »harmonischer Filter« in Erscheinung treten. Der Schnitt zwischen den Gruppen 22 und 23 (FWR II laut Bezeichnung in der Skizze) bedeutet einen Texturwechsel (welcher maßgeblich durch einen Wechsel in der *rhythmischen* Mikrogestaltung beeinflusst wird)[7].

---

6   Imke Misch, *Zur Kompositionstechnik Karlheinz Stockhausens: »Gruppen« für 3 Orchester (1955–1957)*, Saarbrücken 1999, S. 65–67 und 73.
7   Zu den multiparametrischen Tabellen für die »Formwechsel Rhythmus«, vgl. Misch ebd., S. 108–109.

Abbildung 5: »Gruppen«, Rekonstruktion der chronologisch zweiten Schicht des Zeitplans. Die zusätzlichen Eintragungen beziehen sich auf die Formwechsel in den Bereichen »Rhythmus« (FWR gefolgt von römischer Zahl, aber auch die arabischen Zahlen 1–4 in den beiden ersten Systemen) und »Instrumente« (bzw. »Intervall« – FWI mit arabischer Zahl).

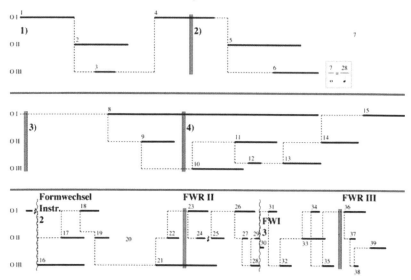

Worauf es im vorliegenden Kontext ankommt, ist die Tatsache, dass der Schnitt zwischen den Gruppen 15 und 16 von Stockhausen bei der Überarbeitung seiner ersten Partitur zum Einfügungsort für einen ersten solistischen Einschub, nämlich der Streicher, gewählt wird, will sagen einer ausgedehnten eigenständigen Passage, die auf den strukturellen Zeitplan nicht zurückführbar ist. Dadurch verändert sich aber die Raumstrategie maßgeblich, insbesondere wenn man als Anhaltspunkt die Fassung der Uraufführung vom 23. März 1958 heranzieht, in der besagtes erstes Solo einzig in Orchester I erklang (gewissermaßen zur Verdeutlichung der großformalen Hierarchie der Raumgliederung). Der Kontrast in der Klangtextur zwischen den vorausgegangenen statistischen Gruppen und dem nunmehr dominierenden Prinzip des Solos mit Orchesterbegleitung lässt den Übergang von Gruppe 15 zum Streichersolo deutlich als Schnitt erkennen, ein Schnitt, der durch die Lokalisierung im gleichen Orchester aber sozusagen (zumindest anfänglich und intentional) ›übermalt‹ wird[8].

---

8   Andere darüber hinaus von Stockhausen verwendete Strategien, die dazu dienen, diesen Schnitt zunächst zu kaschieren, können in meinem Aufsatz »Gravitationsfeld *Gruppen*: Zur Verschränkung der Werke *Gesang der Jünglinge, Gruppen* und *Zeit-*

Für den nunmehr als ersten Formteil begrenzten Abschnitt ergibt sich somit folgende Raumform: Rechtsdrehung, Pendeln vor stabilem Hintergrund in Orchester I, abschließende kurze Linksdrehung mit gleichsam kadenzierender Funktion, die in den Ausgangspunkt, Orchester I, zurückführt.

Abbildung 6: Raumverlauf in der überarbeiteten (definitiven) Fassung des ersten Einschubs (Streichersolo, Gruppen 16–22) von »Gruppen«

15	16	17	18	19	20	21	22			23
I	I	I	I	I	I------	I	I	I	I	I
	II				II-----		II	II		
			III		III--		III			

Als Konsequenz aus dieser Situation, die sich einzig dem ›Zufall‹ der kaskadierten Entscheidungen verdankt und vom Komponisten als qualitative Resultante unmöglich vorhersehbar war, überarbeitete Stockhausen nach der Uraufführung den ersten Einschub dahingehend, dass nunmehr alle drei Orchester daran beteiligt sind. An der Übersicht über den neuen (und definitiven) Raumverlauf innerhalb des ersten Einschubs ist deutlich zu erkennen, dass die ›räumliche Kadenzfunktion‹, die sich aus den aufeinanderfolgenden Arbeitsschritten ergeben hatte, nunmehr als wahrhafte kompositorische Geste an Schlüsselstellen wieder aufgegriffen wird (ansatzweise bereits beim Ausklingen der Orchester in Gruppe 20, deutlicher dann in den Tuttiakkorden in Gruppe 22), was den Raum in der Komposition *Gruppen* nun in der Tat auch zu einem eigenständigen Parameter emporsteigen lässt.

---

maße und deren Auswirkung auf Stockhausens Musikdenken in der zweiten Hälfte der fünfziger Jahre«, *Musiktheorie* 12/1 (1997), S. 37–51 nachgelesen werden. Bemerkenswert ist ferner, dass Stockhausen am Ende des Solos wiederum eine räumliche Kontinuität herstellt, was ihn dazu veranlasst, die frühere Gruppe 16 vom dritten ins erste Orchester (Partitur Gruppe 23) zu verschieben.

5. GESANG DER JÜNGLINGE
Ein Plädoyer für eine kompositionsgenetisch informierte
Aufführungspraxis

Zu Beginn der 1990er Jahre hörte ich den *Gesang der Jünglinge* mehrfach
im Konzert, mit Stockhausen selbst am Mischpult. Mein Eindruck war eindeutig, dass an der Verräumlichung irgendetwas musikalisch nicht richtig
sein konnte. Als ich im Herbst 1991 mit dem Studium der Kompositions-
skizzen begann, lag die Antwort unmittelbar auf der Hand: während Stockhausen im Konzert eine Vierkanalfassung vorführte, war die zweite Realisationspartitur nach der ersten Minute (Formteil A) in Form von fünf Kanälen
skizziert. Dies klärte allmählich über die Verwirrungen in der Literatur auf,
wo je nachdem von vier oder fünf Lautsprechergruppen die Rede war, bzw.
jener Mythos des zentral über dem Publikum hängenden fünften Lautsprecher zelebriert wurde, bis hin zu solch wahnwitzigen Deutungen wie, dass
dort die Stimme Gottes zu erklingen habe (was ja alleine schon durch den
gesungenen Text widerlegt wird). Eine gravierende Ausnahme in dieser Partitur stellt somit der Beginn dar, der mit nur vier Kanälen auskommt, und
wovon eine von Richard Toop besorgte Abschrift bereits mehrfach veröffentlicht worden war[9]. Zunächst sollen aber jene Fakten angeführt werden,
die für eine fünfkanalige Fassung als Mindestannäherung an Stockhausens
Intention plädieren.

In Formteil B erklingen in den fünf Kanälen gleichermaßen Chorscharen,
deren Aufeinanderfolge nur durch in die aus der Zeitstruktur resultierenden
Pausen hineingesetzten Impuls-Sinus-Komplexe unterbrochen wird. Wenngleich bis kurz vor Ende des Formteils (von den Takten 15–41 erst in den
Takten 35–36) ein qualitativer Unterschied zwischen Spur 1 und den vier
anderen zu existieren scheint, da die Impuls-Sinus-Komplexe lediglich in
den Spuren 2–5 erklingen, so spricht doch alles für eine räumliche Gleichverteilung von fünf Lautsprechern in einer einzigen Ebene. Bei Takt 35–36
wird eine Impulsschar mit zunächst auseinanderstrebenden Frequenzbändern
über alle fünf Kanäle verteilt (wobei zuletzt Lautsprecher 1 einbezogen
wird), bevor das abschließende Tutti aller Lautsprecher in Takt 40 die Chorscharen zusätzlich zwischen den Kanälen (1–2–3–5) rotieren lässt, wodurch

---

9   Richard Toop, *Stockhausen's Electronic Works: Sketches and Work-Sheets from
    1952–1967*, Interface 10 (1981), S. 149–197 (Partiturtranskriptionen, S. 178–179);
    Robin Maconie, *The Works of Karlheinz Stockhausen*, zweite Ausgabe, Oxford 1990,
    S. 60–61.

die immer komplexer werdende Polyphonie gleichsam in einer gesättigten Schlussgeste gipfelt[10].

Gleich zu Beginn von Formteil C steht eine sich allmählich im Frequenzraum zusammenziehende Impulsschar, die eine Rotation durch alle Lautsprecher mit abnehmender Geschwindigkeit zu Gehör bringt. Und auch in den darauffolgenden Abschnitten von Formteil C erscheinen Rauschbänder, welche sich kontinuierlich drehend durch den Raum bewegen. Dies kann sinnvoll nur dann zu Gehör gebracht werden, wenn fünf Lautsprecher in regelmäßigen Abständen um das Publikum herum aufgestellt sind. Hier wurde mir klar, dass der von mir empfundene musikalische Fehler darin bestand, dass durch die aus den technischen Beschränkungen des Jahres 1956 heraus geborene Notlösung der Reduktion auf vier Kanäle für den Effekt der »hinkenden Rotationen« verantwortlich war[11].

Kommen wir nun zum problematischen Beginn der Komposition. Die Partitur zeigt also 4 Kanäle[12]. Vor der ersten Spur der Realisationspartitur steht die Angabe »L1 Hoch«[13]. Am unteren linken Rand steht ein Quadrat

---

10 Karlheinz Stockhausen, *Gesang der Jünglinge: Faksimile-Edition 2001*, Kürten 2001, S. 65.

11 Aufgrund ungenügend präziser Synchronisation zwischen der Vierspurmaschine und dem Monotonband mit Spur 5 bei der Uraufführung nahm Stockhausen folgende quadrophonische Neuabmischung vor: die drei ersten Kanäle blieben unverändert, Kanal 4 vereinigte nunmehr die früheren Spuren 4 und 5.

12 Stockhausen, *Gesang der Jünglinge, Faksimile-Edition 2001*, a.a.O., S. 87.

13 Zum Sachverhalt eines höher zu hängenden Lautsprechers fügte Stockhausen eine ausgedehnte Klammer in der Audioversion des Aufsatzes ein. Dieser Auszug sei hier vollständig transkribiert, selbst wenn er mehrere nachweisliche Fehler enthält. »Die vier Spuren des vierspurigen Originalbandes wurden durch vier Lautsprechergruppen aus den vier Saalecken projiziert. Die fünfte Spur, auf einem separaten Tonband, sollte mit einem Lautsprecher von der Mitte der Decke herunter klingen. Aber schon bei der Uraufführung wurde aus Sicherheitsgründen verboten, einen Lautsprecher an der Decke zu befestigen. Deshalb stellte ich einen fünften Lautsprecher vorne in die Mitte des Podiums. Etwas später kopierte ich die fünfte Spur mit auf die erste und vierte Spur. Die vier Spuren werden wiedergegeben: 1 hinten links, 2 vorne links, 3 vorne rechts, 4 hinten rechts. Man sollte den *Gesang der Jünglinge* unbedingt als vierkanalige Projektion hören, möglichst in einem quadratischen Auditorium bei ausgeschaltetem Licht, nur mit einem kleinen Mond in der Mitte über dem Podium an die Wand projiziert. Ich empfehle dazu noch, die Augen zu schließen. Ohne dieses Raumerlebnis weiß man kaum, worüber ich in diesem Vortrag »Musik im Raum« spreche. Es ist noch nicht möglich, diese Raummusik im Rundfunk zu senden, aber selbst eine stereophone Wiedergabe lässt die innere Räumlichkeit der Musik spüren. Man sollte auch bei stereophoner Wiedergabe das Licht löschen, die Augen schließen, und sich in die stereophone Mitte setzen. Hören Sie nun die elektronische Musik *Gesang der Jünglinge* von 1956 stereophon.« (Track 1, 1'39" bis 3'24") Zur Vervollständigung sei hier

mit 5 Zahlen und 4 Kreuzchen: 2–3–4–5 ergeben eine leicht nach rechts ge-
drehte Raute, die aber deutlich zu erkennen gibt, dass die Lautsprecher auf
keinen Fall in den Saalecken zu positionieren sind; bei 1 ist das Kreuzchen
umkreist und es folgt eine Eintragung, die als kleines h mit Punkt gelesen
werden kann. Daraus ist zu schließen, dass Stockhausen beabsichtigte, diesen Lautsprecher *dort* höher zu hängen. Von der musikalischen Struktur von
Formteil A her ist das absolut schlüssig, denn Spur 1 ist sichtlich als durch-
gehende Schicht gedacht, die sich durchaus real von den drei anderen »ab-
hebt«. In Spur 1 sind zunächst alle Ereignisse von Dichte 1 (einzelne Impulse, gehaltenes Rauschen, ein solo gesungenes Wort: Jubelt); erst ab Takt 5
verdichten sich die Ereignisse in dieser Schicht zu elektronischen Akkorden;
in Takt 9 ist der Vokaleinsatz weiterhin solistisch, und erst in Takt 12 wird
auch das vokale Element zweistimmig verdichtet, bei synchronen Tonhö-
henänderungen in beiden »Stimmen«. In den anderen Spuren erklingen währenddessen Massenerscheinungen: zu Beginn eine dreifache Impulsschar,
anschließend diverse Chorscharen, wobei die Raumfigur der Takte 10–11
das symmetrische Pendant zur elektronischen Figur des Beginns darstellt.
Während zu Beginn die Impulsschar die Dichte der Lautsprecherverteilung
von 3 zu 1 abklingen lässt, baut sich nun ein in den ganzen Raum in Beschlag
nehmender Klang in umgekehrter Reihenfolge auf und klingt anschließend
in gleicher Reihenfolge (4–3–2) wieder aus.

Daraus kann gefolgert werden, dass Stockhausen, als er die Synchroni-
sationsarbeit am neuen Anfang von *Gesang der Jünglinge* im Herbst 1955
begann (bekanntlich komponierte und realisierte er ja bereits im Frühsom-
mer 1955 knapp eine halbe Minute Musik, welche dann aber an den Beginn
des Schlussteils F verschoben wurde), wohl die Frage nach den technischen
Bedingungen für einen höher anzubringenden Lautsprecher gestellt haben
wird, eine Frage, auf die er von den technischen Verantwortlichen sichtlich
eine kategorische Absage bekam, so dass bereits während der Synchronisati-
onsarbeit für die unmittelbar folgenden Abschnitte ein Umdenken einsetzte.
Die Zeichnung zur Lautsprecheranordnung auf der ersten Seite der zweiten
Realisationspartitur lässt aufgrund der ungleichen Verteilung der die Lautsprecher symbolisierenden Zahlen auf zwei getrennte Arbeitsschritte schließen: zunächst sah Stockhausen vier Lautsprecher vor, jeweils leicht gegenüber der Mitte der Saalwände versetzt, wovon eben einer in einer höheren
Ebene anzubringen war, doch dann fügte er die Zahl 5 hinzu, wodurch sich
eben die ungleiche Verteilung ergibt. Während in Formteil B noch ein Zwei-

---

angemerkt, dass die Stereoabmischung auf der Grundlage des Vierspurtonbands hergestellt wurde.

fel bestehen kann bezüglich der Platzierung von Lautsprecher 1, muss Stockhausen spätestens ab Formteil C von einer Lautsprecheraufstellung in einer einzigen Ebene um das Publikum herum, also ohne jegliche Stimme aus der Höhe ausgegangen sein, denn von nun an gibt es zwischen den verschiedenen Spuren keine qualitativen Unterschiede mehr, die durch eine räumliche Trennung in zwei vertikalen Ebenen adäquat dargestellt werden würden.

Von den gut 13 Minuten der fertigen Komposition entsprechen schließlich allerhöchstens die ersten 2'45" dem ursprünglichen Gedanken einer Aufstellung mit einem in der Höhe angebrachten Lautsprecher, so dass insgesamt eine Aufstellung mit fünf gleichmäßig in einer Ebene verteilten Lautsprecher als der eindeutig beste Kompromiss erscheinen muss. Wollte man nun aber den von Stockhausen zunächst intendierten Effekt praktisch umsetzen, so genügt es, die Spur 1 von Formteil A auf eine sechste Spur zu verschieben und einen entsprechenden sechsten Lautsprecher frontal in der Höhe anzubringen.

Marc Battier zeigt in seinem Artikel zu den verschiedenen von Pierre Schaeffer Jahr um Jahr angemeldeten Patenten, dass für Olivier Messiaens *Timbres-durées* 1953 ebenfalls eine »Mehrspurfassung« hergestellt wurde, die den Besonderheiten des *pupitre d'espace* in seiner Version aus dem Jahre 1952 angepasst war, nämlich mit drei unterschiedlichen Lautsprechern in einer Ebene auf Ohrhöhe und einem über den Zuhörern hängenden Lautsprecher. Bekannt ist, daß Stockhausen im Frühjahr 1952 in Paris verschiedenen Konzerten der Veranstaltung *L'Œuvre du XX*e *siècle* beiwohnte und dort wahrscheinlich auch die Vorführung der damaligen Kompositionen der *musique concrète* unter Verwendung des *pupitre d'espace* hörte. Bedenkt man ferner noch, dass im 3. Kapitel Daniel, aus dem Stockhausen den Text des Lobgesangs entnahm, von drei Männern, die das Gesetz des Königs Nebukadnezzars missachteten und aus diesem Grund in die Flammen der Feuerofens geworfen wurden, sowie vom herabsteigenden »Engel des Herrn« mit seinen Gefährten die Rede ist, so gewinnt die Idee eines zentralen Lautsprechers in der Höhe in Stockhausens Vorstellung einige Plausibilität, aber als Ort der Stimme des Engels. Andererseits muss angemerkt werden, dass die drei Männer ihren Gott anflehen bevor die Engel in den Feuerofen herabschweben, was mit der Dramaturgie im *Gesang der Jünglinge* (auffordernde Solostimme, antwortende Chöre) nicht übereinstimmt.

Die von mir bevorzugte Hypothese hält indes stärker an den schriftlichen Quellen fest, nämlich an der Tatsache, dass eine Aufstellung eines höher angebrachten Lautsprechers in frontaler wenn auch teils seitlich verschobener Position jene Raumdisposition nachstellt, die durch das Verhältnis von Priester auf der Kanzel und Gemeinde im Kirchenraum gegeben ist. Eine solche Disposition reibt sich nicht mit der musikalischen Dramaturgie der Komposition, sondern lässt diese erst wirklich plastisch erscheinen, und scheint als einzige dem Formteil A einen unmittelbar hörend nachvollziehbaren Sinn zu geben.

Ein weiterer essentieller Punkt betrifft die Verteilung der Kanäle über die Lautsprecher. Die Norm, die Stockhausen selbst später angibt, besagt, dass die Lautsprecherzählung hinten links mit 1 beginnt und dann im Uhrzeigersinn verläuft. Das ist auch genau, was Stockhausen zu Beginn der 1990er Jahre bei Konzerten mit dem Vierspurband von *Gesang der Jünglinge* tat. Stellt man aber die Mischpultpläne in Rechnung, die sich ebenfalls im Skizzenkonvolut von *Gesang der Jünglinge* befinden[14] in Rechnung, so ergibt sich die Notwendigkeit einer Gesamtrotation um ca. 90 Grad, so dass die beiden Lautsprecher 1 und 2 eine Front bilden und die weiteren Lautsprecher entsprechend äquidistant im Raum verteilt werden (3 rechts 2/3 hinten, 4 Mitte hinten, 5 links 2/3 hinten). Dies wird in den folgenden Transkriptionen besonders klar, wenn man die Mischpultpläne für die damaligen Vierkanalkompositionen des WDR-Studios, insbesondere György Ligetis *Artikulation*, mit jenem für *Gesang der Jünglinge* vergleicht. Bei diesen Mischpultplänen bedeuten die Spalten sichtlich die Spuren des mehrkanaligen Eingangssignals (es handelt sich immer um vier Spuren) während die Zeilen die Ausgänge zu den Lautsprechern bezeichnen. Kombiniert mit den Lautsprecherskizzen bzw. Lautsprecheraufstellungsplänen, die ebenfalls im Skizzendossier enthalten sind[15], ergibt sich folgende logische Platzierung und Schaltung auf der Grundlage von fünf gleichmäßig im Raum verteilten Lautsprechern. Da für Ligeti 1+2 das gleiche Signal abstrahlen, müssen diese Lautsprecher die beiden Frontlautsprecher sein; die anderen Lautsprecher befinden sich folglich an den verbleibenden Seitenwänden (und eben nicht in den Ecken). Bei Stockhausen ist bezeichnend, dass Eingang 4 mit zwei Ausgängen, nämlich 4 und 5 gekoppelt erscheint: das legt nahe, dass Stockhausen in den späten fünfziger Jahren eine mehrkanalige Aufführungspraxis für *Gesang der Jünglinge* entwickelt hatte, bei der er von Hand die Kanäle 4 und 5 entsprechend der Partitur live getrennt hat, so dass die Raumerfahrung effektiv mit der intendierten Raumkomposition übereinstimmen konnte.

---

14 Dossiers zu *Gesang der Jünglinge* [Fotokopieausgabe aus dem Jahre 1983], Abteilung V, Blatt 86.

15 Stockhausen, *Gesang der Jünglinge: Faksimile-Edition 2001*, a.a.O., S. 23 (Quadrat in der Mitte), 31 (kopfstehend) und 32 (ebenfalls kopfstehend).

Abbildung 7: Mischpultpläne

I. Evangelisti, Koenig, Ligeti   ...   III. Stockhausen

X				
X				
	X			
		X		
			X	

X			
	X		
		X	
			X
			X

Eine Trennung der Kanäle 4 und 5 ausgehend von der 4-Spur-Fassung, so wie ich sie bereits vor mehr als 15 Jahren vorgenommen habe, ist also nichts anderes als eine im Studio fixierte Entsprechung zu dieser Aufführungspraxis Stockhausens.

Abschließend noch eine Beobachtung aus dem weiteren Verlauf von *Gesang der Jünglinge*, und zwar zu den qualitativen Unterschieden, die zwischen einer Abstrahlung über vier oder fünf Lautsprechern bestehen. Bei fünf wie auch bei vier Lautsprechern gibt es prinzipiell nur zwei Raumintervalle, nämlich 1: eine kontinuierliche Bewegung zwischen zwei benachbarten Lautsprechern, und 2: ein Sprung im Raum (was wenigstens einem nicht verwendeten Lautsprecher entspricht). Während jedoch bei insgesamt vier Lautsprechern ein solcher Sprung stets eine Diagonale zur Folge hat, was das Erkennen einer Raumbewegungsrichtung ausschaltet, ist bei fünf Lautsprechern eine Unterscheidung zwischen 2 nach links und 2 nach rechts sehr wohl möglich – wenn auch ungleich schwieriger als bei einer Aufeinanderfolge von Einerintervallen in eine einzige Richtung.

Betrachtet man die von Stockhausen gewählten Verteilungsreihenfolgen in Formteil B unter diesem Gesichtspunkt, so erkennt man, dass jede Reihenform zwei kontinuierliche Fortschreitungen und zwei Sprünge beinhaltet. Während in den meisten Fällen beide Drehrichtungen unterschiedlich miteinander kombiniert erscheinen, wählt Stockhausen für die letzte Anordnung vor der alle Lautsprecher beanspruchenden Impulsschar der Takte 35–36 eine Reihenfolge, welche ausschließlich aus Rechtsdrehungen besteht – was eine Vorwegnahme der kontinuierlichen Rotationsverläufe des nachfolgenden Formteils C bedeutet.

In Formteil F gibt es Raumdispositionen, die bei vier Lautsprechern nicht zur Geltung kommen können, welche aber sehr wohl zur Intention Stockhausens bei der Komposition gehörten. Gemeint ist die Gegenüberstellung von Raumfläche (will sagen eine privilegierte Kopplung von zwei benachbarten Lautsprechern) und Raumpunkt (ein isolierter Lautsprecher). Wenn bei vier Lautsprechern Klänge aus drei Lautsprechern erklingen, so ist räumlich nur schwer auszumachen, ob es sich dabei um 3 Raumpunkte oder gegebenenfalls einen komponierten Halbkreis handelt: der Gedanke einer Gegenüberstellung von Raumfläche zu isoliertem Raumpunkt kommt hier nicht einmal auf. Bei fünf Lautsprechern ist aber gerade diese Möglichkeit gegeben: Raumfläche und Raumpunkt können deutlich getrennt hörbar gemacht werden, nämlich aufgrund der zwischen ihnen liegenden Raumlücke auf jeder Seite. Genau eine solche Situation hat Stockhausen zwischen 10'28" und 11'35" geschaffen[16]. Hier wird die Gruppenform als formbildende Instanz durch die Verräumlichung gemäß konzentrierter Klangfarbengruppierungen aufgehoben, denn Stockhausen konzentriert in jeweils einem Lautsprecher alle Vertreter einer selben Klangfarbe. Zunächst erklingen alle gesungenen Elemente in Lautsprecher 2, kontrapunktiert durch unterschiedliche elektronische Klänge in Lautsprecher 5. Es folgt eine gemischte Situation in eben diesen beiden Lautsprechern (2 und 5). Der signifikante Sprung erscheint in den folgenden Gruppen mit Gegenüberstellung von homogenen elektronischen Klangfarben in einerseits Lautsprecher 2 und 3, und andererseits in Lautsprecher 5: bei einer Anordnung mit Lautsprecher 1 vorne links resultiert diese Situation in einem ungleichen Stereobild (links 5, rechts 2+3), wodurch die Opposition von Fläche und Punkt unmissverständlich wahrgenommen wird. Der Abschnitt endet mit abschließenden Impulsen in allen fünf Lautsprechern.

Wenn es heute kaum noch vorstellbar ist, Monteverdi auf einem modernen Konzertflügel zu begleiten, so sollte dieses Gefühl für historisch, ästhetisch und kompositionsgenetisch informierte Aufführungspraxis, welche ja gerade sinnvollerweise nicht in archäologische Nachbildungen mündet, auch jenem ersten Meisterwerk der elektronischen Musik zugute kommen, welches aus den Zufällen der kontextuellen Bedingungen heraus bisher weitgehend höchstens in seiner entstellten quadrophonen Raumfassung bekannt ist. Hörend nachvollziehbarer musikalischer Sinn ergibt sich bei *Gesang der*

---

16 Eine Mitlesepartitur zu diesem Abschnitt habe ich bereits in meinem Aufsatz »Timbre Diversification in Serial Tape Music and its Consequence on Form«, in: Contemporary Music Review 10/2 (1994), S. 13–23 (beim Partiturbeispiel auf S. 19 wurde die Reihenfolge der beiden Systeme vertauscht: der Abschnitt beginnt mit »Schnee«, unteres System, und endet mit »Schnee«, oberes System), veröffentlicht.

Jünglinge erst ab fünf Lautsprechern und wiederhergestellter Fünfkanalfassung, mit Lautsprecher 1 frontal links. Der visionärsten Intention des Komponisten kann man sich ferner noch annähern, wenn der Beginn der Komposition in einem vorne höher angebrachten Lautsprecher erklingt und die weiteren Spuren dieser Raumstrategie entsprechend auf die Lautsprecher 3–4–5 verschoben werden. Das Argument, eine solche Übersteigerung der Uraufführungssituation sei bloßer Unsinn, da der Komponist das Stück selbst ja nie in dieser Fassung gehört habe, ist für mich ungültig: einzig die in der Musik selbst verankerte Wahrheit zählt.

ENGLISH SUMMARY

FROM FINDING TO INVENTING
Stockhausen's Theory of »Music in Space« Considered
through His Compositions *Gesang der Jünglinge*,
Gruppen, Kontakte, and *Carré*

In 1958 Karlheinz Stockhausen first presented his ideas and theory on »Music in Space«, an essay he revised and extended several times during the following years. In this chapter the different versions of the essay, as well as the different versions of spatial aspects in the aforementioned compositions, will be analyzed with a view towards a fuller understanding of Stockhausen's spatial ideas and strategies, as well as the ways in which he musically developed them.

In the early sketches to **Kontakte**, Stockhausen assigned sounds to particular locations, varying the amount of change in location from section to section. When realizing the project, a literal realization of the localization, as conceived in the earliest sketches, was of less importance than a qualitative variation in location of a comparable extent. Furthermore, as is well known, Stockhausen imagined a »rotation table« (*Rotationstisch*) to realize part of the spatial distribution of sound in a single step, to be applied after completing the montage of the succession of sounds on tape. (This procedure was significantly different from the complex tape editing required in *Gesang der Jünglinge*). This allowed him to further develop the concept of spatial movement (which was not limited to successively assigning sounds to points in space) with two specific parameters: direction and speed of the rotations – realized by hand. To give each section a supplementary individuality, he gave each a specific spatial behaviour on the four-track tape.

Considering the point in time when the first sketches to **Carré** were drafted, it is surprising that space cannot be found amongst the eight basic parameters in the overall sketch. In the next step (i.e., the cards summarizing the different qualities of each moment, which were the basis for Cornelius Cardew's elaboration of the score), the drawings with spatial distribution appear prominently.

The overall form of *Carré* is divided into four parts with changing spatial behaviour: (1) fixed positions, (2) clockwise rotation, (3) anti-clockwise rotation, and (4) a section with no indication of spatial behaviour. The rotations are of specific interest, since Stockhausen intended to combine perceptible movements with a serial, equal distribution of the four »sound points«. Each orchestra (including its choir) sounds twelve times, thrice alone and three more times each in combinations of two, three, or all four orchestras. The only problematic situations are combinations of two diagonally opposed sound points; otherwise, the rotations have very distinct realizations, but a rotation in the reverse direction never really occurs. These rotations coordinate the events both between and inside the successive moments.

Gruppen is, of course, about chromaticism in the time domain, but the idea of the orchestra's division into three groups was present from the very beginning. A certain, albeit very basic, serial treatment of space consists in changing the predominant orchestra over the complete duration of the piece, beginning with a concentration on Orchestra I, ending with a concentration on Orchestra III, and with Orchestra II playing a central role in the middle of the composition.

The situation is rather simple at the beginning of the piece: independently of the durations of the sound groups, and of the silences separating the groups, rotation is continuously clockwise. After Group 6 (numbering follows sketches), there is a very long silence depending on the proportions between the groups, and the following Group 8 (Stockhausen assigned the intervening group number to the silence) is of an equivalent duration, so that the only possible movement for the following groups is to alternate between the two remaining orchestras. As soon as possible (with the end of Group 8), Stockhausen inverts the rotation (i.e., now anti-clockwise) until a new long group stops the process at Group 25.

The next step of elaboration of the composition leads Stockhausen to subdivide the overall form according to two types of characteristic fields: (1) one of four types of textures; and (2) a succession of harmonic fields, wherein the successive intervals of the basic row »colour« the omnipresent chromaticism. The changes between these assignments occur when there is a tritone in the time plan. Independently of the somewhat expositional first part of the composition (with relation to texture), the first harmonic change has to occur between Groups 15 and 16, and in a still later stage, this will also be the point where Stockhausen will insert the first »solo« – in the first performance this was for the strings of Orchestra I.

This creates an interesting situation from the spatial perspective, since the rotation began in Orchestra I; the long Group 8 sounded in this same orchestra and the reverse movement, initiated in Group 13, has now lead back to Orchestra I.

One consequence of this splitting up of the anti-clockwise rotation is the fact that the newly determined Part A is predominated by clockwise rotations and that only the final spatial gesture is anti-clockwise. This lends the exceptional situation a somewhat cadential function, which will also reoccur at the end of the first insert (the string solo) when, after the first performance, Stockhausen decided to rethink this section, having all three orchestras taking part.

So what was, at first, only a practical way of making the temporal polyphony audible through the spatial separation of the sounding instrumental groups became, progressively, an independent parameter, even if its treatment is »serial« to only a very limited degree.

The spatial display of today's four-track version of **Gesang der Jünglinge** seems to be inappropriate with regard to the composition's spatiality. It is well known that, owing to technical problems (i.e., the synchronization of a four-track tape with an additional monophonic tape), Stockhausen mixed Tracks 4 and 5 onto a single track (Track 4). Although in the late 1950s (as shown by documents among the sketches) he separated the former tracks by manipulations at the mixing table, later on he simply played the four-track tape.

Some 15 years ago I separated out Tracks 4 and 5 according to the score, thus realizing in the studio what Stockhausen had done in performance during the late 1950s. But even in this version, there was still something that was not yet clear, and it was the musical-dramatic situation alluded to in Part A. Returning to the sketches recently, I came to my current position, which is that the only musically valid version in accordance with the composer's intentions is a six-track version. The major modifications are the following: (1) rotation of the basic pentagram, so that Loudspeakers 1 and 2 sound in frontal position; (2) transfer of the beginning to a sixth loudspeaker placed higher (and possibly a bit more centred than Loudspeaker 1, but not completely in the middle of the stage); and (3) adaptation of the ›congregational‹ choral responses to the ›priest‹ in Loudspeaker 1 by rotating the other three tracks one position, to have the solo in the front and the responses filling the rear space.

Finally, one qualitative difference between having four and five sound points is the fact that with five points, as Stockhausen used in the last part of **Gesang**, it is possible to play with sonic oppositions that are not only punctual, but which confront spatial qualities such as planes and points. With four loudspeakers, a plane realized through the combination of two loudspeakers, when counterpointed against a point in an additional loudspeaker, will sound as an enlarged plane. With five loudspeakers such an opposition becomes far more apparent.

Space as a Carrier of Materials, Meaning, and Metaphor in Karlheinz Stockhausen's Music-Theatre Composition *Sirius*

ELIZABETH L. ANDERSON

RECEPTION BEHAVIOUR FRAMEWORK

My analysis of certain aspects of *Sirius* is based on my reception behaviour framework for electroacoustic music that I developed in my doctoral dissertation[1] (see figure 1). The framework arose from my fascination with the communicative power and scope of acousmatic music. It owes much to the listening strategies conceived by François Delalande at the *Groupe de Recherches Musicales* in Paris[2], which were important to the orientation of my research to discover sounds in acousmatic music that could be considered to

---

1   Elizabeth L. Anderson, *Materials, Meaning, and Metaphor: Unveiling Spatio-Temporal Pertinences in Acousmatic Music*, doctoral dissertation, London 2011, http://openaccess.city.ac.uk/3530/ (30.9.2014).

2   Delalande conducted his listening experiment with the movement *Sommeil* from Pierre Henry's acousmatic work, *Variations pour une porte et un soupir*, with the goal to investigate listening strategies. When analyzing his findings, Delalande discovered three primary types of listening strategies. They include: (1) Taxonomic listening, a strategy where listeners aim to make a global survey of a work in order to understand its general structure, (2) Empathic listening in which the listener focuses on the 'physiological' product of the sound and centers, initially, on personal sensations and feelings, and (3) Figurativisation, where listeners search for a contrast between sonic constructions that are associated with the image of a living, moving entity and other elements that have a contextual function such as a stage, scene, or décor (François Delalande, »Music Analysis and Reception Behaviours: *Sommeil* by Pierre Henry«, in: Journal of New Music Research 27/1–2 (1998), pp. 13–66, here: pp. 13, 26, 37, 52 and 47).

be what Denis Smalley refers to as »carriers of meaning«[3]. I conducted a listening experiment in 1999 to test François Delalande's listening strategies. In view of the problems encountered in attempting to analyse my findings using Delalande's strategies, I conceived a reception behaviour framework that comprises four strategies[4]:

Figure 1: Framework for reception behaviours

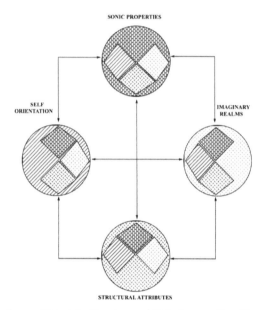

Elizabeth L. Anderson, *Materials, Meaning, and Metaphor*, op.cit, p. 31

Sonic Properties

Listeners who adopt this strategy center on the sound world they hear in the work. Sonic properties includes discussion of source-based sounds, different levels of abstraction with regards to particular sounds, extensive sonic topologies as well as discussion of one or more of the components of the sound[5]. In sonic properties, the discussion of sound is cultivated, often ex-

3   Denis Smalley, »Spectromorphology: Explaining Sound-Shapes«, in: Organised Sound 2(2) (1997), pp. 107–126, here p. 111.

4   Elizabeth L. Anderson, »Materials, Meaning and Metaphor in *Bâton de pluie* from *La Main Vide*«, in: *Le monde sonore de François Bayle* (= Signale aus Köln: Beiträge zur Musik der Zeit 18), edited by Christoph von Blumröder, Vienna 2012, pp. 162–180, here p. 162.

5   Ibid., p. 163.

clusively, though observations about the sound world may at times include personal assessments, forays into the listening imagination, or traits that suggest an appreciation of structure[6].

Structural Attributes

This listening strategy is an expansion of Delalande's strategy of »taxonomic behaviour«. Like taxonomy, a discussion of structural attributes aims to take into account the global design of the work. Structure is discussed characteristically using formal terms, and listeners may embrace descriptions of morphological units to enable the process. However, metaphors and imagery can additionally be utilized if their ultimate goal is to describe and otherwise illuminate structure. The latter is liable to be a predominant behaviour with listeners who lack a ›formal‹ vocabulary[7].

Self-Orientation

Self-orientation, an expansion of Delalande's strategy, »empathy«, is an expression of opinions and thoughts that centre on or emanate from the self in so far as the ›listening consciousness‹ is mobilised by personal estimation or judgement. Listeners who use this strategy may observe their own emotional and physiological reactions to the sounding flow and, more broadly, to the listening experience. These responses are qualified as ›physiological sensations‹ and ›emotions‹. Self-orientation also refers to a type of perception of the sounding flow, or the listening experience, that allows for more neutral deliberations resulting in contemplation or reflection. These deliberations are qualified as *evaluations*[8].

Imaginary Realms

This strategy has its origin in Delalande's »figurativisation«, a type of listening where form is perceived to unfold through narrativity, which additionally furnishes a basis for perceptual construction[9]. Imaginary realms is an enlargement of »figurativisation« because it allows for variations in »figurativisation« and, additionally, embraces other reception behaviours, notably fiction, fantasy, and surrealism, in which the listener exercises imagination as an *end* in itself. It is true that listeners may respond to an acousmatic work by addressing the sound world, structure, or their physiological sensations,

---

6   Elizabeth L. Anderson 2011, op.cit., p. 32.

7   Ibid., pp. 34–35.

8   Ibid., p. 37.

9   François Delalande, op.cit., p. 52.

emotions or opinions using imaginative terms. However, the listening strategy, imaginary realms, differs insofar that the images fabricated by the listening consciousness are not perceived to be inherent in the work nor in a culturally or universally appreciated or defined construction, although certain spectromorphological qualities apprehended during listening may influence the inception of the image and the manner in which it unfolds[10].

Further to the four listening strategies, listeners can engage in different listening patterns within the reception behaviour framework. An »independent« listening strategy is one that does not operate in tandem with another strategy. A »hybrid« listening strategy is the combination of two or more strategies one of which is frequently more pronounced. »Dynamic« listening occurs when a listener's focus repeatedly shifts from one strategy to another, which often is hybridised, in the course of the listening experience. A »combination« of strategies, independent, hybrid, or dynamic, is a somewhat rare conglomerate a listener may adopt in the course of the listening act[11].

Finally, space has an essential role in the four listening strategies. This is because sound is acoustic energy and it dictates spatial impression through the materiality of the aural trace. In electroacoustic sound, spatial impression is linked to two elements engendered by the aural trace: physical, otherwise known as three-dimensional, space, in which spatial motion and distribution occur, and spectral space[12]. Thus, it is through the three-dimensional and spectral space conveyed by the sounding flow of an electroacoustic work that the listener could perceive the work's sonic properties and structural attributes. It is also through these spaces that a listener can develop a personal response to the sounding flow, which has its own psychological or physical space, or construct images, each of which has their respective space.

KARLHEINZ STOCKHAUSEN'S *SIRIUS*

Sirius, for soprano, bass, trumpet, bass clarinet and octophonic electronic sounds, is based on the twelve melodies (formulas) of the signs of the zodiac Stockhausen composed for *Tierkreis* (*Zodiac*). However, in *Sirius*, he focuses on four melodies, one during each of the four main movements in the work that represent the four seasons: *Libra* (autumn), *Capricorn* (winter),

---

10 Elizabeth L. Anderson 2011, op.cit., pp. 40–41.
11 Elizabeth L. Anderson 2012, op.cit., p. 163.
12 Elizabeth L. Anderson 2011, op.cit., p. 186.

Aries (spring), and *Cancer* (summer). *Sirius* embodies some of the musical techniques and characteristics of Stockhausen's style, notably serialism. The work is also modular insofar as the order of its main movements may start with any of the four seasons. It features singing (soprano and bass, who represent Summer and Winter respectively) as well as spoken voice and *Sprechgesang*. Stockhausen wrote most of the text, which was inspired by the mystic Jakob Lorber and is in German and English. A section of Lorber's spiritual vision of the cosmos from *Der Kosmos in geistiger Schau* is used in the *Annunciation*. Two instruments (trumpet and bass clarinet) represent Spring and Autumn respectively. With the exception of the source-bonded recordings, all the sound material in the electronic part was created with an EMS Synthi 100 synthesizer[13]. This synthesizer was equipped with a three-track sequencer which allowed the formulas for *Zodiac* to be stored as voltage sequences thereby permitting for extreme malleability in their playback[14]. For example, it was possible to combine the melodic shape of one formula with the rhythmic shape of another and to expand melodies temporally independently of rhythm and timbre[15]. However, when one of the four *Zodiac* formulas is audible in its »…original melodic and rhythmic form, […] all parameters are […] driven by the two voltage-sequences (channels) of only 1 of the 3 sequencer tracks«[16]. Additionally, Stockhausen's use of source-bonded recordings in the octophonic electronic part, in which the sounds of wood being chopped, wind, footfalls on ice, a burbling brook, and the lighting and burning of a wood fire, provide links to the real world. The multichannel nature of the electronic part also imparts a sense of three-dimensional space and movement. Finally, as suggested by Stockhausen, the work proposes a description of cosmic space and travel through music[17].

Compositional Techniques used in *Sirius*

I shall now briefly discuss some of the compositional techniques that Stockhausen applied to *Sirius*. Stockhausen notes that one of the most significant discoveries in recent years is the ability to address and perceive the musical parameters (melody, rhythm, dynamics timbre and spatial contours) separa-

---

13 Karlheinz Stockhausen, *Sirius,* Booklet accompanying the score, Kürten 1981, p. 36.

14 Ibid., p. 38.

15 Ibid.

16 Ibid.

17 Cf. Karlheinz Stockhausen, *Sirius,* Booklet for the Compact Disc 26A & B, Kürten 1992, pp. 3–21.

tely. In *Sirius*, Stockhausen works with formulas, which are musical forms in which these aspects are integrated, comparable to the figure of a man comprising all the features of his shape and details. He proposes that if we treat these parameters separately, the result is a completely new approach to music composition and perception[18].

Following, each melody in the *Zodiac* has its own formula. Thus, each melody is based on a different twelve-tone row and starts on a different pitch, ascending chromatically from *Aquarius* (which starts on a D♯) to *Capricorn* (which starts on a D♮). Following its prescribed formula, each melody is performed at a different tempo; the slowest is 53,5 beats per minute (BPM) and the fastest is 101 BPM[19]. As a compositional tool in *Sirius*, Stockhausen uses *Glieder* and *Gruppen*, which I understand as musical cells and groups of notes respectively. In most cases, the lengths of the *Glieder* are identical to the lengths of the *Gruppen*[20].

Each of the *Zodiac* melodies comprises thirteen different *Glieder*, the last *Glied* repeating the first note of the tone row. The formulas dictate the musical parameters of the melodies. For example, in the *Cancer* formula, the ending notes of the *Glieder* follow the specific tone row for *Cancer*. Additionally, in *Cancer*, the *Glieder* possess varying durations and melodic shapes, which alternate between movement and immobility[21].

In contrast, the formula for the *Libra* melody is organized on the model of a pendulum, a movement-oriented interpretation of the notion of balance. Thus the *Glieder* and *Gruppen* are shorter at the beginning of the melody, become progressively longer until the middle of the melody, and then become progressively shorter in the second half of the melody. The durations of the notes in the tone row also follow this principle of organization. The intervals between the notes in the tone row also become progressively larger in the first half of the row and progressively smaller in the second half (an example of the use of progressively larger intervals, always alternating upward and downward movement, is illustrated by the first four notes in the row: the first note is a B♮, the second moves up a minor second to C♮, the third moves down a minor third to A♮, the fourth moves up a perfect fourth to D♮). In the melody, however, each *Glied* starts with the beginning tone in *Libra*, and subsequently features a note in the tone row. For example the first *Glied* features the movement from B♮, up to C♮, the second *Glied* features

---

18 Cf. Karlheinz Stockhausen, *Kompositions-Kurs über »Sirius«*, Kürten 2000, p. 6.
19 Ibid., p. 4.
20 Ibid., p. 7.
21 Ibid., pp. 6–7.

the movement of B♮ down to A♮, the third *Glied* features the movement of B ♮ up to D♮. This pattern reinforces the notion of spectral centrality while simultaneously conveying progressively larger or smaller spectral swaths depending on the part of the melody that one analyses[22].

Remarks about the Performance and Spatial Layout of *Sirius*

Figure 2: Symbolic and structural layout of »Sirius«

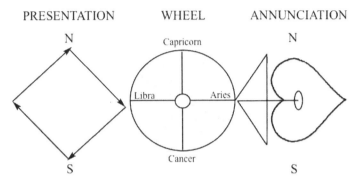

Computer-made symbolic and structural layout of *Sirius* using Stockhausen's diagram[23] as a guide

The performance of *Sirius* is divided into four sections:

- *The Presentation (die Vorstellung)* of the four soloists who are the musical embodiments of the four cardinal points, the elements (air, fire, water, and e-arth), the sexes, the four times of day (morning, noon, evening and night), and the four stages of growth (seed, bud, blossom and fruit)[24].
- *»The Wheel (das Rad)* of the constellations and seasons is the clock of *Sirius*. According to the seasons of the performance, the *Wheel* begins with one of the four main melodies, *Aries*, *Cancer*, *Libra* and *Capricorn*, which transform into one another, sometimes together [...]. Each of the four melodies dominates for approximately a quarter hour, and the twelve melodies divide the hour like the twelve numbers in a clock. The wheel turns clockwise«.[25]

---

22 Ibid., pp. 8–9.
23 Karlheinz Stockhausen 1981 (booklet), op.cit., p. 27.
24 Karlheinz Stockhausen 1992, op.cit., p. 7.
25 Ibid., p. 9.

- The bridge between the final season of the *Wheel* and the *Annunciation*[26].
- *The Annunciation (die Verkündigung)*[27]. Because the *Wheel* can start with any of the four seasons, there are four different possible bridges between the *Wheel* and the A*nnunciation*, depending on the order in which the work unfolds[28]. In a performance of *Sirius*, the four soloists are placed in the four cardinal points and the octophonic electronic part is projected over sixteen loudspeakers in such a way that two channels of sound separate each of the four performers[29].

Figure 3: Spatial disposition for a performance of Sirius

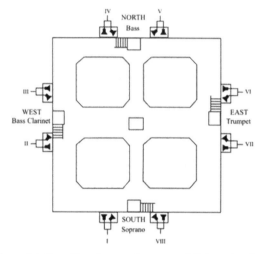

Computer-made spatial disposition for a performance of *Sirius* using Stockhausen's diagrams[30] as a guide

Figure 3 illustrates the spatial disposition of soloists, loudspeakers and tape channels for a performance of *Sirius*. The soloists perform from podiums that are arranged in a cruciform. Each of the eight channels of the electronic part is played through pairs of loudspeakers which are connected in parallel to one output on the mixing desk in the center of the performance space. For each pair, one loudspeaker is directed inwards toward the soloist and the

26 Ibid., p. 17.
27 Ibid., p. 7.
28 Ibid., p. 17.
29 Karlheinz Stockhausen 1981 (booklet), op.cit., p. 41.
30 Ibid. pp. 41–43.

other is directed toward the audience[31]. The sound of each of the soloists is mixed via microphone and mixing desk to the respective channels of the tape part that is projected from loudspeakers to the left and right behind them[32].

Spatial analysis of extracts of *Sirius*

I shall analyse the following four extracts from the Summer version of *Sirius*:

- Two excerpts from the *Presentation*
- An excerpt from the *Bridge after Aries*
- An excerpt from the *Annunciation* at the end of the work.

Due to the length of the work, which is 96 minutes[33], I chose to restrict myself to these short passages. My analyses are based on these passages as apprehended in the stereo version of the complete recording of the work and in the octophonic version of the electronic part. For all musical excerpts I refer to the timing of the actual recording rather than the timing indicated in the score.

Excerpt 1: 0'38"–2'15"; from the *Presentation* – Octophonic electronic part

Given the absence of soloists at the beginning of the *Presentation*, I chose to examine only the octophonic version of this passage, which is an octophonic recording of sounds emitted from the rotating loudspeaker that Stockhausen used at the beginning and end of this work. I shall now analyze this excerpt through my reception behaviour framework, focusing primarily on its spatial aspects and starting with sonic properties. From a spatial perspective, sonic properties divides into spectral space, suggesting a vertical space of a certain nature, and three-dimensional space, of a more physical nature. In this sound example, spectral space and three-dimensional space collude to suggest not only the rotations but also the spectral directions of these clock-wise and counter-clockwise rotations. For the most part, the upper limit of spectral space rises stepwise from F5 to Eb6, before alternating with downward glissandi:

---

31 Ibid., p. 43.
32 Ibid., p. 41.
33 Ibid., p. 27.

Figure 4: Score corresponding to excerpt N°1 from the Presentation

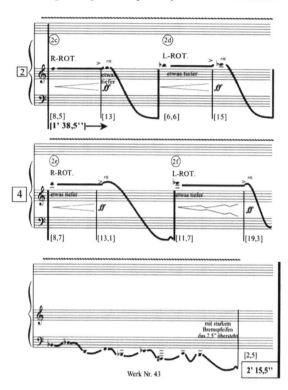

Computer-made score of part of page 1 of the *Presentation* in *Sirius* using the *Sirius* score[34] as a guide

The circular setting of the eight loudspeakers surrounds the listener with sound and establishes a three-dimensional spatial structure from the outset. The structural attributes of the extract, unfolding in four similar gestures, display an apparent symmetry. However, when analyzed more closely, each gesture is slightly different from the other three regarding duration, occupancy of spectral space and inner structure (cf. figure 4). This may suggest that these gestures represent the four messengers that arrive from *Sirius*.

Self-orientation explores opinions, emotions and sensations that stem from the self. From the spatial viewpoint, listeners find themselves inside a

---

34 Karlheinz Stockhausen, *Sirius*, score, Kürten 1981, p. 1. These scores have been made on Finale with the help of David Baltuch.

vast vortex of sounds. These sounds may be perceived as evidence of civilization through their motoric nature and therefore may evoke a landing, and thus a previous journey.

Through imaginary realms, listeners may unleash their imagination beyond or in lieu of the above mentioned evocative process. For example, they may envision the shape and size of the spaceship producing this motoric sound, or infer reasons for the repeated downward glissandi, each of which starts from a different pitch and deploys in space in alternating clock-wise and counter-clockwise rotations. For example, one could imagine that the spaceship attempts different landings, like a bee trying out different flowers until it finds an acceptable place to land, not without some final low pitch grumbles, which could be construed as some sort of technical adjustment regarding the landing expressed in a humorous way.

Excerpt N 2a: 7'23"–10'01"; from the *Presentation* – Stereo integral version[35]

This extract sets the agenda for the entire work. However, I shall limit my investigation to a brief study of space in this extract through my reception behaviour framework. The discussion of sonic properties in this extract addresses five new parameters: the tessituras, timbres, dynamics and the use of text in the soloists' parts and the discreet sustained pitched sounds in the electronic part (cf. figure 5): The tessituras in the soloists' parts encompass a vast swath of spectral space. The soloists' respective timbral qualities, conveyed primarily through slowly enunciated text by the vocalists, which is accompanied by sustained tones in the trumpet and bass clarinet parts, reflect their symbolic spatial setting as allocated by Stockhausen. The text, written by Stockhausen himself, describes a spatial frame: North, East, South and West as understood on Earth, and cosmic space, notably Sirius and other suns, from the perspective of the messengers from Sirius. The emphasis on these themes is underscored in the electronic part, which contains sustained sounds on channels 11, IV VI and VIII. This second extract is also characterized by synchronized dynamic surges in the electronic and instrumentalist parts.

---

35 My perception of which is informed by the corresponding octophonic electronic part.

Figure 5: Score corresponding to excerpt N°2a from the Presentation

Computer-made score of part of page 4 of the *Presentation* in *Sirius* using the *Sirius* score[36] as a guide

The spatial distribution of the soloists and the discrete sustained pitched sounds in the electronic part are structuring elements. The antiphony between the vocalists, supported by the sustained sounds in the instrumental accompaniment and the dynamic surges on different channels in the electronic part, which, near the beginning of this extract, are simultaneous to the pronunciation of the names of the four seasons by the vocalists, may suggest a brief clockwise motion. The triplet rhythm played by the instrumentalists at the beginning of the extract, anticipating the *Libra* theme, could be perceived to initiate this clockwise motion. Afterwards, synchronized dynamic surges

---

36 Karlheinz Stockhausen 1981 (score), op.cit., p. 4.

in the instrumental and electronic parts help to highlight, spatially, the antiphonal nature of the discourse between the soprano and the bass.

From a self-orientated perspective, the narrative developed by the vocalists places the listener in the center of a vast space. This narrative is supported by the solemnity of the singers' pronunciation, confirming the impression of divine proclamation stated by the soprano at the end of the extract, possibly inducing in the listener a sentiment of awe. The instrumental style, consisting of sustained notes, glissandi and dynamic surges, and the pitched, sustained sounds in the electronic part contribute to the expansive spatial atmosphere of the passage and a sense of expectation.

Through imaginary realms we can build on pre-existing themes such as religion, gender, phases of growth, the elements, time of day and the seasons, but from a perspective that is novel to us. We rediscover these themes through the messengers from Sirius, or rather through our understanding of their discourse. It is through our imagination that we can envision the enormity of cosmic space and the attributes of the divine conveyed by these messengers.

Excerpt 2b: 7'23"–8'07"; from the *Presentation* – Octophonic electronic part

Given the repetitive nature of the electronic part in this extract, I shall only discuss the first 44" (cf. figure 5), which contain the salient qualities of the entire passage. The source-bonded recording of the wind evoques a large space in which such movements of the wind are possible and refers to the boundless element air. The sustained pitched sounds in the electronic part can be perceived as a steady spatial presence, and they help build dramatic tension. The dynamic surges of these sustained pitched sounds in channels IV, VI, VIII and II, which underscore the spoken text, further accentuates this presence. I think these surges evoke stars twinkling in the cardinal points of the night sky. I imagine an icy void, ready to be filled with energy and matter.

Excerpt 3a: 83'59"–85'14"; from the *Bridge after Aries* – Stereo integral version[37]

From a spatial perspective, the discourse between the soloists is fixed in this excerpt from the *Bridge after Aries*, whereas the discourse between the channels in the electronic part seems to float in a circular pattern. From my viewpoint, this suggests a superposition of two three-dimensional spatial

---

37 My perception of which is informed by the corresponding octophonic electronic part.

schemes: the diamond spatial form of the *Presentation* and the circular form
of the moving *Wheel* (cf. figure 2).

Figure 6: Score corresponding to excerpt N°3a from the Bridge after Aries

Computer-made score of part of page 6–7 of the *Bridge after Aries* in *Sirius* using the *Sirius* score[38] as a guide

What is striking, sonically, about this extract is its musical texture, which is
initially intricate, and yet spatially transparent, and thus imparts a
diaphanous quality. Toward the end of the extract (cf. figure 6), the texture
thins out when sustained sounds are audible in the tape and instrumentalists'
parts, and their spectrally inert qualities provide a ›spectral web‹ over which
the spoken bass part can be heard. Three formulas from the *Zodiac* can be

---

38   Karlheinz Stockhausen 1981 (score), op.cit., pp. 6–7.

heard simultaneously as performed by the soloists: the *Cancer* formula is sung by the soprano and the *Aries* and *Libra* formulas are played by the trumpet and bass clarinet respectively.

As I noted previously, because the *Wheel* can start with any of the four seasons, there are four different possible bridges between the *Wheel* and the *Annunciation*, depending on the order in which the work unfolds[39]. The beginning of each of the four bridges contains musical material from the four seasons they precede, respectively. At the end of each bridge, sustained sounds are introduced which feature in the electronic part in the *Annunciation*. For example, in the *Summer* performance of *Sirius*, where the first season on the *Wheel* is *Cancer/Summer*, the material in the *Bridge after Aries* is derived from *Cancer/Summer*. Thus, the first 95 measures in the *Bridge after Aries* are identical to the first 95 measures in *Cancer*. On a spatial level, I propose that this cyclical type of formal closure may be modeled on the rotations and orbits of planets and stars in the universe.

From a self-oriented perspective, this passage conveys to me a sense of joyful exuberance and dance through the frequent use of triplets and jumps in the musical discourse, and the unexpected character of the superimposed formulas, each of which is at this point, a familiar *leitmotif.* The psychological and emotional space is redolent of festivity. I imagine all previous constituents of the narrative – the cardinal points, the elements, the seasons, the phases of growth, the times of day and the sexes – colluding in harmony in divine banquet.

In the *Bridge after Aries,* the soloists' parts cover a large swath of spectral space. Given their physical positions in the performance space, this suggests that the cosmic spatial dimensions they represent are full as well. The electronic part adds to this impression of sonic opulence and activity. As a result, the images that could come to the mind of listeners could be replete with activity.

Excerpt 3b: 83'59"– 84'14"; from the *Bridge after Aries* – Octophonic electronic part

The electronic part of this extract displays the same qualities as the integral recording. However, it possesses several layers of dynamics whereas the soloists' parts present a unified dynamic field. This dynamic diversity may convey to the listener the impression of a physical space that is larger than the actual performance space, the louder sounds appearing closer and the softer sounds further afield.

---

39 Karlheinz Stockhausen 1992, op.cit., p. 17.

Excerpt 4a: 88'45"–89'44"; from the *Annunciation* – Stereo integral version[40]

Figure 7: Score corresponding to excerpt N°4a from the Annunciation

Computer-made score of part of page 5 of the *Annunciation* in *Sirius* using the *Sirius* score[41] as a guide

Following a pattern of dynamic indications in the electronic part in the previous excerpt, Stockhausen indicates different dynamics in the soloists' parts in this section of the *Annunciation* (cf. figure 7): the bass is marked *forte*, the soprano *mezzo forte* and the instruments are marked *piano*. The soprano sings the vowels of the text sung by the bass, which may convey the impression of an aural shadow, and therefore the impression of the space allowing such a shadow. The bass sings in a brilliant upper register and the soprano in

---

a lower mellower register, reinforcing the distance between the object and its shadow.

Excerpt 4b (88'45"–89'44"); from the *Annunciation* – Octophonic electronic part

In this extract (cf. figure 7), the octophonic electronic part includes a recording of the piano part on channels I, III, V and VII, which synchronizes with the soloists. The electronic part also contains high-pitched sustained sounds on channels II, IV and VI which slowly rise in pitch through upward moving glissandi as well as a sustained pitched sound on channel VIII. These two elements, the piano and the glissandi, contribute to a sensation of lessening gravity. Near the end of the extract, the sound of the octophonic recording of sounds emitted from the rotating loudspeaker becomes audible.

CONCLUSIONS

I would like to conclude this presentation with a reflection on the meaning that Stockhausen may have assigned to *Sirius*. As Stockhausen proposed, in *Sirius*, the messengers from Sirius aim to describe cosmic space, the elements, the sexes and manifestations of time through music to people from Earth. The performance space becomes a metaphor of the cosmic space, and Stockhausen's use of texts by the mystic Jacob Lorber in the *Annunciation* serves to further the reflection about the cosmic meaning of our human existence.

François Bayle's *valeur obscure*

JOHN DACK

INTRODUCTION

My intention in this chapter is to investigate François Bayle's unique approach to the use of space in electroacoustic music[1]. My principal focus will be on a specific aspect of Bayle's spatial thinking: I shall concentrate on his metaphoric or symbolic use of space and not so much on how sounds are located or moved, although I accept, of course, that the two subject areas cannot be disentangled. Bayle has made many insightful comments on this metaphoric use of space. Naturally, he has inherited a rich tradition of electroacoustic music and thought. I do not think it is too fanciful to refer to a »tradition« even though it is little more than sixty years old. It is one to which he has made significant contributions. His comment that »a sound that has come out of a transducer is not a sound like all the rest«[2] clearly has roots in early studio practice. But the emphasis on the nature of sounds fixed on a medium and, more importantly, the consequences of that situation have given rise to Bayle's strikingly original theories. Due to my concentration on the *valeur obscure* I shall not comment on other concepts such as the *i-son* nor on the influences from Peirce's semiotics. Both subjects need to be analyzed at

---

1   I would like to acknowledge the kind assistance I have received from François Bayle in the writing of this chapter. An interview in Paris was unfortunately impossible to organize. However, François Bayle kindly responded to many questions both by email and telephone. Without his advice and invaluable insights my chapter would be infinitely poorer. I would also like to acknowledge the advice from my colleague, Christine North, when translating Bayle's texts and supplementary verbal comments.

2   François Bayle, »Space, and more«, in: Organised Sound 12(3) (2007), pp. 241–249, here p. 241.

some point in the future. But in this chapter it is the specific aspects of Bayle's use of space as outlined above that will be my main concern.

In his book *musique acousmatique, propositions... positions* Bayle referred to space as *une valeur obscure*[3]. This expression can be translated as »an obscure [or dark?] value«, which made the juxtaposition of the two words, in my opinion, simultaneously striking but also enigmatic. How can a value be ›obscure‹ (or ›dark‹)? Would perhaps other English words such as ›unknown‹ or even ›concealed‹ make this term more comprehensible when rendered into English? (Though a certain resistance to immediate understanding might also be a deliberate quality of Bayle's language.) Furthermore, what precisely is meant by ›value‹ in reference to space? The more I considered these two words, the more difficult and enigmatic did their meaning become. So let me start with the full quotation by Bayle:

»If there is an obscure value, it is certainly that of space. And, perhaps one could even rely on this first idea, as a start: the space of sounds, or the values of the obscure.

Functionally speaking listening is vigilance. Inverting the function of the gaze – turned towards the outside – it locates what is inside, what is behind, what is hidden.

Space hides and listening wants to see.

What is true in life is even more so in reverie – so, being struck by sound which seeks to feel, to foresee... Valorized musical listening replays vigilance symbolically.«[4]

These are the opening lines of the chapter *L'odyssée de l'espace* (»The Odyssey of Space«) (note the cultural and symbolic significance of the word »odyssey« regarding movement and searching). In this quotation I believe several features of Bayle's distinctive practice regarding space can be identified. I shall, therefore, examine this richly packed extract – which is admittedly short – in the form of an *explication de texte*.

---

3   François Bayle, *musique acousmatique, propositions... positions*, Paris 1993, p. 101.

4   »S'il est une valeur obscure, c'est bien celle de l'espace. Et peut-être même que l'on pourrait prendre appui sur cette première idée, pour commencer: l'espace des sons, ou les valeurs de l'obscur. Fontionnellement l'écoute est vigilance. Inversant la fonction du regard - tournée vers le dehors – elle reprère ce qui est dedans, ce qui est derrière, ce qui est caché.
L'espace cache et l'écoute veut voir.
Ce qui est vrai dans la vie l'est encore avantage dans la rêverie – celle de l'ouïr qui cherche à sentir, à pressentir... L'écoute valorisée, musicale, rejoue symboliquement la vigilance.« (Bayle, op.cit., p. 101)

BACKGROUND

At the outset I think it is necessary to explain my personal interest in Bayle's work and my methodology. It was both a pleasure and privilege to have consulted the composer personally, although I am acutely aware of the dangers of stumbling headlong into the ›intentionalist fallacy‹. I hope I have avoided this. Composers' opinions regarding their work are usually extremely interesting but I stress that any interpretation of Bayle's practice and theories will be my own. Bayle explains himself perfectly eloquently in his writings and one might argue that in many ways he has no need of secondary commentaries – like this one. Nevertheless, I was also motivated by the belief that Bayle scholarship is growing and I hope this text will contribute to the increasing interest in both his compositions and his writings.

During a panel discussion of the 2007 symposium at the University of Cologne Denis Smalley stated that:

»there are hundreds of electroacoustic composers out there in universities and colleges across the United States and Britain, who are always on the lookout for theoretical ideas, to be able to reconcile theory and practice. The more of François Bayle's thinking that gets out there the better. And there isn't much out there so far because there isn't much, dare I say it, in English.«[5]

I sincerely hope that this chapter will help remedy this unfortunate situation. I was also invited to contribute to this symposium and I examined a particular aspect of his use of space within the context of the Romantic trope of ›distance‹ or *der ferne Klang*. I then applied this to a short analysis of Bayle's composition *La fleur future* from *La main vide* (1993/95). This might have seemed a deliberately eccentric strategy. Why did I choose to refer to Novalis, for example, when one can read many perfectly good explanations regarding the effects of space on listeners, both physiologically and psychologically, from psychoacoustic research? The answer was, of course, that scientific positivism is valuable, but we also need to discuss the metaphorical, the ambiguous, the poetic as well as concepts such as the *au-delà*. A positivist approach offers little in the way of explaining these subjects.

---

5   »Hommage à François Bayle«, roundtable with Ludger Brümmer, Philippe Mion, Dennis Smalley, Hans Tutschku, Annette Vande Gorne, and Markus Erbe, 12 Oct. 2007, in: *The Sound World of François Bayle* (= Signale aus Köln: Beiträge zur Musik der Zeit 18), ed. by Marcus Erbe and Christoph von Blumröder, Wien 2012, pp. 315–330, see p. 322.

They are nevertheless present in Bayle's music and his theories. It is no wonder, therefore, that Célestin Deliège in his monumental *Cinquante ans de modernité musicale* referred to him as a *musicien poète*[6]. In examining Bayle's work through Romantic thought I did not make the outrageous (and unsupportable) claim that electroacoustic composers who use spatial techniques are, at heart, Romantics. My approach was based on what is surely a primal human attitude regarding sounds placed within spatial contexts, and I believed that the movement *La fleur future* exemplified an aesthetic trope which has similarities with one originating in the nineteenth century. This is just one approach that has been assimilated by Bayle. His work can, therefore, be located within these historical developments. I also suggested, of course, that such an attitude had never really been adopted, only to be then casually abandoned, by composers. It is always there in the ›background‹ (to continue the spatial metaphor) informing their work.

In fact, it might be more sensible to ask how could contemporary composers not use space in their music, so ubiquitous has it become in many genres of music? The answer is surely simple: practical and often insurmountable difficulties in performance practice existed before the use of electroacoustic technology. I am not for one moment suggesting that composers of Renaissance polyphonic music did not exploit spatial environments in a sophisticated manner. It was nonetheless limited and literal as they had to work within certain fixed architectural spaces. Thus, it could be argued that spatial thinking as hinted at in the late-nineteenth century could only be fully realized as a musical practice *per se* in the twentieth. Robert Schumann could only allude to space in the title of his piano piece *Wie aus der Ferne* (1837). On the other hand, Gustav Mahler could be more explicit when in several of his symphonic scores he demanded that brass instruments be placed at the back of the stage in the auditorium – literally *in der Ferne aufgestellt*. The effect of distance and an invisible orchestra is even more pronounced in Mahler's music when he places them off-stage[7]. However, an extensive, thorough use of space was impractical until the development of electroacoustic technology.

---

6   Célestin Deliège, *Cinquante ans de modernité musicale*, Sprimont 2003, p. 439.
7   This subject area was discussed by Fabian Kolb in this book.

UNE VALEUR OBSCURE

Let me return to a question I posed earlier: what is an »obscure value« when referring to space? ›Value‹ in an electroacoustic context might initially seem to refer to the Schaefferian dualism of *valeur/caractère* (value/ characteristic). Bayle frequently acknowledges Schaeffer's theoretical and musical heritage at the *Groupe de Recherches Musicales*; it continues to inform much musical thought in the worldwide electroacoustic community. But making a potentially superficial connection would fail to give justice to the insights of composers like Bayle. When composers produce theoretical and aesthetic texts, they often reveal interesting aspects of their creative work and show how it builds on previous theories. Luckily we can refer to Bayle's writings, which are often poetic in their use of language. (I do not think Deliège's description of Bayle as *musicien poète* referred only to the music.) So, can space be a ›value‹ in the specifically Schaefferian sense? The terms value and characteristic are certainly central to Schaeffer's generalized theory of music. In conjunction with the dualism of permanence and variation, a relationship was posited by Schaeffer that identifies a fundamental perceptual strategy in music. Indeed, it is so fundamental to music that Michel Chion referred to *permanence des caractères, variations des valeurs* as a *loi du musical* (law of the musical)[8]. This is not an extravagant claim in my view. In this sense, Chion, after Schaeffer, asserted that the values, which form part of a musical discourse, could be defined as the salient features of sounds that are promoted to the principal carriers of meaning. If the listener perceives, for example, pitch and duration as the changing values, within the context of stable instrumental colour (as in most traditional music) they are no longer ›merely‹ characteristics. The permanence of instrumental colour (I am avoiding the term ›timbre‹) allows the changing values of pitch and duration to be perceived by the listener. We should note, of course, that characteristics are in any case rarely ›merely‹ characteristics. They contain many pertinent features of a sound and the value/characteristic relationship is subtle. For example, if performances of the same work by different musicians are compared, the unique ›touch‹ or articulation of a violinist or pianist is assessed according to characteristics. The values would obviously remain the same, apart from minor modifications in expressive timing, but the specific articulation, control of dynamics, etc. of either musician would be noticeably different, even though these would still be generally regarded as characteristics. Thus, the role of characteristics should not be underestimat-

---

8   Michel Chion, *Guide des objets sonores*, Paris 1983, p. 74.

ed. An excessively rigid hierarchy is problematic. It is perhaps more accurate to consider that at certain moments a perceptible feature is granted the status of a value or characteristic depending on the context within which it is placed and on how it is controlled by the composer. For example, in his *Etude aux allures* (1958) Schaeffer attempted (successfully) to promote what is usually a characteristic (the generalized vibrato that is ›allure‹) to that of a value. As stated earlier, pitch and duration are the most obvious example of values in European classical music. They are, moreover, the result of their origins in the unified families of sounds produced by instruments. This raises another important point: sounds come from something, somewhere, even if both the source and location are virtual. Of course, the standard discourse on pitch and duration can be transformed to one where the changes of spectral content are more important and this feature might, in theory, be perceived as a value. But there is a clear difference between this discussion of ›value‹ within the context of the value-characteristic dualism and the description of space as a ›value‹ in its own right.

If space is a value in the specifically Schaefferian sense, we might legitimately ask: what are the individual elements of space compared to discrete steps of a pitch scale? Could they be specific positions in space: hard left, mid-right, centre? Or could they be various kinds of movement: from back to front, from left to right? Or even categories of spatial environments such as reverberant or dry? Indeed, such spaces might be purely imaginary, where the composer arranges the perceptible coexistence of dry and reverberant spaces. This is impossible in the real world, of course. How can the discrete steps of pitch be compared in any way to these depictions of space? Personally, I don't think they can. While Bayle does not contradict the Schaefferian dualism outlined previously, he also asserts that the *valeur obscure* is »never measurable or decipherable«[9]. In doing this, he provides an elaboration of the notion of space as a value, and he opens up a whole area of discourse quite distinct from Schaeffer. Each section of a composition will occupy or express its own ›spaces‹. Once combined and mixed at the point of composition or diffusion, these spaces are impossible to ›decipher‹. Naturally, Bayle as a composer is familiar with the issues of monitoring an acousmatic work in a familiar studio environment, while being constantly aware that these carefully constructed spaces will have to be placed within a different, probably public, venue[10]. It is precisely at the point of diffusion that a composition's qualities must be judged. The musician at the mixing desk has to cope

---

9   Personal communication by email, 27 June 2014: »jamais mesurable ni déchiffrable.«
10   I am reminded here of Smalley's three indicative fields of space.

with different diffusion systems and the acoustics of the venue. Only then can the composer's spaces be placed within the performance space.

What is striking about Bayle and his development of the *acousmonium* as well as the performance practices of spatiality is his notion that the diffusion system can »project« imaginary »screens.« This is conceptually distinct from the immersive practices of many diffusion systems. Of course, at performances by Bayle (and I have been fortunate to witness some of them) speakers are placed in all parts of the auditorium, such as the rear and mid-points of the hall. The bias is usually to the front, with the famous tweeter »trees« usually situated in the audience seating area. Nevertheless, with the audience facing the front there is a sense of transformation of what I can only describe as musical space. *Screens* or *planes* develop from lines, which in turn grow from points. Moreover, *screens* can develop into *volumes* or spaces. Space, therefore, can be the ultimate result of a transformed point. Thus, these virtual *screens* and the concept of »projection« invoke a visual discourse. One can imagine spaces formed of separate *screens*, which fade and emerge at various distances. Such *screens* can be combined and superimposed as necessary, presenting shifting planes of depth. In reference to painting, Bayle claimed the spaces thus created are »a bit like the colour of indistinct paints of Rothko, composed of dozens of translucent layers«[11]. It comes as no surprise that these spaces cannot be »deciphered«.

Bayle is clearly aware of the effects of inverting word order in a text to communicate new meanings. Note that in the first phrase of the quotation under examination we read: »an obscure value«. The following sentence concludes with: »values of the obscure«. The word »obscure« in the latter case is presented not as an adjective but as a noun. Thus, the »obscure« is revealed as containing values (in the plural). If »obscure« is translated as »dark«, as suggested earlier, it invokes the shadowy, indistinct places where we can detect things such as sound sources, but these sound sources are impossible to see and thus difficult to comprehend effortlessly. This is for Bayle »an acousmatic value par excellence«[12]. I cannot resist referring once more to Romantic composers and writers and their fondness – I might even say obsession – with the dark and the night. Here is Novalis (again!) and his *Hymns to the night* in particular the fourth one, where he claims, »Wears not everything that inspires us the colour of the Night? [...] Thou wouldst vanish into thyself – in boundless space thou wouldst dissolve, if she did not hold

---

11 Personal communication by email, 27 June 2014: »un peu à la manière de la couleur des laques troubles de Rothko, composées de dizaines de couches translucides.«

12 Personal communication by email, 27 June 2014: »une valeur acousmatique par excellence.«

thee fast«[13]. The Romantics knew that the dark of the night was where we, as perceiving subjects, could allow the imagination – a mental faculty greatly prized by the Romantics – to create connections, to dwell on the ambiguous and unknown even unknowable sounds. The listener can fantasize about the sources of these sounds and about the spaces in which they are placed. Indecipherable and formlessness should not be regarded as negative. Let us recall Bayle's comment that the »valeur obscure« is »never measurable or decipherable«. These non-rational qualities were valued by the Romantics and the post-Romantics, particularly the Symbolists. The imagination is stimulated and identification is revealed as slippery and elusive. Darkness and suspension of vision is hardly a new situation for acousmatic composers and for those who are drawn to this performance practice in electroacoustic music. So, it is the »obscure« as darkness that contains within itself values, true acousmatic values. This encourages the sensitizing of attention or ›vigilance‹, which is raised to a heightened degree. We listen, according to Bayle, to, »the sound as a hard object; space as the place where sounds ›happen‹«[14]. Note that in the quotation from *Musique acousmatique*, Bayle asserts that *écoute est vigilance* (»listening is vigilance«). Listening becomes an active, re-creative activity where we as listening subjects, perceive and reconfigure sounds that are difficult to comprehend, but which can take us beyond ourselves and the phenomenal world. Here I am referring not only to the Kantian sublime, but also to the sublime of Romantic literature. This might not be spatiality in the literal sense, but we all occupy our own mental space. Any challenge to this will imply movement within and beyond known mental and metaphoric space.

When Bayle writes: »What is true in life is even more so in reverie – the reverie of being struck by sound which seeks to feel, to foresee... Valorized musical listening replays vigilance symbolically.« We should note he uses the verb *ouïr*, which can be translated as »struck« by sound«. In reverie we experience sound without necessarily being conscious of it. In particular, ›reverie‹ is not experiencing a dream (which is, of course, *rêve* in French). It is that state so dear to the Romantics (once more!) of daydreaming – although this is a rather trivial term in English. When one experiences a reverie, the conscious, rational mind is suspended. Instead sounds strike us before our attention – our vigilance – is alerted, at which point we turn to the sounds to listen in an active attempt to understand and make sense of them.

---

13 http://www.logopoeia.com/novalis/hymns. Revised version of the 1897 translation by George MacDonald. Accessed June 2014.

14 Personal communication by email, 4 July 2014: »Le son comme objet dur. L'espace comme lieu du son.«

In an interesting comment, Bayle wrote »The spatio-temporal disengagement (what I hear is neither here nor now: the only one here and now is me...)«[15]. Consequently, the listening subject becomes an active participant.

Another example of Bayle's inversion is the play on hearing and listening, on the one hand, and vision, on the other. Unlike vision, which turns to the outside, according to Bayle listening attempts to hear what is ›inside‹ sounds, what is ›behind‹, what is ›hidden‹. »Space hides«, according to Bayle's quotation. This might seem contradictory. Surely in composing with space, the main purpose should be to clarify relationships and to reveal structurally important sections? But it is the function of space to provide the environments to hide and conceal, in order to stimulate our imagination. As an autonomous object the sound grabs our attention and once we are alerted we begin to hear ›inside the sound‹, we hear ›living things which are hidden‹. This aspect of spatiality is, of course, on a small scale when compared to larger spatial environments. Nevertheless, it illustrates clearly that space exists on a continuum between the large and small. For a composer, both are important and are often related either to support or contradict each other. Some sounds, by their very behaviour, catch our attention and cause us – even demand from us – that we subject them to intense scrutiny, despite the time-based nature of aural perception. Unlike Schaeffer's *sons convenables* (»suitable sounds«), which clarify the dualism between value and characteristic, a listener is more likely to be drawn into the Schaefferian *sons excentriques* (»excentric sounds«). Sounds like the *sons excentriques* challenge us in their awe-inspiring features of unpredictable spectral and dynamic complexity. These are sounds that are (too) long in duration or (too) complex in their spectral and dynamic evolutions. When I asked Bayle about such sounds, he referred to them in a communication with me as *sacripants* (»rogues« in English!). Because they do not conform to the normative criteria of the *sons convenables*, they invite us to perceive their inner development. Faced with these sounds, we literally go beyond what we know.

In these comments, one subject area seems to be missing completely. What role does technology play in these processes of spatio-temporal disengagement? In concluding this chapter I return to comments made at the beginning. Without technology – first analogue then digital – these techniques could not occur. It is a truism that »technology is not neutral«[16]. Bayle wrote,

---

15 Personal communication by email, 4 July 2014: »Le débrayage spatio-temporel (ce que j'écoute n'est ni ici ni maintenant: le seul qui est ici et maintenant c'est moi...).«

16 François Bayle, *L'image de son/Klangbilder* (= Signale aus Köln: Beiträge zur Musik der Zeit 5), ed. by Imke Misch and Christoph von Blumröder, Münster 2003, p. 2: »La technologie n'est donc pas neutre«.

in reference to Michel Foucault and Giorgio Agamben, »I call everything a ›device‹ that has, in one way or another, the capacity to capture, to orientate, to determine, to intercept, to model, to control, and to ensure gestures, behaviours, opinions, and the discourse between human beings«[17]. There is a fascinating study to be undertaken on Bayle's reaction as a composer to the change from using mainly analogue stereo techniques to digital multichannel composition. This would apply not only to the composer's space in the studio, but also to the point of diffusion when the music is presented to the public[18]. Bayle refers to the relationship between the hand and the ear. In his diffusion practice he confirms that his natural inclination is to transform and modify at each concert. The faders on the mixing desk, for example, relate actual linear movement to sonic modifications of spectral or dynamic qualities.

This chapter can do no more than scratch the surface of Bayle's musical thinking, which can be, like many French texts, both playful and intellectually rigorous. I hope to extend these investigations in future research projects.

---

17 Personal communication by email, 4/7/2014: »J'appelle dispositif tout ce qui a, d'une manière ou d'une autre, la capacité de capturer, d'orienter, de déterminer, d'intercepter, de modeler, de contrôler et d'assurer les gestes, les conduites, les opinions et les discours des êtres vivants.«

18 This subject has been referred to in an extremely interesting article by Jan Simon Grintsch (idem, »La fonction perceptive de l'espace composé dans l'œuvre de François Bayle«, in: *Lien: Revue d'Esthétique Musicale: L'Analyse Perceptive des Musiques Électroacoustiques*, Musiques et Recherches, pp. 107–111) as well as in a panel discussion in Cologne by Ludger Brümmer which is transcribed in the proceedings of the aforementioned 2007 symposium (cf. *The Sound World of François Bayle*, op.cit).

Raum in Luigi Nonos
1° Caminantes ... Ayacucho (1987)

CHRISTINA DOLLINGER

Die bewusste kompositorische Einbeziehung des Raumes spielt in Luigi Nonos gesamtem Schaffen eine so herausragende Rolle, dass seine Musik immer auch als Raumkunst aufzufassen ist. Daher geht der folgende Beitrag zunächst auf den besonderen Zugang des Komponisten zum Raumklang ein, um dann im zweiten Teil anhand des 1986/87 entstandenen Werks *1° Caminantes ... Ayacucho* einige wesentliche Merkmale seiner Raummusik herauszuarbeiten[1].

I. RAUM IM WERK LUIGI NONOS

Nonos Interesse für den Raumklang wurde bereits in der Kindheit geweckt. Er führte sein ausgeprägtes räumliches Hörvermögen später auf die besondere Klangkulisse seiner Heimatstadt Venedig zurück, die vom Hall der Glocken in den Gassen und deren Echo über den Kanälen gekennzeichnet ist[2]. Bereits in sehr jungen Jahren war Nono fasziniert von der Akustik des Markusdoms und beschäftigte sich in einem intensiven Quellenstudium mit der musikalischen Tradition Venedigs, vor allem mit der Venezianischen Mehrchörigkeit.

---

1 Vgl. dazu ausführlich: Christina Dollinger, *Unendlicher Raum – zeitloser Augenblick: Luigi Nono, »Das atmende Klarsein« und »1° Caminantes ... Ayacucho«*, Saarbrücken 2012.

2 »Luigi Nono« in: Klaus Kropfinger, »... Kein Anfang – kein Ende ... Aus Gesprächen mit Luigi Nono«, in: Musica 42, (1988), S. 165–171, hier S. 166.

In den 1950er Jahren förderte ein weiteres Umfeld entscheidend den räumlichen Aspekt in seinem Schaffen: die Darmstädter Ferienkurse als wichtiges Forum für die neue Tonbandmusik einerseits und für Experimente mit neuen Aufstellungen in der Ensemble- und Orchestermusik andererseits. Im Jahr 1950, als Nono erstmals teilnahm, hielt Robert Beyer seinen zukunftsweisenden Vortrag über die Bedeutung des Raums für die elektronische Musik[3]. Gleichzeitig fand ein Kompositionskurs mit Edgard Varèse statt, in dem Nono dessen Konzept einer spatialen Musik kennenlernte.

Eine wichtige Rolle für Nonos musikalische Raumerfahrung spielte außerdem der Dirigent Hermann Scherchen, in dessen elektronischem Studio in Gravesano er sich mehrmals aufhielt. Die von Scherchen herausgegebenen *Gravesaner Blätter* widmeten sich den Themen räumliche Wahrnehmung und neue Hörräume. Mit Sicherheit hatte auch Nonos Freundschaft mit Karlheinz Stockhausen, der während des Ferienkurses 1958 seinen berühmten Vortrag »Musik im Raum« hielt, in den fünfziger Jahren Einfluss auf sein eigenes Raumverständnis.

Schon in seinen frühesten Werken knüpfte Nono unmittelbar an die Tradition der Venezianischen Mehrchörigkeit an, deren musikalische Auffassung er entscheidend weiterentwickelte. Dies geschah zunächst im Hinblick auf die besondere Aufteilung und Aufstellung des Klangkörpers. Ihr folgten die Bewegung des Klangs im Raum und zunehmend eine semantische Dimension.

Bereits die Stimmenanordnung in der Partitur des zweiten Lorca-Epitaphs *Y su sangre ya viene cantando* aus dem Jahr 1952 zeigt eine mehrchörige Anlage, allerdings noch ohne eine spezifisch räumliche Aufstellung. Eine solche findet sich erstmals im *Diario polacco '58* als symmetrische Anordnung vier gleich besetzter Instrumentalchöre (Abbildung 1).

Nono bezieht sich immer wieder explizit auf die Venezianische Mehrchörigkeit, nicht ohne den zentralen Unterschied zu betonen:

»Diese Ping-Pong-Auffassung, bei der die Musik von rechts nach links und von links nach rechts wechselt, wie der Ball beim Ping-Pong-Spiel, und alles sich im Effekt auflöst, ist meiner Musik fremd. Ich setze den Klang räumlich zusammen durch die Benutzung verschiedener, im Raum getrennter Ausgangspunkte.«[4]

---

3   Der Raum als formbildendes Moment in der Tonfotografie – seine Bedeutung für die elektronische Musik. URL: http://www.internationales-musikinstitut.de/images/stories/PDF/Darmstaedter_Ferienkurse_1946–1966.pdf, S. 29 (6.7.2014).

4   Luigi Nono, »*Diario Polacco '58* (1959)«, in: Jürg Stenzl (Hrsg.), *Luigi Nono: Texte, Studien zu seiner Musik*, Zürich 1975, S. 124.

Abbildung 1: Orchesteraufstellung in »Diario Polacco«

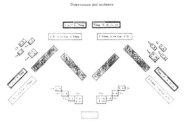

aus: Partitur *Diario polacco '58* Mainz 1958

In seinen großen Bühnenwerken hebt Nono entsprechend seinem politisch egalitären Denken die Trennung von Bühne und Auditorium auf. Anknüpfend an Meyerholds und Piscators Idee eines ›totalen Theaters‹ der 1920er Jahre schwebte Nono ein engagiertes Theater vor, in dem das Publikum Teil des Geschehens wird. In seiner *Intolleranza 1960* ist die Verteilung der vier Lautsprechergruppen im Raum so konzipiert, dass das Publikum vom Klang der vom Tonband kommenden Chorpartien umschlossen wird und sich so im Zentrum des Geschehens wiederfindet. Für Nonos ›Hör-Tragödie‹ *Prometeo* (1984/85) konstruierte der Architekt Renzo Piano im Inneren der Kirche San Lorenzo in Venedig einen besonderen ›Hörraum‹, in dem die Musiker um das Publikum herum auf verschiedenen Ebenen postiert waren.

In den frühen fünfziger Jahren spielte Nono erstmals mit dem Gedanken, das statische Raumkonzept der Venezianischen Mehrchörigkeit durch eine Bewegung der Klangquellen im Aufführungsraum aufzubrechen. Ursprünglich war im zweiten *Lorca-Epitaph* eine wandernde Soloflöte vorgesehen. Fünfzehn Jahre später, im *Musica Manifesto n. 1* (1968/69), verwirklichte Nono dann ein ähnliches Vorhaben und ließ Schauspielerin und Sängerin rezitierend im Zuschauerraum umhergehen. Der Einsatz von Live-Elektronik ermöglichte schließlich in den achtziger Jahren eine Klangbewegung im Raum, ohne dass einer der Musiker seine Position verlassen musste.

Ab 1981 begann Nono im Experimentalstudio des SWF in Freiburg die neuen live-elektronischen Mittel systematisch zu erforschen. Mit ihnen waren erstmals die virtuelle Platzierung von Klangquellen im Raum, Klangbewegungen und Nachhallvariationen in Echtzeit möglich. Auf dieser Basis konnte Nono den Raumaspekt über die äußere Wahrnehmungsebene hinaus in semantische Dimensionen hinein weiterentwickeln.

Die semantische Dimension des Raumes

Nonos musikalisches Werk steht in einer starken Wechselwirkung mit anderen Disziplinen, u.a. der Architektur, der Bildenden Kunst, der Literatur und der Philosophie. So befasste er sich anhand der umfangreichen Abhandlung von Alexander Gosztonyi[5] auch mit den philosophischen Hintergründen des Themas Raum. Im Archivio Luigi Nono sind die seitenlangen Notizen einsehbar, die Nono sich bei der Lektüre gemacht hat. Sie sind ein chronologischer Gang durch die Philosophiegeschichte von der Antike bis ins 20. Jahrhundert. Besonders scheint Nono der nichteuklidische Ansatz des 19. Jahrhunderts, der die Dreidimensionalität in Frage stellte, fasziniert zu haben. Der Gedanke einer ›n-dimensionalen‹ Räumlichkeit entsprach seiner eigenen Suche nach immer neuen Vorstellungsräumen, wie sie in *1° Caminantes... Ayacucho*, unserem Beispielwerk, besonders deutlich wird.

In Nonos Musik sind der äußere Klang-Raum als physikalische Größe und innere Räume in Form unendlicher Vorstellungsräume eng aufeinander bezogen. Indem er in seinen Kompositionen akustische Räume gestaltet, schafft er insofern immer zugleich auch geistige Räume, als Musik für ihn eine Form des Denkens darstellt:

»[...] Musik komponieren ist nicht bloß technische Sache, ist nur vom Handwerk, ist vom Denken. [...] Das kommt auch in der Unterweisung von Renaissancezeit [...], wo man hat immer gesprochen von verschiedenen Denken, musikalisch. Ist nicht nur technisch, nur Formel, Schemata, Paradigmata, ist eine besondere Denken vom Menschen, der in eine besondere Zeit lebt [...].«[6]

Musik ist für Nono Ausdruck des denkenden und des fühlenden Menschen als eines Zeugen seiner jeweiligen Epoche. So wird das Hören, das Jahrhunderte lang dem Primat des Sehens untergeordnet war, zu einem wieder neu zu entdeckenden Erkenntnismodus: »Hören [bedeutet] nicht nur das Hören traditioneller Musik [...], sondern auch das Hören der Stadt, das Hören der akustischen Umwelt, in der man lebt. Es geht um das Reagieren auf die Ge-

---

5   Alexander Gosztonyi, *Der Raum, Geschichte seiner Probleme in Philosophie und Wissenschaft*, Freiburg 1976.

6   »Nono im Gespräch zur UA seines Streichquartetts *Fragmente – Stille, An Diotima*«, in: Kay-Uwe Kirchert, *Wahrnehmung und Fragmentierung: Luigi Nonos Kompositionen zwischen »Al gran sole carico d'amore« und »Prometeo«*, Saarbrücken 2006, S. 204f.

genwart [...], um das Kennenlernen auch der *anderen Klänge*, die existieren und die geschaffen werden können.«[7]

Dies hat nicht zuletzt auch eine politische Dimension: »Andere Gedanken, andere Geräusche, andere Klänge, andere Ideen«[8] zu hören, ist für Nono notwendige Voraussetzung, um festgefahrene Mentalitäten zu durchbrechen und in neue geistige Räume vorzudringen. Seine Musik will einen Beitrag dazu leisten. Nur wenn sich das Individuum ändert, lassen sich aus Sicht des späten Nono auch die gesellschaftlichen Verhältnisse verändern.

Nonos Bedürfnis, seinen geistigen Horizont permanent zu erweitern, wird verkörpert im Bild des Wanderers. Die Worte »*Caminantes, no hay caminos, hay que caminar*« (frei übersetzt als: »Wanderer, es gibt keinen Weg, Weg entsteht im Gehen«)[9], die er 1985 auf einer Klostermauer in Toledo entdeckte, wurden zum Motto seiner gesamten letzten Schaffensphase. Wandern bedeutet zu suchen, sich nicht auf vermeintliche Sicherheiten zu verlassen, sondern offen zu sein für das Unbekannte. Auf ein solch unvoreingenommenes Hören zielt Nonos Komponieren. Die vielfältigen Klangbewegungen im Raum fordern dazu auf, die Ohren wandern zu lassen. Dabei lassen sich die verschiedenen Klangquellen häufig nicht genau lokalisieren – der Raumklang wird zum bewusst eingesetzten Mittel, um das traditionelle Hören und damit eingefahrene Denkstrukturen aufzubrechen.

II. 1° CAMINANTES ... AYACUCHO

Das großbesetzte *1° Caminantes ... Ayacucho* für Alt, Bassflöte, Orgel, kleinen und großen Chor, Orchester in drei Gruppen und Live-Elektronik vereint eindrucksvoll all die bisher genannten räumlichen Aspekte. Es entstand 1986/87 als Auftragswerk der Münchner Philharmoniker im Zusammenhang mit der Einweihung des neu erbauten Konzertsaals im Münchner Gasteig.

---

7 Luigi Nono, »Andere Möglichkeiten des Hörens«, in: Dissonanz #60 (1999), S. 11.

8 Luigi Nono, »L'erreur comme nécessité«, in: SMZ 123 (1983), S. 270f.

9 Es handelt sich um ein abgewandeltes Zitat aus Antonio Machado, »Proverbios y Cantares«, in: *Campos de Castilla*, Madrid 1912.

Raum als kompositorischer Ausgangspunkt

Der architektonische Raum

»Studien über das akustische Raum von Gasteig« vermerkte Nono auf einer farbigen Aufstellungsskizze des Werks[10]. Dass der Raum den entscheidenden kompositorischen Ausgangspunkt darstellt, zeigt auch eine Notiz auf einem der ersten Skizzenblätter[11]:

<blockquote>

»München Aprile 1987

Tr, Cr a2, Trb (A – C)

Archi + Fl – Cl (B)

Percussione A – C

Coro FR A – C

Coro BR B«

</blockquote>

Abbildung 2: Die Großbuchstaben A, B und C hinter den Besetzungsangaben beziehen sich auf die folgenden drei Raumchöre

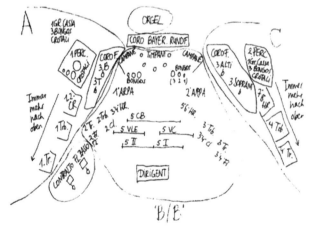

aus: Hella Melkert, »Jedem Klang sein Universum: Zu *Caminantes ... Ayacucho* (1978) von Luigi Nono«, in: MusikTexte 64, April 1996, S. 20 – 28, hier S. 20.

---

10 Abgebildet in: Gabriele E. Meyer, (Hrsg.), *100 Jahre Münchner Philharmoniker*, München 1994, S. 458f.

11 Skizzenblatt 55.02./ 07 inf.

Es war der architektonische Raum der Münchner Philharmonie, der Nono in Anlehnung an die Venezianische Mehrchörigkeit zur Aufteilung des Klangkörpers in mehrere ›Chöre‹ inspirierte. Nonos Projekte begannen stets mit dem ›Erhören‹ des Raumes, mit akustischen Versuchen und dem Studium der baulichen Voraussetzungen, wie Hans Peter Haller, der damalige Leiter des Freiburger Experimentalstudios, schilderte[12].

Noch bevor er sich dem konkreten musikalischen Material widmete, skizzierte Nono bereits Raumwege und verschiedene Möglichkeiten, die Raumchöre miteinander kommunizieren zu lassen[13]:

Takt	Version 1	Version 2	Version 3
T. 1–30	A+C	B	A+B+C
T. 31–60	B	A+C	B+A
T. 61–90	B ⇨ A	B+C	B+C
T. 91–120	B ⇨ C	B+C	B
T. 121–138	A+B+C	A+B+C	A+C

In der ersten Version lässt Nono den Klang von den beiden seitlichen ›Chören‹ A und C aus in die Mitte (B) wandern und von dort erst auf die eine, dann die andere Seite zurückkehren, um im letzten Abschnitt alle drei ›Chöre‹ miteinander zu verbinden. Dagegen beginnt die zweite Version aus der Mitte heraus, die dritte gleich mit allen drei Raumchören.

Die semantische Dimension:
Giordano Brunos Gedicht *A i principi dell'universo*

Auch in *1° Caminantes ... Ayacucho* geht Nono weit über ein musikalisches Ausloten des Aufführungsraumes und seine live-elektronische Überschreitung hinaus und öffnet hier ganze Gedanken-Universen. Noch vor Beginn der Kompositionsarbeit hatte er sich mit den Schriften Giordano Brunos beschäftigt, der um 1600 die Hypothese eines unendlichen Weltraums ganz ohne Mittelpunkt formulierte. Schon in seinen frühesten Skizzenblättern fin-

---

12 »Auch in München in der neuen Philharmonie haben wir schon sehr früh ähnliche Klangproben durchgeführt, die zu wichtigen Entscheidungen für die räumliche Konzeption der Komposition *Caminantes ... Ayacucho* von Luigi Nono und deren Aufführung am 25. April 1987 beitrugen.« (Hans Peter Haller, »Nono im Konzert«, in: MusikTexte 35 (1990), S. 62–68, hier S. 67).

13 Skizzenblätter 55.03.01/20 und 21.

den sich als Arbeitstitel die Initialen G.B. und mehrfach auch ein italieni-sches Zitat, das in der deutschen Übersetzung lautet: »Die Fixsterne seien unendliche andere Sonnen anderer Planetensysteme – jede dieser unendli-chen Welten unterscheidet sich von der anderen.«[14]

Als Textgrundlage für *1° Caminantes ... Ayacucho* wählte Nono schließ-lich das erste von fünf Gedichten, die Brunos metaphysischem Grundlagen-werk *De la causa, principio e uno* vorangehen. Die im Gedicht angelegte Aufwärtsbewegung von der irdischen zur göttlichen Sphäre bot sich Nono für eine Raumkomposition geradezu an. Verschlüsselt in Bilder der antiken Mythologie, wie sie in der Renaissance wieder aufgegriffen wurden, spricht Giordano Bruno von einer Erlösung des Menschen durch den Weg der Er-kenntnis. Die auffällige Licht-Metaphorik als Sinnbild der Wahrheit verweist auf den Ur-Gegensatz vom absoluten göttlichen Licht und der Finsternis der Welt, wie er für gnostische Vorstellungen kennzeichnend ist[15].

Diese inhaltliche Räumlichkeit des Gedichts und der äußere Auffüh-rungsraum bestimmen gemeinsam die Werkstruktur von *1° Caminantes ... Ayacucho* nahezu auf allen Ebenen.

Raum in den kompositorischen Schichten des Werks

Innerhalb dieser Komplexität von Raumbezügen wird im folgenden zwi-schen äußeren Raumklängen und einer inneren, symbolischen Räumlichkeit unterschieden. Beide sind eng mit der Textausdeutung verbunden.

Symbolischer Raum

Die räumliche Dualität des Gedichts zwischen Unten und Oben, einer be-grenzten irdischen und einer unendlichen himmlischen Sphäre, findet sich gleich auf mehreren musikalischen Ebenen wieder. So steckt die Orgel mit ihren extrem tiefen und extrem hohen Haltetönen den Ambitus ab. Während der gesamte Part von Orgel, Chören und Orchester fast vollständig auf dem Fünftonkomplex *c–g–a–b–h* beruht, durchwandern die beiden Solisten, die

---

14 »Le stelle fisse infiniti altri soli siano di altre sistemi planetari – ciascuno di questi in-finiti mondi si diversificano tra lore« G[iordano] B[runo]: Le stelle fisse infiniti altri soli siano di altri sistemi planetari – ciascuno di questi infinitimondi si diversificano tra lore«. Notiz Nonos (u.a. auf Skizzenblatt M05.222/04v), inhaltlich bezogen auf Giordano Brunos Schrift *De l'infinito, universo e mondi*, 1584.

15 Giordano Bruno, *Von der Ursache, dem Prinzip und dem Einen*, aus dem Italienischen übersetzt von Adolf Lasson, hrsg. v. Paul Richard Blum, 7. Aufl., Hamburg 1993, S. XIX.

Altstimme und die Bassflöte, als einzige den gesamten Tonraum. Sie sind die ›Caminantes‹, die Wanderer, des Werktitels.

Innerhalb der rhythmischen Gestaltung ist das auffälligste Merkmal der Kontrast kurzer, punktueller Einwürfe und breit ausgedehnter Klangflächen, der auf eine ursprünglich strenge Organisation der Tondauern zurückgeht[16]. Er macht zwischen lang gehaltenen Clusterflächen und kurzen Akzenten, zwischen Stillstand und Ereignis, einen Zeit-Raum erfahrbar.

Einen weiteren symbolischen Raum eröffnet die Kontrastdramaturgie auf der dynamischen Ebene. Mit schockierendem, schmerzhaftem *Fortissimo* und kaum wahrnehmbaren *Pianissimo*-Klängen lotet Nono die klanglichen Grenzen aus, ja er überschreitet sie sogar, indem er die Dynamikskala am unteren Ende zur Stille hin öffnet. Damit dringt er in neue Räume vor, die sich für den Hörer durch das Lauschen nach innen öffnen, die intendierten Gedankenräume.

Solche Gedankenräume entstehen auch im Bereich des gesungenen Textes. Die Partien von Chören und Altsolistin enthalten nahezu den identischen Text, jedoch über weite Strecken« zeitlich verschoben. Durch die Überlagerung verschiedener Textfragmente öffnet Nono in Form klanglicher und neuer inhaltlicher Bezüge auch Räume innerhalb des Textes. Schon in seinen Vokalkompositionen der fünfziger Jahre wird die Linearität des Textes in ähnlicher Weise aufgehoben. So entsteht die von Nono in seinem Vortrag »Text – Musik – Gesang« von 1960 beschriebene »Vielschichtigkeit der Beziehungen nach allen Richtungen«[17].

Aus diesem Denken resultiert ein räumliches Formkonzept, in dem die Vorstellung von einer eindimensional fortschreitenden Zeit überwunden wird. Es gibt keinen rein linearen Zusammenhang mehr, keine Entwicklung ›von links nach rechts‹, sondern ein räumliches Beziehungsnetz. Die Skizzen zeigen deutlich, dass Nono zunächst ein Gesamtkonzept entwirft, das er in vielen einzelnen Schritten aufbricht. Besonders deutlich wird dies am Part der Solisten, der zunächst getrennt komponiert und dann in Fragmenten eingeschoben wird. Gerade in den Takten 111 bis 136 lässt sich die Verquickung der beiden unabhängigen Texturen anhand der starken Kontraste in der Dynamik und besonders im Tempo gut beobachten: Mit Tempo M.M. 30 in den Solofragmenten und M.M. 120 im Orchester wählte Nono bewusst die beiden Extreme des Werks.

---

16 Die mit »*A veloce*« und »*B calmo*« bezeichneten Rhythmusbasen finden sich erstmals in *Con Luigi Dallapiccola*, anschließend in mindestens sieben weiteren Werken, u.a. im Streichquartett und im *Prometeo*.

17 Luigi Nono, »Text – Musik – Gesang«, in: Jürg Stenzel, *Luigi Nono*, a.a.O., S. 49.

»No hay caminos, hay que caminar« – es gibt keinen Weg, nur das Gehen, bezieht sich auch direkt auf die formale Gestaltung. Der Hörer muss bereit sein, ins völlig Ungewisse aufzubrechen, frei von Erwartungen. Nonos Musik verlangt eine viel unmittelbarere Art der Wahrnehmung, die zunächst mehr körperliche Erfahrung ist als intellektuelles Verstehen: Die *fortissimo*-Eruptionen in *1° Caminantes ... Ayacucho* gehen durch Mark und Bein. Durchdrungen vom Raumklang, der von allen Seiten auf ihn einströmt, wird der Hörer selbst zum Teil des Klangs. Er ist nicht mehr Zeuge eines rhetorischen Diskurses, dessen Argumentation sich Schritt für Schritt nachvollziehen ließe, und auch kein Wanderer, der eine mehr oder weniger vorgegebene Route mittels Karte abläuft, sondern ein Pionier, der sich einen Weg durch unerforschtes Gelände bahnt.

Zusammengehalten wird das 35 Minuten lange Werk durch eine großangelegte Aufwärtsbewegung vom C_1 im Kontrabass am Beginn hin zum h^5 in der Orgel und dem verklingenden a^2 im Sopran, eine ›Erhöhung‹, die keine dramatische Entwicklung ist, sondern die letzten Takte mit ihrem Ausklingen in höchster Lage zu einem utopischen Moment werden lässt.

Komponierter Raum

Innerhalb der besonderen Aufstellung der Musiker repräsentiert das Orchester mit seiner differenzierten Anordnung am deutlichsten den Aspekt des Raumes. So sind nicht nur die ›Chöre‹ A und C als Ganze in ihrer Besetzung symmetrisch zueinander angelegt, sondern auch Streicher, Bläser und Schlagwerk innerhalb des ›Chores‹ B spiegelbildlich platziert (B und B'). Hinzu kommt, dass die acht Blechbläser der beiden ›Chöre‹ A und C nach oben ansteigend auf seitlichen Emporen sitzen und damit den Raum gewissermaßen dreidimensional machen.

Eine gezielte Instrumentierung erzeugt in Verbindung mit der rhythmischen Ebene äußere Raumwirkungen. Gerade ganz zu Beginn des Stückes wird das sehr deutlich: Die zeitlich kurz aufeinanderfolgenden Schläge der Großen Trommeln und Bongos ›eröffnen‹ für den Zuhörer in den ersten Takten den Raum. Es beginnt die Trommel des ›Chores‹ A auf der linken Seite des Saales. Nach zwei Takten Pause wiederholt sie ihren Schlag, dem direkt die große Trommel des ›Chores‹ C von der rechten Seite her antwortet. Gleich anschließend in Takt 5 geht die Bewegung in den Bongos zurück von rechts nach links, dabei erklingt zusammen mit dem zweiten Bongo-Schlag von links auch die große Trommel von rechts – der Raum ist in seiner Breite aufgespannt.

Abbildung 3: Takt 1–5 Schlagwerk

In der Verwendung gleich zweier Vokalchöre schwingt in *1° Caminantes ... Ayacucho* ein weiteres Mal die Tradition der Venezianischen Mehrchörigkeit mit. Während der große Chor sich zentral in der Mitte befindet, sind Männer- und Frauenstimmen des Solistenchores auf der linken und rechten Seite doppelchörig positioniert. Schon dadurch ist die besondere Raumwirkung des kleinen Chors begründet, dessen Klang im Gegensatz zu dem des großen Chores außerdem mittels *Halaphon* im Aufführungsraum bewegt wird.

Einen Großteil der äußeren Raumwirkungen erzielt Nono also ganz unmittelbar durch die besondere Aufstellung des Klangkörpers. Mit Hilfe der live-elektronischen Möglichkeiten werden sie unterstrichen und erweitert. In der einzigen bislang existierenden Druckfassung des Werks, einer Kopie der handschriftlichen Partitur, fehlen alle Angaben zur Ausführung des live-elektronischen Parts. Die Lautsprecherdisposition der Uraufführung lässt sich durch Fotos rekonstruieren. Abbildung 4 zeigt eine schematische Darstellung.

Abbildung 4: Lautsprecherverteilung im Raum

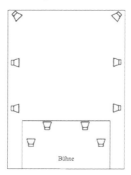

Die beiden Lautsprecher vorne links und rechts auf der Bühne sind den beiden Solisten vorbehalten, während die übrigen im Konzertsaal ansteigenden

Lautsprecher den Solistenchor wiedergeben[18]. Im Gegensatz zum Chorklang, der nur verstärkt, aber nicht verändert wird, ist im Skizzenmaterial für Alt und Bassflöte ein »Wandern mit Filter und Hall« vermerkt. Dies ist besonders deutlich bei den Luftgeräuschen der Flöte wahrnehmbar, die durch den Halleffekt eine räumliche Wirkung erhalten.

Der Klang des Solistenchores ist zum einen statisch über bestimmte Lautsprecherkombinationen im Raum zu hören, wobei nicht immer alle Lautsprecher angesteuert werden. So verwendet ein ›Fernprogramm‹ nur die beiden Lautsprecher ganz hinten im Saal. Seh- und Höreindrücke des Publikums müssen sich also nicht zwangsläufig decken. Der Klang kann zusätzlich aus einer völlig anderen Richtung als derjenigen kommen, in der sich der Standort der Sänger befindet.

Zum zweiten wird der Chorklang mittels *Halaphon* über die im Raum verteilten Lautsprecher zeitgleich mit seiner Entstehung bewegt, nicht nur auf der horizontalen Ebene, sondern auch vertikal im Raum als die musikalische Entsprechung der in Giordano Brunos Gedicht angelegten Aufwärtsbewegung. Zusätzlich zur Bewegungsrichtung lässt sich auch die Geschwindigkeit der Raumbewegung variieren.

Um die von Nono intendierten neuen Klangräume zu schaffen, muss jede Aufführung seiner live-elektronischen Werke an die Bedingungen des konkreten Aufführungsraumes angepasst werden. Auch Nono und die Techniker des Freiburger Studios erarbeiteten für jeden Aufführungsraum von neuem die Aufstellung der Lautsprecher und der Musiker, die Klangbewegungen und Verzögerungszeiten. Der Raum ist ein so wesentlicher Bestandteil der Komposition, dass die Angaben zur Live-Elektronik in der Partitur in einigen Punkten unvollständig bleiben müssen.

Obwohl Nono häufig selbst Klangregie führte (so auch bei der Uraufführung von *1° Caminantes ... Ayacucho*), hat er seine eigenen Realisierungen des live-elektronischen Parts nie als die allein gültigen betrachtet. »Immer, wenn ich allein am Regiepult saß«, betont Haller ausdrücklich, »hat er mich gebeten, meine persönlichen Klangvorstellungen zu verwirklichen.«[19]. Heutige Aufführungen gelingen demnach nur, wenn sie die musikalische Aussage des Werks umsetzen, nicht, wenn sie Nonos Klangregie eines bestimmten Konzerts kopieren. Um dieser Forderung gerecht zu werden, ist ei-

---

18 Nach der Aussage André Richards in einem Telefongespräch mit der Verfasserin am 17.3.2010.

19 Hans Peter Haller, *Das Experimentalstudio der Heinrich-Strobel-Stiftung des Südwestfunks Freiburg 1971–1989: Die Erforschung der Elektronischen Klangumformung und ihre Geschichte*, Baden-Baden 1995, Bd. 2., S. 154.

ne umfassende Kenntnis von Nonos musikalischem Denken unabdingbare Voraussetzung.

MAKROKOSMOS MIKROKOSMOS

Auf allen Ebenen der Komposition *1 ° Caminantes ... Ayacucho* sind zwei Raumdimensionen wirksam: der äußere Aufführungsraum, die Philharmonie im Münchner Gasteig (besonders vor dem Hintergrund ihrer Einweihung), und der Text mit seinem inhaltlichen Raumbezug bzw. die Vorstellung seines Autors Giordano Bruno von unendlichen Universen. Zur Raumkomposition machen das Werk viele einzelne Faktoren, die an dieser Stelle noch einmal zusammengefasst und ergänzt werden:

1. teilt Nono den Klangkörper in mehrere Gruppen oder ›Chöre‹ auf, die
2. im Aufführungsraum in besonderer Weise angeordnet sind. Die Aufstellung bezieht auch die Vertikale mit ein. Ebenfalls im Raum gestaffelt angeordnet sind die Lautsprecher der Live-Elektronik.
3. werden Klangbewegungen im äußeren Raum sowohl durch gezielte Instrumentierung als auch durch den Einsatz des *Halaphons* erzeugt.
4. bezieht sich der Raum-Gedanke auch auf eine Art Innenraum des Klangs: Nonos berühmter *suono mobile*, sein »beweglicher Klang«, meint nämlich nicht nur die äußere Bewegung im Aufführungsraum, sondern ebenso diejenige im Mikrokosmos des ›Klanginneren‹: das permanente Changieren des Klangs durch mikrotonales Einfärben sowie feinste Dynamikabstufungen und variierende Instrumentierung. So erscheint die Grundkonstellation des Fünftonkomplexes in ständig neuem Licht. Kennzeichnend ist dabei ein subtiles Ineinandergreifen vom unveränderten und unverstärkten Live-Klang des großen Vokalchores und des Orchesters und der mit Hilfe live-elektronischer Verfahren in Echtzeit veränderten Klänge der Solisten.
5. wird ganz besonders in *1 ° Caminantes ... Ayacucho* deutlich, dass Nonos Raumkompositionen auf geistige Räume verweisen wollen, die sich schon zwischen den beiden Titelworten auftun: *Caminantes*, Wanderer, verkörpert für Nono die Geisteshaltung des permanenten Suchens als Gegensatz zum Stillstand. Mit *Ayacucho*, einer seit der spanischen Eroberung im 16. Jahrhundert immer wieder rebellischen Region im Süden Perus, setzt er den abstrakten philosophischen Gedanken die Tat entgegen, das Aufbegehren gegen Unterdrückung damals wie heute.

Dazwischen ist Raum für nahezu unendlich viele Anknüpfungspunkte, wie Nonos Einführungstext im Programmheft der Uraufführung eindrucksvoll deutlich macht. Was Nono lapidar mit »Einige Informationen über *Caminantes ... Ayacucho*« betitelte, entpuppt sich als eine Montage vielfältig miteinander verknüpfter Stichworte. Sie beziehen sich u.a. auf die Multiperspektivität des Denkens, die Bedeutung des Hörens und das Anknüpfen an die Raummusik-Traditionen der Vergangenheit. Geht man den einzelnen, knapp hingeworfenen Gedanken nach, so öffnet sich jener »ins Unendliche expandierende geistige Kosmos«[20] den die semantische Ebene von *1° Caminantes ... Ayacucho* widerspiegelt.

Nonos Raummusik wird so zu einem Medium, sich auf Neues und Unbekanntes einzulassen. Sie hält gewissermaßen den Raum in Form von Gedanken- und Erfahrungsräumen für denjenigen Hörer offen, der in diese Universen einzutauchen bereit ist.

---

20 Gerhard R. Koch, »Klangarchitektur als Wanderschaft in die Unendlichkeit: Luigi Nono in München: eine große Uraufführung und eine Initiative«, Frankfurter Allgemeine Zeitung, 30.4.1987.

ENGLISH SUMMARY

Space in Luigi Nono's 1° Caminantes ... Ayacucho

The compositional inclusion of space plays an outstanding role in Nono's entire creative activity, so that his music can always also be interpreted as spatial art. Nono traced his distinct spatial hearing abilities back to the unique sound scenery of his hometown Venice, which is marked by echoes of church bells in the alleys and over the canals and he thought intensively about Venetian polychorality since his early years. Since his earliest works, he was directly tied to this tradition, and later he decisively developed their musical conception (see figure 1). In the 1950s, another sphere decisively promoted the spatial aspect in Nono's works: the Darmstadt Summer Course for New Music.

Nono's musical thinking is closely connected to his political intentions, which rely on the concept of equality. In his great stage works this lead to a revocation of the separation between stage and auditorium. In *Intolleranza 1960*, the distribution of the loudspeakers is conceived such that the audience is enclosed by the electronic sounds from tape and, therefore, is seated in the centre of musical activities. For *Prometeo* (1984/85), the architect Renzo Piano constructed a special ›listening space‹, in which the musicians were positioned around the public and on different levels.

Movement of sounds in space is another important point of Nono's spatial thinking. In the second of the *Tre epitaffi per Federico García Lorca* (1952), a wandering solo flute was planned from the beginning. In the *Musica-Manifesito n. 1* (1968/69), the actress and singer recite while walking around the auditorium. In the 1980s, using equipment for live electronics of the Experimental Studios of the Südwestfunk (SWF) in Freiburg, movement of sound in space became possible without requiring the musicians to leave their places. Since that time Nono began to systematically study new equipment for live electronics. From his perspective, the rising virtual spaces are not an end in themselves. Rather, they are a further development of the aspect of space, growing beyond the bare level of perception to a semantic dimension.

Nono studied the philosophical background of 'space' in the 1980s through Alexander Gosztonyi's work, *Der Raum: Geschichte seiner Probleme in Philosophie und Wissenschaft* (Freiburg 1976). Because music was a way of thinking for Nono, he understood the sound space as a physical quantity, and the philosophical space in form of never-ending spaces of imagination strongly apply to each other. Through the composition of acoustical rooms, Nono – in his own view – simultaneously creates mental spaces. Hearing different thoughts and sounds is a necessary precondition for Nono to break through deadlocked mentalities and to get through to new mental spaces. This is personified through the image of the rambler. The words, »Wanderer, there is no path, paths evolve in the walking«, (*Caminante, no hay caminos, hay que caminar*) became the motto of his entire final creative phase. ›Rambling‹ means searching, being open for the unknown. The diverse movements of sound in space require the ear to move. In doing so, different sound sources may not always be localized – the space sound is a method deliberately inserted to rupture the traditional hearing and the well-worn structures of thinking.

In *1° Caminantes ... Ayacucho*, for alto solo, bass flute, organ, small and large choirs, orchestra (in three groups), and live electronics, impressively combines all the named spatial aspects. Following the Venetian polychoral style, Nono was inspired by the architectural space of the Munich Philharmonic Hall to divide the orchestra into several ›choirs‹. Before he began to work on the musical material, he sketched the room paths and possibilities to let these ›choirs‹ communicate with each other (see figure 2). For his composition Nono was inspired by Giordano Bruno's Poem *A i principi dell'universo*. Around 1600, the Italian philosopher Giordano Bruno had formulated the hypothesis of infinite outer space, completely without a centre. The element of an upward movement describes the redemption of the human through the path of insight and realization.

The spatial duality of the poem between the finite earthly realm and the infinite divine sphere can be found in the form of extreme contrasts at the levels of pitch, rhythm, and dynamics. In addition, there is Nono's specific working with the text, which opens up new spaces of thoughts in the text through new references with regard to content and ambiguities. In the field of form, there is no longer a linear connection. A spatial net of relations, in the form of a fragmentary figure, replaces it.

Orchestra and small choir are placed in a differentiated symmetric order in the room. A well-aimed instrumentation, in connection with the rhythmic level, generates outer spatial effects. The spatial effects through live electronics are emphasized and extended through live electronics. Today, no information regarding the electronics is to be found in the printed score. Pictures from the concert hall show ascending loudspeakers, through which the sound of the small choir is moved – the sound is unchanged, only amplified through the *Halaphon*.

Klangarchitektur /

Sound Architecture

»... every movement is possible«

Spatial Composition in Iannis Xenakis's *Hibiki-Hana-Ma*

RALPH PALAND

Iannis Xenakis regarded music not only as a temporal art, but also as a spatial one, and he declared that sound displacement was »part of our perception of the world, our universe, and space must be integrated into sound structures«[1]. Space had a prominent role in his theoretical writings, in his architectural works and, of course, in his instrumental and electroacoustic compositions.

With regard to the implementation of sonic spatiality, Xenakis attaches, from the start, particular importance to electroacoustic resources. In his essay »Notes Towards an ›Electronic Gesture‹«, written in 1958, he stated: »Thanks to electro-acoustic techniques, we may note that the conquest of geometric space, a new step into the realm of Abstraction, is indeed realizable.«[2] In this text, which reflects the architectural and musical experiences of the Philips Pavilion, with its huge sound diffusion system of nearly 350 loudspeakers, distributed over the curved walls in the form of nine sound routes[3], he differentiates between two general types of sonic spatiality: a ›static‹ one, based on the simultaneous emission of sounds from different

---

1   Iannis Xenakis, »Topoi« [ca. 1970–1971], in: idem, *Music and Architecture* (= The Iannis Xenakis Series 1), edited by Sharon Kanach, Hillsdale, New York 2008, pp. 142–147, here p. 143.

2   Iannis Xenakis, »Notes towards an ›Electronic Gesture‹«, in: idem 2008, pp. 131–134, here p. 134.

3   Cf. Peter Révai, »Die technische Einrichtung des *Poème électronique*«, in: Dieter A Nanz (ed.), *Edgard Vàrese und das Poème électronique: Eine Dokumentation*, Basel 2006, pp. 43–51, here pp. 46–48.

points, and a ›cinematic‹ one, based on sound movements[4]. Both types are generally also feasible with instrumental resources, and for a time Xenakis regarded the spatial scattering of the musicians among the audience, in the manner of his orchestral works *Terretektorh* or *Nomos gamma*, as a more convincing way to realize spatialization of either type than the use of electroacoustic diffusion techniques. In a note written in the late 1960s he postulated that in instrumental compositions a »radically new kinetic conception of music, which no modern electro-acoustical means could match«[5] had been achieved. But not long afterwards, Xenakis modified his opinion and no longer regarded electroacoustic sound diffusion as a deficient mode of musical spatiality but as an autonomous approach, which would be able to constitute a »new type of space«, in which the three-dimensional distribution of the loudspeakers would create »homogeneity« or »a multi-directional isotropy« of sound »without any focalization, without any privileged focal points«[6].

SPACE IN XENAKIS'S ELECTROACOUSTIC MUSIC

Against this background, it is disappointing to see how little material exists that documents the concrete spatial strategies Xenakis pursued in his electroacoustic works. »Even if the composer himself has described in depth many of his composition techniques, no detailed info[rmation] on spatialization strategies in multichannel setup is available.«[7] To make things worse, Xenakis produced »multiple versions of all his tape pieces, up to *La Légende d'Eer*, mixing for different numbers of channels, accounting for different playback situations, and so forth«[8]. Particularly the cinematic aspect of spatiality is hard to grasp: though most of his electroacoustic compositions are

---

4 With the differentiation between ›static‹ and ›cinematic‹ spatiality Xenakis refers apparently to terms and concepts which have been developed by Jacques Poullin and Pierre Schaeffer in the early 1950s (cf. in this volume: Marc Battier, »Recent Discoveries in the Spatial Thought of Early *musique concrète*«).

5 Iannis Xenakis, *Formalized Music: Thought and Mathematics in Music*, Revised Edition, Hillsdale, New York, 1992, p. 236.

6 Xenakis 2008, op.cit., p. 142.

7 Andrea Valle, Kees Tazelaar and Vincenzo Lombardo, »In a Concrete Space: Reconstructing the Spatialization of Iannis Xenakis' *Concret PH* on a Multichannel Setup« [2010], http://smcnetwork.org/files/proceedings/2010/40.pdf (15.9.2014), pp. 1–8, here p. 4.

8 James Harley, »The Electroacoustic Music of Iannis Xenakis«, Computer Music Journal 26(1), (2002), pp. 33–57, here p. 37.

preserved in multichannel formats, effectively only a few tapes contain information about sound movements. Most of these pieces belong to Xenakis's early electroacoustic output from the late 1950s and the early 1960s[9]: *Diamorphoses* from 1957; *Concret PH* from 1958, originally composed as a three-track-tape for automated spatialization with the huge loudspeaker system of the Philips Pavilion; and *Orient-Occident* from 1960, an adaption of a monophonic soundtrack to the film of the same title by Enrico Fulchignoni[10]. But as the four-track versions of these three pieces were produced no earlier than 1969[11], spatialization of the sound processes seems, at least for *Diamorphoses* and *Orient-Occident*, not to be a constitutive aspect of the original musical conception, even if Xenakis may certainly have appreciated spatialization as an additional possibility of staging these processes on an impressive auditive scene and to clarify the complex layer or the sound textures. And *Bohor*, realized in 1962 and commonly regarded as one of the first eight-track pieces produced at GRM (despite the fact that it is simply a doubling of only four independent channels) is, as a whole, constructed exclusively from static sound layers[12].

At first sight, the spatial design of the electroacoustic music for Xenakis's *polytopes* is similar to that of *Bohor*. Although pieces like *Persepolis*, *Polytope de Cluny*, or *La Légende d'Eer* (as part of the *Diatope*) are fixed on seven or eight tracks, the multichannel recordings are not used for realizing sound movements by panning. But there is one crucial difference to most of Xenakis's earlier tape music: In *Polytope de Cluny* as well as in the *Diatope*, spatialization is not fixed on tape but is the result of automated sound distribution during the performance. In these pieces, Xenakis worked with individual systems of multiple loudspeakers, distributing the speakers according to the specific architectural conditions of the performance place. Although he employed twelve loudspeakers to diffuse the eight tracks of *Polytope de Cluny* into the historical rooms of the Paris *Hôtel de Cluny*, in the tent he de-

---

9 Xenakis's electroacoustic works from the late 1970s to the 1990s, which are realized with the UPIC system and the GENDYN algorithm, reduce spatiality on a kind of pseudo-stereo.

10 Makis Solomos, »›Orient-Occident‹: From the film version to the concert version«, in: Ralph Paland and Christoph von Blumröder (ed.): *Iannis Xenakis: Das elektroakustische Werk* (= Signale aus Köln: Beiträge zur Musik der Zeit 14), Vienna 2009, pp. 118–131.

11 Concerning the different remixes of these pieces and some problems with their dating, cf. James Harley, *Xenakis: His Life in Music*, New York 2004, p. 257 (footnotes 21 and 22).

12 Tobias Hünermann, »Iannis Xenakis: *Bohor*«, in: Paland, von Blumröder (ed.), op.cit., pp. 152–166, here p. 154.

signed for his *Diatope* he used eleven loudspeakers for the projection of the seven tracks of *La Légende d'Eer*[13]. Two earlier works by Xenakis follow a similar concept, so that they could be understood, at least in some ways, as precursors of the *polytopes*: first, the aforementioned *Concret PH*, originally composed in three tracks as a short interlude between the performances of the *Poème électronique* by Edgard Varèse and Le Corbusier in the Philips Pavilion[14]; second, *Hibiki-Hana-Ma*, also composed for a multimedia show during a World's Fair, in this case originally designed as twelve-track piece for a spectacle of music and light in the so-called Steel Pavilion of the Japan Iron and Steel Federation at the Expo 1970 in Osaka.

There are no fixed correlations of tracks and speakers in any of these works. Thus, these tapes do not contain any information about the actual spatial processes during the performance. Neither are there any verbal instructions nor a performance score, which would describe the diffusion of these pieces in a universal, unequivocal manner. There is a significant difference here between Xenakis's concept and the two main streams of early electroacoustic music, the Cologne School and *musique acousmatique*. Both of these traditions aimed for a more-or-less meticulous spatial organization on the recording medium, even if the protagonists of the Cologne School, like Karlheinz Stockhausen, were geared towards the ideal of a pure rendition of the compositional structure, in contrast to acousmatic composers, such as François Bayle, who allowed the mixing engineer an interpretative performance of the stereophonic reference image fixed on tape. To the extent that, in these cases, the recording medium contains virtually all temporal, spectral,

---

13 Interestingly, there exists an eight-channel concert version of *La Légende d'Eer*, which was realized by Xenakis with assistance of Volker Müller and James Whitman in the electronic studio of Westdeutsche Rundfunk (WDR) in Cologne in 1977 (cf. Marcus Erbe, *Klänge schreiben: Die Transkriptionsproblematik elektroakustischer Musik* (= Signale aus Köln: Beiträge zur Musik der Zeit 15), Vienna 2009, pp. 144–162). Although this version, which includes a great deal of sound movement, rotation, etc., produced with the EMS *Quadrophonic Effects Generator* (*QUEG*), two quadrophonic potentiometers (*Unipot*), and a mixing console, and was premiered in 1978 before the first multimedia performance of the *Diatope*, it is still largely unknown. Today, this failure to observe the authorized cinematic version of *La Légende d'Eer* leads to a performance practice that unnecessarily limits the spatiality of the piece to the static replay of the seven tracks on tape. Even the new 5.1 surround mix, produced in 2004 by such a widely regarded expert as Gérard Pape (Mode DVD 148), lacks any spatial movement.

14 According to Valle, Tazelaar and Lombardo, the whereabouts of the final three-track version of *Concret PH* (2'40") are currently unknown. Only an earlier, shorter version seems to be available (idem, p. 3).

dynamic, and spatial relations of the composition in a definitive form, it can be perceived as the material essence of the work.

The aesthetic status of Xenakis's tapes, however, is more problematic. With regard to the *Polytopes*, Sven Sterken characterized Xenakis as an »architect of the ephemeral«[15]; in respect to the sound spatialization of these multimedia works it seems to be also true to think of him as a composer of the ephemeral. If you regard spatial distribution as a constitutive part of the composition, you have to concede that the tapes provide, in some respects, only a raw and preliminary form of the intended work, which is not completed until it is spatially diffused in real time. If, on the other hand, you consider spatiality to be only a secondary aspect of electroacoustic performance practice, you should nevertheless reflect on the aesthetic criteria for successful or less successful diffusion. But how could those criteria be found if the tapes contain only the pure sound material? In any case, it might help to have a look at the materials and documents preserved from Xenakis's first performances. Although these materials are closely related to the specific technical equipment of the respective location, they might feature some more universally applicable strategies for spatialization.

HIBIKI-HANA-MA AND THE TECHNICAL MEANS OF THE *SPACE THEATRE* AT OSAKA WORLD'S FAIR

Among the aforementioned forerunners of the *Polytopes*, *Hibiki-Hana-Ma* seems to be of particular interest: in Osaka, Xenakis had access to the most advanced audio technologies of the time, a huge sound system, which included, according to the pavilion's leaflet, »more than 1,000 speakers«[16]. In such a configuration the loudspeaker »becomes an agent in a mass of agents, its character subsumed into the essential group activity [...] the loudspeaker acts not as a virtual source of a ›stereo image‹ but as an individual source within a mass of sources«[17]. Twelve years after the brilliant experience of the Philips Pavilion, these possibilities inspired Xenakis to deal anew with questions of electroacoustic space composition.

---

15 Sven Sterken, »Spiel mit dem Raum: Iannis Xenakis, Architekt des Ephemeren«, in: MusikTexte, Vol. 90, 8/2001, pp. 36–42.

16 Leaflet *Space Theatre/Steel Pavilion: Expo '70* [1970], edited by the The Japan Iron & Steel Federation, n.p., n.d., p. 3. I would like to thank Martha Brech for providing me this historical leaflet and also another accompanying booklet (cf. Footnote 21) from the archives of the Electronic Studio of the *Technische Universität Berlin*.

17 Simon Emmerson, *Living Electronic Music*, Surrey 2007, p. 160.

Hibika-Hana-Ma was initially commissioned as an orchestral work, intended for recording and automated replay in the so-called *Space Theatre* of the Steel Pavilion at the Osaka World's Fair, alternating with pieces by Toru Takemitsu and Xenakis's former student Yuji Takahashi. But what Xenakis heard about the technical equipment of the pavilion, soon motivated him to transform this commission into an electroacoustic work, although recorded orchestral sounds play an important role in the piece[18].

Figure 1: Space Theatre of the Steel Pavilion

From: Leaflet *Space Theatre/Steel Pavilion: Expo '70*

The Steel Pavilion was designed by the noted Japanese architect Kunio Maekawa, a former student of Le Corbusier, as a building with two main sections, connected by a *Corridor of Lights*. First, the *Foyer*, which was made of steel and glass and in which sound sculptures of Bernard and

18 Sharon Kanach, »From hand to ear (or seeing is hearing): Visualization of Xenakis's creative process: methods and results«, in: Paland, von Blumröder (ed.), op.cit., pp. 83–98, here pp. 90–92.

François Baschet were performed and a Foucault Pendulum was on display. The second section was the *Space Theatre*, a cubical concert hall with a floor space of about 1600 square meters and a height of 17 meters, in which a circular arena with a moveable stage was set (figure 1)[19].

Furthermore, several lasers and mirrors were installed. These were used for light choreographies by the Japanese artist Keiji Usami, accompanying the musical presentation. This combination of music and laser spectacle had an important influence on Xenakis's artistic thinking, which seems to be reflected in the multimedia conceptions of *Polytope de Cluny* and the *Diatope*. But the most fascinating aspect of the *Space Theatre* for Xenakis was its sound diffusion system, designed by Takashi Fujita, the chief engineer of the NHK Engineering Laboratory. The technical potential of the *Space Theatre* triggered in Xenakis a complete rethinking of spatial composition: »For the first time, there was a possibility to treat sound in space and that created a new dimension that is not extra-musical but right and the heart of music making.«[20] Only a stone's throw from the German Pavilion with its spherical auditorium[21], the *Space Theatre* of the Steel Pavilion represented an alternative realization of musical spatiality.

Xenakis's early sketches, however, indicate that the composer's ideas were based at first on partly incorrect information about the technical details of the Osaka sound diffusion system. So he initially assumed that there were 18 separate channels available, although there were, in fact, only 12. In one of his sketches, he noted euphorically his ›conclusion‹ from this premise: »then any movement is possible«[22]. This underscores once more the importance Xenakis particularly attached to the ›cinematic‹ aspect of sound projection. In July 1969, after he had been informed about the actual technical conditions of the Steel Pavilion, Xenakis reworked his spatial conception. In the studio of the Japan Broadcasting System in Tokyo he realized a twelve-channel raw version of *Hibiki-Hana-Ma* without any sound movement, using two synchronized six-track machines. Afterwards he worked out

---

19 *Space Theatre/Steel Pavilion*, op.cit., pp. 4–5.

20 Xenakis 2008, op.cit., p. 143. In contrast to the famous Philips Pavilion of the Brussels World's Fair 1958, the Steel Pavilion has not been demolished after the event. Since 2010 it serves under the new name *EXPO'70 Pavilion* to commemorate the Osaka World's Fair 1970. The audio system of the *Space Theatre*, however, does not exist anymore.

21 Concerning the technical equipment of spherical auditorium of the German Pavilion cf. in this volume: Enda Bates, »Before and after Kontakte: Developments and Changes in Stockhausen's Approach to Spatial Music in the 1960s and 70s«.

22 Xenakis Archives of the Bibliothèque national de France, OM 12/9. I would like to thank Sharon Kanach for her kind support of my research.

the spatialization. First, he designed various sound dispositions and movements on the ground and under the ceiling, to be realized by automated activation of the single loudspeakers following certain spatial ›patterns‹. Several sketches show how meticulously Xenakis compassed various sound trajectories from loudspeaker to loudspeaker.

Evidently the ground and the ceiling loudspeakers were each arranged in two corresponding hemicycles. The sketches of the ground patterns are based on twelve semicircles, each with 18 speaker positions, whereas the ceiling patterns work with six semicircles, each with 8 speaker positions. This amounts to 216 autonomous speaker groups on the ground and 48 autonomous groups on the ceiling; 264 speaker groups in total[23], each with two symmetrically corresponding speaker positions in the two hemicycles. Indoor photographs of the Steel Pavilion show that some of the spherical loudspeaker housings, hanging under the ceiling, were equipped with several speakers, so that a total of 800 to 1,000 speakers, as is mentioned in different sources[24], seems to be absolutely plausible.

Apparently, every speaker group on the ground was able to emit the signals from up to four sound channels simultaneously, whereas the speaker groups on the ceiling could transmit up to eight channels. In the case of the ground speakers, four channels were distributed with what Xenakis termed *automated patterns* and four with *fixed patterns*, whereas the ceiling speakers emitted the signals in form of two automated patterns and two fixed patterns.

With regard to the latter, Xenakis's preserved sketches contain only the fixed ground patterns (figure 2 on the right). Each of them is built up of segments either 40° or 50° and alternates with equivalent segments of the other fixed pattern. All loudspeakers of the respective segments worked simultaneously, so that they generated four static sound arrays, regularly rotating with the four arrays of the other fixed pattern. It is assumed that the fixed ceiling patterns looked similar: in all probability the four channels were routed to four sectors, only without the doubling of each section.

Among the manuscripts of the Xenakis archives in the Bibliothèque nationale de France there are three pages with automated patterns: five figures depict those for the ground (figure 2 on the left and figure 4) and eight those for the ceiling (figure 3).

---

23 Xenakis (1992, op.cit.) speaks from »approximately 150 independent groups« (p. 379 (footnote 19)), in 2008 (op.cit*.)* he mentions »250 groups of speakers«, (p. 142).

24 While the Pavilion's leaflet (op.cit, p. 3) and the according booklet (op.cit, p. 5) mention more than 1000 loudspeakers, Xenakis speaks from ca. 800 (2008, op.cit., p. 142).

Figure 2: Hibiki-Hana-Ma, automated and fixed ground patterns

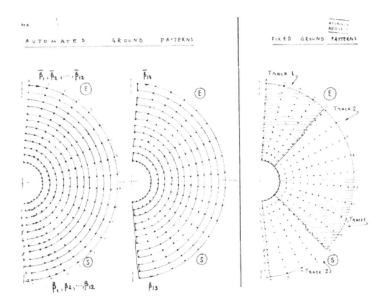

From: Xenakis 2008, op.cit., p. 146

Most of the figures represent sound paths, resulting from the successive activation of nearby loudspeaker groups: in the ceiling, for example, the six
semicircles with different distances to the centre of the space theatre (in the
diagram designated as ξ_1 to ξ_6), or the eight radial routes (ζ_1 to ζ_8), or the
closed loop line (ξ_8). Although these movements are regularly structured,
others are characterized by a labyrinthine meandering, for example ψ_1
through ψ_4 and their inversions, $\overline{\psi}_1$ to $\overline{\psi}_4$. Another type of automated pattern
is based on the concurrent displacement of specific loudspeaker constella-
tions onto new spatial positions, as is to be seen in the automated ground pat-
tern α_1 and its inversion $\overline{\alpha}_1$, in which a radial route, represented by twelve
simultaneous loudspeakers, rotates clockwise or anticlockwise around the
centre of the space theatre.

Figure 3: Hibiki-Hana-Ma, automated ceiling patterns

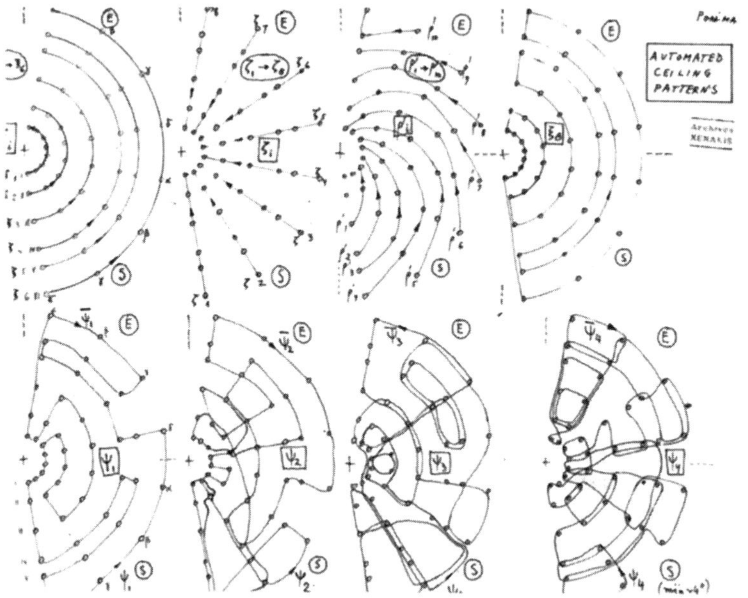

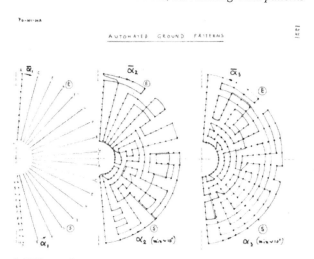

From: Kanach 2009, op.cit, p. 97

Figure 4: Iannis Xenakis: Hibiki-Hana-Ma, automated ground patterns

From: Kanach 2008, op. cit., p. 146

Obviously, the sound system of the Steel Pavilion allowed cinematic spatialization of an impressive diversity and complexity. But it also had, of course, some technical constraints, so that not every movement was effectively possible: Apparently, in the *Space Theatre* it was feasible to play the automated patterns in various speeds. Some of Xenakis's annotations indicate, however, that the peak speed of the sound movements was limited owing to technical reasons. For some particularly long patterns, composed of a particularly large number of successive position changes, Xenakis notes a minimum duration. Pattern α_3, for example, has to run through its 240 positions in ten seconds at least. From this it follows that a loudspeaker displacement has to take a minimum of 1/24 second. This appears plausible, as the control commands for the loudspeakers were fixed on film[25], and the frame rate of this medium was usually twenty-four pictures per second. Another limitation of the technical equipment is quite obvious: due to the separation of the ground and the ceiling speakers, automation of vertical movements was impossible. And with the structure of Xenakis's automated patterns in mind, there could possibly be a further restriction: all sound paths are exclusively based on sequences of directly adjacent loudspeakers without any jumping over one or more space positions. But until further technical details are known, it cannot be conclusively determined whether this issue resulted solely from the technical limitations of the sound system, or whether a specific aesthetic concept of the composer was involved, for instance, the idea to work only with continuous space figures.

SPATIAL STRATEGIES IN *HIBIKI-HANA-MA*

To apply the fixed and the automated patterns on the music of *Hibiki-Hana-Ma*, Xenakis created a thirteen-paged ›cinematic score‹. It shows the distribution of the sound materials over the twelve tracks, their overall dynamic shaping, and, in particular, their spatialization using the ›fixed‹ and the ›automated patterns‹ in the temporal process[26] of the piece. Each sound material is marked by a Latin letter; Greek letters, partly tagged with numeral indices and specifications of the requested duration, refer to the spatial patterns. On the basis of this ›cinematic score‹, all spatial activities during the performances of *Hibiki-Hana-Ma* in the Osaka Steel Pavilion are generally documented, and so analysing the precise relation between the spectro-

---

25 Xenakis 2008, op.cit., p. 143.
26 Page 13 ends at 17'20". As *Hibiki-Hana-Ma* actually lasts 17'39", it seems as if the concluding page of the cinematic score has been lost.

morphological and the spatial processes of the piece would surely be instructive. But this intention is unfortunately hampered by some problems. First, the original twelve-track version of *Hibiki-Hana-Ma* appears to have been lost and the only available multitrack version seems to be an eight-track downmix Xenakis realized at GRM in 1992[27]. A more serious deficit is the fragmentary state of the sources regarding automated ground and ceiling patterns. As the annotations in the ›cinematic score‹ show, there must definitely have been more than the automated patterns depicted on the aforementioned three pages. Because of this fragmentary state of sources, reliable statements about the spatial process as a whole are impossible at present. It seems, at least, feasible to illustrate and discuss exemplarily local spatial strategies of selected passages. So the analytical focus concentrates on the spectro-morphological and spatial organization of the opening section and on the relation between static and cinematic spatialization in the overall formal process.

Spectro-morphological and spatial organization of the opening section

Compared with the extensive and continuous sound processes Xenakis developed in his previous electroacoustic compositions, such as *Diamorphoses* or *Bohor*, the opening section of *Hibiki-Hana-Ma* is surprising. The first three minutes work exclusively with two distinct types of textures:

1. A dull, thunderous layer of overlapping upward and downward *glissandi* with a core range of circa 30 to 500 Hz.

2. Bundles of string *glissandi* at different speeds and with an extended range up to 3,000 Hz. These are partly in a fast tempo and diverging directions, and partly in a slow tempo and gradually descending, but they are all rather closely miked and, thus, lacking any spatial information.

At the beginning, these spectrally opposed textures are not melted into a homogenous sound continuum, but are rather abruptly contrasted. From this it follows that the formal organization of this part is characterized by rough cuts and unexpected disruptions. The first 26 seconds of the piece exclusively use a dense layer of the first, dull texture type, which is varied by different dynamics and spectral filtering. Suddenly the second texture type ap-

---

27 Daniel Teruggi, »Against oblivion«, in: Paland, von Blumröder (ed.) op.cit. pp. 28–31, here pp. 30–31.

pears, but only for two seconds, before the music is cut by a silence of two seconds. After that, the dull texture starts again, but only three seconds later the strings return for two more seconds and then disappear abruptly, while the dull texture continues for a further nine seconds before being interrupted again by a silence of two seconds.

Figure 5: Hibiki-Hana-Ma, cinematic score, page 1 (0'00"-1'20")

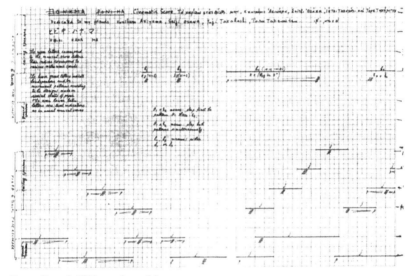

From: Kanach 2009, op.cit., p. 96

With regard to the spatial distribution, the two types are joined with two types of sound movement (figure 5): the dull texture is emitted solely from the fixed speaker arrays, at first from those at ground level. In doing so, it alternates slowly and with slight overlapping between the sectors of channels 1 and 2. After six seconds, the same spectro-morphological type is also successively emitted from the fixed ceiling sectors 1 to 4. Although these textures appear simultaneously in various fixed channels, they differ in their microstructure, as well as in their dynamic level and the region around the central frequency. Even without any elaborated loudspeaker displacement, this distribution of strongly related sound textures is likely to have generated the suggestion of a spatial fluctuation of sound. It is thus the relatively large portion of lower, and hence hardly localizable frequencies, that might have caused an especially strong impression of sonic enveloping. The spatial form of the two string entries, in contrast, might have been much more sharply defined. Indeed, the reference to the automated patterns can not be clearly deciphered: it looks like »S [or 5?]γ(VI→I)«, and this could designate either a specification of a lost (and consequently unknown) ceiling pattern γ (gamma), or it may possibly indicate the simultaneous use of the loudspeakers on angle position γ of the six circle lines (I to VI) in the south quadrant (S). In any case, this texture is definitely emitted by just one channel, in a linear form and in a well-contoured array with no, or at best minimal, sound movement. In the opening 45 seconds of *Hibiki-Hana-Ma*, the spectro-morphological contrast between the two texture types is translated into a spatial relation of figure (string sounds) and ground (dull sounds).

Relation between static and cinematic spatialization in the overall formal process

The following entries of the string textures show a gradual increase of spatial activity. While the slowly descending string *glissandi* from 0'44" to 1'04" were based on the fivefold run through another unknown ceiling pattern (written as θ_{13}), the next entry with an augmented variant of the short first string textures uses a sequence of two counter-rotating ceiling patterns, namely the four-second semi-circular movements ζ_4, answered by the counter-rotating movement $\bar{\zeta}_4$. And the following wild, unleashed glissando field (from 1'28" to 1'40") is based on the layer of up to four textures, played at different speeds and with different ceiling patterns, culminating in the labyrinthine sound paths of ψ_2, ψ_3, and ψ_4. As far as can be reconstructed from the fragmentary sources, the spatialization in this opening section develops from static sound distribution over circular figures to a complex polyphony of autonomous spatial movements. Moreover, on closer inspection it seems that this process characterizes not only the internal development of a single section, but also the overall formal directionality of *Hibiki-Hana-Ma*.

In fact, in the course of the work more and more passages appear that work completely without fixed spatial patterns. The first of them occurs from 4'06" to 4'55" (figure 6). Xenakis exposes a new spectro-morphological type here, a bright, shimmering, tonally enriched sound field with slight internal fluctuations. The weightless, levitating character of this section results not least from overlaying two sonically related textures with differently pronounced frequency bands. Corresponding to this interior differentiation, both textures are moved in diverging forms, one at the ground with five propeller-likes rotations (α_1) and the other under the ceiling with an unknown pattern (σ_1).

Figure 6: Hibiki-Hana-Ma, cinematic score, page 4 (4'00"-5'20")

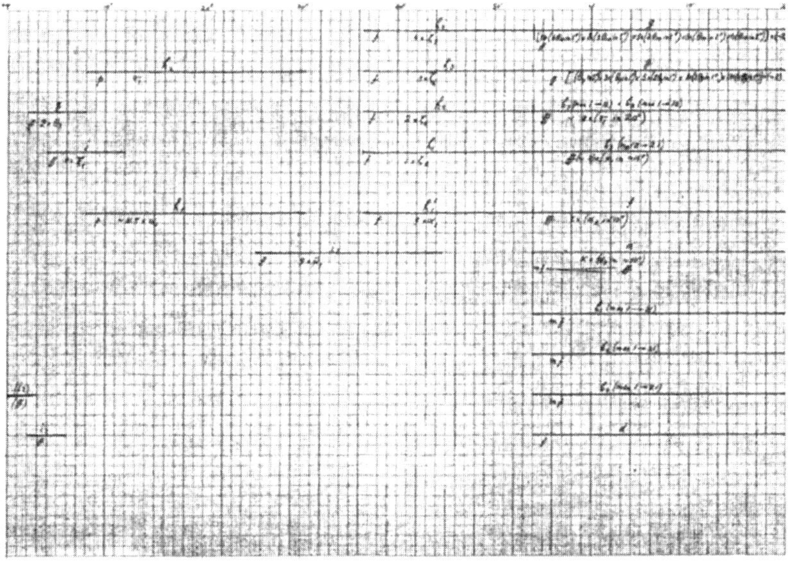

From: Kanach 2008, op.cit., p. 147

The following passages without fixed patterns get longer and longer (6'33" to 7'45", 11'39" to 14'48"), while, in the progress of the piece, static sound diffusion increasingly takes a back seat. Only in the final section (14'48" to 17'39"), which is characterized by a complex layer of heterogeneous sound textures, all patterns, both fixed and moving, melt into an impermeable spatial polyphony that leads to an irresistible vortex of sound, while the six cinematic tracks work with automated patterns, which are replayed with alternating moving direction and with increasing speed (figure 7). The ceiling tracks 1 to 4 work with the closed loop line ξ_8, as well as with σ_3, σ_1, σ_4, and their inversions. The ground tracks 5 and 6 work with the labyrinthine α_3, with the closed loop line β_3, and their inversions. Starting at different points in time, many of these patterns run at first in 20 seconds, than in 16, 12, 10, 6, 4, and ultimately in 2 seconds[28].

---

28 The patterns of track 2 and 4 end with a running time of 4", but it is to be assumed, that the value of 2" is reached on the missing last page of the score (cf. footnote 21). Pattern α_3 ends with a running time of 10", because this is the fastest speed which is technically possible for this pattern composed from 240 speaker positions. This should also be the case for β_3 (216 speaker positions), but here Xenakis notes a final running time of 4", which seems to be a fault.

Figure 7: Hibiki-Hana-Ma, cinematic score, page 13 (16'00"-17'20")

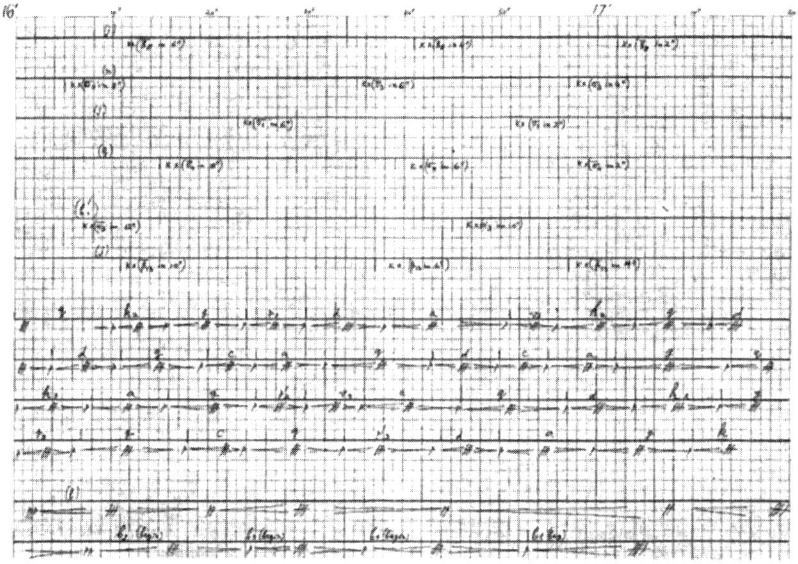

From: Xenakis 2008, op.cit., p. 147

The interplay of fluctuating and sharply contoured sound movements, the gradual increase of spatial activity, the aggregation and acceleration of the spatial patters – all these aspects demonstrate that, despite all the uncertainty about several details of the cinematic score, there exists a clear relationship between the spectro-morphological and the spatio-morphological processes of the work. Even if in the Osaka *Space Theatre* some movements were surely not possible, the performances of *Hibiki-Hana-Ma* must have been an overwhelming experience of musical spatiality.

CONSEQUENCES FOR TODAY'S PERFORMANCE PRACTICE

But from all these spatial processes in the Osaka version of *Hibiki-Hana-Ma*, there is nothing to be found in Xenakis's eight-track mix from 1992, which limits itself to the static diversification of the sound material. In view of the multifaceted interdependencies between the spectro-morphological, formal, and spatial structure of the Osaka version, it is hardly imaginable that Xenakis later might have deemed cinematic sound diffusion as an insignificant aspect of performance practice. This raises the general question of the extent to which the sound projectionist of Xenakis's music has to take into account the spatial structure of the work, as fixed on the multitrack tape.

In his reflections about the performance practice of Xenakis's electroacoustic output, Gerard Pape compares the role of the tape projectionist to that of a classical conductor[29]. He postulates that the projectionist must carve out the overall ›macro-form‹ of an electroacoustic work as well as the subtleties of its ›micro-forms‹ by means of ›dynamic variation‹[30]. The fragmentary analysis of *Hibiki-Hana-Ma* may have already shown that sound distribution in Xenakis's music, far from being merely ornamental, is able to fulfil similar structural and dramaturgical functions. Surely it is not the goal to copy the spatial structure developed for the unique circumstances of the Osaka Steel Pavilion (including its multimedia presentation) and to repeat it, one point for point, at completely different performance places and occasions. Equally, the awareness of the ephemeral nature of the original performance situation is not a valid argument for establishing a practice that reduces spatialization to the static reproduction of material tracks. In fact, not only the cinematic score of *Hibiki-Hana-Ma*, but also the Cologne version of *La Légende d'Eer* and the spatial concept for the Brussels version of *Concret PH*, as far as it can be developed from the sources[31], show that Xenakis was definitely interested in elaborating complex spatial movements when he had access to adequate technical equipment. Today, these works could serve as models for a creative performance practice that nevertheless respects the composer's claim that »space must be integrated into sound structures«. Further careful studies into Xenakis's concrete elaboration of sound movements in his electroacoustic music could be a first step towards this aim.

---

29 Cf. Gerard Pape, »*Interpreting Xenakis' Electroacoustic Music: ›La Légende d'Eer‹*«, in: Sharon Kanach *(ed.), Performing Xenakis* (= The Iannis Xenakis Series 2), Hillsdale, NY, 2010, pp. 369–372, here p. 369.

30 Ibid., p. 371.

31 Valle, Tazelaar and Lombardo, op.cit., pp. 2–4.

The Complexity of Xenakis's Notion of Space

MAKIS SOLOMOS

INTRODUCTION

Xenakis is often described as a ›space‹ composer. When saying that, we think of the three-dimensional quality of his music, which works with sound masses and juxtaposition of textures, and which has a quasi-tactile dimension – in a way, Xenakis is a ›sound sculptor‹. But we also think of the fact that he was one of the first composers to work with sound spatialization both in instrumental music and in electroacoustic music, putting the listener ›inside‹ an orchestra (*Terretektorh*), realizing complex, automated spatializations of electroacoustic sounds (the *Polytopes*), etc. There are also other domains where the notion of space can be inferred from Xenakis's music and thought.

In fact, the notion of space itself, as it is used in music – as well as in many other fields – has many senses; as the French writer Georges Perec would say, there are »spaces of space«[1]. There is, for instance, an opposition between physical space and metaphorical space (or space as a tool for representation); there is also an opposition between virtual and real space; space can be used as immersion or, on the contrary, for constructing localizations; and so on[2].

Thus Xenakis's thought can help us to analyse the various aspects of space in music. In this chapter, we will see that we can define at least four different notions of space: the first notion concerns the philosophical level, in relationship to the ideas of time and energy; the second notion is rooted in

---

1   Georges Perec, *Espèces d'espaces*, Paris 1974.
2   In my recent book (*De la musique au son: L'émergence du son dans la musique des XXe–XXIe siècles*, Rennes 2013), I explore some of the meanings of space in music, in particular in Chapters 3 (»Immersion«) and 6 (»Sound-Space«).

the compositional level; the third is related to physical space; and finally, the fourth notion appears when physical space becomes place.

Time, Space, and Energy

First, there is a philosophical or ontological level, where space is, for Xenakis, a crucial notion. Let's start with Xenakis's philosophy of time. He acknowledges the centrality of unmeasured time, i.e. the pure time flow. He even thinks of it almost as an equivalent to music itself:

»When you use tools like paper while writing and conceiving musical forms, you can think in terms of spatial qualities, but that is less important during composition itself. Music develops in time. [...] Musical time can't be reduced to a stopwatch. [...] The exact measurement, in seconds, of musical time and durations is of little interest. [...] It is the interior of time that counts, not its absolute duration. [...] Time is independently and simultaneously articulated by various musical events.«[3]

Xenakis makes a difference between ›flow‹ and ›duration‹, meaning unmeasured and measured time. Only the latter is reversible:

»A duration is something that can be moved around within time, it is therefore reversible, commutative. [...] The difference between any two points is a concept which stems from comparisons and mysterious judgments I make about the reality of the temporal flow, which I accept *a priori*. The distance between the two points is what is then identified as a duration. I displace this duration anywhere; therefore, it is reversible. But the temporal flow itself is irreversible.«[4]

In these lines, the phrase »mysterious judgments I make about the reality of the temporal flow, which I accept *a priori*« is crucial. Xenakis admits that he does not know what time is (time flow). In one of the latest interviews, he says: »I never understood what is time. Time remains something mysterious

---

3 Iannis Xenakis interviewed by Anne-Maria Harley, »Musique, espace et spatialisation«, in: Circuits 5/2 (1994), pp. 9–20, here p. 13.

4 Iannis Xenakis, *Arts/Sciences: Alloys*, translated from French by Sharon Kanach, Hillsdale (N.Y.) 1985 (originally published as *Arts/Sciences: Alliages*, Tournai 1979), pp. 74–75.

for me. Time is everywhere, it rains, it snows[5], it is part of nature. This is why I cannot understand what time is.«[6]

That may explain why he focused more and more on measured time – time that can be ›constructed‹: »There is the temporal flow, which is an immediate given, and then there is metrics, which is a construction man makes upon time.«[7] He often defines time (time flow) as an empty blackboard: »Time could be considered as a blank blackboard, on which symbols and relationships, architectures and abstract organisms are inscribed«[8]. There, time is an abstract dimension enabling one to ask the question of time in terms of construction. Therefore, when he says that time is the same as music, it would be ›measured time‹ that he means, not ›time flow‹. This contrasts sharply with the centrality of unmeasured time in the philosophy of Henri Bergson (although Bergson's word for unmeasured time was ›duration‹). Xenakis is more interested in the possibility of making, building, or constructing something within time (or, upon time). We might even say that he aims to ›construct‹ time. It is no surprise, then, that during the 1960s and 1970s he had a strong interest in Jean Piaget:

»Piaget's book provided me with my first justification that I was right to do calculations with time. He proved that the perception of time stopped developing at the age of twelve. Up until the age of six one can't see this process clearly, but between six and twelve I think there are three stages. He showed that time has an ordering structure and that time intervals can be added and permutated, and consequently that they have a group structure. I concluded from all this that time is nothing but a kind of structure. And because it is a structure it can be counted, expressed with real numbers, and shown as points on a straight line.«[9]

In the 1960s, Xenakis spoke of ›amnesia‹. The chapter of *Musiques Formelles* devoted to »symbolic music« begins, »we shall begin by imagining that we are suffering from a sudden amnesia[10]. We shall thus be able to re-ascend to the fountain-head of the mental operations used in composition

5   The French word temps means both ›time‹ and ›weather‹.
6   Omer Corlaix and Bastien Gallet, »Entretien avec Iannis Xenakis«, in: Musica Falsa No. 2, Paris 1998, p. 29.
7   Iannis Xenakis 1985, op.cit., p. 97.
8   Iannis Xenakis, *Formalized Music*, edited by Sharon Kanach, Hillsdale (N.Y.) 1992, p. 192.
9   Bálint András Varga, *Conversations with Iannis Xenakis*, London 1996, pp. 82–83.
10   The English translation »we are suffering from a sudden amnesia« is not a very good translation. Original French: »Nous commencerons par nous considérer brusquement amnésiques.«

and attempt to extricate the general principles that are valid for all sorts of music.«[11] In a sense, we may say that Xenakis ›fights‹ with time. And, anyway, we should not forget his notion that the temporal dimension also includes »outside-time« structures. »Whatever we think is by definition outside time because it is in our memory and doesn't disappear with the passage of time (unless we forget it). We have no power over the time-flow but we feel it passing: the notion of time is also outside time.«[12]

Elsewhere, Xenakis considers time as an epiphenomenon, and space as a more fundamental reality. On this, we should carefully look into Xenakis's only article explicitly devoted to the issue of time[13]. The beginning reads: »Isn't time simply an epiphenomenal notion of a deeper reality? Thus an illusion that we unconsciously have accepted since our earliest years and even since the earliest, ancient ages?«[14] He then hypothesizes that ›displacement‹ is a more fundamental notion, adding that »if the notion of displacement were more fundamental than that of time, one could undoubtedly reduce all macro- and microcosmic transformations to extremely short chains of displacement«[15]. Furthermore, referring to the experiment of »correlation of the movement of two photons emitted in opposite directions by a single atom«[16], he notes,

»Now, this experiment could be a starting point for the investigation of more deeply seated properties of space, freed from the tutelage of time. In this case, could the ›nonlocality‹ of quantum mechanics be explained perhaps not by the hypothesis of ›hidden variables‹ in which time still intervenes, but rather by the unsuspected and extravagant properties of nontemporal space, such as ›spatial ubiquity‹, for example?«[17]

Yet, not even space seems to be the ultimate reality. Xenakis's preliminary conclusions, in fact, are as follows:

»As space is perceptible only across the infinity of chains of energy transformations, it could very well be nothing but an appearance of these chains. In fact, let us consider the movement of a photon. Movement means displacement. Now, could this displacement be

---

11 Iannis Xenakis 1992, op.cit., p. 155.
12 Bálint András Varga, op.cit., p. 83.
13 Iannis Xenakis »Sur le temps« (1988), reprinted in: idem, *Kéleütha*, edited by Alain Galliari, preface and notes by Benoît Gibson, Paris 1994, p. 94; Chapter 10 of *Formalized Music*, op.cit, is closely related to this article.
14 Iannis Xenakis 1994, op.cit., p. 94.
15 Ibid.; cf. Iannis Xenakis 1992, op.cit., p. 256.
16 Ibid.; cf. Iannis Xenakis 1992, op.cit., p. 257.
17 Ibid.; cf. Iannis Xenakis 1992, op.cit., p. 257.

considered an autogenesis of energy, an energetic parthenogenesis of the photon by itself at each step of its trajectory (continuous or quantized)? This continuous auto-creation of the photon, could it not, in fact, be space?«[18]

SPACE AS AN OPERATIVE CATEGORY

Let us now analyse a second level, where the question is about ›geometrical‹ space, and, for instance, the use of graphs for composing music. It is thanks to this kind of space that Xenakis invented new types of sound morphologies (the morphology of *glissandi*) or that he invented transfers from the microscopic to the macroscopic time level. More generally, we could say that, in this context, space is a tool for representing and composing music, and thus an operative category.

Figure 1: Analysis of Beethoven's Appassionata

The following is an analysis of a fragment of *Sonata*, Op. 57 (Appassionata), by Beethoven (see Fig. VI–1). We do not take the timbre into account since the piano is considered to have only one timbre, homogeneous over the register of this fragment.

Fig. VI–1

Assume as unit vectors: h, for which $1 \triangleq$ semitone; $\bar{g}$, for which $1 \triangleq 10 \; db$; and $\bar{u}$, for which $1 \triangleq \eighthnote$. Assume for the origins

 on the h axis,

$ff = 60 \; db$ (invariable) on the $\bar{g}$ axis, and
5 ♪ on the $\bar{u}$ axis.

ALGEBRA OUTSIDE-TIME (OPERATIONS AND RELATIONS IN SET A)

The vector $X_0 = 18h + 0\bar{g} + 5\bar{u}$ corresponds to G.
The vector $X_1 = (18 + 3)h + 0\bar{g} + 4\bar{u}$ corresponds to $B\flat$.
The vector $X_2 = (18 + 6)h + 0\bar{g} + 3\bar{u}$ corresponds to $D\flat$.
The vector $X_3 = (18 + 9)h + 0\bar{g} + 2\bar{u}$ corresponds to E.
The vector $X_4 = (18 + 12)h + 0\bar{g} + 1\bar{u}$ corresponds to G.
The vector $X_5 = (18 + 0)h + 0\bar{g} + 1\bar{u}$ corresponds to G.

From: Iannis Xenakis 1992, op.cit., p. 164

---

18 Ibid.; cf. Iannis Xenakis 1992, op.cit., pp. 257–258, incomplete.

It is interesting to notice that, in one of his very few attempts to analyze music that was not composed by himself, Xenakis used algebraic space. I refer to his analysis of Ludwig van Beethoven's *Appassionata* in *Musiques Formelles* (see figure 1).

As for his own music, the most radical utilization of a geometrical space can be found in *Nomos alpha* (1965–66, for cello), where Xenakis uses the group model (in the mathematical sense) of a cube and its 23 rotations (see figure 2). More generally, Xenakis used space in the geometrical sense as a way to understand music and to compose it, as shown by Peter Hoffmann[19].

Figure 2: The group model (a cube and its 23 rotations) used in »Nomos alpha«

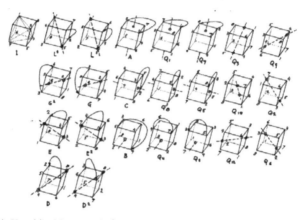

From: Iannis Xenakis, *Musique, Architecture*, Tournai 1971, p. 98

Xenakis's use of graphs for composing is a special case. As is well known, it is due to these kinds of graphs that he invented the notion of massive glissandi – a totally new sound morphology in the mid-1950s – such as those found at the end of *Metastaseis* (see figure 3). The graph tool allowed him to develop his own vision of global sound phenomena, of masses of microsounds, which, owing to their complex interlocking, form a new global sound.

This is, of course, related to his experience in architecture. As Xenakis writes:

---

19 Peter Hoffmann, »L'espace abstrait dans la musique de Iannis Xenakis«, in: *L'espace: Musique/Philosophie*, edited by Jean-Marc Chouvel and Makis Solomos, Paris, pp. 141–152 (German translation: »Weltlinie im musikalischen Universum: Abstrakte Räume in der Musik von Iannis Xenakis«, in: MusikTexte No. 90, Köln, 2001, pp. 23–29.

»In music, you begin with a theme or a melody and then you have a whole arsenal at your disposal that is more or less given for developing elaborations, be they polyphonic or harmonic (this applies as much to a classical sonata as a piece of serial music). You start from the mini to attain the global. In architecture, however, you must simultaneously conceive the details and the ensemble, otherwise, it all falls apart. This approach, this experience at Le Corbusier's studio and side with him obviously influenced me (even though I sensed it all along), or at least helped me conceive my music like an architecture project: globally and in detail at the same time. What constitutes architecture's force is these proportions: the coherent relationship between details and the whole [...].«[20]

Figure 3: Xenakis's graph for the first version of the end of »Metastaseis«

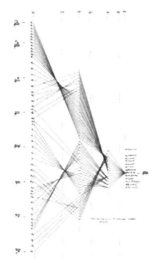

From: Iannis Xenakis 1971, op.cit., p. 8

It is also thanks to graphs that Xenakis moves from »microtime« to »macrotime«, such as those that gave birth to his notion of Brownian motion. In the end of the 1960s in Bloomington, Xenakis started investigating stochastic sound synthesis with random walks (in the mathematical sense of the term), producing graphs such as the one shown in figure 4. In these graphs, it is a question of microtime. At the beginning of the 1970s, since he did not have access to sufficiently powerful computers to synthesize sound on the basis of the graphs, he used them to compose instrumental music instead. The first work composed with Brownian motions is *Mikka* (1971, for solo violin):

---

20 Iannis Xenakis, *Music and Architecture*, edited by Sharon Kanach, Hillsdale (N.Y.) 2008, p. 72.

Xenakis used stochastic sound pressure curves and changes the coordinates, computing macrotime instead of microtime[21].

Figure 4: Stochastic sound pressure

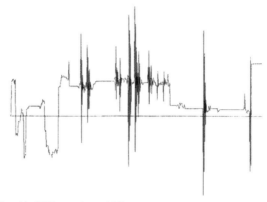

From: Iannis Xenakis 1992, op.cit., p. 251)

PHYSICAL SPACE – SOUND SPATIALIZATION

The third level is the physical notion of space, which is related to sound spatialization. In this domain, Xenakis, after Edgard Varèse and around the same time as Karlheinz Stockhausen, is an important pioneer of this notion, which became increasingly important for music. Xenakis began very early to work with the idea that physical space can be composed. This can already be seen in his orchestral work *Pithoprakta* (1955-56): the ›grains‹ of the piece's beginning (string players striking the body of their instruments) move from one group to another; and at the end of the piece, the strings come to play a single note, which travels from one group to another. Of course, the composition of space is most important in the 1958 composition *Concret PH*, the ›instrumental interlude‹ of *musique concrète* composed by Xenakis to be played with *Poème électronique*. Here Xenakis designed the complex »sound routes« that spatialized sound using the over 400 loudspeakers available. In the same year he published the article »Notes towards an ›Electronic

---

21 Cf. Makis Solomos, »The Unity of Xenakis's Instrumental and Electroacoustic Music : The Case of ›Brownian Movements‹«, in: *Perspectives of New Music* 39(1) (2001), pp. 244–254.

Gesture«»[22], which reviews the experience of the performance given in the Philips Pavilion and puts forward new proposals for sound spatialization.

In 1962, *Bohor* is one of the first compositions to treat space in the sense of immersion. This electroacoustic work was composed for four two-track tape recorders, which, during the concert, were launched at the same time, inevitably became desynchronized. These desynchronizations were not ›errors‹ because the idea was not to realize ›travels‹ of sound from one loudspeaker to another, as in the *Poème électronique*, but to totally immerse the listener – it is also why Xenakis performed the piece extremely loudly. In 1963–1964, *Eonta* (for five brass instruments and piano) uses space, this time with a concern for staging: the instrumentalists (brass) are sometimes required to move and change their position in the concert hall.

Then, with the orchestral works *Terretektorh* (1965—1966) and *Nomos gamma* (1967–1968), the research into space became even more important and came to have a quasi-political meaning. Xenakis upsets the world of the orchestra and its audience by having the orchestra leave the stage; the musicians are distributed around the hall and the audience is placed inside the orchestra! Figure 5 shows the well-known layout of the orchestra in *Terretektorh*.

It is also important to quote Xenakis's note program:

»The scattering of the musicians brings in a radically new kinetic conception of music which no modern electro-acoustical means could match. For if it is not possible to imagine 90 magnetic tapes relaying to 90 loudspeakers disseminated all over the auditorium, on the contrary it is quite possible to achieve this with a classical orchestra of 90 musicians. The musical composition will thereby be entirely enriched throughout the hall both in spatial dimension and in movement. The speeds and accelerations of the movement of the sounds will be realized, and new and powerful functions will be able to be made use of, such as logarithmic or Archimedian spirals, in-time and geometrically. Ordered or disordered sonorous masses, rolling one against the other like waves... etc., will be possible.

Terretektorh is thus a ›Sonotron‹: an accelerator of sonorous particles, a disintegrator of sonorous masses [...]. It puts the sound and the music all around the listener and close up to him. It tears down the psychological and auditive curtain that separates him from the players when positioned far off on pedestal, itself frequently enough placed inside a box. The orchestral musician rediscovers his responsibility as an artist, as an individual.«[23]

---

22 Iannis Xenakis 2008, op.cit., pp. 131–134.
23 Iannis Xenakis 1992, op.cit., pp. 236–237.

Figure 5: Terretektorh's orchestra

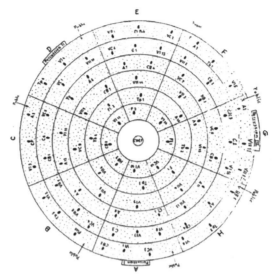

From: Iannis Xenakis, *Terretektorh*, score, Salabert editions

It is in *Persephassa* (1969, for six percussionists), where the six musicians surround the audience, that Xenakis's spatial composition culminates in the frame of instrumental music. It happens especially in the final part (bars 352–456) – a kind of amplification of the end of *Nomos gamma* – constituting a composition inside the composition, that John Batigne, a member of the *Percussions de Strasbourg* (the original performers of the piece), compares to a ›turnstile‹, indicating that it was the most difficult part of the piece to perform without a conductor[24].

Figure 6 shows a transcription showing the spatial movement. Notice that this extract gives rise to an enormous accelerando and a giant crescendo (some high nuances that go beyond the overall crescendo are shown in bold-face). As for the spatial movement, the six musicians (indicated by letters in the transcription) who have at their disposal six membrane instruments, siren, metal and wood Simantrons, cymbal, gong, tam-tam, and wood block, to which are added, towards the end of the piece, pebbles and *affolants* (thin steel sheets) transmit to each other a minim with a shift of a crotchet. The movement is twofold: one for the membrane instruments, the other for the remaining instruments (except the siren, which is not involved in this space

---

24 Jean Batigne, »Sur *Persephassa* et *Pléiades*«, in: *Regards sur Iannis Xenakis*, edited by Hugues Gerhards, Paris 1981, pp. 175–183, here p. 181.

game). The transcription (where a line indicates the continuation of the same figure) shows that the spatial motion goes through two phases. In bars 352–420 each membrane instrument enters gradually.

Figure 6: Transcription of »Persephassa« (bars 352–456)

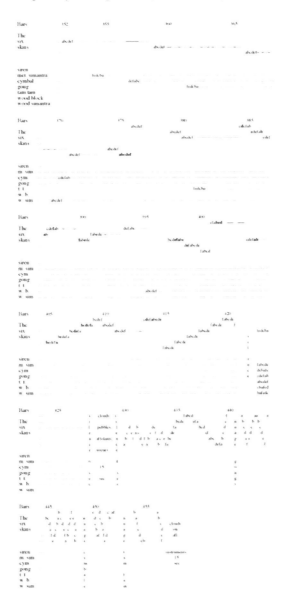

The spatial movement is circular: A-B-C-D-E-F for skins and for four other instruments, in reverse movement for the others. Bars 423–426, which follow after a general silence, constitute an area of disruption. After a ›cloud‹ (improvised dense sounds with pebbles, *affolants*, and sirens) framed by two silences, only the membrane instruments remain in the spatial movement. First the initial circle is rebuilt (bars 430–439), but the membrane instruments change with each percussionist at both ends and with two, three or four in the middle. A ›cloud‹ of gongs introduces a continual alternation of two circular directions and a sinusoidal path of (relative) pitches (bars 441–448). With a ›cloud‹ of cymbals, the unique and reverse movement is restored bars (450–452). Finally, between a ›cloud‹ of tam-tams and the long (15-second) conclusive ›cloud‹ on all instruments, all types of spatial movement are deconstructed (B-A-F-E-D-C-B) very briefly (bars 454-455), and give rise to a single circle in the initial direction.

In Xenakis's subsequent instrumental production, space is far from absent (for example, in *Retours-Windungen*, 1976, for twelve cellos, or in *Alax*, 1985, for three instrumental groups), but it is not used in such a striking manner. In fact, the ›spectacular‹ aspect of space composition, which combines spatial trajectories and immersion, culminates with the *Polytopes*: *Polytope de Montréal* (1966–1967), *Polytope de Persépolis* (1971), *Polytope de Cluny* (1972–1974), *Polytope de Mycènes* (1978), and *Diatope (Polytope de Beaubourg*, 1978)[25].

SPACE AS PLACE: *POLYTOPES*

The last notion of space concerns the *Polytopes*. In these multimedia (or intermedia) productions, we can speak about ›place‹, i.e., a specific physical space and simply not any arbitrary physical space. Indeed, Xenakis realized each *Polytope* for a specific location, indicated in the *Polytope's* title. In a way, we could say that there is a single work, called ›*Polytope*‹, and that

---

25 The bibliography on Xenakis's sound spatialization is becoming increasingly important. Here a sampling of some extensive works on this topic: Helena Maria Da Silva Santana, *L'orchestration chez Iannis Xenakis: l'espace et le rythme fonctions du timbre*, Ph.D. dissertation, Université de Paris IV, Villeneuve D'Ascq 1999; Boris Hofmann, *Mitten im Klang: Die Raumkompositionen von Iannis Xenakis aus den 1960er Jahren*, Ph.D. dissertation, Technische Universität Berlin (= Sinefonia 10), Hofheim 2008; and Renaud Meric, »Concret PH, un espace mouvant«, in: *12e Journées d'Informatique Musicale 2005*, edited by Anne Sedes and Horacio Vaggione, Paris 2005, pp. 147–155.

each precise *Polytope* is a concretization of this work in a specific place. It is particular truth for the *Polytope de Cluny* and the *Diatope*: many aspects of the first (both in the visual spectacle and in the music) can be found in the second.

The most interesting feature of the idea of space as place is the position of the listening audience (figure 7).

Figure 7: Listening-audience during Polytope de Cluny's performance

From: Archives Xenakis

We could compare this position with the position of the listeners in the well-known painting »Beethoven and His Admirers« (figure 8).

Figure 8: Albert Grafle, »Beethoven and intimates, listening to him playing«

From: Beethoven-Archiv, Bonn

More generally, Xenakis's idea that music and sound are deeply linked to space – and even more, to place – can be viewed as an antithesis to the idealistic aesthetics, which, if we follow Georg Wilhelm Friedrich Hegel, can be analysed as a negation of space:

»Mit dem Ton nun verläßt die Musik das Element der äußeren Gestalt und deren anschauliche *Sichtbarkeit* und bedarf deshalb zur Auffassung ihrer Produktionen auch eines anderen subjektiven Organs, des *Gehörs,* das wie das Gesicht nicht den praktischen, sondern den *theoretischen* Sinnen zugehört und selbst noch ideeller ist als das Gesicht. Denn die ruhige, begierdelose Beschauung von Kunstwerken läßt zwar die Gegenstände, ohne sie irgend vernichten zu wollen, für sich, wie sie da sind, ruhig bestehen, aber das, was sie auffaßt, ist nicht das in sich selbst Ideellgesetzte, sondern im Gegenteil das in seiner sinnlichen Existenz Erhaltene. Das Ohr dagegen vernimmt, ohne sich selber praktisch gegen die Objekte hinauszuwenden, das Resultat jenes inneren Erzitterns des Körpers, durch welches nicht mehr die ruhig materielle Gestalt, sondern die erste ideellere Seelenhaftigkeit zum Vorschein kommt. Da nun ferner die Negativität, in die das schwingende Material hier eingeht, einerseits ein Aufheben des räumlichen Zustandes ist, das selbst wieder durch die Reaktion des Körpers aufgehoben wird, so ist die Äußerung dieser zwiefachen Negation, der Ton, eine Äußerlichkeit, welche sich in ihrem Entstehen durch ihr Dasein selbst wieder vernichtet und an sich selbst verschwindet. Durch diese gedoppelte Negation der Äußerlichkeit, welche im Prinzipe des Tons liegt, entspricht derselbe der inneren Subjektivität, indem das Klingen, das an und für sich schon etwas Ideelleres ist als die für sich real bestehende Körperlichkeit, auch diese ideellere Existenz aufgibt und dadurch eine dem Innerlichen gemäße Äußerungsweise wird.«[26]

That does not mean that Xenakis's aesthetic is ›materialistic‹, nor that in his music or in his *Polytopes* there is no longer anything called ›meaning‹! In fact, his aesthetics represent a break with the idealistic idea that the meaning of a musical or artistic work lays »behind« the sounds or the other physical media. This idea considerably reduced the possible meanings through a parallelism between music and language. As Luigi Nono clearly shows in an important discussion with Massimo Cacciari, the interest in physical space, as well as for place, in contemporary music can be interpreted as the need to re-introduce the multiplicity of meaning through the indissolubility of meaning and physical media–sound and space, when it is question of music (see Nono, 1993). Going back to Xenakis, we could say that it is not a coinci-

---

26 Georg Wilhelm Friedrich Hegel, *Vorlesungen über die Ästhetik*, III: »Das System der einzelnen Künste: Die Musik: Allgemeiner Charakter der Musik« http://www.textlog. de/hegel_aesthetik.html 1835–1838.

dence that he gave us his most beautiful definition of music in the *Diatope*'s program notes, his most accomplished *Polytope*:

»Music is not a language. Every musical piece is like a complex rock formed with ridges and designs engraved within and without, that can be interpreted in a thousand different ways without a single one being the best or the most true. By virtue of this multiple exegesis, music inspires all sorts of fantastic imaginings, like a crystal catalyst. I, myself, wanted to deal with the abysses that surround us and among which we live. The most formidable are those of our own destiny, of life and death, of visible and invisible universes. The signs that convey these abysses to us are made up of lights and sounds that provoke our two predominate senses. This is why I have conceived the Diatope as a place for the condensation of these signs and signals from our various worlds. Rational knowledge blends with intuitive knowledge, or revelation. It is impossible to dissociate them. These abysses are unknowable; that is to say, knowledge of them is an eternal and desperate search, composed of milestones or hypotheses that have marked our various epochs.«[27]

* * *

In this article, I have tried to show four different notions of space that we find in Xenakis's thought and artistic production: the philosophical level, where, for him, space is a more deep reality than time (but lesser deep than energy); the compositional level, where geometrical space is an operative category (materialized, for instance, in the graphs used by Xenakis to compose music); the physical level, where we speak about sound spatialization; and finally, a level with a more concrete notion of physical space, the level of what we can call ›place‹, and which allows us to understand the need for space in terms of aesthetics as a way to rediscover the multiplicity of meaning.

---

27 Iannis Xenakis, *Music and Architecture*, op.cit, p. 261.

Biographies

Elizabeth Anderson is a composer of electroacoustic and instrumental music. In 2011 she received her PhD at the City University London for her thesis on *Materials, Meaning and Metaphor: Unveiling Spatio-Temporal pertinences in acousmatic Music* and lives in Brussels.

Enda Bates is a composer, musician and producer specialized on spatial music. In 2010 he received his PhD for his thesis on *The Composition and Performance of Spatial Music* from Trinity College Dublin, where he currently is an associated lecturer in the Music and Media Technology Programme.

Marc Battier is a composer of electroacoustic music and a musicologist who is based in Paris where he is professor at Sorbonne University. In 2003 he cofounded the Electroacoustic Music Studies (EMS) conference. He published and edited several books on electroacoustic music.

Dorothea Baumann is a musicologist and qualified professor at Zurich University. She studies spatial music and the acoustics of architectural spaces since many years. In the past years she specialized in acoustics of Renaissance architecture and spatial music of this era and edited the book *Music and Space* (Frankfurt a.M. 2011).

Martha Brech is a musicologist specialized in analysis and history of electroacoustic music She is qualified professor at the Technische Universität Berlin and currently finished her book on the history of auditive space and spatial technology of the early electroacoustic music (*Der hörbare Raum*, Bielefeld 2015).

Christa Brüstle is a musicologist specialized in the aethetics, performance and history of 20th century music and media art who wrote and edited several books on this subjects. She is a qualified professor for this field and currently researches at the Kunst Universität Graz.

Henrik von Coler is a composer and a sound engineer. He received a Diploma in communication engineering in Hamburg and a M.S. in Audiocommunication and Technology at the Technische Universität Berlin. Since 2013 he researches at the Staatliches Institut für Musikforschung in Berlin for a doctoral thesis.

John Dack is a musicologist specialized on the history and analysis of electroacoustic music who published many articles in this field and translated Pierre Schaeffer's books into English. He is a senior lecturer at the Middlesex University London and a member of the Electronic and Digital Arts Research Cluster.

Pascal Decroupet is a musicologist specialized on the analysis and aesthetics of 20th century music, the work of Karlheinz Stockhausen and other serialists. He has published and edited many books and articles in this field and currently is a professor at the University in Nice.

Helga de la Motte-Haber is a musicologist specialized in contemporary music, sound and media art as well as in psychology of music and systematic musicology. She published extensively in these fields and is a professor of the Technische Universität Berlin and received an honorary doctor of the Hochschule für Musik und Darstellende Kunst in Hannover.

Christina Dollinger is a musician (flute) and musicologist specialized on Luigi Nono. In 2012 she received her doctoral degree at the University of Würzburg for her thesis on *Unendlicher Raum – zeitloser Augenblick: Luigi Nono's »Das atmende Klarsein« und »1° Caminantes ... Ayacucho«.*

Simon Emmerson is a composer of electroacoustic music and musicologist. Since 1986 he published several CDs and books on this subject, founded some and currently is professor in Music Technology and Innovation at De Montfort University, Leicester.

Inga Mai Groote is a musicologist specialized in theory, analysis and (social) history of late medieval and renaissance music who published about later music, too. Currently she is an associate Professor of Fribourg University (Switzerland).

Fabian Kolb is a musicologist specialized on music of the classical and romantic era. In 2010 he received his doctoral degree at the University of Cologne for his thesis on the French symphonic tradition between 1871 and 1914. He currently is a lecturer at the musicology department of the University of Mainz.

Sonja Neumann is a musician and a musicologist specialized in modern music and history of music technology who received her doctoral degree at the University of Hamburg. She currently is a member of the scientific staff of Deutsches Museum in Munich.

Ralph Paland is a musicologist, organist and music pedagogue who received his doctoral degree at Cologne University in 2006. He published several articles and books in the field of contemporary and electroacoustic music (recent publication *Flo Menezes – Nova Ars Subtilior: Essays zur maximalistischen Musik*, 2014).

Susan Schmidt Horning is a cultural historian specialized in history of technology and sound studies. In 2013 she published *Chasing Sound: Technology, Culture, and the Art of Studio Recording from Edison to the LP*. Currently she is an associate professor at St. John's University, New York.

Julia H. Schröder is a musician and musicologist specialized in contemporary and electroacoustic music, media and sound art. In 2011 she received her doctoral degree at the Technische Universität Berlin. In 2015 she published a book on listening perspectives in modern music.

Makis Solomos is a musicologist specialised on contemporary music, the music of Iannis Xenakis and philosophy of music. In 2013 he published his latest book *De la musique au son: L'émergence du son dans la musique des XXe-XXIe siècles.* Currently he is professor at University Paris VIII.

Annette Vande Gorne is a composer of electroacoustic music and audio art and mixed styles specialized on music concrete and spatial music. She published several books and articles on this topic. In the 1980ies she founded an acousmonium of more than 60 loudspeakers at the Conservatory of Brussels where she still teaches as a professor.

Index

Musik und Klangkultur

Frédéric Döhl, Daniel Martin Feige (Hg.)
Musik und Narration
Philosophische und musikästhetische
Perspektiven

September 2015, ca. 280 Seiten, kart., ca. 32,99 €,
ISBN 978-3-8376-2730-5

Reinhard Gagel, Matthias Schwabe (Hg.)
**Improvisation erforschen – improvisierend
forschen/Researching Improvisation –
Researching by Improvisation**
Beiträge zur Exploration musikalischer
Improvisation/Essays About the Exploration
of Musical Improvisation

April 2016, ca. 420 Seiten, kart., zahlr. Abb., ca. 39,99 €,
ISBN 978-3-8376-3188-3

Jörn Peter Hiekel, Wolfgang Lessing (Hg.)
Verkörperungen der Musik
Interdisziplinäre Betrachtungen

2014, 234 Seiten, kart., zahlr. Abb., 29,99 €,
ISBN 978-3-8376-2753-4

Leseproben, weitere Informationen und Bestellmöglichkeiten
finden Sie unter www.transcript-verlag.de

Musik und Klangkultur

Camille Hongler, Christoph Haffter,
Silvan Moosmüller (Hg.)
Geräusch – das Andere der Musik
Untersuchungen an den Grenzen
des Musikalischen

2014, 198 Seiten, kart., 24,99 €,
ISBN 978-3-8376-2868-5

Sylvia Mieszkowski, Sigrid Nieberle (Hg.)
Unlaute
Noise/Geräusch in Kultur,
Medien und Wissenschaften seit 1900

Januar 2016, ca. 300 Seiten, kart., ca. 34,99 €,
ISBN 978-3-8376-2534-9

Christian Utz
Komponieren im Kontext der Globalisierung
Perspektiven für eine Musikgeschichte
des 20. und 21. Jahrhunderts

2014, 438 Seiten, kart., zahlr. Abb., 39,99 €,
ISBN 978-3-8376-2403-8

Leseproben, weitere Informationen und Bestellmöglichkeiten
finden Sie unter www.transcript-verlag.de

Musik und Klangkultur

Leseproben, weitere Informationen und Bestellmöglichkeiten
finden Sie unter www.transcript-verlag.de